Mastering the
Instructional
Design
Process

WILLIAM J. ROTHWELL
H. C. KAZANAS

Mastering the Instructional Design Process

A Systematic Approach

Jossey-Bass Publishers · San Francisco

For international orders, please contact your local Paramount Publishing
International office.

Printed on acid-free paper and manufactured in the
United States of America

The paper used in this book meets the State of California
requirements for recycled paper (50 percent recycled waste,
including 10 percent post-consumer waste), which are the
strictest guidelines for recycled paper currently in use in
the United States.

Credits are on page 387.

Library of Congress Cataloging-in-Publication Data

Rothwell, William J., date.
   Mastering the instructional design process : a systematic approach
   William J. Rothwell, H. C. Kazanas. — 1st ed.
      p.   cm. — (The Jossey-Bass management series)
   Includes bibliographical references and indexes.
   ISBN 1-55542-427-9
   1. Employees—Training of.   2. Instructional systems—Design.
I. Kazanas, H. C.   II. Title.   III. Series.
HF5549.5.T7R659   1992
658.3′12404—dc20   91-31612
                                                     CIP

FIRST EDITION
HB Printing   10 9 8 7 6 5 4   *Code 9224*

The Jossey-Bass Management Series

Consulting Editors
Human Resources

Leonard Nadler
Zeace Nadler
College Park, Maryland

Contents

Tables, Figures, and Exhibits

Tables

Figures

Exhibits

Preface

Managers in the United States are pursuing efforts to improve human performance with growing fervor. In some respects, this pursuit has become the modern business world's equivalent of the medieval quest for the Holy Grail. Of course, there are good reasons for this. American businesses face increasing foreign competition from the Pacific Rim and a unified European Economic Community, declining rates of productivity growth, eroding public confidence in product or service quality, advancing technology, and shifting social attitudes about work and organizational loyalty. Many managers are eager to take whatever steps they can to meet these challenges. Many have also taken to heart the conclusions of best-selling authors Tom Peters, Charles Garfield, and Rosabeth Moss Kanter that the long-term success of their ventures will increasingly depend on their ability to cultivate improvements in employee performance.

For some managers, efforts to improve employee performance have led to headlong plunges into flashy fads and quick fixes — modern-day snake oil remedies. Others, however, are meeting the challenges they face by a more thoughtful approach: supporting and participating in efforts to analyze employee performance problems systematically, identify the root causes of those problems, consider various solutions to them, and implement the solutions in ways designed to minimize the unintended consequences of corrective action.

Instructional designers are often the standard-bearers of these calculated, long-term efforts to improve employee performance. They work under the guise of many job titles and are sometimes called performance technologists, trainers, training and development specialists, instructional developers, staff development specialists, or instructional designers. Whatever their titles, they share a common goal of improving human performance through instructional or noninstructional solutions. Perhaps the best-known instructional solution is training, though employee education and employee development are usually categorized as instructional solutions as well. Noninstructional solutions include the preparation and use of job aids, the redesign of organizational structures and reporting relationships, the redesign of jobs and tasks, the refocusing of employee selection methods, the reengineering of job- and task-related feedback methods, and the design and implementation of employee reward programs.

The examples and references incorporated in this book grow out of our own experiences in instructional design. Since our experiences have not been universal, we have attempted to focus on what we know. Overall, our goal is to give instructional designers a tool for developing their own skills in down-to-earth ways.

The Foundation of the Book

In the past, books on instructional design have often reflected the personal views of the authors and have not been based on an underlying foundation of solid research. However, *Mastering the Instructional Design Process: A Systematic Approach* is based on Foshay, Silber, and Westgaard's competency study titled *Instructional Design Competencies: The Standards* (1986) — abbreviated throughout this book as *The Standards*. Prepared through the cooperation of highly respected professionals in the instructional design field, *The Standards* was sponsored by the International Board of Standards for Training, Performance, and Instruction (IBSTPI).

The Standards identifies sixteen competencies for instructional design work, sequenced in the typical order in which they are used. (See the Resource Aid in the back of the book.) Each competency consists of component performances. These performances are the behaviors that instructional designers must be able to carry out to demonstrate each competency. While the competencies and their component performances may vary among organizations because of differences in corporate cultures, *The Standards* does provide a solid foundation for understanding and describing the instructional design field.

Mastering the Instructional Design Process: A Systematic Approach is intended to take up where *The Standards* leaves off. While *The Standards* focuses on *what instructional designers do,* this book focuses on *how to demonstrate competencies of instructional design work.* Its purpose is thus to point the way toward developing and improving competencies associated with instructional design work.

Audience

This book is for current instructional design professionals and professionals in the making, regardless of their formal job titles. It is intended as a desk aid to help professionals carry out their work and as a text for students. A comprehensive list of references appears at the end of the book, and we suggest that readers use it to pursue subjects of interest to them.

Mastering the Instructional Design Process: A Systematic Approach should also be of interest to others — such as human resource professionals and operating managers — who have reason to analyze employee performance problems systematically, pinpoint root causes of those problems, consider various solutions to the problems, and implement the solutions in ways designed to minimize the unintended side effects of corrective action.

Overview of the Contents

This book generally follows the structure of *The Standards*. However, Chapter One serves as an introduction and is not based on *The Standards*. It sets the stage for the remainder of the book by defining instructional design, describing instructional design as an emerging profession, and summarizing key issues that affect human performance in organizations.

Chapter Two reviews noninstructional solutions to human performance problems. Not based on the *The Standards*, the chapter is unique: noninstructional solutions are rarely treated in books on instructional design. However, we have decided to discuss them because we feel that instructional designers should be familiar with occasions in which it would be appropriate to request assistance from experts in other fields.

Chapter Three, the last chapter in Part One, focuses on determining which projects are appropriate for instructional design solutions. After defining what we mean by a performance problem and after discussing the ways of labeling the parts of a problem, we distinguish between comprehensive and solution-specific models for analyzing employee performance problems. A comprehensive problem-solving model is useful for scanning the "big picture" of an organization; a situation-specific model provides instructional designers with guidance for dealing with common symptoms of employee performance problems that prompt managers to request the aid of instructional designers. Most of the chapter is devoted to a detailed explanation of a comprehensive problem-solving model created by Thomas Gilbert and a situation-specific problem-solving model created by Robert Mager and Peter Pipe.

Parts Two, Three, and Four comprise Chapters Four to Thirteen. They are unified by a common, albeit simplified, model of the instructional design process.

Part Two consists of four related chapters on analyzing instructional needs, learners, work settings, and work. Chapter Four, based on the *The Standards*, focuses on conducting a needs assessment. Appropriate only when an employee performance problem has been attributed to a deficiency in knowledge, skills, or attitudes and can be most cost-effectively addressed through instruction, needs assessment is an evaluation of instructional requirements. The chapter is divided into five sections that address developing a needs assessment plan, conducting a needs assessment, identifying instructional problems, judging needs assessment plans, and justifying needs assessment.

Assessing the relevant characteristics of learners is the topic of Chapter Five. In this chapter — which is based on *The Standards* — we explain how to select, carry out, judge, and justify learner characteristics for assessment.

Closely related to Chapter Five, Chapter Six focuses on analyzing characteristics of a work setting. In this chapter, we explain how to achieve a better match between learners and the settings in which instruction is designed, delivered, and applied. To that end we cover methods of determining work-setting resources and constraints and judging and justifying setting analysis.

Chapter Seven defines job, task, and content analysis — collectively called work analysis — and summarizes methods of performing them. Work analysis is conceptually related to needs assessment, since both are centered on work-related requirements. The chapter also describes how instructional designers may judge and justify a job, task, or content analysis.

Part Three comprises three chapters on performance objectives and measurements. Performance objectives and measurements are, of course, developed from results of needs assessment, learner analysis, setting analysis, and work analysis. They are intended to guide the remaining steps in the instructional design process by describing precisely what targeted learners should know, do, or feel on completing a planned learning experience. Writing statements of performance objectives is the topic of Chapter Eight. The chapter explains how instructional designers can distinguish performance objectives from instructional/organizational goals or learner/trainer activities, state objectives in performance terms, judge performance objectives prepared by others, and justify objectives that have been prepared.

Developing performance measurements is the topic of Chapter Nine. Established to monitor learner achievement, performance measurements build accountability for results into instruction from the outset. In this chapter, we explain how performance measurements and performance objectives are related, how to generate performance measurements, and how to state a rationale for the way a measurement instrument is constructed or a judgment about a performance measurement is made.

Chapter Ten addresses the sequencing of performance objectives, a step of instructional design that should occur after work tasks have been analyzed and inventoried, performance objectives have been formally stated, and performance measurements have been established (*The Standards,* 1986). The purpose of this step in the instructional design process is to ensure that, during instruction, workers are introduced systematically to what they must know or do. We explain how to state rules for sequencing performance objectives, how to apply the rules, how to judge the sequencing of performance objectives, and how to justify decisions made about sequencing performance objectives.

Part Four comprises three chapters on instructional strategies, materials, and evaluation. It rounds out the discussion of steps in the instructional design process. Specifying instructional strategies is the topic of Chapter Eleven. Building on earlier chapters about preceding steps in the instructional design process, it explains how instructional designers should choose appropriate methods and media for achieving desired results. We divide the chapter into three related sections: (1) specifying the instructional strategy; (2) judging the appropriateness of instructional strategy; and (3) justifying decisions made about instructional strategy.

Designing instructional materials, a familiar and important topic to many instructional designers, is the topic of Chapter Twelve. In this chapter, we advise instructional designers to follow six simple steps when designing these materials: (1) prepare a working outline; (2) conduct research; (3) examine existing instructional materials; (4) arrange or modify existing materials; (5) prepare tailor-made instructional materials; and (6) select or prepare learning activities.

Evaluating instruction is the topic of Chapter Thirteen. In keeping with *The Standards* (1986), however, we devote primary attention to formative evaluation that is conducted before instruction is delivered to the targeted learners on a widespread basis. We describe how to develop a formative evaluation plan, carry out the plan, generate ideas for revising instruction, and judge and justify formative evaluation.

Part Five consists of six chapters. Two of them focus on managing instructional design, three of them center on communication skills for instructional designers, and one sums up the lessons learned about being an effective instructional designer. Chapter Fourteen summarizes important issues associated with designing an instructional management system. We focus on methods of ensuring that entrance into instruction is quick and easy, that learners entering instruction are diagnosed as to their readiness, and that learners are directed to appropriate sections with a minimum of time and effort. We also discuss ways of making sure that each step, section, or experience within the instruction is provided with transitions and references, that each instructional element is easily identified in terms of both content and purpose, and that competence is documented.

Planning and monitoring instructional design projects is our focus in Chapter Fifteen. We describe how to develop a project management plan for an instructional design project and how to judge and justify project plans.

In Chapter Sixteen, we provide helpful hints about ways to cultivate and apply effective visual, oral, and written communication skills. Like many professionals, instructional designers must be able to formulate and articulate their thoughts. However, their need to exercise communication skills is probably greater than in many other fields. Chapter Sixteen is divided into three sections: (1) using effective visual communication; (2) using effective oral communication; and (3) using effective written communication.

In Chapter Seventeen we describe methods that instructional designers can use to interact effectively with others. More specifically, the chapter focuses on techniques for establishing rapport with others, stating the purpose of interpersonal interactions, asking questions, providing explanations, listening actively, dealing with conflict, handling resistance to change, keeping people on track, securing commitment, and selecting appropriate behaviors for effective interpersonal interaction.

In Chapter Eighteen we offer suggestions about promoting the use of instructional design in organizational settings. More specifically, we begin the chapter with a brief case study to dramatize important issues in promoting instructional design. We then turn to describing ways to make others aware of instructional design. We conclude the chapter with a few words of advice about justifying these promotional efforts.

Chapter Nineteen concludes the book with our personal observations about what it takes to be effective in the instructional design field. We offer eight key points for you, the reader, to keep in mind. The chapter, and the book, ends with an activity that is intended to help you contemplate the future — and the competencies necessary to succeed as the future unfolds.

As mentioned earlier, the Resource Aid in the back of the book presents the sixteen competencies for instructional design work described in *The Standards*.

Acknowledgments

We would like to express our thanks to the members of the International Board of Standards for Training, Performance, and Instruction (IBSTPI) for their encouragement of this project and their permission to use *The Standards* as the foundation for this book. (A description of IBSTPI appears on the next page for those who are curious about what the board is and what it stands for.) While any mistakes in this book are entirely the responsibility of the authors and not the International Board, we are indebted to the board members for their support.

We would also like to thank our spouses — Marcelina Rothwell and Nuria Kazanas — for enduring the many hours we did not spend with them as we labored on this project. Without their help, encouragement, and inspiration, this book could not have been written.

January 1992

William J. Rothwell
Springfield, Illinois

H. C. Kazanas
Champaign, Illinois

The International Board
of Standards for Training,
Performance, and Instruction

The International Board of Standards for Training, Performance, and Instruction (IBSTPI) was founded as a not-for-profit corporation in 1984. Its mission is to promote high standards of professional practice in the areas of training, performance, and instruction by (1) articulating and promoting the integrity of professional practice through research, development, definition of competencies, and education, and (2) stretching the boundaries of the fields through exploration, promotion, and integration of new ideas, research, and practices from other disciplines.

The board grew out of the work of the Joint Certification Task Force, which was composed of people actively involved in the Association for Educational Communications and Technology (AECT) and the National Society for Performance and Instruction (NSPI). Created in 1977, the task force included over thirty professional practitioners and academics with expertise in various facets of training, performance, and instruction. The task force developed an initial set of competencies for the instructional design professional, published an index linking current publications to the competencies, and created a prototype assessment procedure. Members of the task force spoke at professional meetings and published articles on competencies and certification.

After researching the certification programs of various professional groups and with the advice of legal counsel, the task force created the IBSTPI. This action was taken with the approval and encouragement of the boards of directors of NSPI, AECT, and the Division of Instructional Development within AECT.

IBSTPI considers itself a service organization to practitioners, consumers, managers, educators, researchers, and vendors in the training and performance improvement field. IBSTPI provides these groups with competencies for effective practice, research information, curriculum guides, assessment tools, and training. To date, IBSTPI has developed and distributed competencies for the professional instructional/training designer, bibliographical references, competencies for instructors, a code of ethics, competencies for training managers, and supporting materials. The board continues to be engaged in ongoing research into new standards, advances in technology, and measurement systems.

The Authors

William J. Rothwell is assistant vice president and management development director for The Franklin Life Insurance Company, a wholly owned subsidiary of American Brands in Springfield, Illinois. He received his B.A. degree from Illinois State University in English and completed his M.A. degree and all courses for the doctorate in English at the University of Illinois, Urbana–Champaign. In addition, he earned his M.B.A. degree from Sangamon State University in Springfield, Illinois, and received his Ph.D. degree from the University of Illinois, Urbana–Champaign, in education with a specialty in human resource development. He has twelve years of full-time professional work experience in managing human resource development in the public and private sectors and has taught college part time for seven years.

Rothwell is a member of the American Society for Training and Development, the National Society for Performance and Instruction, the Society for Human Resource Management, and the Organization Development Institute. He has been accredited as a Senior Professional in Human Resources (SPHR), a Registered Organization Development Consultant (RODC), and a Fellow of the Life Management Institute (FLMI). He has been a frequent speaker at national conferences, has held local and national leadership positions in the American Society for Training and Development, and has authored or coauthored over sixty-five articles, seven books, and five training packages. Among other publications, he coauthored two volumes of *The ASTD Reference Guide to Professional Training Roles and Competencies* (1987 and 1992, with H. J. Sredl), coauthored *The Workplace Literacy Primer* (1990, with D. C. Brandenburg), and authored *The Structured On-the-Job Training Workshop* (1990), in two volumes. He has also served as a human resource development consultant for numerous organizations, both public and private.

H. C. Kazanas is professor of education at the College of Education at the University of Illinois, Urbana–Champaign. He received his B.Sc. and M.Ed.

degrees from Wayne State University in industrial education and his Ph.D. degree from the University of Michigan in education.

Kazanas's present professional interests are in management development, training employees on the job, and the effects of work values on productivity. He is an active member of several professional organizations, including the American Society for Training and Development and the National Society for Performance and Instruction, and has served on many committees and held leadership roles, including that of president of the National Association of Industrial and Technical Teacher Educators. He has received several outstanding service awards. Kazanas has published eighty articles in twenty-eight different journals in education and human resource development. He has contributed several book chapters and monographs and has authored or coauthored eleven books relating to technical training in manufacturing and human resource development. One of his technical books has been translated into Spanish and Arabic. With William J. Rothwell, he has coauthored *Strategic Human Resources Planning and Management* (1988) and *Strategic Human Resource Development* (1989). He has two other books forthcoming with William J. Rothwell: *Developing Supervisory Skills: An Orientation Workbook for New Supervisors* and *Developing Supervisory Skills: A Guide for Classroom Presenters and On-the-Job Coaches.*

Kazanas has worked for ten years in the manufacturing industry as a machinist and production supervisor and twenty-five years as an educator in human resource development. He has been a consultant in human resource development with such national and international organizations and agencies as the U.S. Department of Labor, the U.S. Department of Education, the U.S. Agency for International Development, Motorola, Westinghouse, the World Bank, the United Nations Development Program, the International Labor Office, and UNESCO. He has worked in Asia, Africa, Europe, and South America. Kazanas has taught at Eastern Michigan University, the University of Missouri–Columbia, and the University of Illinois. He has served as graduate program coordinator and department chair at the University of Missouri–Columbia and the University of Illinois, respectively. During his academic career he has coordinated and directed many research studies in such areas as work values, attitudes and productivity, strategic human resource planning, on-the-job training, management job rotation programs, and individualizing instruction.

Mastering the
Instructional
Design
Process

PART I

Detecting and Solving
Human Performance Problems

CHAPTER ONE

The Role
of Instructional Design
in Solving Performance Problems

The field of *instructional design* is associated with analyzing employee performance problems systematically, identifying the root cause(s) of those problems, considering various solutions to address the root causes, and implementing the solutions in ways designed to minimize the unintended consequences of corrective action. Richey (1986, p. 9), for example, defines instructional design as "the science of creating detailed specifications for the development, evaluation, and maintenance of situations which facilitate the learning of both large and small units of subject matter." Further, "current usage in the private sector is converging on the term 'instructional design' for this field" (*The Standards,* 1986, p. 1). It encompasses not just preparation of job-related instruction but also the selection of such noninstructional solutions to employee performance problems as the preparation and use of job aids, the redesign of organizational structure and reporting relationships, the redesign of jobs and tasks, the refocusing of employee selection methods, the reengineering of job- and task-related feedback methods, and the design and implementation of employee reward programs (Jacobs, 1987). As we use the term, instructional design is (1) an emerging profession, (2) focused on establishing and maintaining efficient and effective human performance, (3) guided by a model of human performance, (4) carried out systematically, (5) based on open systems theory, and (6) oriented to finding and applying the most cost-effective solutions to human performance problems. In this chapter, we will explore each of these characteristics to lay the groundwork for the remainder of the book.

Instructional Design: An Emerging Profession

Instructional design is an emerging profession because people can, and do, enter jobs as instructional designers and work in that capacity for their entire careers. Employment advertisements for instructional designers frequently appear in such publications as the National Society for Performance and Instruction's *News and Notes*. The following is an example of such an advertisement:

> Instructional designers are sought to assess training needs and tasks, identify instructional content and strategies, and assist in the development, writing, and revision of course materials. Instructional Designers conduct needs assessments, define learning objectives, work with subject experts, prepare job aids, select media (for example, computer-based training, video, print-based), develop curriculum plans, write instructor and participant materials, and conduct pilot tests of materials. A degree in the field of Instructional Technology, with courses in learning theory, systematic course development, and media use, is desired. Excellent organizational, interpersonal, time management, and oral and written communication skills are required.

This advertisement captures the major duties — and summarizes employers' expectations — of most instructional designers in just a few lines. It is consistent with Briggs's (1977b, p. xx) description of an instructional designer as "a person who engages in the planning, analysis, and development of instruction and instructional materials, in contrast to a person who operates the instructional system. A teacher may be both designer and system operator, while a curriculum developer may be only the designer."

Many organizations employ instructional designers. Jobs bearing this title are quite often positioned at the entry level. They occupy the first rung on a career ladder leading to such higher-level jobs as Instructor, Project Supervisor of Instructional Design, and Manager of Training and Development. But variations of this career ladder, as well as of specific titles and duties, do exist. Alternative job titles may include Performance Technologist, Instructional Developer, Education Specialist, Employee Educator, Trainer, Instructional Technologist, or Instructional Systems Specialist. Because of these variations in titles and duties, instructional design should be regarded as only an emerging and not an established profession.

Instructional Design: Focused on Establishing and Maintaining Efficient and Effective Human Performance

The chief aim of instructional design is to improve employee performance so as to increase organizational efficiency and/or effectiveness. For this reason, instructional designers should be able to define such fundamentally important terms as *performance, efficiency,* and *effectiveness.*

What Is Performance?

Performance is perhaps best understood as the achievement of results, the outcomes (*ends*) to which purposeful activities (*means*) are directed. It is not synonymous with *behavior,* the observable actions taken and the unobservable decisions made to achieve work results.

There are several types of performance, of course. *Human performance* is the result of human skills, knowledge, and attitudes. *Machine performance* is the result of machine activities. *Company performance* is the result of organizational activities.

When asked to think about employee performance, most people in the United States think first of individual performance. There are at least two reasons why. First, people are sensitized to appraisals of individual performance because most organizations make it an annual ritual, often linked to decisions about pay increases. This practice has made a lasting impression on nearly everyone. Second, American culture has long prized rugged individualism, implying that very little lies beyond the reach of determined heroes and heroines acting alone. However, recent trends point toward greater emphasis in the future on the performance of groups, departments, divisions, or organizations.

Defining Efficiency and Effectiveness

Traditionally, two aspects of performance have been considered — efficiency and effectiveness. These terms have no universally accepted definitions. But *efficiency* is usually understood to mean the ratio between the resources needed to achieve results (inputs) and the value of results (outputs). Some have said that the central question of efficiency can be posed simply: "Are we doing things right?" In this question, the phrase "doing things right" means "without unnecessary expenditures of time, money, or effort."

Effectiveness, on the other hand, usually means the match between results achieved and those needed or desired. Its central question is this: "Are we doing the right things?" In this question, the phrase "right things" typically means "what others expect or need from the organization, group, or individual."

Instructional Design:
Guided by a Model of Human Performance

Instructional design is guided by a model of human performance. In the most general sense, of course, a *model* is a simplified or abstract representation of a process, device, or concept. A model of any kind is designed to help understand a problem, situation, process, or device. This applies to a model of human performance, which is a simplified representation of factors involved in producing work results. It is intended to provide labels to key factors involved in performance and clues to pinpointing underlying causes of performance problems. For these reasons, "you should always work from a model of human performance" (Zemke and Kramlinger, 1982, p. 17).

Many human performance models have been constructed (Bailey, 1982; Cummings and Schwab, 1973; Nash, 1983). They can be categorized as *comprehensive* or *situation-specific*. A *comprehensive performance model* includes as many factors as possible affecting human performance in organizational settings. An example is shown in Figure 1.1. Table 1.1 defines and briefly describes the factors appearing in Figure 1.1.

A *situation-specific performance model* focuses on an existing or suspected problem. One of the best known was first described by Rummler (1976). (See Figure 1.2.) According to Rummler, five factors should be considered whenever a human performance problem is identified. They include (1) the

Figure 1.1. A Comprehensive Model of Human Performance in Organizations.

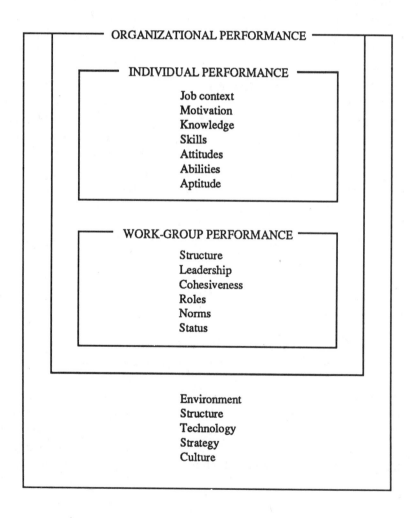

Table 1.1. Factors Affecting Performance.

Factor	Brief definition	Questions to consider about the influence of the factor on performance
INDIVIDUAL PERFORMANCE		
Job context	The environment of the job, including supervisor(s), equipment and tools to be used, customers and co-workers.	Do people have the necessary equipment, tools, and resources to perform?
Motivation	The desire to perform.	Do people want to perform?
Knowledge	Facts and information essential to performing a job or task.	Do people have the necessary facts and information they need to take action and make decisions?
Skills	Abilities to do things associated with successful job performance.	Can people do the things associated with successful job performance?
Attitudes	Feelings about performance that are voiced to other people.	How do people feel about their behavior?
Abilities	Present capabilities to behave in certain ways.	Do people possess the necessary talents and mental or physical characteristics?
Aptitude	The future capability to behave in certain ways.	Are people physically and/or mentally capable of learning how to perform?
WORK-GROUP PERFORMANCE		
Structure	The way work is allocated to members of a work group.	Is responsibility for results clearly assigned? Are people aware of what they are responsible for? Are they held accountable for achieving results?
Leadership	The way directions are given to members of a work group.	Is it clear who is in charge? Does the leader consider *how people feel* (attitudes) as well as *what must be done to achieve results* (tasks)?
Cohesiveness	The extent to which members of a work group are unified, pulling together as a group.	Are people willing to work together to achieve desired results?
Roles	The pattern of expected behaviors and results of each member of a group.	Do members of a group understand what they are responsible for doing?
Norms	Accepted beliefs of the work group.	How do members of a work group feel about the results they are to achieve? methods of achieving those results?
Status	The relative position of people in a group.	Do people have the formal authority to act in line with their responsibilities? Are other people willing to follow the lead of those who know what to do?
ORGANIZATIONAL PERFORMANCE		
Environment	The world outside the organization.	How well is the organization adapting to—or anticipating—changes outside it that affect it?
Structure	The way work is divided up and allocated to parts of the organization.	Is work divided up appropriately?

Table 1.1. Factors Affecting Performance, Cont'd.

Factor	Brief definition	Questions to consider about the influence of the factor on performance
Technology	Actions taken by people to change objects, people, or situations. Often refers to "how the work is done."	Is the organization applying work methods that reflect current information about how to do the work?
Strategy	The means to achieve desired ends. It denotes an organization's long-term direction.	Is the organization competing effectively?
Culture	Beliefs and attitudes shared by members of an organization.	Do members of the organization share common beliefs and attitudes about what they—and the organization—should do?

Figure 1.2. A Situation-Specific Model of Human Performance.

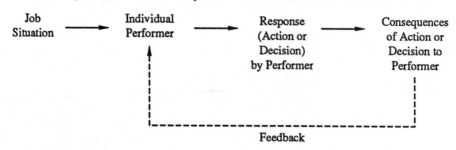

Feedback

Source: Rummler, G. "The Performance Audit." In R. Craig (ed.), *Training and Development Handbook: A Guide to Human Resource Development.* (2nd ed.) New York: McGraw-Hill, 1976, p. 14-3. Reproduced with the permission of McGraw-Hill, Inc.

job situation, (2) the performer, (3) the behavior, (4) the consequence, and (5) the feedback of the consequence back to the performer. Rummler (1976, p. 14-3) observes that "in any job there is a *situation* or occasion requiring a particular *performer* to make a particular response or take some action, which results in some consequence to the performer. The performer may consider that consequence to be positive or negative or to have little value. And last, information on that consequence is fed back to the performer."

Rummler's model is very useful in analyzing human performance problems. After all, the cause of the problem *must* be determined, and each factor in this simple model can be examined as a possible cause. If it is not clear *when* the desired performance is necessary, the cause stems from the job situation. If performers are physically or mentally unable to perform, the cause stems from the performers. If performers lack the necessary skills or tools or other resources, the cause stems from the response (behavior). If the consequences of performing are punishing or do not exist, the cause of the problem stems from the consequences. If performers are given no information about the value of their performance, then the problem's cause stems from inadequate or nonexistent feedback.

We will discuss models for analyzing human performance in greater detail in Chapter Two. For now, suffice it to say that instructional designers base what they do on a human performance model. Applying such a model to problem solving is the foundation of instructional design. After all, the field is associated with analyzing employee performance problems systematically, identifying the root cause(s) of those problems, considering various solutions to address the root causes, and implementing the solutions in ways designed to minimize the unintended consequences of corrective action.

Instructional Design: Carried Out Systematically

Instructional design is not just a field. It may also be regarded as a process for examining problems and identifying solutions. The process should not be carried out intuitively; rather, its success depends on systematic application. In other words, it is a *planned process* "by which needs are identified, problems are selected, requirements for problem solutions are identified, solutions are chosen from alternatives, methods and means are obtained and implemented, results are evaluated, and required revisions to all or part of the system are made so that the needs are eliminated" (Kaufman, 1972, p. 2). Instructional designers place their faith in an iterative, systematic process in which all steps in the process, taken together, are more powerful than any single step. Over forty systematic instructional design models have been constructed to guide instructional designers in their work (Andrews and Goodson, 1980).

Instructional Design: Based On Open Systems Theory

Instructional design is based on open systems theory. An *open system* receives *inputs* from the environment, transforms them through *operations* within the system, submits *outputs* to the environment, and receives *feedback* indicating how well these functions are carried out. To survive, any open system must gain advantages from its transactions with the environment.

Inputs include raw materials, people, capital, and information. Operations are activities occurring within the organization that add value to raw materials. Outputs are services or finished goods released into the environment by the organization. Figure 1.3 illustrates these basic components of an open system.

All open systems share common characteristics. First, they are dependent on the external environment for essential inputs and reception of their outputs. Second, there is a pattern to the flow of inputs and outputs. Third, all but the simplest open systems are composed of subsystems and interact with environmental suprasystems. A subsystem is a system within a system. A suprasystem is an overarching system that includes more than one system.

Figure 1.3. The Basic Components of an Organization as an Open System.

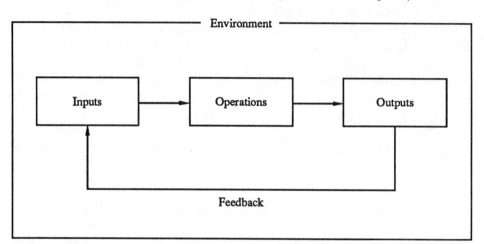

As Katz and Kahn (1978) explain in their classic treatment of open systems theory, most organizations consist of four generic subsystems. (They are generic because they are found in most organizations, regardless of industry or reporting relationships.) The first is the *production subsystem,* which focuses on getting the work out. The second is the *adaptive subsystem* which includes any functions concerned with helping the organization change its internal operations to adapt to external environmental change. The third is the *maintenance subsystem,* which is concerned with streamlining internal operations and increasing efficiency. The fourth and last is the *managerial subsystem,* concerned with directing and coordinating the other three subsystems. Although organizations vary somewhat, the production or operations department exemplifies the production subsystem in most firms; the marketing department exemplifies the adaptive subsystem in most firms; the human resources department exemplifies the maintenance subsystem in most firms; and the top management team exemplifies the managerial subsystem in most firms.

Most organizations function within many suprasystems. Perhaps the most obvious is the *industry suprasystem,* composed of all organizations involved in the same basic type of work. There are also other, equally important, suprasystems. The *governmental/legal suprasystem,* for instance, is made up of all government agencies regulating the industry of which one organization is part. It also includes the applicable laws, rules, and regulations with which the organization must comply. The *marketing/competitive suprasystem* is made up of all competitors, present and future. The *economic suprasystem* consists of the national and international economic environment within which the organization functions. The *technological suprasystem* is composed of the tools, state-of-the-art know-how, and work methods used in delivering the organization's services or producing goods. The *supplier suprasystem* comprises all suppliers providing inputs to an organization. Each suprasystem exerts influence on organizational performance.

Open systems theory is important to instructional designers for two reasons. First, instructional designers recognize the critical importance of adapting to changes in the environment and even anticipating them. Organizational and individual effectiveness depends on how well work results match environmental demands. Hence, one question that should be asked in any performance improvement effort is this: *How much will this project contribute to the organization's ability to adapt to changing environmental conditions?* If the answer is "not much" or "we don't know," then it could well be that performance improvement activities should be directed to other projects.

Second, instructional designers recognize that any *corrective* action taken to change one subsystem will affect others. The parts of any organization (system) are as interdependent as strands of a spiderweb. It follows, then, that a change in one part will affect others, just as an entire spiderweb vibrates when one strand is disturbed. For example, if a change is made in the kinds of people selected into a job category, it will affect the kind of training they should receive. Large system changes in organizations will have effects that are partially predictable—and partially unpredictable.

Instructional Design: Oriented to Finding and Applying the Most Cost-Effective Solutions to Human Performance Problems

Instructional designers sometimes assume, mistakenly, that their role is to "offer job-oriented instruction." Sometimes others in the organization share the same misconception of their role. In fact, human performance problems cannot always be addressed via instruction. It should only be used when the performance problem stems from a lack of knowledge or skills or the wrong attitudes and when instruction is the most cost-effective solution. Since we will use the terms *knowledge, skills,* and *attitudes* throughout this book, perhaps some definitions are in order at this point. *Knowledge* is simply "what the employee knows. It is important in terms of jobs and training because people usually perform better if they understand what they are doing and why" (McArdle, 1989, p. 34). *Skills* involve the abilities to do something— such as operate a machine. "Skills imply actions; others can observe them" (McArdle, 1989, p. 34). The term *attitudes* denotes how people feel about what they do. Instructional designers "generally accept that how people feel about what they are doing and the organization for which they are working has some effect on their performance" (McArdle, 1989, p. 34).

Instruction should not be used as the solution when a performance problem stems from lack of motivation, feedback, incentives, or some other cause. It is also a costly solution because it demands substantial investments of time and money to prepare instructional materials, test them, revise them, deliver them, and evaluate them. Employees who receive off-the-job instruction lose time doing work and are usually paid while learning, which adds to the cost. At the same time, instructional designers and others involved in the preparation of instructional materials must be paid, which further adds to the cost.

For all these reasons, job-oriented instruction is a costly way to improve performance. It should only be used as a solution of last resort. Indeed, instructional designers should be certain that there will be a favorable return on *any* investment in performance improvement efforts. To this end, they may apply any one of many different methods of *cost-benefit forecasting and analysis* to estimate the expected return (payoff) on the investment (Kearsley, 1986; Swanson and Gradous, 1988). First they estimate the cost of the performance problem. Then they estimate the expected costs to rectify the problem. Finally, they compare the two. If a return on investment takes too long, instructional designers should direct their attention to other projects in which the benefits are more certain, payoffs are higher, or results can be achieved faster.

Conclusion

The instructional design field is an exciting one that has real potential to improve employee performance and thereby enhance organizational productivity, increase competitiveness, and eliminate the problems faced by workers who lead lives of quiet desperation amid a sometimes chaotic and irrational organizational setting. Instructional designers view their roles as more than just "preparing instruction." Instead, they see what they do as linked inexorably to one of continuous improvement of organizational conditions and operations. Their challenging role is to analyze employee performance problems systematically, identify root cause(s) of those problems, consider various solutions to address the root causes, and implement solutions in ways designed to minimize the unintended consequences of corrective action.

Our goal in the following chapters is to describe the competencies of instructional design work and provide the means by which practitioners can develop, or sharpen, their abilities.

CHAPTER TWO

Alternatives
to Instructional Solutions:
Five Frequent Options

Noninstructional design solutions—which we will abbreviate as noninstructional solutions from this point on—address employee performance problems through means other than training, education, or development. While most books on instructional design do not treat these solutions, we include this chapter to give instructional designers a rudimentary knowledge of them. When they choose these solutions, however, instructional designers should usually consult other professionals—such as human resources specialists—who have the appropriate expertise in this area.

Even though as many as fifteen noninstructional solutions to employee performance problems have been catalogued (Hutchison, 1990), we focus on just five of them in this chapter: (1) feedback methods, (2) job performance aids, (3) reward systems, (4) employee selection practices, and (5) organizational redesign. We have chosen to focus on these five solutions because instructional designers have traditionally used them, separately or in combination, more than others (Jacobs, 1987). In our summary of each noninstructional solution, we will (1) describe what it is, (2) explain when it should be used, and (3) summarize how to apply the solution to employee performance problems.

Feedback Methods

Feedback is a continuous process of providing information about an activity, sometimes during the activity itself (Nadler, 1977). It serves two primary purposes. First, it influences the *quantity* of performance by stimulating people to continue doing more or less of what they are already doing (Tosti, 1986). Second, it influences the *quality* of performance by stimulating people to change how or what they do (Tosti, 1986). Feedback can be either *incidental,* growing out of specific situations in a spontaneous way, or *inten-*

tional, growing out of situations deliberately designed to provide people with evaluative information about how or what they do. Substantial research evidence exists to support the value of improving feedback (Jacobs, 1988).

When Should Feedback Be Used to Address a Performance Problem?

Use feedback when each of the following questions can be answered yes (Mager and Pipe, 1984, pp. 100–105): (1) Is the performance problem caused by deficiencies in knowledge, skills, or attitudes? (2) Could the employee perform in the past? and (3) Is the skill used often? If these questions can be answered with a yes, turn next to examining the quantity and quality of feedback that employees are already receiving. Consider these questions (Rummler, 1983, p. 14): (1) Do employees receive enough information on the consequences of performing as desired? If the answer is no, provide feedback. (2) Are employees receiving accurate information on the consequences of performing as desired in a way that leads them to believe that their performance is correct? If the answer is no, improve the clarity and accuracy of feedback performers are receiving. (3) Are employees receiving *timely* information on the consequences of their performance so that it can be used in time to improve what they are doing or how they are doing it? (If the answer is no, improve the timeliness of the feedback.)

How Should Feedback be Used in Solving Performance Problems?

Coaching, production wall charts, memorandums, team meetings, quality circles, performance appraisals, or customer surveys can be used to change the quantity or quality of feedback that employees receive about what they do, how well they do it, what results they achieve, or how well their work results match up to desired results (Jacobs, 1987).

Coaching occurs during work activities and is thus appropriate for improving employee behavior on a short-term—even minute-by-minute—basis (Blanchard and Johnson, 1981). Although employees can (and sometimes do) coach each other, coaching is often done by supervisors, who offer their employees timely, immediate, and concrete feedback about performance. "Coaching sessions" may last between a minute and a half hour (Stowell and Starcevich, 1987). Effective coaches are supportive, expressing through body language as well as spoken word their confidence that the employee is capable of superior performance (Halson, 1990). Effective coaches are also able to make a point quickly, reinforce the importance of the point, establish a plan for improvement with the employee on the spot, gain employee commitment and willingness to change, deal effectively with excuses, describe the consequences of performing problems, and maintain confidence in employee abilities over time (Stowell and Starcevich, 1987).

Production wall charts are visual displays that provide immediate, concrete feedback to employees about their performance, often on a daily basis.

They are thus appropriate for increasing feedback on how much or how well individuals or work groups are producing. The typical wall chart illustrates individual or work-group piece rates, error rates, scrap rates, and various other information on a graph. Employees are thus able to see tangible results from their work and can improve or change it based on the feedback they receive (Bullough, 1981).

Memorandums are short written directives to employees. They provide practical, how-to-do-it guidance on handling common or unique problem situations. In many cases, they are prompted by a mistake made by an otherwise good, experienced performer and thus serve as feedback intended to change what employees do or how they do it (American Society for Training and Development, 1986b).

Team meetings are vehicles for giving feedback to all members of a work group about what they are doing or how well they are performing. Team meetings also provide a means of increasing group cohesiveness by building a sense of "psychological closeness" among members of a group (Dyer, 1977). High group cohesiveness is equated with increased group performance when group goals coincide with organizational goals (Gibson, Ivancevich, and Donnelly, 1985). Much has been written about methods of conducting successful team meetings — and "team building," the process of increasing the cohesiveness of a work group (see Guest, 1986).

Quality circles were originally exported to Japan from the United States and eventually reimported after publicity about the success of Japanese management techniques became widespread. They are usually designed to provide managers, not employees, with feedback about ways to increase organizational performance. In a typical quality circle, employees meet during working hours to identify work problems and solutions to those problems. A trained quality circle coordinator provides suggestions to the organization's management and feedback about the suggestions from management to employees (Barra, 1984; The Conference Board, 1988; DeWar, 1982; Ingle, 1982).

Performance appraisal is an excellent tool, in theory at least, for providing individuals with structured feedback. Just as *job descriptions* outline major job activities (Bishop, 1988a; Bureau of Law and Business, 1982), appraisals measure how well employees carried out those activities in a given time period. Performance appraisal is continuous — supervisors are always appraising employee performance — even when no formal performance appraisal process exists in an organization (Sherman, Bohlander, and Chruden, 1988). In most organizations, formal appraisals are often conducted on a cycle, usually once a year. While too infrequent to substitute for the spontaneous feedback provided by supervisors to employees on daily work performance, appraisals are appropriate for uncovering long-term performance trends and developmental opportunities (Baird, Beatty, and Schneier, 1982).

Unfortunately, performance appraisals are not always effective in providing structured feedback to employees. There are many reasons why.

Some appraisal systems are designed to accomplish too much. They may be intended to provide evaluative feedback on past performance, plan future career advancement, justify salary actions, and assess training needs. Sometimes the appraisal systems themselves lack top management support, fail to provide a method for establishing performance standards at the beginning of the appraisal cycle, discourage give-and-take discussions between employee and supervisor in favor of one-sided meetings led by the supervisor, and lack clear job relatedness (Lazer, 1980). To be effective, an appraisal system must be designed to overcome these common problems.

Customer surveys provide feedback to all members of the organization — managers and employees alike — about how well the organization is meeting the needs of people it is intended to serve (Becker and Wellins, 1990). This information can be most useful in planning for future performance improvement, for both the individual and the organization (Lee, 1989). Customer surveys can be conducted by enclosing written questionnaires with products, telephoning customers some time after product (or service) delivery, visiting customers on-site, offering toll-free hot-line numbers for questions or help, or providing large-scale written questionnaires to an organization's mailing list of past customers.

Job Performance Aids

According to Harless (1986, p. 108), a job performance aid is "a mechanism that stores information external to the user, guides the performance of work, and meets these requirements: (1) Can be accessed and used in real time (employed during actual performance of the task); (2) Provides signals to the performer when to perform the task or increments of the task (stimuli); (3) Provides sufficient direction on how to perform each task (responses); and (4) Reduces the quantity and/or time the information may be recalled (reduces access of memory)." In emphasizing the simplicity and value of job performance aids — sometimes simply called *job aids* — Harless (1985, p. 5) once remarked that "inside every fat course is a thin Job Aid crying to get out."

Job aids provide employees with guidance on how to perform in the work context (Finnegan, 1985). They cost significantly less to prepare and use than training. They are also easier than training to revise under swiftly changing work conditions. Of course, job aids can be used in conjunction with training to help ensure transfer of training from classroom to job. This is why canny instructional designers sometimes deliberately set out to create "trainee workbooks" or "job checklists" that lend themselves easily to being taken out of a training classroom and used immediately on the job (Harless, 1986).

When Should Job Performance Aids Be
Used to Address Performance Problems?

Job aids are appropriate when the consequences of errors are great, procedures are complicated, work tasks are not frequently performed, the time for training is limited, and the budget for training is also limited (Finnegan, 1985). But they are inappropriate when employees have no time during work tasks to refer to them or when an employee's credibility with customers will be undercut by referring to a job aid during performance of a work task. Nor are they appropriate when the consequences of errors are not great, work procedures are simple, and employees frequently perform the task.

How Should Job Aids Be Designed and Used?

Virtually anything that provides on-the-spot, practical guidance can be considered a job aid — such as cues built into the questions on an application form that explain what information is being requested (Smillie, 1985). Examples of job aids include cleaning instructions sewn into clothing, lights on automobile instrument panels, operators' manuals provided with personal computers, and warnings on medicine bottles (Sredl and Rothwell, 1987). However, the most familiar job aids include checklists, decision aids, algorithms, procedure manuals, and work samples (American Society for Training and Development, 1989d; Jacobs, 1987; Lineberry and Bullock, 1980).

Checklists are simple to design and are widely applicable to any activity — such as an organization's procedures — that must be performed in a sequence. To create a checklist, begin by listing tasks of an activity or procedure in the order they are supposed to be performed in. Label the column above the tasks "Tasks to Perform." Then add another column for responses, such as "yes," "no," and "not applicable to this situation." Label the column "Responses: Did You Do?" Be as short in your task descriptions as possible to keep the checklist simple. If most employees are making the same mistakes, add notes.

Algorithms are usually visual representations, often resembling flowcharts, of steps to take in an activity or procedure (Horabin and Lewis, 1978). If employees follow an algorithm precisely, they should not be able to deviate easily from correct performance (Jackson, 1986). Developing an algorithm closely resembles the process of developing a checklist. Start with a task analysis and identify alternative actions in each step of an activity or procedure. Then flowchart the steps, depicting precisely what choices are available to a performer and what consequences will result from each choice. Use an algorithm only for *short* procedures, since lengthy ones will require many pages to flowchart.

Procedure manuals are books filled with step-by-step instructions for carrying out work activities. They are intended to serve as practical "how-to" references, organized around typical work duties or problem situations, and are meant to be consulted by performers as need arises. To develop a procedure manual, begin with a comprehensive list of organizational policies or work-related problems. Conduct a separate task analysis or procedure analysis on each policy or problem activity. Then write step-by-step guidelines on what to do to comply with each policy or solve each work-related problem.

Procedure manuals are often written with the aid of the *playscript technique,* which takes its name from highly structured scripts used in theatrical productions. A procedure that is described by means of the playscript technique lists steps in chronological order from beginning to end and uses columns with headings such as "When?," "Who?," and "Does What?" Items in the "When" column describe the conditions under which action should be taken or the time it should be taken. Items in the "Who" column affix responsibility for taking action. Items in the "Does What?" column describe what steps should be taken. While potentially useful for providing on-the-spot guidance to workers, procedure manuals are often tough to keep up to date. (When out of date, they create more of a performance problem than they solve!)

Work samples are examples of work that can be used by employees to save time or imitate a previously successful work product. It is easy to cite examples of them. Lawyers use work samples when consulting books filled with prewritten contracts. Secretaries use work samples when they pull a letter from the file and revise it to handle a similar situation. Auditors use work samples when they prepare an "exemplary audit report" and then follow it when subsequently asked to prepare reports. If employees can *see* an example of something that has been done correctly, they can often replicate it closely in similar situations in the future.

Reward Systems

A reward system is the organization's way of tying employee actions to positive consequences. You might think of it as the means by which an organization attracts people to join, keeps them working, and motivates them to train or perform (Bishop, 1988b; Gibson, Ivancevich, and Donnelly, 1985). Rewards are the positive consequences that (presumably) greet individual performance that is in line with organizational goals. A significant amount of research has been conducted on reward systems from the standpoint of human motivation (Brown, 1989; Rosenbaum, 1982; Society for Human Resource Management, 1989a). Motivation means simply "the desire to perform." It governs human choices of behavior and action (Vroom, 1964), and it is related to rewards because people choose to perform what they are rewarded for doing. While theories of rewards and human motivation differ, everyone agrees that employees tend to do what they are rewarded for doing, will avoid what they are punished for doing, and will neglect what they are neither punished nor rewarded for doing (Kerr, 1975; Leibman and Weinstein, 1990).

Managers do not always consider employee rewards or motivation when carrying out such typical management functions as planning, organizing, scheduling, delegating, controlling, budgeting, communicating, or staffing (Lawler, 1977). As a result, rewards do not always match up with desired performance (Kerr, 1975), and the impact on performance is predictably negative. In contrast, organizations typified by a culture of "excelïence" tend to match rewards to organizational goals and desired results (Kerr and Slocum, 1988; Peters and Waterman, 1982).

When Should Rewards Be Used in Addressing a Performance Problem?

Rewards or work consequences should be reviewed when planning any change that will affect the organization, work group, individual, or job. Instructional designers should be sure to pose the following question before the change is implemented and consider the answer carefully: "What's in it for the performer if he or she does what is asked?" To perform successfully, people must feel they will be able to succeed. They must also expect to receive some reward—and must *value* this reward (Vroom, 1964).

When troubleshooting existing performance problems, instructional designers should pose these questions to identify a problem caused by a poorly designed reward system: (1) Is the problem caused by obstacles in the work environment rather than by a lack of skills on the part of the individual? (2) Before performing, does the employee *expect* not to be rewarded—or even to be treated negatively—as a result of performing as desired? (3) Are the consequences of performing without much perceived *value* to the employee? (4) Do employees find the consequences of performing as desired negative (punishing), *or* neutral (no results), *or* positive (important)? If the answer to the question as well as to any other question is yes, then the performance problem is caused by a poorly designed reward system.

How Should Incentive Systems Be Used to Address a Performance Problem?

In what should be considered a classic article on incentive systems, Kemmerer and Thiagarajan (1989, p. 11) note that all incentive systems "should be *intentional, external,* and *standardized.*" By *intentional,* they mean that incentives should be deliberately designed to encourage a performance that is consistent with job or organizational goals. By *external,* they mean that rewards should generally be controlled and monitored by management levels within the organization. By *standardized,* they mean that all reward systems "should specify a standard procedure that identifies the employees, activities, and incentives—and the relationships among them" (p. 11). Employees in an organization may be categorized into groups, the activities and accomplishments of each group may be identified as they contribute to organizational goals, and each group may be rewarded in line with its accomplishments.

Whenever approaching a performance problem, instructional designers should always consider the consequences to performers of achieving results desired by an organization. Any intentionally designed incentive system may have been established to achieve from one to four possible goals: (1) contribute to attracting people to an organization, (2) encourage people to remain with the organization, (3) encourage people to behave in certain ways—

such as follow standard operating procedures, or (4) encourage people to achieve work results desired by an organization. *If the consequences of performing result in none of these, then it is unlikely that the performance is being intentionally encouraged by the organization. But it should be, if the performance is valued.*

Various incentives may be matched to desired work results. In general, they can be classified as *monetary incentives* (sometimes called *extrinsic rewards*) or *nonmonetary incentives* (or intrinsic rewards). The following comprehensive list, adapted from Kemmerer and Thiagarajan's article "What Is an Incentive System?" in *Performance and Instruction,* includes illustrations of each type. While some experts on incentive theory may dispute the accuracy of the categories presented below, the list does provide an excellent overview of incentives for performing.

Monetary Incentives	Nonmonetary Incentives
Salary	*Working Conditions*
Base salary	Celebrations and
Beginning salary	rituals
Holiday payment	Choice of project
Market adjustment	Collegiality
Overtime payment	Flexible calendar
Salary scales	Flexible schedule
Weekend payment	Geographical location
	Informality
Differential Pay	Job enrichment
Merit pay	Nature of work
Pay for knowledge	Organizational
Pay for length of service	culture
Pay for performance	Size of organization
	Staff support
Allowances	Type of community
Clothing allowance	Type of customers
Cost-of-living allowance	Type of organization
Entertainment allowance	Workload
Family allowance	
Hardship allowance	*Training*
Housing allowance	Mentoring
Relocation payment	Off-site training
Training allowance	On-the-job training
Travel allowance	Participation in professional
	conferences
Time off with Pay	Support for personal devel-
Disability payments	opment
Family illness leave	Support for professional de-
Jury duty	velopment

Monetary Incentives

Maternity leave
Military duty
Paid vacation
Paternity leave
Personal leave
Sabbatical
Sick leave
Vacations

Deferred Income

Investment trust
Pension plan
Postretirement consulting
Profit sharing
Social security
Stock option

Loss-of-Job Coverage

Guaranteed annual income
Outplacement assistance
Severance pay
Unemployment insurance

Other Perquisites

Athletic leagues
Automobile
Cash bonus
Children's education
Club membership
Commission
Company apartment
Expense account
Financial counseling
Free housing
Free meals
Gift
Legal service
Liability insurance
Loan
Medical examinations
Parking insurance
Parking
Physical fitness program

Nonmonetary Incentives

Training facilities and
  equipment
Training materials

Facilities, Equipment, and Materials

Access to supplies
Appropriate facilities
Cafeteria
Equipment use and training
Ergonomic design
Executive washroom
Job aids and documentation
Office size
Type of furniture

Management

Access to information
Compatible values
Dynamic leadership
Freedom to innovate
Frequent feedback
Lunch with a manager
Participatory decision
  making
Participatory goal setting
Performance appraisal
Recognition by manager

Career Opportunities

Career counseling
Career ladder
Committee assignments
Entrepreneurial support
Job security
Job title
Membership in elite team
Opportunities for profes-
  sional growth
Opportunities for promotion
Patents
Royalties
Tenure
Type of industry

Monetary Incentives

Product samples
Spouse travel
Stock bonus
Subsidized housing
Survivor protection
Tax service

Employee Selection Practices

Effective employee selection practices involve matching people to jobs or assignments for which they are qualified by virtue of their education, experience, attitudes, and abilities (Myers, 1986). Employee recruitment, a related activity, involves seeking individuals who are qualified for jobs or assignments and encouraging them to participate in the selection procedure. In these processes, managers in most organizations begin by analyzing work activities. They then infer from those activities the knowledge, skills, and attitudes necessary for applicants to learn the job quickly, recruit people from sources where they can acquire the necessary knowledge or skills, and screen individuals until the best-qualified candidate is matched to the job (Arvey and Faley, 1988; Eder and Ferris, 1990; Schmitt and Robertson, 1990). Human resource managers are particularly well equipped to provide insight into methods of improving selection and recruitment practices.

If there is a single step that most organizations can take to improve human performance, improving selection and recruitment methods might well be it. As Leibler and Parkman (1986, p. 176) note, "the place to begin *preventing* performance problems and reducing their associated cost is in the selection of personnel." They argue that instructional designers should apply their expertise to improving human performance by describing jobs, analyzing them, and determining selection criteria.

Selection methods influence training because the knowledge, skills, and attitudes that individuals bring to a job influence what they must learn to perform competently. If experienced people are hired for jobs, training time should be reduced. Of course, the organization will generally have to pay a premium on salaries for experienced people. If inexperienced people are hired, training time should be increased. The organization will also be able to pay less for salaries.

When Should Selection Practices Be
Used to Address a Performance Problem?

Corrective action should be taken to improve organizational selection practices when most or all of the following symptoms are evident: (1) turnover is high; (2) involuntary termination rates are increasing from their historical rates in the organization; (3) employees are complaining that, at the time they were recruited for or placed in their current positions, they were not expecting the work activities they subsequently encountered in their jobs; and (4) supervisors and managers are complaining that their employees are ill-equipped, even after training, to perform duties for which they were hired.

How Should Selection Methods Be Used to Address a Performance Problem?

If instructional designers have reason to believe that performance problems in an organization stem in whole or in part from selection methods — or believe changes in selection methods can contribute to solving existing performance problems — then they should focus their attention on each major step in the organization's selection process. They should begin by examining recruitment, job analysis, selection tools, and selection results.

Recruitment is the process of attracting people to the organization. There are two labor pools from which to recruit: (1) inside the organization, and (2) outside the organization. Examine methods presently being used to recruit from both sources. Is any *long-term, continuous effort* being made to identify and target sources of talent, both internal and external, for entry-level vacancies in the future — or do decision makers wait until vacancies exist and then scurry around madly looking for people to fill them? If the latter is the case, work to improve external recruitment by establishing internship programs with local schools, work-study programs with government agencies, and adopt-a-school efforts to build ties with local sources of talent. Run job advertisements even when no vacancies exist simply to keep a large and current inventory of applications on file to use as the need arises. Make sure that recruitment efforts are targeted, as much as possible, at sources of talent appropriate for meeting the organization's needs. At the same time, establish internal job posting and career improvement programs so that employees can gradually qualify for higher-level positions in the organization (Rothwell and Kazanas, 1988b).

Job analysis is the process of identifying job activities in the organization (Ghorpade, 1988; Levine, 1983; McCormick, 1979). The result of a job analysis is a *job description,* which literally describes what people should be responsible for doing and what results they should achieve (Bishop, 1988a; Jones, 1984). When addressing a performance problem that may be caused by poor selection methods, examine the *completeness, accuracy,* and *currency* of existing job descriptions (Bishop, 1988a). Do they provide clues, as they should, for identifying the knowledge, skills, and attitudes needed for successful job performance? Do they provide criteria for evaluating the education and experience of applicants relative to the knowledge, skills, and attitudes needed for successful job performance? If not, work toward updating job descriptions — or making them more complete or accurate. Start by consulting *The Dictionary of Occupational Titles* (Bureau of Labor Statistics, 1977).

Then refer to other references that can aid in preparation of job descriptions (Bruce, 1986; Bureau of Law and Business, 1982; Business Research Publications, 1976; Jones, 1984; Ulery, 1981; Workman and Sperling, 1975).

Selection tools are methods for structuring information or evaluating applicants relative to work requirements. They include application blanks, selection tests, and structured guides for interviewing job applicants. Written preemployment tests, in particular, have been the subject of substantial litigation since the Civil Rights Act of 1964 because the results "exhibit a sizeable mean difference in test scores between black and white employees. . . . " (Arvey and Faley, 1988, p. 317). Even though recent court cases have made the legal status of preemployment tests equivocal, there is research evidence to support the desirability of using multiple selection tools instead of relying simply on unstructured job interviews. In some cases, major improvements can be made in selection practices simply by substituting highly structured for unstructured employment interviews through the use of a job performance aid called an *employment interview guide* (Eder and Ferris, 1990; McMurray, 1979; Schmitt and Robertson, 1990; Webster, 1982).

Selection results are consequences of recruitment and selection methods. Typical results may include separation (firings or resignations), retention in the present position, or movement within the organization. Take care to examine separations, both voluntary and involuntary, before and after any change in selection procedures. Try to predict, in advance, what effects will be created by a change in selection methods.

Selection results may also include the proportion of protected groups within the organization compared to those in the general population from which the organization recruits and hires. While recent Supreme Court cases have raised doubts at this writing about the future of *disparate impact* — defined as otherwise neutral selection practices that have a consequence of adversely affecting employment of protected groups — socially responsible organizations support voluntary efforts to seek out and employ members of protected labor groups such as women, minorities, and the disabled.

For this reason, many organizations take *affirmative action* to recruit, hire, train, and promote people in protected labor categories. Any changes in selection practices should be made only after considering what effects (if any) they will have on efforts to support social equality in human resources practices.

Organizational Redesign

"*Organization design* refers to managerial decision making to determine the structure and processes that coordinate and control the job of the organization" (Gibson, Ivancevich, and Donnelly, 1985, p. 487). *Organizational redesign* is the process of *changing* "assigned goals, responsibilities, and reporting relationships within a given organization" (Rummler, 1986, p. 212). Although typically connoting changes in the organization's structure (reporting relationships), organizational redesign in a broader sense may include *any* change in the structure of an organization, division, department, work unit, or job. It may thus incorporate *job redesign,* meaning changes in "the contents, methods, and relationships of jobs to satisfy both organizational and individual requirements" (Gibson, Ivancevich, and Donnelly, 1985, p. 16).

There is a substantial body of literature on organizational design and redesign, including much impressive research (Carr, 1990; Chase and Tansik, 1983; The Conference Board, 1989c; Nystrom and Starbuck, 1983; Pearce and David, 1983; and Rummler, 1986). This research leaves little doubt that organizational design affects organizational and individual performance. Less certain is what the relationship is, how much it is affected by the personal motives of those establishing organizational designs, and what unpredictable results can stem from changes made to those designs. As Gibson, Ivancevich, and Donnelly (1985, p. 419) point out, "it is entirely reasonable to acknowledge that in many instances organizational structures do not contribute positively to organizational performance because managers are unable by training or intellect to design a structure that guides the behavior of individuals and groups to achieve high levels of production, efficiency, satisfaction, adaptiveness, and development." But inappropriate organizational designs can create severe problems. Some experts have suggested that these will have an increasingly negative impact on U.S. productivity. They recommend that modern organizations be redesigned to allow greater individual discretion than has been common in designs more appropriate for the early Industrial Revolution than for the Information Age (National Center on Education and the Economy, 1990).

When Should Organizational Redesign Be Used to Address a Performance Problem?

Consider organizational redesign as a possible solution to performance problems when the following symptoms are evident: (1) confusion about job responsibilities; (2) vague or unclear job descriptions; (3) outdated organization charts; (4) unclear relationships between the organization's stated strategic goals and its structure; (5) complaints from supervisors and managers about overseeing too many people or too many different jobs; (6) pockets of "burned out" employees doing boring work, too much work, or too little work; (7) inefficient workflow, resulting in inefficient steps, unnecessary complexity, or other wasteful uses of resources; or (8) inability by the organization to adapt swiftly to dynamic conditions in the external environment — such as new competitors or unusual requests from suppliers.

How Should Organizational Redesign Be Used to Address a Performance Problem?

Rummler (1986) outlines specific steps for instructional designers to follow in organizational redesign. First, he suggests determining where there *is* a need to redesign the structure of jobs in the organization or the collection of activities a job is made up of. Redesign should be considered, he notes, only when the organization is experiencing a performance problem in responding to external demands or in using resources efficiently. Second, he recommends examining the primary responsibilities of each major structural component of the organization—division, department, or work unit—to identify key problems affecting each component and describe the flow of work passing through the organizational system. Third, he suggests preparing alternate and improved models of workflow. Fourth, he emphasizes the importance of establishing a mission (purpose statement) and goals (desired results) for the new, major structural components illustrated on the organization chart. Fifth, he recommends drawing up a new organization chart (structure) for the organization based on environmental demands and efficient workflow. Sixth and finally, he urges that the process of establishing new missions and goals down the organization's chain of command be continued until each division, department, and job is included.

Rummler's suggestions for organizational redesign are quite logical. Similar suggestions are offered in the literature of Strategic Business Planning (Galbraith and Nathanson, 1978) and job redesign (Hackman and Oldham, 1980). Unfortunately, organizational redesign is as much a *political* issue affecting the power of individual managers as it is an *efficiency* issue affecting an organization's ability to survive in its environment. Consequently, logical approaches do not always prevail and are sometimes sacrificed to the wishes of self-interested mangers (Gibson, Ivancevich, and Donnelly, 1985).

Jacobs (1987, p. 32) describes several ways to carry out organizational redesign. He suggests (1) changing reporting relationships; (2) improving information sharing; (3) defining job responsibilities; (4) changing job responsibilities; (5) changing goals, objectives, or standards; and (6) increasing information available about workflow systems.

Changing reporting relationships means altering who reports to whom. It is the one method most commonly associated with organizational redesign. It should be used carefully because changing the leaders of various organizational components can have unintended side effects. For instance, subordinating one activity or department or manager to another inevitably reduces the emphasis placed on the subordinated activity or department and creates another management layer through which approvals must pass.

Improving information sharing means finding ways to increase relevant, job-related information about workflow in an organization. To achieve this goal, conduct a *communication audit* (Goldhaber and Rogers, 1979). Using a standardized questionnaire and approach to analyzing organizational communication, examine what information—and how much—flows between work units. In addition, examine how and when information is communicated.

Defining job responsibilities has to do with analyzing what people do, how they do it, and what results are desirable in line with organizational goals. When responsibilities or work goals are vague, employee and organizational performance can be improved simply by describing what people do. In practical terms, it means creating job descriptions when they do not exist, revising those that are outdated, or communicating to employees what job responsibilities they are accountable for.

Changing job responsibilities is sometimes appropriate to address performance problems caused by boring jobs (Buchanan, 1979). Use *job enrichment* to add tasks to jobs so that they will become more interesting and will require employees to exercise increased responsibility. Job enrichment is a method of creating a *qualitative* change in responsibilities. To address performance problems caused by jobs with a limited range of tasks, use *job enlargement* to add more of the same kinds of tasks to the job. This is a means of creating *quantitative* change in responsibilities. To address performance problems caused by shortages of staff in key positions — a common problem as organizations downsize — use *job rotation* to relieve monotony and cross-train several workers for key jobs.

Changing goals, objectives, or standards is a means of shifting accountability for a job, work unit, department, division, or organization. A goal is derived from a statement of purpose that addresses the reason for the existence of a job or organization. It is usually expressed in general — rather than in specific, measurable — terms. An objective is derived from a goal. It is specific and measurable. It describes what must be achieved in a given period of time and how good achievement is defined. A standard is a minimum expectation of performance, usually expressed in measurable terms. By changing goals, objectives, or standards, decision makers can also change the direction of an organization or organizational component.

Increasing information available about workflow systems means helping people understand how each part of an organization contributes to the products made or services delivered. There are many ways to achieve this purpose. In some organizations, for instance, managers provide their employees with published "directories" that list "who to call for help" on specific, common problems. In other organizations, company newspapers run articles periodically on each department so that employees will know what each department does and how work flows through it.

Conclusion

Noninstructional solutions should be chosen when employee performance problems are caused by deficiencies in the environment. They should also be used when they are more cost effective than such instructional solutions as training, education, or development for addressing deficiencies in knowledge, skills, or attitudes. As we pointed out in this chapter, five noninstructional solutions are frequently used: (1) feedback methods, (2) job performance aids, (3) reward systems, (4) employee selection practices, and (5) organizational redesign. Each is appropriate for addressing only certain performance problems, and we provided guidelines for selecting when to use each noninstructional solution. We also described specific ways to improve feedback methods, prepare job performance aids, redesign reward systems, reexamine employee selection practices, and redesign organizational reporting relationships.

CHAPTER THREE

Determining Projects
Appropriate for
Instructional Design Solutions

This chapter is based on the first instructional design competency identified in *The Standards* (1986). It focuses on analyzing employee performance problems systematically and identifying their root cause(s), activities that instructional designers typically call *performance analysis* or *front-end analysis*. (We use the term *performance analysis* throughout.) Performance analysis is carried out to distinguish problems, situations, or projects appropriate for instructional solutions — such as job-specific training — from those that are more appropriately addressed through noninstructional solutions.

We begin the chapter by defining employee performance problems and labeling their most common features. We then distinguish between two types of problem-solving models, comprehensive and situation-specific, and describe how to apply them. A simple example of a problem-solving situation is provided. Finally, we conclude with brief discussions about judging and justifying performance analyses.

Defining Employee Performance Problems
and Labeling Their Parts

The word *problem* is formed from two Greek words — *pro,* meaning "forward," and *ballein,* meaning "to throw" (McCall and Kaplan, 1985, p. 10). It literally means "something thrown forward," a result of a discrepancy between the actual (*what is?*) and the ideal (*what should be?*) that requires present or future action. The actual is called *condition,* meaning "the existing state of affairs." The ideal is called *criterion,* meaning "the desired state of affairs." The difference between condition and criterion is a *gap.* The reason for the gap is the problem's *cause;* the consequences of the gap are the problem's *symptoms.* These components of a problem are illustrated in Figure 3.1.

Figure 3.1. Components of a Problem.

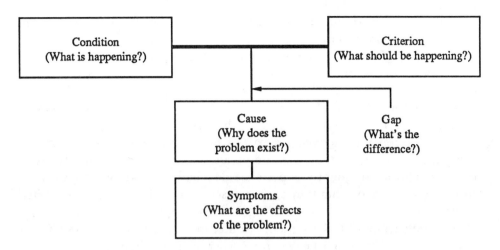

To be successful in determining which performance problems are appropriately addressed through instruction, instructional designers must be able to distinguish between these components.

First, collect information about the *condition*. It should be easily identified. Simply ask people about the problem. When people describe what is happening or how employees are performing, they are providing information about condition. Second, identify *criterion*. It may not be as easily identified as condition. Criterion refers to the desired or ideal state, what should be happening or how people should be performing. There are essentially two kinds of criteria: (1) *performance standards,* which are minimally acceptable job performance benchmarks (Springer, 1980), and (2) *performance objectives,* which are desirable job performance targets (Odiorne, 1979). Inexperienced employees usually require training to perform to standard. Experienced employees are expected to perform at least to standard. In contrast, performance objectives require results that are greater than minimal requirements. Performance standards, like objectives, should be measurable and expressed as results to be achieved in an identifiable time period. Standards are usually established from historical information, organizational plans, or management expectations. Objectives should be established by mutual agreement of employees and their immediate supervisors.

Unfortunately, managers do not always establish clear expectations for performance — that is, performance standards or objectives. Nor do they always communicate their expectations to workers. In these situations, the performance problem results from a lack of criteria. Employees cannot perform competently when managers do not know what they want! In these cases, instructional designers can often solve the problem by helping managers establish and communicate performance standards or objectives to workers (Brennan, 1990).

After identifying condition and criterion, identify the *gap* (difference) between them. What is the difference? How important is it? If it is not important, time and resources should be devoted to other, more significant projects; if it is important, then consider the problem's *cause. Always remember that the only effective solution to any problem must address its cause.* While human performance is complicated and many causes for a performance problem are possible (Fournies, 1988), all causes can be reduced to three fundamental ones (Rummler, 1983): (1) a deficiency of knowledge, (2) a deficiency of environment, or (3) a combination of the first two.

A deficiency of knowledge exists when people do not know how to perform or what results they seek. For example, newly hired or newly transferred employees frequently experience deficiencies of knowledge because they are not aware of what they are supposed to do or how they are expected to perform.

A deficiency of environment—sometimes called a deficiency of execution—exists when people face barriers to performance. Such barriers include poor or inadequate feedback, poorly designed jobs, or negative (punishing) consequences for good performance. For example, a deficiency of environment may be created when an employee is asked to perform her job while, at the same time, performing the job of a vacationing employee. In this case, she has been burdened with double duty and may not perform either job successfully.

A combination of deficiencies of knowledge and environment exists when part of a performance problem results from an employee's lack of knowledge or skills or poor attitude and part results from obstacles posed by the environment. Suppose that, in the example in the previous paragraph, the employee is asked to perform someone else's job but has never been trained to do it. In that case, she will experience both a deficiency of knowledge (the other job) and a deficiency of environment (performing two jobs at once).

Symptoms, the last component of a problem labeled in Figure 3.1, are the consequences of a performance problem. Quite often, managers confuse a symptom with a problem. Typical symptoms include (Rummler, 1983, p. 10):

- Tasks are not being performed to standards.
- Employee performance gets worse over time.
- Employees do not believe there is reason for them to perform as desired.
- Deadlines are not being met.
- There is a work backlog.
- Employees are performing up to standards, but work is rejected because of a mismatch with quality control requirements.
- Some work tasks are "forgotten."
- Employees perform only when they are observed by their supervisors.
- Managers have reason to believe employees are deliberately exerting less effort than they are capable of.

Each item in this list is a *symptom* because underlying causes will only be revealed after further investigation. However, these symptoms typically result from a deficiency of environment, not a deficiency of knowledge. Hence, instruction will not be appropriate as a solution because it addresses deficiencies of individual knowledge. To solve these problems, instructional designers should apply noninstructional solutions.

Models for Performance Analysis

Over the years, several well-known instructional designers have devoted considerable attention to performance analysis. Through experience they have developed models for troubleshooting human performance problems. These models differ somewhat because their creators were not always trying to achieve the same results.

Two Categories of Models

There are two categories of problem-solving models: (1) *comprehensive models,* which are useful for scanning "the big picture" of an organization to identify problems, and (2) *situation-specific models,* which provide guidance in dealing with the kind of run-of-the-mill symptoms that prompt managers to request the aid of instructional designers. A comprehensive model is appropriate for those occasions in which much information must be reviewed quickly, such as full-scale instructional design projects involving an entire organization. On the other hand, a situation-specific model is appropriate for troubleshooting management requests to solve immediate operational problems.

Applying a Comprehensive Problem-Solving Model: Gilbert's Performance Matrix

Perhaps the best example of a comprehensive model is Gilbert's *performance matrix.* Gilbert (1978, p. 110) describes it as "a way to organize our points of view so we shall set first things first when we design a performance system . . . and troubleshoot problems in existing systems." It is called a *matrix* because it allows instructional designers to examine six different hierarchically ordered performance levels. Each level corresponds to a different value system or vantage point by which performance can be viewed. Each level contains three related "cells"—models, measures, and methods. Gilbert uses the term *model* to mean a criterion, ideal, goal, expectation, standard, or objective. A *measure* is analogous to condition or actual results. A *method* is a solution, a way to narrow or close a gap between what is (*measure*) and what should be (*model*).

When the matrix is applied to organizational settings, Gilbert suggests using only the three bottom levels of the matrix—Policy (Institutional systems), Strategy (Job systems), and Tactics (Task systems). Gilbert (1978,

p. 136) believes these levels are "most demanding of detailed analysis when we design such subcultures as schools or institutions in the world of work." Gilbert calls this modified matrix the Performance Engineering Model (PEM).

Gilbert's disciple Rummler (1976) has described in detail how to apply the PEM. He suggests that instructional designers begin their analysis at the Policy level, asking questions about models, measures, and methods to determine which performance improvement programs will have the highest possible payoffs. They should then ask questions about the Strategy level to identify how to define and improve jobs. Finally, they should ask questions about the Tactics level to determine what specific actions must be taken to help people become more efficient in their jobs. The appropriate questions to ask appear in the modified Performance Engineering Matrix presented in Table 3.1.

Begin the investigation by asking the questions appearing *at the top left of the PEM*. Then work to the right and down. There is one important reason for applying this top-down approach: *"the source of performance problems usually originates from the organizational level just above where the problem is first perceived to exist"* (Jacobs, 1987, p. 29). For instance, many job problems (at the Strategy level) stem from organizational, departmental, or division problems (Policy level). Similarly, many task problems within jobs (Tactical level) stem from job problems (Strategy level). To solve these problems, the cause(s) at higher levels *must* be addressed first.

Applying a Situation-Specific Problem-Solving Model: Mager and Pipe's Performance Analysis

Gilbert's Performance Engineering Model is a powerful tool. But it is not the only one useful in troubleshooting performance problems. In fact, the problem-solving model of Mager and Pipe may actually be better known than Gilbert's. Mager and Pipe's model, summarized in their book *Analyzing Performance Problems or "You Really Oughta Wanna"* (1984), is particularly useful to instructional designers as they handle the daily requests for assistance they receive from managers and supervisors. Their model is shown in Figure 3.2.

Review this model step by step, starting at the top and reading down. The first step is to collect as much information as possible about the performance problem. Ask questions such as these:

> What is the problem?
> How many people are affected?
> When did the problem first become evident?
> What are the consequences of the problem?
> What is happening at present?
> How do you know there is a problem?
> Who is affected by it?

Table 3.1. The Performance Engineering Matrix.

Levels	Models *What should be?*	Measures *What is?*	Methods *How can performance gaps be closed?*
POLICY (Organizational, Divisional, Departmental, and Work-Unit Level)	• How should work be organized? • How should work be allocated? • How should work flow into, through, and out of the organization, work unit, or job? • How can economic benefits be maximized?	• What are present conditions? • What gaps exist between what is and what should be? • What gaps are of most economic importance?	• What general methods could be used to solve the performance problem(s)? • What are the estimated costs of each general method that can be used to solve the problem? • What performance improvement method is likely to have the greatest worth?
STRATEGY (Job Level)	• What are the most important work outputs of the job? • How should the job be structured? • What are the requirements associated with major duties/results of the job? • What are the standards for each work output?	• What is the present status of the job? • What deficiencies exist in job outputs? • What are the *causes* of important discrepancy between what is and what should be?	• What performance improvement method(s) can be used to narrow or close performance gaps? (Consider information, training, guidance, motivation, reward systems, etc.)
TACTICS (Tasks-Within-Jobs Levels)	• What do people have to know or do to achieve desired results and carry out desired tasks? • What environment is needed for the job? • What can be done to match the right people to the right jobs?	• What media should be used? • What time schedules should be used to develop designs? • What are the costs of implementing solutions?	• What materials, tools, and resources are needed to solve performance problems (that is, narrow or close gaps between what is and what should be)?

Source: Rummler, G. "The Performance Audit." In R. Craig (ed.), *Training and Development Handbook: A Guide to Human Resource Development.* (2nd ed.) New York: McGraw-Hill, 1976, p. 14-11. Reproduced with the permission of McGraw-Hill, Inc.

Figure 3.2. Mager and Pipe's Performance Analysis Model.

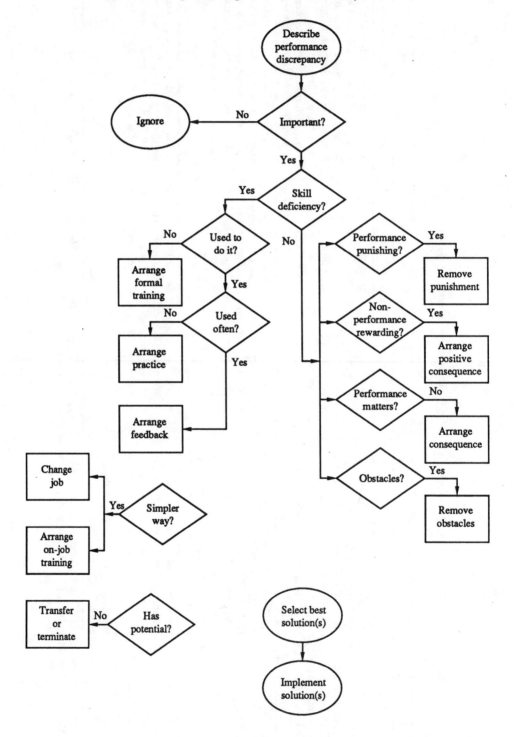

Source: Mager, R., and Pipe, P. *Analyzing Performance Problems or "You Really Oughta Wanna."*
Belmont, Calif.: Lake Publishing Company, 1984, p. 3. Used by permission of the publisher.

Where is the problem evident?
Are some locations affected more than others?
What should be happening?
How wide is the gap between what is and what should be?

Use the answers to these questions to *describe* the performance discrepancy.
Next consider the relative importance of the performance problem.
Continue to pose questions to people familiar with it:

Why is the discrepancy important?
How much will it cost to fix the problem? (Estimate cost of training
    in salaries, lost work time, and preparation of training materials.)
What will happen if no action is taken to correct the problem?
How much is the discrepancy costing the organization in lost produc-
    tion, wasted materials, lost time, or employee turnover?
What is the estimated benefit of correcting the problem? (Subtract the
    estimated cost of correcting the problem from the estimated benefit
    to the organization of correcting the problem.)

Use the answers to these questions to compare the expected benefits (sav-
ings) of correcting the problem less the cost of correcting it. If the problem
does not meet the test of importance, ignore it and devote attention to other
problems. If the problem meets the test of importance, go on to the next step.

Next, consider whether the performance discrepancy is caused by deficiencies in knowledge, skills, or attitudes or in the environment. Ask this
crucial question: *Could people perform properly if their lives depended on it?* The
answer to this question is crucial and can provide guidance in selecting an
appropriate way to close the performance gap.

If it is a deficiency in knowledge, skills, or attitudes — that is, people
could not perform competently even if their lives depended on it — then ask
another series of questions to identify an appropriate solution. First, are people
accustomed to performing? If not, consider formal training. For example,
training is appropriate when reducing the unproductive breaking-in period
of new employees. If people are accustomed to performing, determine whether
they are used to performing *often*. If not, address the performance problem
by giving employees the opportunity to practice. If they are performing often,
the problem may be solved by improving the quantity and quality of feedback that employees receive about what they do (Jacobs, 1988).

Before deciding on a final solution, double-check the analysis. Consider: Is there a simpler way to address the problem than has been identified to this point? For instance, would it be easier and faster to change
the job? Or to provide employees with checklists, procedure manuals, or
other job performance aids that can be used as the job is performed? Would
on-the-job training solve the problem more quickly and inexpensively?

Finally, analyze the performer before offering off-the-job training, arranging practice, arranging feedback, changing the job, or arranging on-

the-job training. Do all performers have the ability to benefit from the corrective action that is contemplated? If not, transfer employees who are unable to learn job requirements. These performers may require retraining for other jobs first. As a solution of last resort, terminate people who cannot be matched to available jobs in the organization.

If a performance problem is caused by a deficiency of environment — that is, people could perform if their lives depended on it but are not doing so for some reason — then ask other questions to find the best solution. Begin with this one: Why are people not performing? First, consider whether people are *punished* in some way for performing. For example, does their good performance yield them nothing but more work — or the sneers of co-workers? (If so, they will *not* perform as desired until the punishment is removed.) If people are not punished for performing, are they rewarded in some way for *not* performing as desired? For example, are they praised by co-workers for devoting their energies to other activities? If so, then non-performance is rewarding and the consequences should be changed. Make it so that performance *is* rewarding. Finally, consider whether employees face obstacles that prevent them from performing. If they do, remove the obstacles.

At this point, select and implement solutions to the performance problem. As part of this process, prepare detailed estimates of the benefits expected to result from correcting the performance problem. In addition, estimate the likely costs of taking corrective action.

Quite often the *means* of implementing a solution is as important as the *results* to be achieved. For this reason, take pains to brief key decision makers about the cause of the performance problem and gain their support for implementing an appropriate solution. Encourage them to participate in this process, recognizing that their participation will be time consuming and will undoubtedly add to the time and cost of solving the problem. However, their support will also increase the likelihood that the solution will be successful.

Performance Analysis: An Example

Joel Finlay is an instructional designer employed by the XYZ Corporation. Working out of the Corporate Training Department, Joel is a troubleshooter who responds to special requests for assistance made by any of the corporate divisions. His primary function is to diagnose performance problems and identify appropriate solutions. Based on his recommendations, division or corporate management will either ask for additional assistance from the Training Department or will contract externally with vendors for help in rectifying a performance problem.

Joel was recently asked for assistance by XYZ pharmaceuticals, manufacturers and marketers of many popular over-the-counter cold remedies. Joel was told this divison was experiencing a decline in sales. The Director of Human Resources for this division, who initially contacted Joel, felt that the problem was caused by high turnover among the salesforce and that the problem could be solved by intensive sales training. Before Joel arrived at the division's headquarters, he asked the Director of Human Resources to schedule meetings with the Vice President of Marketing and several other key managers in the division so that, when Joel arrived, he could use his time economically.

In that initial meeting, Joel explained to the managers that his purpose was not solely to deal with the (purported) turnover problem, which might only be a symptom of some other problem, but rather to help the managers identify opportunities for performance improvement in the division. He went on to explain that, to be of maximum value, he needed to collect background information about the division.

Joel began his questioning at the top left of Gilbert's performance matrix. He asked the managers to describe for him how the division is structured, how work flows into and out of it, and what activities are of greatest economic value to it. He then went on to ask them about present conditions (sales, turnover, profits, and so on) and desired conditions (sales standards and targets). From this quick overview, Joel could see that the division's primary source of revenues depended on the salesforce. Each salesperson was given an exclusive territory, worked solely on commission, and made commissions by servicing all product outlets in the assigned area.

Switching to the Strategy (Job) level of Gilbert's performance matrix, Joel then asked about the *outputs* of the salesperson's job. From detailed questioning, Joel was able to determine that the managers could not identify important outputs. They tended to speak in terms of *activities* (*behaviors*) rather than *results*. Joel also learned that some salespersons had territories so large — such as the entire Chicago area — that one person could not possibly service it effectively. By this point, Joel had gathered enough information to recommend (1) clarifying work standards by outputs, and (2) restructuring the salespersons' jobs so that their territories could be handled effectively.

Not wishing to disappoint his clients, Joel then shifted his attention to salesforce turnover. Joel called this the *presenting problem*. (For Joel, a *presenting problem* is one that triggers an initial plea for help from managers.) Joel examined the turnover issue by using Mager and Pipe's Performance Analysis Model. He asked the managers to describe the nature of the problem, how present turnover differed from historical rates, what locations (if any) were affected by turnover most, what information had been collected through exit interviews with departing salespersons, when turnover rates had begun increasing, and what corrective actions had already been taken to deal with turnover.

From answers to these and similar questions, Joel determined that turnover was an important problem for the XYZ Pharmaceutical Division. However, it did not stem from a deficiency in knowledge or skills or an attitude problem; rather, it seemed to stem from many obstacles faced by salespersons in their jobs. Joel made a note to himself to check that tentative conclusion against written exit interview questionnaires completed by terminating salespersons.

Joel found the managers receptive to his initial conclusions. They agreed to work with him to verify his conclusions — or arrive at new ones based on a review of exit interview questionnaires and talks with experienced salespersons.

Judging Performance Analysis

According to *The Standards* (1986, p. 24), instructional designers should be able to judge the quality of decisions made by others. There are several reasons why. First, the ability to think critically and thus evaluate decisions and actions made by others is usually a demonstration of proficient skill. Second, and more to the point, instructional designers must occasionally review the work of their professional colleagues to ensure that it was performed properly.

Judging performance analysis is particularly important because it is essential that employee performance problems be analyzed systematically and their causes determined before appropriate solutions can be identified.

On occasion, instructional designers do find themselves assigned to the middle — or even near the end — of a project rather than at the beginning. In these cases, a performance analysis has usually been completed by others. How do newcomers to a project know, then, that the performance analysis was properly completed? The answer is that they do not — at least not without reviewing, and critically evaluating, the steps in the performance analysis that was conducted.

In some instances, instructional designers who are assigned late to a project may need to conduct their own abbreviated performance analysis, a condensed version of a complete performance analysis. This is also an excellent way for a newcomer to be oriented to the project. To conduct an abbreviated performance analysis, instructional designers should begin by asking a number of important questions:

1. What was happening at the time the performance problem was first noticed?
2. What should have been happening?
3. How important was the gap between what was happening and what should have been happening?
4. What was the cause of the gap? Why was it happening?
    a. Was the problem attributable to deficiencies in knowledge, skills, or attitudes?
    b. Was the problem attributable to a deficiency in the environment?
    c. Was the problem caused by a combination of knowledge and environmental deficiencies?

5.   What actions have been taken to solve the problem?
6.   What has happened on the instructional design project?
7.   When did the project begin?
8.   Who has been working on the project?
9.   What important decisions have been made on the project?
10. How committed is management to achieving results?
11. What are the history, structure, and pertinent policies of the organization or group within the organization?
12. Who are the key decision makers associated with this instructional design project? What preferences do they seem to have for solving the problem?

An abbreviated performance analysis helps a team of instructional designers avoid groupthink—the deterioration of mental efficiency, reality testing, and moral judgment resulting from a group's desire to minimize interpersonal conflicts and preserve solidarity (Janis, 1973). By raising questions, a newly assigned instructional designer can bring out concerns and doubts that may be shared by several team members who have been reluctant, for fear of starting group conflict, to voice their opinions. This can be an effective way of preventing groupthink.

Justifying Performance Analysis

According to *The Standards* (1986), instructional designers should always be able to explain the underlying rationale for their decisions and actions. At least two approaches can be used by instructional designers to justify the results of their performance analyses. They are compatible and can thus be used together. The first approach is to educate clients about instructional design. This approach works best when there is extended contact between instructional designers and their clients. To use this approach, instructional designers should take every opportunity to brief their clients on the theory of performance analysis and the distinction between problems that lend themselves to solution through training, education, and development and problems that better lend themselves to other solutions. There are many opportunities for such briefings, such as during an initial meeting with a prospective client, during problem identification interviews, and in written project status reports. Instructional designers may also circulate articles on performance analysis, give talks to organizational groups, and write short articles for in-house publications. It is usually easier to justify results of performance analysis if managers have been educated about the process.

A second approach is to explain the assumptions underlying the decisions made in analyzing a specific problem, in identifying its cause(s), and in determining appropriate solutions. This approach seems to work best when the time for client contact is limited. Instructional designers using this approach should state their assumptions about problem solving up front, describe the steps taken to analyze the problem, and explain the reasons for choosing an appropriate solution. This approach appears to work best in written reports or oral presentations.

Conclusion

As we have noted in this chapter, any employee performance problem consists of several parts. *Condition* means "the existing state of affairs"; *criterion* means "the desired state of affairs." The difference between condition (what is happening?) and criterion (what should be happening?) is a *gap*. The reason for the gap is the problem's *cause;* the consequences of the gap are the problem's *symptoms*.

Various problem-solving models have been devised to provide guidance in troubleshooting. A *comprehensive model* is appropriate for large-scale examinations of organizations or work units. Some instructional designers use a comprehensive model when entering an organization for the first time. Perhaps the best example of a comprehensive model is Gilbert's Performance Engineering Model. A *situation-specific model* is useful to instructional designers as they handle the daily requests for help they receive from managers and supervisors. It is appropriate for small-scale examinations of problems stemming from operations. Perhaps the best known is Mager and Pipe's Performance Analysis Model.

By applying these models appropriately, instructional designers can determine the cause(s) of employee performance problems. All performance problems stem from just three possible causes: (1) deficiencies in knowledge, skills, or attitudes; (2) deficiencies in the environment; and (3) a combination of (1) and (2). There are two classes of solutions: instructional and noninstructional. Instructional solutions rely on training, education, or development to address performance problems. They should be chosen only when (1) performance problems are caused by deficiencies in individual knowledge, skills, or attitudes, and (2) alternatives have been ruled out. On the other hand, noninstructional solutions rely on methods other than training, education, and development to address performance problems. They should be chosen when problems are caused by environmental deficiencies or when they are less costly to use than instruction, as pointed out in Chapter Two.

PART II

Analyzing Needs, Learners, Work Settings, and Work

CHAPTER FOUR

Conducting
a Needs Assessment

After our discussion of noninstructional and instructional solutions to employee performance problems discussed in Chapters Two and Three, let us turn now to needs assessment. As we do so, we should begin by explaining that, over the years, instructional designers have devised over forty models to guide the process of developing instruction (Andrews and Goodson, 1980). Each model is based on a highly structured process called *instructional systems design* (ISD) that traces its roots to workplace research on effective training originally conducted by the U.S. military (Carnevale, Gainer, and Villet, 1990). These models have at least one feature in common: they base instruction (training) on job requirements in a dynamic, sequential, and multistage process. Once the cause of an employee performance problem has been pinpointed and a noninstructional solution has been ruled out, instructional designers then follow a series of predictable steps to prepare workplace training. One model for this process is shown in Figure 4.1. This chapter — and the nine chapters following it — describe each step of the model.

Conducting a needs assessment is the first step in the ISD model. It is also the second competency identified for instructional designers in *The Standards* (1986). The purpose of needs assessment is to uncover, more precisely than performance analysis does, what the performance problem is, who it affects, how it affects them, and what results are to be achieved by training. Needs assessment is very important because all subsequent steps in the ISD model depend on its results.

In this chapter, we define terms associated with needs assessment, describe essential steps in developing needs assessment plans, review typical problems likely to arise during needs assessment, suggest ways of overcoming these problems, explain how to identify instructional problems based on needs assessment results, and provide a simple case study highlighting important issues in needs assessment. We conclude the chapter by offering some advice on judging and justifying needs assessment.

Figure 4.1. A Model of Steps in the Instructional Design Process.

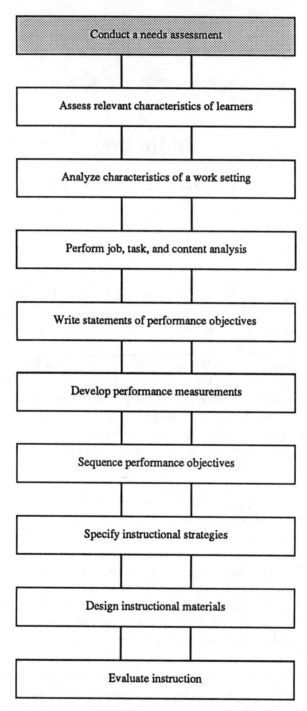

Source: Foshay, W., Silber, K., and Westgaard, O. *Instructional Design Competencies: The Standards.* Iowa City, Iowa: International Board of Standards for Training, Performance, and Instruction, 1986, p. 3. Used with permission of the publisher.

Defining Terms

To understand needs assessment, instructional designers should first understand the meaning of key terms associated with it. Such terms include *need, needs assessment, needs assessment planning,* and *needs assessment plan.*

A Definition of Need

A need is a performance gap separating what people know, do, or feel from what they should know, do, or feel to perform competently. The word should always be used as a noun, not as a verb (Kaufman, 1986). The reason: when need is used as a verb in the sentence "we need some training on time management," it implies something merely desirable (a want) rather than something essential to competent performance. A need should always be linked to the essential knowledge, skills, and attitudes an individual must possess to perform work competently and thereby accomplish the desired results.

A Definition of Needs Assessment

A needs assessment is an evaluation of instructional requirements. It is undertaken to "identify, document, and justify gaps between what is and what should be and place the gaps in priority order for closure" (Kaufman, 1986, p. 38). It is a traditional starting point for developing instruction (Sredl and Rothwell, 1987).

Kaufman and English (1979) identify six types of needs assessment arranged in a hierarchical order of complexity. The first, and least complex, is alpha assessment. It focuses on identifying the nature and cause of a performance problem. (An alpha assessment is synonymous with performance analysis.) A beta assessment is the second type. It is based on the assumption that an employee performance problem exists but that alternative solutions must be weighed for their relative cost-benefit and practicality. A gamma assessment, the third type, examines differences between alternative solutions to a performance problem. The fourth type is a delta assessment, and it examines specific performance gaps between *what is* and *what should be.* An epsilon assessment, the fifth type, examines discrepancies between desired and actual results of an event. A zeta assessment is the sixth type. It involves continuous assessment and evaluation in which regular feedback is used to monitor solutions and make corrective changes if they are necessary.

A Definition of Needs Assessment Planning

As the process of developing a blueprint for collecting needs assessment information, needs assessment planning should not be confused with a needs assessment plan. Planning is a process; a plan is a tangible product. For needs assessment planning to be handled successfully, key line managers and other interested groups should participate in each step of designing the needs assessment plan and interpreting the results. Participation in needs assessment, as in many organizational activities, is essential to building ownership among key stakeholders (Rothwell and Kazanas, 1987).

In the broadest sense, needs assessment planning can be categorized into two types: (1) *comprehensive* and (2) *situation-specific*.

Comprehensive needs assessment planning is broad, covering large groups inside or outside an organization (Rothwell and Kazanas, 1989). Sometimes called macro needs assessment (Laird, 1985), it is to be appropriate for determining the continuous and relatively predictable training needs of all newly hired employees, since they must be oriented to their jobs. The results of a comprehensive needs assessment are used to establish an organization's curriculum — an instructional plan — covering basic training for each job category. A curriculum provides long-term direction to organized learning activities (Rothwell and Kazanas, 1988a, 1989).

Situation-specific needs assessment planning is narrower. Sometimes called micro needs assessment (Laird, 1985), it is appropriate for correcting a specific performance problem that affects only a few people. For instance, a microtraining need exists when one supervisor reveals no knowledge of "progressive discipline" in the firing of an employee!

More often than not, instructional designers devote their attention to situation-specific needs. There are several reasons why. First, relatively few organizations establish an instructional plan or training curriculum across all job categories. As a result, they lose the advantages that could be gained by pursuing a long-term direction for instructional activities in the organization (Rothwell and Kazanas, 1988a). Second, situation-specific needs often have built-in management support. Since the performance problem already exists, has visible symptoms, and affects an identifiable target group, instructional designers find they already have a constituency of interested managers who are eager to support efforts — and furnish resources — to solve the problem.

A Definition of Needs Assessment Plan

A needs assessment plan is a blueprint for collecting information about instructional needs. By its very nature, a needs assessment plan assumes that sufficient justification already exists to solve a performance problem (Kaufman, 1986). In form it usually resembles a research plan, a proposal for conducting a research study (Isaac and Michael, 1984).

According to *The Standards* (1986, p. 27), a needs assessment plan should address seven key issues:

1. *Objectives*. What results are desired from the needs assessment?
2. *Target audience*. Whose needs will be assessed?
3. *Sampling procedures*. What methods will be used to select a representa-

tive group of people from the target audience for participation in the needs assessment.

4. *Data collection methods.* How will information about needs be gathered?
5. *Specifications for instruments and protocols.* What instruments should be used during needs assessment, and how should they be used? What approvals or protocols are necessary for conducting the needs assessment, and how will the instructional designer interact with members of the organization?
6. *Methods of data analysis.* How will the information collected during needs assessment be analyzed?
7. *Descriptions of how decisions will be made based on the data.* How will needs be identified from the results of data collection and analysis?

Steps in Developing Needs Assessment Plans

To develop a needs assessment plan, instructional designers should first clarify why they are doing the assessment. Beyond that, the appropriate place to start depends on the problem that is to be solved, the number of people affected by it, and the time span available for the intended solution. For example, the appropriate starting point for an alpha needs assessment is not the same as that for a delta assessment. Likewise, the starting point for a comprehensive needs assessment differs from a situation-specific needs assessment.

Instructional designers who set out to develop a plan for a comprehensive needs assessment, adequate for establishing a long-term instructional plan for an organization or an employee job category, are embarking on an ambitious undertaking akin to corporate Strategic Business Planning (Rothwell and Kazanas, 1989). They should begin by locating a current organization chart and information about Strategic Business Plans, job categories in the organization, common movements from each job category to others, existing performance problems in each job category, and individual training needs. They should then identify, for each job category, the knowledge, skills, and attitudes necessary for employees to perform competently. They should use the skills list as the basis for a curriculum by job category. More information on this challenging but difficult process can be found in Galosy (1983) and Rothwell and Kazanas (1989).

On the other hand, instructional designers who are developing a situation-specific needs assessment plan, designed to close a performance gap through instruction, should begin by clarifying what they know about it. For example:

Question	*Related Issues*
What is happening now?	How are people presently performing?
	What results (levels of outputs/quality) are now being achieved?

What should be happening?	What are the relevant work standards or performance objectives?
	What relationship, if any, exists between the organization's Strategic Business Plan and employee performance?
	How do managers want people to behave or perform?
	What results should be achieved by employees?
	How much does management want this ideal state to exist?
How wide is the performance gap between "what is" and "what should be"?	How can the gap be measured?
	What historical trends are evident? Is the gap increasing over time?
How important is the performance gap?	What effects (consequences) of the gap are evident in the organization?
	How does the gap affect individuals inside the targeted group? outside the targeted group?
How much of the performance gap is caused by deficiencies in knowledge, skills, or attitudes?	Can the problem be broken down into parts?
	Are some parts of the problem (that is, subproblems) caused by deficiencies in knowledge, skills, or attitudes, while others are caused by deficiencies in the environment?
What solutions are cost effective and feasible?	How should subproblems caused by environmental deficiencies be solved?
	How should subproblems caused by deficiencies in knowledge, skills, or attitudes be solved?
What unintended side effects of taking corrective action can be predicted?	Will efforts to investigate problems or subproblems change them because people will modify their behaviors during the investigation process?
	Will data collection efforts create expectations, realistic or otherwise, about management actions or solutions?

> Will decision makers interpret
> results of needs assessment in
> conformity with logical conclu-
> sions reached — or will they im-
> pose their own personal in-
> terpretations on results?

Having answered these questions, instructional designers should then move on to establish objectives, identify the target audience, select sampling procedures, decide on appropriate data collection methods, specify instruments and protocols, choose methods of data analysis, and describe how decisions will be made based on the data. We now turn to a discussion of each step.

Establishing Objectives of a Needs Assessment

Needs assessment objectives spell out the results sought from needs assessment. In a written needs assessment plan, they should appear immediately after a succinct description of the performance problem to be investigated. Needs assessment objectives, much like instructional objectives, provide direction. They reduce the chance that instructional designers might get sidetracked studying tangential issues during the assessment process. In addition, they also clarify why the problem is worth solving and what the ideal assessment outcome(s) will be.

To establish needs assessment objectives, instructional designers should begin by clarifying what results are to be achieved from the needs assessment. This is a visioning activity that should produce a mental picture of the desired conditions existing at the end of the assessment process. Once the vision has been formulated, instructional designers should then write a short (one- to two-page) proposal for conducting the needs assessment. This proposal should be used as a selling tool and as a formal request. Most important, it should be used to build ownership for the assessment among key decision makers.

Results can be thought of in several ways. One desirable result of needs assessment is agreement among stakeholders about the outcomes of the needs assessment — and the instruction that should follow it. A second desirable result is a sense of what learners must know, do, or feel to overcome the deficiency of knowledge causing the performance problem. A third and final result is a clear sense of the final work product of the needs assessment. By thinking about the final work product, instructional designers begin to clarify just how the results should be presented to stakeholders. For example, should the needs assessment results be described in the format of a lengthy and detailed report, a short memo, a letter of medium length, an oral report, or some combination?

Objectives can take different forms in a needs assessment plan. For example, they can be presented as questions about a performance problem, statements of desired results, or statistically testable hypotheses. Questions are appropriate when the aim is to use information collected during needs assessment to stimulate organizational change (Nadler, 1977). Statistically testable hypotheses are appropriate only when assessment will be carried out with extraordinary rigor—which is rare (Digman, 1980; "Employee Training in America," 1986; Feuer, 1986)—and the information collected during assessment will be subjected to statistical analysis. Any good book on social science research will contain sections on establishing "research objectives" (Isaac and Michael, 1984), a topic that can be readily translated into advice about preparing "needs assessment objectives." Some books on training also contain sections on needs assessment objectives (see Westgaard and Hale, 1985).

Identifying the Target Audience

Whose instructional needs are to be addressed in solving the performance problem? Who must be persuaded by the results of needs assessment to authorize instructional projects and provide resources for carrying them out? To answer these questions, instructional designers have to identify target audience(s). Of course, any needs assessment really has at least two target audiences—performers and decision makers.

Performers are employees whose instructional needs will be identified through the needs assessment process. They correspond to subjects in a research project. Any needs assessment will have to identify who is presently affected by the performance problem, how much they are affected, and where they are located. In microtraining needs assessment projects focusing on a single work unit, it may be possible to identify only a few individuals whose needs should be examined. But in most macrotraining needs assessment projects, it will be necessary to consider instructional needs by employee job categories (Rothwell and Kazanas, 1989). Each job class may be viewed as a different market segment for instruction—and each segment may differ in needs. For example, if performance problems stem from lack of employee knowledge about such organizational "rules" as dress code or hours of work, employees may lack knowledge of them, while supervisors and managers may lack knowledge of how to deal with the discipline issues stemming from those problems.

Decision makers are the individuals whose support will be crucial if the needs assessment plan is to be carried out successfully. They may include instructional designers who will use results of the needs assessment and supervisors of employees who will receive instruction. It is essential to identify who will receive results of the needs assessment, because their personal values and beliefs will affect interpretation of the results.

Establishing Sampling Procedures

A sample is a small, representative group drawn from a larger group called a population. Sampling is the process of identifying smaller groups for examination. It is used to economize the time and expense of gathering information about needs.

Any sample will deviate to some extent from the "true" nature of the population from which it is drawn, a principle known as *sampling error*. Sampling error cannot be eliminated, but it can be predicted and conclusions can be reached in a way that takes its effects into account. A *sampling procedure* is the method used to select a sample.

Instructional designers commonly use any of four types of sampling procedures: (1) convenience or judgmental sampling, (2) simple random sampling, (3) stratified sampling, and (4) systematic sampling. To determine which one to use, instructional designers should consider the objectives of the needs assessment, the degree of certainty needed in the conclusions, the willingness of decision makers in the organization to allow information to be collected for the needs assessment study, and the resources (time, money, and staff) available.

Convenience or judgmental sampling is probably used more often than many instructional designers would care to admit. It is a type of nonprobability sampling in that the subjects for review are chosen for convenience or accessibility rather than representativeness. Sampling of this kind is tempting because it is usually fast and inexpensive. Unfortunately, convenience or judgmental samples do not necessarily yield unbiased results because the choice of case may be biased from the outset. To carry out convenience or judgmental sampling, instructional designers (1) select some number of cases to include in the sample based on convenience (they are easiest to obtain), access (capable of examination), or intuition (best guess of appropriate number to sample), and (2) choose the sample based on the results of step 1.

Simple random sampling is a type of probability sampling in which each subject in the population has an equal chance of being selected for study. This sampling procedure is appropriate when the population is large and it does not matter which cases in the population are selected for examination. To carry out simple random sampling, instructional designers should (1) clarify the nature of the population, (2) list the population, (3) assign an identification number to each member of the population, and (4) select the sample by using any method that permits each member of the population an equal chance of being selected (for example, use a random number table or the random number feature on certain calculators).

Stratified sampling is more sophisticated. It is appropriate when the population is composed of subgroups differing in key respects. In needs assessment, subgroups may mean people in different job classes, hierarchical levels, structural parts of the organization, or geographical sites. They may also mean classifications of people by age group, level of educational attainment, previous job experience, or performance appraisal ratings. The important point is that stratified sampling ensures each subgroup in a population is represented proportionally in a sample. For instance, suppose 10 percent of an organization consists of salespersons. If it is important in needs assessment to ensure that 10 percent of the sample consists of salespersons, then stratified sampling is appropriate. In simple random sampling, that may not occur. To carry out stratified random sampling, instructional designers should (1) clarify boundaries of the population, (2) identify relevant subgroups within the population, (3) list members of each subgroup, (4) assign numbers to each member of each subgroup, (5) determine what percentage of the population is made up of members of each subgroup, and (6) select the sample at random (each subgroup should be represented in proportion to its representation in the population).

Systematic sampling is an alternative to other methods. It is very simple to use. Suppose that it is necessary to assess the training needs of 10 percent of all employees in an organization. First make a list of everyone in the organization. Then divide the number of persons by 10 percent. Finally, select every tenth name on the list. If names are listed in random order, the resulting sample will be as good as a simple random sample. But if there is any order to the list whatsoever, the resulting sample may be biased as a result of that order.

Many novices — and, on occasion, even those who are not novices — express concern about sample size. On this subject, misconceptions are common. For instance, some people claim a sample size of 5 or 10 percent of a population is adequate for any purpose. Others may (jokingly) claim that any needs assessment is adequate if at least 345 cases are reviewed — because 345 is the minimum number of cases necessary to achieve a representative sample of the entire U.S. population at a low confidence level! However, population size has nothing to do with appropriate sample size.

Three issues should be considered when selecting sample size. First, consider degree of confidence. To be 100 percent certain, examine the entire population. But if lower degrees of confidence can be tolerated, the percentage of the population to be examined can be reduced. Second, consider maximum allowable error, indicating what number it may not exceed. Third, consider standard deviation. It measures variations in the population. When these numbers have been computed, appropriate sample size can be determined. For more information on this subject, see Kalton (1983).

Determining Data Collection Strategy and Tactics

How will information about instructional needs be collected? Answer this question in the needs assessment plan, making sure that the data collection methods chosen are appropriate for investigating the performance problem (Weller and Romney, 1988). Five methods are most often used to collect information about instructional needs: (1) interviews, (2) direct observation of work, (3) indirect examinations of performance or productivity measures, (4) questionnaires, and (5) task analysis ("Employee Training in America," 1986, p. 35). Other possible data collection approaches include (1) key informant or focus groups, (2) nominal group techniques, (3) delphi procedure, (4) critical incident method, (5) competency assessment, (6) assessment center, and (7) exit interviews. Rossett (1988) also lists others.

Interviews are structured or unstructured conversations focusing on needs. They are relatively simple to plan and conduct. Instructional designers should focus these conversations on key managers' perceptions about the performance problem and the planned instruction necessary to solve it. A key advantage of interviews is that they allow instructional designers the flexibility to question knowledgeable people, probing for information as necessary. On the other hand, a key disadvantage of interviews is that they may be time consuming and expensive to carry out—especially if travel is required. To plan interviews, instructional designers should

1. Prepare a list of general topics or specific questions
2. Identify people who are knowledgeable about training needs
3. Meet with the knowledgeable people and pose questions about training needs
4. Take notes during—or immediately following—the interview

For more information on planning and conducting interviews, see Antaki (1988) and Davis (1982).

Direct observations of work are, as the phrase implies, firsthand examinations of what workers do to perform and how they do it. They may be planned or unplanned; they may or may not rely on specialized forms to record the actions or results of performers. For more information on direct observation, see Isaac and Michael (1984), Jorgensen (1989), and Patton (1987).

Indirect examinations of performance or productivity measures are called indirect because they do not require instructional designers to observe workers performing; rather, they judge performance from such tangible results or indicators of results as production records, quality control rejects, scrap rates, work samples, or other records about the quantity and/or quality of work performed. Indirect examinations may be structured (in which results of observations are recorded on checklists) or unstructured (in which the researcher's feelings and perceptions about results are recorded). For more information on indirect examinations, see Brinkerhoff and Dressler (1989), Priestley (1982), and Webb, Campbell, Schwartz, and Sechrest (1966).

Questionnaires, sometimes called *mail surveys*, consist of written questions about instructional needs. They solicit opinions about needs from performers, their supervisors, or other stakeholders. They are sometimes developed from interview results to cross-check how many people share similar opinions or perceptions about needs. They may be structured (and use scaled responses) or unstructured (and use open-ended, essay responses). For more information on questionnaires, see American Society for Training and Development (1986h), Converse (1986), Fowler (1988), and Frey (1989).

Task analysis is a general term for a series of techniques by which work procedures or methods are carried out. We will have more to say about this approach to data collection in Chapter Seven.

Key informant groups or *focus groups* rely on highly knowledgeable people or committees composed of representatives from different segments of stakeholders. *Key informant groups* are especially knowledgeable about a performance problem and/or possible instructional needs; *focus groups* are committees, usually created informally, that are established to identify instructional needs through planned participation of representatives from key stakeholders. For more information on key informants or focus groups, see Krueger (1988), Morgan (1988), and Nickens, Purga, and Noriega (1980).

The *nominal group technique* (NGT) takes its name from the formation of small groups in which the participants do not, during the earliest stages of data collection, actively interact. Hence, they are groups in name only— that is, they are only nominal groups. To use NGT in data collection, instructional designers should

1. Form a panel of people representative of the targeted learners (or their superiors)
2. Call a meeting of the panel
3. Ask each panel member to write opinions about training needs on slips of paper
4. Permit no discussion as the opinions are being written
5. Record items on a chalkboard or an overhead transparency for subsequent panel discussion
6. Combine similar responses
7. Solicit discussion from panel members about what they have written
8. Ask panel members to vote to accept or reject the opinions about training needs recorded on the chalkboard or transparency

For more information on the nominal group technique, see Martinko and Gepson (1983) and Ulschak, Nathanson, and Gillan (1983).

The *delphi procedure* takes its name from the famed Delphic Oracle, well known during ancient Greek times. Similar in some ways to NGT, the delphi procedure substitutes written questionnaires for small-group interaction as a means of collecting information about training needs. To use the delphi procedure to collect data, instructional designers should

1. Form a panel of people representative of the target group
2. Develop a written questionnaire based on the training needs and/or performance problems to be investigated
3. Send copies of the questionnaire to panel members
4. Compile results from the initial "round" of questionnaires
5. Prepare a second questionnaire and send it and the results of the first round to the panel members
6. Compile results from the second "round"
7. Continue the process of feedback and questionnaire preparation until opinions converge—usually after three rounds

For more information on the delphi procedure, see Rath and Stoyanoff (1983) and Van Gundy (1981).

The *critical incident method* takes its name from the process of collecting information about crucially important (critical) performance in special situations (incidents). Critical incidents were first used as a method of collecting information about the training needs of pilots during World War II and have subsequently been used to identify special training needs of CIA agents (Johnson, 1983). To use the critical incident method, instructional designers should

1. Identify experts — such as experienced performers or their immediate supervisors
2. Interview the experts about performance that is critical to success or failure in performing a job
3. Ask the experts to relate anecdotes (stories) from their firsthand experience about situations in which performers are forced to make crucially important decisions
4. Compare stories across the experts to identify common themes about what performers must know
5. Use this information to identify training needs

For more information on the critical incident method, see Pigors and Pigors (1980).

Competency assessment is a data collection method that has been growing in popularity in recent years. Its purpose is to identify the characteristics of ideal (exemplary) performers and use them as the basis for preparing instruction. A major advantage of competency assessment is that it is targeted toward achieving ideal performance more than rectifying individual performance problems or deficiencies. But a major disadvantage is that needs assessments using this form of data collection may be quite expensive and time consuming. To use the competency assessment method, instructional designers should

1. Form a panel of managers or experienced performers.
2. Identify the characteristics of ideal performers. (In this context, characteristics may mean behaviors, results achieved, or both.)
3. Pose the following questions to the panel members: What characteristics should be present in competent performers? How much should they be present?
4. Devise ways to identify and measure the characteristics.
5. Compare characteristics of actual performers to those described in the competency model.
6. Identify differences that lend themselves to corrective action through planned instruction.

For more information on competency assessment, see Rummler (1987).

An *assessment center* is not a place; rather, it is a method of collecting information. Assessment centers are expensive to design and operate, which is a major disadvantage of this approach to data collection. However, their results are detailed, individualized, and job related, and that is a chief advantage of the assessment center method. To use the assessment center, instructional designers may have to rely on the skills of those who specialize in establishing them. The basic steps in preparing an assessment center are, however, simple enough. They require a highly skilled specialist, familiar with employee selection methods and testing validation, to

1. Conduct an analysis of each job category to be assessed
2. Identify important responsibilities for each job
3. Use the results of step 2 to develop games or simulations based on the knowledge and skills needed to perform the job successfully
4. Train people to observe and judge the performance of participants in the assessment center
5. Provide each individual who participates in the assessment center with specific feedback from observers about training needs

For more information on assessment centers, see American Society for Training and Development (1985d) and Moses (1987).

   Exit interviews are planned or unplanned conversations carried out with an organization's terminating employees to record their perceptions of employee training needs in their job categories or work groups. Exit interviews are relatively inexpensive to do and tend to have high response rates. However, they may yield biased results in that they tend to highlight perceptions of employees who have decided to leave the organization. For more information on the use of exit interviews in collecting data about training needs, see Schneider (1983).

   Many instructional designers wonder when to choose one or more of these data collection methods. While there is no simple way to reach a decision about choosing a method, several important issues should be considered (Newstrom and Lilyquist, 1979, p. 56):

1. *Incumbent involvement.* How much does the data collection approach allow learners to participate in identifying needs?
2. *Management involvement.* How much does the data collection approach allow managers in the organization to participate in identifying needs?
3. *Time required.* How long will it take to collect and compile the data?
4. *Cost.* What will be the expense of using a given data collection method?
5. *Relevant quantifiable data.* How much data will be produced? How useful will it be? How much will it lend itself to verifiable measurement?

In considering various data collection methods, instructional designers are advised to weigh these issues carefully. (See Table 4.1.) Not all data collection methods share equal advantages and disadvantages.

Table 4.1. Strengths and Weaknesses of Selected Data Collection Methods.

Methods	Criteria				
	Incumbent involvement	Management involvement	Time required	Cost	Relevant quantifiable data
Interviews	High	Low	High	High	Moderate
Direct observation of work	Moderate	Low	High	High	Moderate
Indirect examinations of performance or productivity measures	Low	Moderate	Low	Low	High
Questionnaires	High	High	Moderate	Moderate	High
Task analysis	Low	Low	High	High	High
Key informant or focus groups	High	Moderate	Moderate	Moderate	Moderate
Nominal group technique	High	Moderate	Moderate	Moderate	Moderate
Delphi procedure	Low	Moderate	Moderate	Moderate	Moderate
Critical incident method	Moderate	Moderate	Low	Low	Low
Competency assessment	Low	High	High	High	High
Assessment center	High	Low	High	High	High
Exit interviews	Low	Low	Low	Low	Low

Source: Newstrom, J., and Lilyquist, J., 1979, p. 56. Reprinted from *Training and Development Journal.* Copyright 1979, The American Society for Training and Development. Reprinted with permission. All rights reserved.

Specifying Instruments and Protocols

What instruments should be used during the needs assessment, and how should they be used? What approvals or protocols are necessary for conducting the needs assessment, and how will the instructional designer interact with members of the organization? These questions must be addressed in a needs assessment plan. The first has to do with specifying instruments; the second has to do with specifying protocol.

Many instruments may be used in needs assessment. Common methods of collecting information about instructional needs rely on commercially available or tailor-made questionnaires, interview guides, observation guides, tests, and document review guides. Commercially available instruments have been prepared for widespread applications (see Peters, 1985; Pfeiffer, 1988), though some consideration of how to use such an instrument in one organizational setting is usually necessary and should be described in the needs assessment. Tailor-made instruments are prepared by instructional designers or others for assessing instructional needs in one organization or one job classification. The process of developing a valid, reliable questionnaire may require substantial work in its own right, and this process should be described in the needs assessment plan.

On the other hand, *protocol* generally means diplomatic etiquette. Protocol must be considered in planning needs assessment. It stems from organizational culture, the unseen rules guiding organizational behavior. In this instance, "rules" should be interpreted as the means by which instructional designers will carry out the needs assessment, interact with the "client," deliver results, interpret them, and plan action based on them. In the process of developing the needs assessment plan, instructional designers should seek answers to such questions as these:

> With whom in the organization should the instructional designer interact during the needs assessment? (How many people? For what issues?)
>
> Whose approval is necessary to collect information? (For example, must the plant manager at each site grant approval for administering a questionnaire?)
>
> To whom should the results of the needs assessment be reported? To whom should periodic progress reports be provided, if desired at all?
>
> How have previous consultants, if any, interacted with the organization? What did they do particularly well—or what mistakes did they make, according to managers in the organization?
>
> What methods of delivering results are likely to get the most serious consideration? (For instance, will a lengthy written report be read?)

Instructional designers should always remember that the means by which needs assessment is carried out can influence the results and the willingness of the client to continue the relationship. For this reason, it is important to use effective interpersonal skills (described in Chapter Seventeen).

Determining Methods of Data Analysis

How will results of the needs assessment be analyzed once the information has been collected? This question must be answered in a needs assessment plan. It is also the one question that instructional designers may inadvertently forget. But if it is not considered, then subsequent analysis will be difficult because instructional designers may find that they did not collect enough information—or they collected the wrong kind to make informed decisions about instructional needs.

Selecting a data analysis method depends on the needs assessment design, corresponding to a research design, that has been previously selected. Among them: (1) historical, (2) descriptive, (3) developmental, (4) case/field study, (5) correlational, (6) causal-comparative, (7) true experimental, (8) quasi-experimental, and (9) action research (Isaac and Michael, 1984).

Historical and *case/field* study designs usually rely heavily on qualitative approaches to data analysis. The instructional designer simply describes conditions in the past (historical studies) or present (case/field study). Hence, analysis is expressed in narrative form, often involving anecdotes or literature reviews (Cooper, 1989). Anecdotes have strong persuasive appeal, and they tend to be selected for their exceptional or unusual nature. They are rarely intended to be representative of typical conditions or situations.

Descriptive designs include interview studies, questionnaires, and document reviews. Data are presented either qualitatively as narrative or quantitatively through simple frequencies, means, modes, and medians. A frequency is little more than a count of how often a problem occurs or an event happens. A mean is the arithmetic average of numbers. A mode is the most common number, and the median is the middle number in a sequence. Perhaps examples will help to clarify these terms. Suppose we have a series of numbers 1, 4, 9, 7, 6, 3, 4. The frequency is the number of times each number occurs. Each number occurs one time, except for 4. The mode of this series of numbers is 4, since it occurs most frequently. The median is the middle number, found by arranging the numbers in order and then counting: 1, 3, 4, 4, 6, 7, 9. The median in this array is 4, since it is the middle number. To find the mean (arithmetic average), simply add the numbers and then divide by how many numbers there are. In this case, the sum of $1 + 4 + 9 + 7 + 6 + 3 + 4$ equals 34 divided by 7 equals 4.8 (rounded). Frequencies, means, modes, and medians are used in analyzing needs assessment data because they are simple to understand and are also simple to explain to decision makers. In addition, they lend themselves especially well to preparation of computerized graphics.

The analysis utilized in other needs assessment designs — such as *developmental, correlational, experimental, quasi-experimental,* or *causal-comparative* — requires sophisticated statistical techniques. For these designs, the most commonly used data analytical methods include analysis of variance, chi square, and *t* test. When these methods must be used, instructional designers should refer to detailed descriptions about them in statistics textbooks (for example, Fitz-Gibbon and Morris, 1987).

Assessing Feasibility of the Needs Assessment Plan

Before finalizing the needs assessment plan, instructional designers should review it with three important questions in mind: (1) Can it be done with the resources available? (2) Is it workable in the organizational culture? (3) Has all superfluous information been eliminated from the plan?

It makes little sense, of course, to prepare an ambitious plan that cannot be carried out due to lack of resources. For this reason, careful thought must be given to the available resources. More specifically, instructional designers should ponder these issues: Given the draft needs assessment plan, what resources will be necessary to implement it successfully? How many — and what kind of — people will be required to staff the effort? What equipment and tools will they need? How long will it take to conduct the needs assessment? What limitations on staff, money, equipment, or access to information are likely to be faced, and is the needs assessment plan realistic in light of available resources and likely constraints?

Just as it makes little sense to establish an ambitious needs assessment plan that cannot be carried out with the resources available, it also makes little sense to plan a needs assessment that will not be supported by the organizational culture. For this reason, the following questions are also worth consideration: How are decisions made in the organization, and how well does the needs assessment plan take the organization's decision-making processes into account? Whose opinions are most valued, and how well does the needs assessment plan take their opinions into account? How have organizational members solved problems in the past, and how well does the needs assessment plan take the organization's past experience with problem solving into account?

Finally, superfluous information should be eliminated from the needs assessment plan, needs assessment processes, and reports on the results. The acid test for useful information has to do with the amount of persuasion that is necessary. Complex plans are unnecessary when decision makers do not require much information to be convinced of an instructional need. Indeed, too much information will only distract decision makers, drawing their attention away from what is important. Simplicity is more powerful and elegant.

Developing a Needs Assessment Plan: A Case Study

Josephine Smith is the Training Director at a large Midwestern bank. She was recently hired for this job. As her first assignment, she was asked to review correspondence leaving the bank. Key officers of the bank have a problem of (in the words of one) "providing a tone in our correspondence that we put customer service first in whatever we do."

Josephine conducted an initial performance analysis (an alpha needs assessment) and found that the "problem" has several components. Each component she calls a "subproblem."

First, the bank uses form letters for most routine correspondence. Loan officers commonly send out these form letters, which were not written with an emphasis on a good "customer service tone." This subproblem is a deficiency in the environment, and Josephine has asked the key officers to form a committee to review the letters and eventually revise them. They have agreed. Second, Josephine's investigation reveals that employees at the bank do not know how to write correspondence with an adequate "customer service" tone. This subproblem is a training need.

Josephine set out to assess training needs by analyzing common problems appearing in nonroutine correspondence sent from the bank. She will use the results of this situation-specific, gamma-type needs assessment to identify the gap between what is (letters as written) and what should be (letters as they should be written). She will, in turn, use that information in establishing instructional objectives for training that will furnish loan officers — her target audience — with the knowledge they need to write letters in desired ways.

Josephine begins needs assessment planning by proposing to her immediate superiors a review of special letters recently mailed from the bank by loan officers. These letters will be compared to criteria, set forth on a checklist, for letters exhibiting an adequate customer service tone. This checklist (an instrument) will be prepared by a committee consisting of Josephine and several key managers in the bank. (The first step in developing the checklist will involve clarification of just what does and what does not constitute a "good customer service tone," a phrase too vague to provide guidance in establishing concrete instructional objectives.) The same committee will then use the checklist to review letters and identify the frequency of common problems of tone in the letters. It will use the results to prioritize training objectives for loan officers.

Solving Problems in Conducting Needs Assessment

Planning a needs assessment poses one challenge; conducting the needs assessment—that is, implementing the plan—poses another. While logic and research rigor are typically emphasized in the planning stage, everyday pressures to achieve quick results and hold down costs most keenly affect instructional designers during the implementation stage. However, implementation problems can usually be minimized if the plan has been stated clearly and key decision makers have received advance notice of the plan and its pending implementation. Indeed, the chances for success increase even more if key decision makers participated in developing the plan and feel ownership in it.

When implementing the needs assessment plan, instructional designers should at least be able to apply appropriate tactics to ensure successful implementation. *Tactics,* perhaps best understood as specific approaches used in day-to-day operations, are necessary for dealing with common problems typically arising during implementation of a needs assessment plan. These problems include (1) managing sample selection, (2) collecting data while not creating false expectations, (3) avoiding errors in protocol, and (4) limiting participation in the interpretation of needs assessment results.

Selecting a sample is usually simple enough. But actually contacting people or finding the "cases" selected is not always so simple. Sometimes people selected are not available because of absences from the job, pressures from work assignments and deadlines, or unwillingness to participate. "Cases"—such as documents or work samples—may be unavailable because they are being used for other reasons or are geographically beyond easy reach.

Perhaps the best way for instructional designers to handle sampling problems is to anticipate them. Sample sizes can be enlarged beyond what is minimally needed so that allowances have been made for unavailable people or cases. Lack of cooperation can be avoided by communicating with others about the purpose of the study, why and how they were chosen to participate, whether their names will be used in the presentation of results, and what will happen with the results.

The more employees who provide data about instructional needs, the higher people's expectations will be that corrective action in the organization will take place. This expectation of change can be a positive force — an impetus for progressive change — when action quickly follows data collection and is visibly targeted on problems that many people believe should receive attention. However, the reverse is also true: the act of collecting data can be demoralizing when corrective action is delayed or when key managers end up appearing to ignore the prevailing views of prospective learners about the direction for desired change. To overcome this problem, instructional designers can choose to limit initial data collection efforts to small groups or to geographically restricted ones so as to hold down the number of people whose expectations are raised.

Errors in protocol can also plague needs assessment efforts. Perhaps the most common one is the instructional designer's failure to receive enough — or the right kind of — permissions to collect data. To overcome this problem, instructional designers should be sure to discuss the organization's formal (or informal) policies on data collection with key decision makers in the organization before sending out questionnaires, interviewing employees, or appearing in work units to observe job activities. They should double-check to make sure they have secured all necessary approvals before collecting data. Failure to take this step can create significant, and often unfortunate, barriers to cooperation in the organization. Indeed, it may derail the entire needs assessment effort.

Some instructional designers like to think of themselves as powerful change agents who are technically proficient in their craft and who, like skilled doctors, should "prescribe the right medicine to cure the ills" of the organization. Unfortunately, this approach is not always effective because it does not allow decision makers to develop a sense of ownership in the solutions. Indeed, they may think of the solution as "something dreamed up by those instructional designers." To avoid this problem, instructional designers may form a committee of key managers to review the raw data and detailed results of their needs assessment before proposing a corrective action plan (Krueger, 1988; Kruger, 1983; "Win New Allies . . . ," 1982). Committee members go over the data and the analytical methods used. They are then asked for their interpretations and suggested solutions.

This approach serves several useful purposes. First, it builds an informed constituency among the audience for the needs assessment report. Members of that constituency will grasp, perhaps better than most, how conclusions were arrived at. Second, they have an opportunity to review "raw" data. (On occasion, striking anecdotes or handwritten comments on questionnaires have a persuasive force that statistical results do not.) Third, by giving members of the committee an opportunity to interpret results on their own, instructional designers build support for the needs assessment's results.

Identifying Instructional Problems

According to *The Standards* (1986, p. 29), instructional designers should be able to "identify instructional problems" based on needs assessment results. Of course, the key to identifying instructional problems is the needs assessment plan itself. It should clarify what performance is desired and provide criteria by which to determine how well people are performing, how well people should be performing, and how much difference there is between the two. By keeping in mind what results are sought throughout the needs assessment process, instructional designers can prepare themselves for identifying instructional needs.

One way to identify instructional needs is to focus, over the course of the needs assessment, on tentative needs that are discernible during the data collection process. To keep track of them, instructional designers may wish to use a needs assessment sheet. (See Exhibit 4.1 for an example.) It is a structured way of recording instructional needs for subsequent review. Accountants use similar sheets when conducting financial, compliance, management, or program results audits. While the final results of the needs assessment may or may not confirm these needs, the needs assessment sheets do provide a means by which instructional designers can communicate with team members. They are also very helpful because they often suggest ways to organize the needs assessment report.

Judging Needs Assessment Plans

According to *The Standards* (1986, p. 30), instructional designers should be able to judge needs assessment plans prepared by themselves or others. Their judgment should be based on the contents and feasibility of the needs assessment plan and the match between instructional problems and data about them.

Judging Contents and Feasibility of a Needs Assessment Plan

Instructional designers should always review their own needs assessment plans — or plans of other instructional designers — to be sure that they contain at least the following: (1) needs assessment objective(s), (2) identification of the target audience, (3) procedures for sampling the target audience and organizational objectives, (4) strategy and tactics for data collection, (5) specifications of instruments or protocols to be used, (6) data analysis methods, and (7) a description of how decisions will be made based on the data.

Instructional designers should then review the details in the needs assessment plan. Are they adequate to guide implementation? Are they feasible? Does the plan possess sufficient detail so that someone knowing little

Exhibit 4.1. A Needs Assessment Sheet.

Directions: For each problem you notice during needs assessment, complete this sheet to keep track of it. For each question appearing in the left column below, provide a tentative answer in the right column. As you collect more data, review this sheet to determine whether the instructional need is—or is not—confirmed.

What Is the Problem? (*Summarize it in a sentence.*)	
What Is Happening? (*Describe the present situation.*)	
What Should Be Happening? (*Describe applicable work standards, objectives, organizational policies, and so on.*)	
What Is the Gap Between What Is Happening and What Should Be Happening? (*Explain it as precisely as possible.*)	
How Important Is the Difference Between What Is Happening and What Should Be Happening? (*Describe costs of the problem, as best you can anticipate them.*)	
What Causes the Difference Between What Is Happening and What Should Be Happening? (*Describe briefly whether it is caused by a deficiency in knowledge or environment.*)	
What Is an Appropriate Solution to the Problem? (*Explain why instruction is or is not justifiable.*)	
What Will Be the Likely Impact of the Solution on the Organization? (*Describe possible negative consequences of any proposed solution and then explain how you plan to anticipate and head off those negative consequences.*)	

about the organization can understand why the needs assessment is necessary? Are there reasons given for the selection of instructional objectives, targeted audience, sampling procedures, data collection strategy and tactics, instruments and protocols, and analytical methods and decision-making methods?

Judging the Match Between Instructional Problems and Data About Them

Instructional designers should also evaluate the match between the results of needs assessment and the conclusions about instructional problems based on them. To address these issues, instructional designers may find it helpful to prepare a simple chart indicating the needs assessment results and the conclusions drawn from them. If there is a match, this chart should be easy to prepare. Otherwise, it may be necessary to backtrack — or advise others to do so — in order to collect additional data or revise conclusions.

Justifying Needs Assessment

Instructional designers should also be able to justify needs assessment. They should thus be able to explain the reason the needs assessment was conducted and justify the objectives, target audience, sampling procedures, data collection methods, instruments and protocols, methods of data analysis, methods of conducting the assessment, and methods of identifying problems appropriate for instruction. In short, they should be able to explain why the needs assessment was carried out, why it was planned as it was, why the plan was implemented as it was, and what the results mean. If instructional designers cannot justify what they do, they will find it difficult to satisfy questions raised by operating managers or clients as they arise.

To provide good justification, instructional designers should keep track of their reasons for making decisions about needs assessment plans, objectives, target audience, sampling procedures, data collection methods, instruments and protocols, methods of data analysis, methods of conducting the assessment, and methods of identifying problems appropriate for instruction. All team members assigned to an instructional design project team should be briefed on these issues so that they can field questions about them.

At the end of the needs assessment, instructional designers should do a postmortem, reflecting on the project from the beginning. They should discuss why the needs assessment was carried out and what was learned from the process. Did team members include all essential elements of a needs assessment plan — such as objective(s), target audience, sampling procedures, data collection strategy and tactics, instruments, protocols, data analysis methods, and descriptions of how decisions will be made based on the data? Did they ensure that the needs assessment plan was practical to implement? Were they able to identify instructional problems congruent with data on discrepancies between what is happening and what should be happening?

Conclusion

In this chapter, we described the first step in the systematic design of instruction — conducting a needs assessment. The purpose of needs assessment, as we explained, is to uncover precisely what the performance problem is, who it affects, how it affects them, and what results are to be achieved by instruction. In the next nine chapters, we will continue to describe steps in the model of instructional design introduced in this chapter.

CHAPTER FIVE

Assessing Relevant
Characteristics of Learners

As the authors of *The Standards* (1986, p. 33) point out, "Obviously, all learners are not alike. Salespeople, engineers, managers, and technicians all differ from each other. Even within occupational groups learners vary. Some learn best by reading, some by listening, and some by trying procedures. When instruction or training is developed, these characteristics must be taken into consideration. To do this, instructional designers must know the specific characteristics of the group of people who will be training." The process of identifying these specific characteristics is called assessing the relevant characteristics of learners, though we will call it simply *learner assessment*. It is the second step in the model of the instructional design process we introduced in Chapter Four. (See Figure 5.1.) It is also the second of four related forms of analysis performed before instructional or training materials are prepared. The first analysis, needs assessment, was described in the last chapter.

In this chapter, we describe selecting learner characteristics for assessment, suggest methods of identifying appropriate learner characteristics, discuss ways of conducting learner assessment, and provide suggestions about developing learner profiles. We conclude the chapter with helpful hints for judging and justifying learner assessment.

Selecting Learner Characteristics for Assessment

Before preparing instructional or training materials, instructional designers should be able to answer this simple question: Who is the intended and appropriate learner? The answer helps define the *target population, target group,* or *target audience*. Traditionally, writers on this subject have advised instructional designers to direct their attention to *typical* or *representative* learners so as to maximize the number (and success rates) of people who subsequently participate in instruction (Blank, 1982). However, growing sensitivity to the

Figure 5.1. A Model of Steps in the Instructional Design Process.

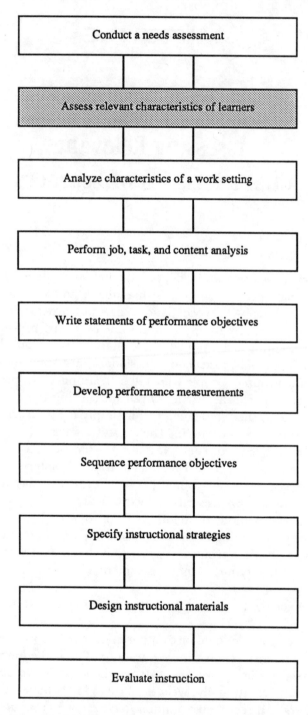

Source: Foshay, W., Silber, K., and Westgaard, O. *Instructional Design Competencies: The Standards.* Iowa City, Iowa: International Board of Standards for Training, Performance, and Instruction, 1986, p. 3. Used with permission of the publisher.

needs of atypical learners — such as those possessing physical, mental, or learning disabilities — may require instructional designers to pay increasing attention to a broader range of learner characteristics. Indeed, somewhere between 3 to 16 percent of all adults in the United States experience learning problems (American Society for Training and Development, 1987d; Lynn, 1979), and that group is too large to ignore.

What Learner Characteristics Should Be Assessed?

Assessing learner characteristics resembles *segmentation,* the process used to categorize consumers by similar features. A well-known technique in the marketing field, it gives advertisers the ability to target messages to the unique needs and concerns of their audiences. In similar fashion, learners are consumers of services provided by instructional designers. Consequently, many fundamental marketing principles apply to the process of assessing learner characteristics. Much as an organization competes against other organizations in the marketplace, so instruction must compete with other priorities for the attention of learners and their supervisors. The key to success in instructional design, as in marketing, is "to make selling superfluous. The aim is to understand the customers so well that the product or service fits them and sells itself" (Drucker, 1973, pp. 64–65).

Three basic categories of learner characteristics are relevant to a specific situation, performance problem, or instructional need: (1) *situation-related characteristics,* (2) *decision-related characteristics,* and (3) *learner-related characteristics.*

Situation-related characteristics stem from events surrounding the decision to design and deliver instruction. The chief focus of the instructional design effort should be directed to those most affected by it. The reason: subsequent delivery of instruction to that group will presumably have the greatest impact. It will also be substantially more cost effective than delivering instruction to all employees when only some really need it.

For example, suppose that customers of one organization complain that they are not being treated courteously over the telephone. Performance analysis reveals it is a problem caused by a lack of knowledge about phone courtesy. In this simple example, the performance problem itself suggests an important learner characteristic: training should be designed only for employees using telephones and dealing directly with customers. Since not all employees in the organization use phones or deal with customers, this learner characteristic alone is helpful in narrowing down the target audience. Moreover, it raises additional questions. For instance, what do these employees have in common that (perhaps) others do not? Why do they talk to customers, for example?

When assessing situational characteristics of learners, instructional designers should begin by asking this question: What are the possible relationships between the performance problem and the learner? Does the performance problem itself suggest unique characteristics of the learners who should receive instruction? If so, what are they? Will those characteristics remain the same—or change—over time (Rothwell and Kazanas, 1989)? If they will change, in what ways?

Decision-related characteristics pertain to those making decisions about learner participation in instruction. When assessing these characteristics, instructional designers should ask the following question: Who makes decisions permitting people to participate in instruction? After all, instructional designers may prepare instruction for a targeted group, but others often decide who actually participates. If this fact is ignored, much time may be wasted preparing instruction to meet the needs of one group, only to find that other groups actually participate!

Instructional designers should thus clarify, before preparing training materials, who will make decisions about participation. There are several ways to do that. One way is to establish a formal committee of people from inside the organization (Rothwell and Kazanas, 1989; Kruger, 1983; "Win New Allies . . . ," 1982). The members of the committee can give advice about who should participate, predict who is likely to participate, and offer practical guidance for attracting appropriate participants by targeting the needs of decision makers.

Learner-related characteristics stem from learners themselves. There are two kinds: (1) prerequisite knowledge, skills, and attitudes, and (2) other learner-related characteristics. Prerequisite knowledge, skills, or attitudes is sometimes called simply a prerequisite. Blank (1982, pp. 44–45) defines a prerequisite as "a characteristic, trait, or ability that students should possess to be successful on the job—but one that they will not get as a result of a training program." Blank identifies four types: (1) physical traits, (2) previously learned skills, (3) previously learned knowledge, and (4) previously learned attitudes.

Physical traits include manual dexterity, grip strength, lifting ability, visual acuity, hearing ability, tolerance to extreme conditions, height, weight, sense of balance, and sensitivity to chemicals or other substances. Employers must take care to make reasonable accommodation, too, for workers with physical and other disabilities who can perform various jobs, but perhaps with modifications (Martinez, 1990). Previously learned skills include the ability to read, write, and compute at a certain minimum level, the ability to use certain types of machines or tools, the ability to drive specific vehicles (forklift, road grader, tractor), and the ability to type. Previously learned knowledge includes awareness of rules—such as those associated with arithmetic, grammar, pronunciation, electricity, chemistry, or medicine. Previously learned attitudes include basic employability skills—such as awareness of the importance of appropriate dress, punctuality, interpersonal relations at work, and organizational policies and procedures (Carnevale, Gainer, and Meltzer, 1988; Rothwell and Brandenburg, 1990b).

There is no foolproof method for establishing instructional prerequisites; rather, it is often a trial-and-error process (Dick and Carey, 1985).

In many cases, instructional designers must simply ask themselves what knowledge, skills, and attitudes they think participants will bring with them to instruction (Blank, 1982). Later, when instructional materials and methods are tested on small groups of learners chosen as representative of the targeted audience, assumptions made about prerequisite knowledge, skills, and attitudes can also be tested. Another approach is to select at random a few prospective participants to see if they do, in fact, possess the necessary prerequisites.

Instructional designers should remember two key points as they identify prerequisites. First, if trainees enter instruction lacking essential knowledge or skills, then these essentials must be furnished to them. Second, competent legal advice should be sought before people are screened out of instruction that is necessary for job advancement or security (Arvey and Faley, 1988) — particularly when physical traits are the prerequisites. The reason: "the adoption of physical requirements such as height and weight has the natural effect of screening out proportionally greater numbers of females and some ethnic-group members other than white males" (Arvey and Faley, 1988, p. 266). When instruction is necessary for job entry or advancement and is denied to some individuals solely because they do not meet previously established prerequisites about physical ability, then it functions as a selection device. As a result, it is subject to the laws, regulations, and court decisions affecting Equal Employment Opportunity and equal access for the disabled (Giorgini, 1983).

Other learner-related characteristics are also worthy of consideration. They center around the learners' demographic characteristics, physiological characteristics, aptitudes, experience, learning styles, attitudes, job categories, value systems, life cycle stages, or career stages. The following list provides an overview of these important characteristics.

Demographic

- Age
- Gender
- Race

Physiological

- Heart condition
- Lung capacity
- General physical condition

Experience

- Length of service with the organization
- Length of service in the job
- Experience with present job activities prior to job entry
- Similar experience

Learning Style

- Classified according to standardized categories

Aptitude

- Special talents/skills

Knowledge

- Education
- Basic skills
- Specialized previous training

Attitudinal

- Feelings about the topic
- Feelings about training
- Feelings about job
- Feelings about the performance problem
- Feelings about the organization

Demographic characteristics are associated with learners' race, gender, and age. Two demographic issues are worthy of special consideration. First, instructional designers should ask whether the instruction they design will be geared to the needs of a particular racial group, gender, or age group — as is sometimes the case in specialized seminars on career planning, communication, retirement, or other subjects. If it will be, then any assumptions made about the learners should be double-checked. These assumptions may be based, knowingly or unknowingly, on stereotypes about the needs or beliefs of the targeted audience and thus may be erroneous. To avoid this problem, some instructional designers may establish an ad hoc panel of advisers to clarify or check the assumptions made about the learners before instruction is designed.

Learner sensitivity to special issues is a second matter to be considered. In recent years, for instance, much attention has been devoted to establishing gender-neutral language so as to avoid stereotypes or other objectionable implications about the gender of employees. Are there other issues to be addressed in the instruction that need to be considered from the standpoint of unique employee groups? If so, they should be identified. Further, means should be established, before instruction is designed, to make sure that learner sensitivities are not violated.

Physiological characteristics pertain to the most intimate aspects of the learner. They may include sensitivity to chemicals, prior medical history, and genetic heritage — including a tendency to certain forms of disease. As medical science has advanced, it has become more than a science fiction writer's dream to assess — and even predict — human sensitivity to substances and inclinations to disease.

Little attention in the literature has been devoted to making assumptions about learners' physiological conditions. Nevertheless, if learners will be exposed to chemicals during instruction, then their physiological characteristics should be considered. Should they be given medical examinations before exposure? Have all government requirements been met so that employees are aware of their "right-to-know" about the substances to which they will be exposed?

Aptitudes are "the future capabilities to perform in certain ways." Some individuals are gifted with talents that others do not possess, and those talents are synonymous with aptitudes. Employers sometimes administer aptitude tests before or after employee selection to assess individual potential. When test scores are available, they can be a rich source of information about learners. While this information may be used in designing instruction, it should be examined with due consideration to organizational policies on employee confidentiality.

Experience means the amount of time the targeted learners have spent in the employing organization, in their jobs, and in their chosen occupations. It is frequently one of the most important learner characteristics to consider in designing instruction. There are several reasons why. First, experience sometimes affects motivation to learn. When people first enter an organization, job, or occupation, they are often highly motivated to learn. They want to reduce the tension existing between themselves and the unfamiliar surroundings (organization) or unfamiliar activities and expectations they face. When instruction will be designed for those with limited experience, there is a greater likelihood that the targeted learners will be motivated to learn. These learners are willing to take instruction very seriously indeed and may (in fact) be depending on it to help them make essential transitions in their lives. Second, experience affects the selection of appropriate instructional methods. Learners with the least experience need the most guidance. Since they "do not know what they do not know," they are prime candidates for directive methods or simulated experiences. On the other hand, learners with the most experience generally rebel against directive instructional methods or unrealistic simulations.

Knowledge is associated with what learners know about the subject of instruction, the performance problem, learning needs, and organizational policies and procedures. What, if anything, is known about the learners' knowledge of these subjects? What assumptions, if any, are safe to make about what they know *before* they enter instruction? Have learners had much or little formal education generally? Have they had specific, previous instruction on the subject at another institution? If so, how was the subject treated?

Learning style means "the typical ways a person behaves, feels, and processes information in learning situations" (Stephen, 1987, p. 41). Much has been written about learning style in recent years (American Society for Training and Development, 1988e; Herrmann, 1987; Kolb, 1984). Several excellent questionnaires are available for assessing the learning style of individuals (see, for example, Hagberg and Leider, 1982; also see Stephen, 1987). They may be administered to representatives of the expected target group before instruction is designed, and then the results of the questionnaires can be used in preparing instruction. Alternatively, learners may be asked at the outset of instruction how they learn best, and the results can be used at that stage to modify instruction (Knowles, 1980).

Attitudinal characteristics refer to learners' "feelings about performance that they voice to other people." The term specifically denotes what learners think about a subject, the performance problem that instruction is designed to solve, their own learning needs, the organization, and other important issues. One way instructional designers can assess attitudes is to prepare and administer a simple attitude survey to representatives of the targeted audience (see Rothwell, 1983a, 1985). Another way is to prepare instructional materials and then administer an attitude survey to participants in a small-group session (Dick and Carey, 1985). Excellent sources of pretested attitudinal items for surveys can be obtained from numerous sources (Mahler, 1974; Robinson, Athanasiou, and Head, 1969; Robinson and Shaver, 1969).

Geographical location may affect learners' needs and willingness to participate in instruction. It may also influence their attitudes about the performance problem and/or instruction designed to address it. After all, learners in different parts of the country may report to different supervisors and may face problems differing in degree or type from learners in other locations. Marketing specialists stress the importance of geographical dimensions as a basis for segmenting markets, "because consumers do have different lifestyles and needs, depending on where they live" (McCarthy, 1978, p. 197). Instructional designers may wish to target instruction to one geographical area first and then, in time, to spread out to others. This method is frequently used in marketing products or services (Kotler, 1984).

Job category means the learners' job duties and responsibilities within the organization. It is very frequently used as the basis for targeting instruction, because job category is an important determinant of what employees need to know and do to perform satisfactorily. Job categories often become the basis for establishing long-term instructional plans to make it easier to orient people to new jobs, upgrade their knowledge and skills as job requirements change, and prepare individuals for promotion or other movements (Rothwell and Kazanas, 1988a).

There is good reason for placing heavy emphasis on job categories when assessing learner characteristics. As Gibson, Ivancevich, and Donnelly (1985, p. 451) note, "the building blocks of organizational structures are the jobs that people perform." A job is thus a key link between individual and organizational needs. Individual needs and characteristics also tend to vary somewhat by job. Hourly employees may not need the same instruction as supervisors, managers, or executives on a given organizational policy or procedure. Consequently, instruction targeted for one employee job category should take the duties and responsibilities of that job category into account.

However, jobs may be categorized in several ways. For instance, some instructional designers prefer to use a general job classification scheme. Examples of general job categories include executives, managers, first-line supervisors, technical employees, salespersons, professionals, and skilled workers (Rothwell and Kazanas, 1989). An alternative classification scheme, established by the Equal Employment Opportunity Commission for mandatory government reports on hiring, training, and other employee activities, lists the following job categories: Officers and Managers, Professionals, Technicians, Sales Workers, Office and Clerical Workers, Skilled Craft Workers, Semi-Skilled Operatives, Unskilled Laborers, and Service Workers. The actual job titles placed in each job category may vary *across* organizations but should remain consistent within *one* organization.

Value systems are "enduring organizations of beliefs concerning preferable modes of conduct or end-states of existence along a continuum of relative importance" (Rokeach, 1973, p. 5). They are closely associated with *organizational culture,* perhaps best understood as the taken-for-granted assumptions about the "right" and "wrong" ways of behaving and performing in a particular setting (Schein, 1985). To be effective, instruction should be designed with multiple value systems taken into account (Zemke and Zemke, 1981). Rokeach included a questionnaire in his book *The Nature of Human Values* (1973) that can be very useful in assessing the value systems of people in organizational settings. Instructional designers may administer this survey before instruction is designed or before it is delivered to a specific group in one instructional session. A more recent book, by Francis and Woodcock (1990), also provides information for assessing individual values.

Life cycle stage pertains to the individual's age and stage of development. In each stage of development, the individual experiences *central life crises* that stimulate interest in learning about issues related to those crises. Consequently, the life cycle stages of prospective participants in instruction are worth some consideration by instructional designers.

The crucial importance of life cycles was first recognized by the developmental psychologist Erikson (1959). It has since been popularized by Levinson (1978) and Sheehy (1974). The importance of life cycle stage in designing instruction was first recognized by Havighurst (1970), described more completely by Knox (1977), and reinforced by Knowles (1984). Knowles, for instance, identifies three specific stages of adulthood and describes typical "life problems" associated with them, based on vocation/career and home/family living. The three stages are (1) early adulthood (ages eighteen to thirty), (2) middle adulthood (ages thirty to sixty-five), and (3) later adulthood (ages sixty-five and over).

During early adulthood, as Knowles points out, most people are exploring career options, choosing a career, getting a job, learning job skills, and making career progress. They are also usually dating, selecting a mate, preparing for marriage and family, and accepting many responsibilities of adulthood — such as purchasing a home, raising children, making repairs, and so on. They are thus primarily interested in learning about improving their employment-related skills, clarifying their personal values, and coping with the responsibilities of the first stage of adulthood. During middle adulthood, most people face somewhat different life problems. They learn advanced job skills and move beyond technical and into supervisory work. They cope with the challenges of teenage children, adjust to aging parents, and plan for retirement. They are chiefly interested in self-renewal and in dealing with change. During later adulthood, most people encounter challenges very different from those of the middle years. They must adjust to retirement. They may have to adjust to the death of a spouse or learn how to deal with grandchildren. Their central learning issues have to do with keeping up to date and coping with retirement.

Career stages or career prospects may also influence learners. Several career theorists have suggested that individuals progress through identifiable career stages (for example, Dalton, Thompson, and Price, 1977; Hall, 1976). Examples of such stages include apprentice, colleague, mentor, and sponsor. These stages and their potential influence on instruction are described in Table 5.1. More detailed summaries and comparisons of the theorists' views may be found in Burack (1984).

Consider the career stage(s) of the targeted learners. After all, learners who view instruction as a vehicle for career advancement — as those in the apprentice stage are likely to do — will tend to want practical, hands-on instruction that can help them advance in their careers. Other learners will not. They will see instruction as serving other purposes — such as being a vehicle for socializing with others or acquiring knowledge for its own sake (Houle, 1961).

Table 5.1. Summary of Stages in the Dalton, Thompson, and Price Model.

Stage	Focus	Affects instruction

Apprentice	Performs technical work
	Deals with authority
	Learns from others about work
	  and about dealing with others
		Interest in techniques and technical
		  issues
		Interest in dealing with others

Colleague	Begins to specialize Regarded as competent Makes contacts	Interest in maintaining professional competence

Mentor	Provides leadership
	Develops more contacts
	Demonstrates ability to
	  get things done
		Interest in guiding/influencing
		  others

Sponsor	Initiates programs
	Guides others
	Continues to develop contacts
		Interest in exerting long-term impact
		  by influencing "up-and-coming"
		  people

Source: Rothwell, W., and Kazanas, H. *Strategic Human Resource Development,* © 1989, p. 362. Reprinted by permission of Prentice-Hall, Inc., Englewood Cliffs, N.J.

Selecting Learner Characteristics: A Case-Study Example

Georgeanna Lorch is an instructional designer who has been hired as an external consultant to design and implement a new management performance appraisal system for Ajax Vending Company, a wholly owned subsidiary of a much larger corporation. The new appraisal system will be used with all supervisors, managers, executives, professionals, and technical workers at Ajax. As part of her contract, Lorch is preparing instruction on appraisal for managers and executives in the company.

Lorch begins assessing relevant learner characteristics by brainstorming — more specifically by completing the Worksheet on Learner Characteristics appearing in Exhibit 5.1. When she has completed the worksheet, she has identified most of the crucial learner characteristics that will affect her project. Later, she discusses — and double-checks — the learner characteristics with members of the organization and randomly selected representatives of the targeted audience.

Determining Methods for Assessing Learner Characteristics

According to *The Standards* (1986), instructional designers must know *when* and *how* to assess learner characteristics.

When Should Learner Characteristics Be Assessed?

Learner characteristics should be assessed at three different points in the instructional design process.

First, instructional designers should consider the targeted learners *before* instruction is prepared to meet identified instructional needs and solve specific performance problems as they exist *at the present time*. As they do that, they should clarify exactly what assumptions they make about the knowledge, skills, and attitudes typical of intended learners. Instruction should be designed accordingly, but it should be made clear how prospective participants may satisfy necessary prerequisites through means other than instruction. These assumptions can be tested later during formative evaluation of the instruction.

Second, instructional designers should consider targeted learners who may need to participate in *future instruction,* perhaps on a regular basis. These learners will be affected by the selection and promotion practices of the organization, which will (in turn) determine the appropriate entry-level knowledge, skills, and attitudes of people moving into the jobs. After all, future learners may have needs — and the organization may experience performance problems — uniquely different from those existing at the time instruction is first designed or delivered. For instance, job duties may change. Likewise, the organization may shift strategic direction and thereby change performance requirements of *every position*. Then, too, new technology and work methods may be introduced. These changes — others can be identified as well — may dramatically affect the appropriate learner characteristics to be

Exhibit 5.1. A Worksheet on Learner Characteristics.

Directions: Use this worksheet to help you structure your thinking on learner characteristics that may—or should—influence your instructional design project. For each learner characteristic listed in column 1 below, identify in column 2 what learner characteristics are unique to the situation. Then, in column 3, describe how the characteristic(s) should be addressed or considered in the instruction that you subsequently design.

Column 1	*Column 2*	*Column 3*
What learner characteristics . . .	*What are the characterisitcs?*	*How should the characteristics be addressed (or considered) in the instruction you subsequently design?*
Are targeted directly at the area of need?		
Pertain to organizational policies?		
Pertain to learner/ organizational needs?		
Can be addressed with available resources?		
Pertain to existing constraints on the instruc- tional design project?		
Are feasible to collect data about in terms of resources and logistical limitations?		
Are translat- able into design specifications?		
Are related to the performance problem that instruction is intended to solve?		
Other		

considered. Hence, instructional designers should *forecast* learner characteristics that may need to be considered for designing effective instruction *in the future* (Rothwell, 1984).

Third, instructional designers should consider characteristics of a specific targeted group of learners *each time the instruction is delivered* (Knowles, 1980). After all, one group or one individual may have a unique profile, perhaps one radically different from the typical or representative characteristics of most learners in the organization. If radical differences between an actual targeted group of learners and the average or typical learners are ignored, major problems will be experienced during delivery.

How Should Learner Characteristics Be Assessed?

Instructional designers may assess learner characteristics using either of two methods: the *derived approach* or the *contrived approach*.

The *derived approach* is simplest to use. Can instructional designers identify learner characteristics of obvious importance to a given performance problem, instructional need, or organizational constraint simply by brainstorming? If so, they can *derive* relevant learner characteristics. If relevant learner characteristics can be identified in this way, then a list of learner characteristics to consider during instructional design will usually suffice. The process can be quite simple.

On the other hand, the *contrived approach* may not be as simple to use. If learner characteristics cannot be derived easily through the derived approach, then instructional designers should contrive a list of characteristics worthy of consideration. They should then go through the general list item by item, asking themselves whether each item is related to the performance problem that is to be solved, the instructional needs to be met, or the organization's policies and procedures. Unrelated items on the list can be ignored; related items, on the other hand, must be pinpointed.

Expensive and time-consuming methods of assessing learner characteristics are simply unnecessary in most cases. Very often, instructional designers and line managers already have a firm knowledge of the people for whom instruction is being designed (Dick and Carey, 1985). All that is necessary, then, is to write out that profile of the prospective learner and verify its accuracy with such others as line managers, supervisors, prospective learners, and members of the instructional design team. Once formalized in writing, it should be reviewed periodically to make sure it remains current.

Developing a Profile of Learner Characteristics

According to *The Standards* (1986), instructional designers should be able to summarize the results of a learner assessment in a *learner profile*. Simply stated, a learner profile is a narrative description of the targeted audience for instruction that sets forth key assumptions that will be made about them as instruction is prepared. To be adequate, this learner profile should be consistent with the results of the learner assessment and complete enough to be used for making instructional decisions.

What Should Be Included in a Learner Profile?

A learner profile should clarify exactly what assumptions will be made about individuals who will, or should, participate in an instructional experience that is intended to rectify a performance problem. It can be thought of as a "role" (or even "job") specification of the learner that summarizes

> *Necessary background knowledge, skill, attitudes, and physical traits.* What should the learner already know or be able to do at the time he or she begins instruction? What should he or she feel about it? What minimum physical traits, if any, are necessary for success in the instructional experience?
>
> *Other necessary learner characteristics.* These include any assumptions made about learners' demographic or physiological characteristics, aptitudes, experience, learning styles, attitudes, job categories, value systems, life cycle stages, or career stages.

It is also wise to indicate reasonable accommodation that can be made for the physically disabled and those suffering from special learning problems.

How Should a Profile of Learner Characteristics Be Developed?

There are three basic ways to develop a profile of learner characteristics for instruction: (1) *normatively,* (2) *descriptively,* and (3) *historically.* The normative profile is established judgmentally, without necessarily considering the existing "market" of learners. Instead, it summarizes characteristics of the "ideal" or "desired" learner. To develop such a profile, instructional designers — or instructional designers working along with operating supervisors and managers — may make arbitrary assumptions about what knowledge, skills, attitudes, physical traits, and other characteristics learners should possess before they enter instruction.

The descriptive profile is established by examining the characteristics of an existing group and simply describing them. It thus summarizes characteristics of the probable or likely learner. To develop such a profile, instructional designers — working alone or in tandem with experienced job incumbents and/or supervisors — select a representative random sample of a "targeted group of learners" and describe their knowledge, skills, attitudes, physical traits, and other relevant characteristics.

The historical profile is established by examining characteristics of those who actually participate in instruction over a period of time. It thus summarizes characteristics of the historical learner. To develop such a profile, instructional designers should track the knowledge, skills, attitudes, and physical traits of those who participated in instruction and who then went on to become exemplary (excellent) performers. With this information, it is possible to develop a predictive profile of those most likely to succeed following instruction.

Judging Learner Assessments

Instructional designers should be able to evaluate learner assessments performed by themselves or other designers. As they do so, they should give special emphasis to the means by which learner characteristics were chosen for assessment, the way information was collected about them, and the quality of the learner profile that was subsequently developed.

To judge learner assessment, instructional designers may begin by first making sure that one was conducted! Beyond that, they can question those who performed the assessment. A good approach is to try to get them to spell out the assumptions they made so that it is clear what the learner should already know, do, or feel at the time he or she begins instruction. Then they can be asked what provisions, if any, have been made for those lacking prerequisite abilities and those with physical handicaps or special learning problems.

Second, if a learner assessment has been made, instructional designers should ask the following questions:

1. What learner characteristics were assessed?
2. How were they assessed?
3. What philosophical consideration underlies existing learner profiles (are they descriptive, normative, or historical)?
4. Was the learner assessment well designed?
5. Should more information about learners be collected?
6. Should additional refinements be made to learner profiles?

Justifying Learner Assessments

According to *The Standards* (1986), instructional designers should be able to explain why a learner assessment was necessary, why some learner characteristics were identified as relevant, and why the assessment was carried out as it was. Competent instructional designers should thus be prepared to explain the work they have done with other people — such as other instructional designers, operating managers, or learners. Often, this requires keeping notes of steps made during the instructional design process. In many cases, the rationale for selecting learner characteristics for assessment and the methods used in this process should be explained in instructional catalogues or other sources available to users of the instruction.

To make this rationale simple and complete, many instructional designers prepare a brief checklist about the learner assessment. It is retained in files about each instructional design project and is thus available to future designers. It is also readily available to those who may have questions about the assessment.

Conclusion

Learner assessment addresses the following deceptively simple question: Who is the intended and appropriate learner? The answer to this question helps define the *target population, target group,* or *target audience.* In this chapter, we have described what learner characteristics may be assessed, suggested how to identify appropriate learner characteristics, provided advice about how to develop learner profiles, and furnished helpful hints for judging and justifying learner assessment.

In the next chapter, we turn to methods of analyzing the settings in which learners must apply what they learn.

CHAPTER SIX

Analyzing Characteristics
of a Work Setting

The process of gathering information about an organization's resources, constraints, and culture so that instruction will be designed in a way appropriate to the environment is called *analyzing characteristics of a work setting.* For simplicity's sake, we will call it *setting analysis.* It is the third step in the model of the instructional design process we introduced in Chapter Four (see Figure 6.1), and it is the fourth competency for instructional designers described in *The Standards* (1986). Setting analysis is also the third of four related forms of analysis performed before instructional objectives and materials are written. The first analysis — needs assessment — was described in Chapter Four; the second analysis — learner assessment — was described in Chapter Five; and the fourth analysis — work analysis — will be described in Chapter Seven.

In this chapter, we explain the importance of setting analysis, identify key environmental factors, and describe how to carry out this form of analysis. Finally, we conclude with some advice for instructional designers about judging and justifying setting analysis.

The Importance of Setting Analysis

Nearly twenty years ago, Steele (1973) emphasized the importance of physical settings in planned organizational change efforts. As he noted, "if one attempts to make changes in the social functioning of an organization, one must pay attention to the physical systems which form part of the context for the social system" (p. 6). As he defined it, *physical system* means *setting* or *environment.* It is "the total surrounding context for the person or the subject of interest" (p. 6).

Those who set out to change organizations require what Steele (1973, p. 8) called *environmental competence,* meaning "(1) the ability to be aware of one's environment and its impact; and (2) the ability to use or change that

Figure 6.1. A Model of Steps in the Instructional Design Process.

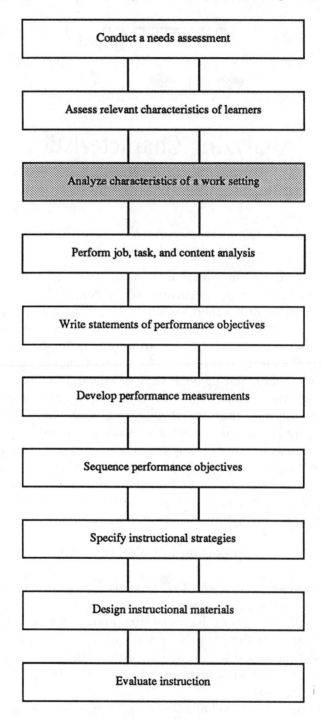

Source: Foshay, W., Silber, K., and Westgaard, O. *Instructional Design Competencies: The Standards.* Iowa City, Iowa: International Board of Standards for Training, Performance, and Instruction, 1986, p. 3. Used with permission of the publisher.

environment. . . . " To demonstrate environmental competence, managers —
or other change agents — should "be more aware of the setting," "ask themselves what they are trying to do there," "assess the appropriateness of the
setting for what is to be accomplished," and "make appropriate changes to
provide a better fit between themselves and the setting" (p. 8).

Of course, the instructional design process is a change effort that is
intended to meet or avert deficiencies in knowledge, skills, or attitudes. It
should therefore be carried out with due appreciation for the environments
in which instruction will be designed, delivered, and subsequently applied.
If this step is ignored, instructional designers may experience stiff resistance
from managers and prospective participants as they prepare instruction.
Worse yet, participants in instruction may later experience much frustration if, when they return to their job settings, they are not allowed to apply
what they learned because their managers do not support it.

The chief reasons for conducting setting analysis are also reempha-
sized in *The Standards* (1986, p. 40):

> The organization in which instruction is to be developed and
> delivered has a significant impact on how that development and
> delivery is done. The resources and constraints of the organi-
> zation (time, money, people, equipment) and its "culture" (val-
> ues, philosophy, mission, goals, and policies) will affect the
> length of time the development can take, which media can be
> used, how and where the instruction will be delivered, which
> instructional and testing strategies can be employed, and simi-
> lar factors. Instructional designers must be able to find out what
> the resources, constraints, and culture of an organization are,
> and then make appropriate decisions throughout the instruc-
> tional development process based on that information.

Identifying Factors and Carrying Out Setting Analysis

Instructional designers should make systematic examinations of the development, delivery, and application environments at the outset of the instructional design process. The *development environment* is the setting in which instruction will be prepared; the *delivery environment* is the setting in which
instruction will be presented; and the *application environment* is the work set-
ting(s) in which learners will be expected to apply what they learn. Each
of these environments should affect instructional development, delivery, and
application.

What Characteristics of the Development Environment Should Be Assessed, and How Should They Be Assessed?

Begin a setting analysis by focusing initial attention on the development environment, since it will affect how the instructional design project proceeds

(American Society for Training and Development, 1985h). First, list characteristics of the setting that may affect the instructional design assignment. Examples may include any or all of the following characteristics that are listed in the left column and briefly described in the right column:

Developmental Characteristics	*Brief Description*
The (apparent) nature of the change desired	The prevailing desire to improve consistency or change the way the organization functions.
The organization's mission	The primary reason for the organization's existence. A short description of the organization's products/service lines, customers, philosophy of operations, and other relevant characteristics that affect why the organization exists and how it interacts with the external environment.
Organizational philosophy and perceived values	Fundamental beliefs about the way the organization should function with its customers, employees, the public, and other key stakeholders. Includes not only what management says "should be done" but also what is "really done."
The organization's goals and plans	Beliefs about what the organization should do in the future and assumptions about the environment(s) in which it is or will be functioning.
The organization's structure	The way that duties and responsibilities have been divided up in the organization—that is, reporting relationships.
Results of a needs assessment/analysis	The difference between what is and what should be, stemming from lack of employee knowledge or skills or poor attitudes.
Resources available for the development effort—people, money, time, equipment, and facilities	The resources available for carrying out instructional development.

| Preselected instructional design methods | Managers' predisposition to approach an instructional need in a specific way, regardless of results yielded by analysis. |

Many other developmental characteristics of the setting may also be considered (Steelcase, 1989).

Second, determine how many of these development characteristics may affect the present instructional design assignment and how they may, or should, affect it. Given the culture of the organization and the performance problem that instruction is intended to solve, consider three major questions:

1. Based on what is known of the organization, how many of these characteristics are relevant to the present assignment?
2. How are the characteristics relevant? What is known about them?
3. How should information about these characteristics be used in such subsequent steps of the instructional design process (depicted in Figure 6.1) as analyzing tasks? Writing statements of performance objectives? Developing performance measurements? Sequencing performance objectives? Specifying instructional strategies? Designing instructional materials? Evaluating instruction?

Third, conduct a reality check to make sure that the most important developmental characteristics have been identified, their key implications noted, and the information recorded for appropriate use during the instructional design project. To do that, discuss the questions above with key decision makers in the organization, other members of the instructional design team, and experienced or exemplary performers in the organization. Note their responses carefully and make the changes they suggest.

What Characteristics of the Delivery Environment Should Be Assessed, and How Should They Be Assessed?

Focus attention next on the delivery environment, since it will affect how instruction is received by managers and employees of the organization (American Society for Training and Development, 1985i). First, decide how the instruction will probably be delivered. (While final decisions about delivery strategies are not usually made until later in the instructional design process, determine whether managers in the organization have predetermined notions — and justifications for them — about how instruction should be delivered, who should participate in it, when it should be delivered, why it should be delivered, and what needs or whose needs are to be met by it.)

There are, of course, many ways to deliver instruction. It may be delivered on or off the job; it may be delivered to individuals (for example, through computer-based training, programmed instruction, or self-study readings) or to groups. The appropriate choice of what to examine in the delivery environment depends on how instruction will be delivered.

Most instructional designers and other training and development professionals, when asked about delivery, usually think first of the classroom (Zemke, 1985)—though that is by no means the best, least costly, or most effective alternative. When instruction is delivered on the job, relevant characteristics are the same as those listed below for the application setting. When instruction is delivered off the job and in a meeting (informal) or classroom (formal) setting, relevant characteristics to consider may include any of the following listed in the left column below and briefly described in the right column (Crowe, Hettinger, Weber, and Johnson, 1986, p. 128):

Delivery Characteristics	*Brief Description*
Learner involvement	The extent to which participants have attentive interest in group activities and participate in discussions. The extent to which participants do additional work on their own and enjoy the group setting.
Learner affiliation	The level of friendship participants feel for each other—that is, the extent to which they help each other with group work, get to know each other easily, and enjoy working together.
Instructor support	The amount of help, concern, and friendship the instructor directs toward the participants. The extent to which the instructor talks openly with students, trusts them, and is interested in their ideas.
Task orientation	The extent to which it is important to complete the activities that have been planned. The emphasis the instructor places on the subject matter.
Competition	The emphasis placed on participants' competing with each other for successful completion of the tasks and for recognition by the instructor.

Order and organization	The emphasis on participants' behaving in an orderly and polite manner and on the overall organization of assignments and classroom activities. The degree to which participants remain calm and quiet.
Rule clarity	The emphasis on establishing and following a clear set of rules, and on participants' knowing what the consequences will be if they do not follow them. The extent to which the instructor is consistent in dealing with participants who break the rules or disrupt the group in its activities.
Instructor control	The degree to which the instructor enforces the rules and the severity of the punishment for rule infractions. The number of rules and the ease of students' getting into trouble.
Innovation	The extent to which participants contribute to planning classroom activities, and the amount of unusual and varying activities and assignments planned by the instructor. The degree to which the instructor attempts to use new techniques and encourages creative thinking on the part of the participants.

Other characteristics may also be considered (Randhawa and Fu, 1973; Richey, 1986).

Use these lists as a starting point for identifying important characteristics of the delivery environment and determining how they may be relevant to delivering instruction. Also refer to the lists in deciding how these characteristics should be considered while you analyze tasks, write statements of performance objectives, sequence performance objectives, specify instructional strategies, design instruction materials, and evaluate instruction. Be sure to conduct a reality check at the end of these steps and when instruction is subsequently delivered.

*What Characteristics of the Application Environment
Should Be Assessed, and How Should They Be Assessed?*

Characteristics of the application environment may affect the instructional design process just as much, if not more, than characteristics of the development and delivery environments. The application environment should be considered before instruction is designed to maximize the likelihood that learners will transfer what they learn from instruction to their jobs (Baldwin and Ford, 1988).

Historically, instructional designers have seldom paid as much attention to the application environment as they could have, concerning themselves instead with results at the end of the instructional experience (Sredl and Rothwell, 1987). One unfortunate result is that not more than 10 percent of the estimated $100 billion spent on workplace instruction each year produces on-the-job change (Georgenson, 1982). To the extent that instructional designers have paid attention to the application environment, they are usually aware that learners are more likely to transfer what they learn from instruction to their jobs when conditions in the two environments are similar, if not identical (Thorndike and Woodworth, 1901a, 1901b, 1901c). Results of more recent research indicate that it may be possible to focus training on broad, underlying skills that can be applied in different but related work tasks (Fleishman, 1972).

Any or all of the following characteristics listed in the left column and briefly described in the right column may influence on-the-job application of instruction (Crowe, Hettinger, Weber, and Johnson, 1986, p. 146).

Application Characteristics	*Brief Description*
Involvement	The extent to which employees are concerned about and committed to their jobs.
Peer cohesion	The extent to which employees are friendly and supportive of one another.
Supervisor support	The extent to which management is supportive of employees and encourages employees to be supportive toward each other.
Autonomy	The extent to which employees are encouraged to be self-sufficient and to make their own decisions.
Task orientation	The degree of emphasis on good planning, efficiency, and getting the job done.

Work pressure	The degree to which the press of work and time urgency dominate the job milieu.
Clarity	The extent to which employees know what to expect in their daily routine and how explicitly rules and policies are communicated.
Control	The extent to which management uses rules and other pressures to keep employees under control.
Innovation	The degree of emphasis on variety, change, and new approaches.
Physical comfort	The extent to which the physical surroundings contribute to a pleasant work environment.

Additional characteristics of the application environment may also be worthy of consideration (Fitz-Enz, 1984, p. 210):

Application Characteristics	*Brief Description*
Leader behavior	The supervisor's way of dealing with people, workflow, and resource issues.
Worker behavior	Work-related interactions with co-workers and supervisor.
Delegation	Extent to which and manner in which the learner's supervisor delegates and encourages new ideas.
Worker capability	Skills, knowledge, experience, education, and potential that the worker brings to the job.
Strictness	Firm and equitable enforcement of the company rules and procedures.
Equipment design	Degree of difficulty experienced in operating equipment.

Job satisfaction	Each worker's general attitude and amount of satisfaction with the job.
External influences	Effects of outside social, political, and economic activity.
Safety	The organization's efforts to provide a safe and healthy working environment.
Self-responsibility	Workers' concern for quality and their desire to be responsible.
Resources	Availability of tools, manuals, parts, and material needed to do the job.
National situation	Impact of national conditions on the worker and the company.
Co-workers	Mutual respect and liking among members of the work group.
Pay and working conditions	Performance reviews, promotions, pay, and work scheduling.
Job stress	Environmental effects, such as temperature and ventilation, plus feelings about job security.
Personal problems	The impact of overtime on personal life and other issues concerning personal life.
Self-esteem	The sense of self-respect — and respect from others — that learners derive from doing the job.
Work problems	Physical and psychological fatigue resulting from work.
The organization	General attitudes toward the organization, its style of operation, and its stability.
Economic needs	Degree to which the job satisfies workers' needs for food, clothing, and shelter.

Responsibility accepted

Desired workload and responsibility versus actual workload and responsibility.

Organizational policies

Rest periods, training, job layout, and departmental characteristics.

Use these lists of characteristics to analyze the application environment. First, determine how many of these application characteristics are relevant to the present instructional design assignment and how they may (or should) affect it to improve the chances that instruction will subsequently be applied by learners on their jobs. Given the culture of the organization and the performance problem that instruction is intended to solve, consider the following questions:

1. Based on what is known about the organization, how many of these characteristics are relevant to the present assignment?
2. How are the characteristics relevant? What is known about how each characteristic affects on-the-job performance?
3. How should information about these characteristics subsequently be used in the instructional design process to improve the chances that learners will apply on the job what they learned during instruction? How should this information influence subsequent steps in the instructional design model?

As in analysis of previous characteristics affecting the development and delivery environments, conduct a reality check to ensure that these questions have been answered appropriately. In addition, make notes to use during the instructional design process. When necessary, recommend that managers make noninstructional changes to the work environment to encourage on-the-job application of learning.

Judging a Setting Analysis

According to *The Standards* (1986), instructional designers should be able to evaluate a setting analysis in order to determine whether it was conducted at the appropriate time and was focused on appropriate issues. Take a few simple steps to make these judgments.

First, make sure that a setting analysis was conducted at all. Instructional designers assigned to a project at the middle or end of the work should ask their teammates what environmental characteristics were examined, why they were chosen, and why other characteristics were ignored. A few other simple questions are also worth asking:

1. What are the constraints, if any, on the project?
2. What resources are available?
3. How have the constraints and available resources of the project been taken into account on the project thus far?
4. How do the resources available and constraints affecting the project influence the development of instruction?
5. How will the available resources and constraints affect delivery?
6. How may they affect application of the instruction by learners?
7. What is the culture of the organization, and how may it affect instructional development, delivery, and application?

If other members of the instructional design team are unable to answer these questions, then set out to investigate characteristics of the work setting and apply the resulting conclusions to subsequent steps in the instructional design process.

Second, check whether the analysis was conducted properly. If the characteristics of the work setting have been investigated, be sure they have been verified. Look for evidence of agreement from independent sources — members of the instructional design team, line managers, and experienced employees — on assumptions that have been made about the development, delivery, and application settings. If the assumptions cannot be verified, then be prepared to review and revise instruction.

On occasion, instructional designers may wish to wait until a rehearsal of the instructional materials and/or delivery methods to verify some important points. At this time, for example, they can question knowledgeable members of the organization concerning the assumptions made about the learners and delivery or application environments. If these members of the organization confirm the assumptions upon close questioning, then there is no reason to make changes. However, if they point out additional issues for consideration, then be prepared to make appropriate changes to the instruction.

Third, make sure that the results of analysis are used during instructional development, delivery, and application. To this end, periodically ask members of the instructional design team how they are using what they know about the setting(s) — and how they feel they should be using this information.

Justifying a Setting Analysis

According to *The Standards* (1986, p. 43), instructional designers should be able to explain why they conducted a setting analysis and the reasons they chose certain features of the design, delivery, and application environments. To explain the reasons for conducting a setting analysis, instructional designers should be prepared to point out to line managers and others that instruction must be tailored to the unique needs of learners and the unique conditions in the organization. There is no one right way to do that. Instead, instructional designers must take their cues from what managers talk about and say they want. The setting analysis can be explained as a way to ensure that instruction matches up to their expectations, organizational goals, and other requirements.

To explain the features of the environments chosen for consideration, instructional designers should be prepared to point to information they have collected from credible sources in the organization. That is why reality checks are worth conducting. They provide support — and ownership — among key decision makers. They also give the setting analysis legitimacy and grounds for justification.

Conclusion

In this chapter, we described the third step in the systematic design of instruction, setting analysis. The purpose of setting analysis, as we explained, is to ensure that instruction is prepared with due regard to the available resources, constraints, and culture of the organization. Setting analysis must focus on three related environments: (1) the *development environment,* meaning the setting in which instruction will be prepared; (2) the *delivery environment,* meaning the setting in which instruction will be presented; and (3) the *application environment,* meaning the work setting(s) in which learners will be expected to apply what they learn. Each environment has its own unique characteristics that may affect subsequent steps in the instructional design process.

In the next chapter, we turn to the last of four related forms of analysis that should be conducted before performance objectives are written.

CHAPTER SEVEN

Performing Job, Task, and Content Analysis

The process of gathering detailed information about the work that people do in organizations is called *work analysis*. A general term, work analysis encompasses three different kinds of investigation—*job analysis, task analysis,* and *content analysis*. Taken together, they are probably the most technical activities of the instructional designer's job because carrying them out requires specialized skills.

Work analysis is expensive and time consuming. For this reason, it is warranted only after performance analysis reveals a performance problem lending itself to an instructional solution and after needs assessment provides information about the performance gap. Work analysis takes up where needs assessment leaves off. Its results become the basis for developing performance objectives to guide later steps in the instructional design process. Work analysis is the fourth step in the model of the instructional design process we introduced in Chapter Four (see Figure 7.1), and it is the fifth competency for instructional designers described in *The Standards* (1986). Work analysis is also the last of four related forms of analysis carried out before performance objectives are written and instructional materials are prepared. The other three forms of analysis were described in Chapters Four to Six.

In this chapter we define job, task, and content analyses. Moreover, we explain how to carry out each of them. Finally, we offer advice to instructional designers about judging and justifying work analysis.

Job Analysis

Jobs are important to employee performance, job satisfaction, and morale. As Gibson, Ivancevich, and Donnelly (1985, p. 451) observe, "The building blocks of organizational structures are the jobs that people perform. There are many causes of individual, group, and organizational effectiveness. A major cause is the job performance of employees. *Job design* refers to the

Figure 7.1. A Model of Steps in the Instructional Design Process.

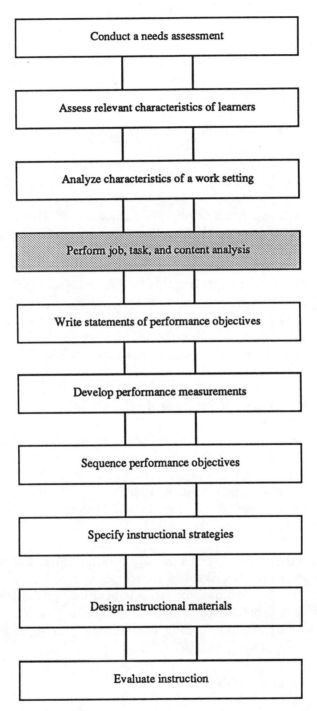

Source: Foshay, W., Silber, K., and Westgaard, O. *Instructional Design Competencies: The Standards.* Iowa City, Iowa: International Board of Standards for Training, Performance, and Instruction, 1986, p. 3. Used with permission of the publisher.

process by which managers decide individual job tasks and authority. Apart from the very practical issues associated with job design . . . we can appreciate its importance in social and psychological terms. Jobs can be sources of psychological stress and even mental and physical impairment." Indeed, "within an organization, each job is designed to facilitate the achievement of the organization's objectives" (Sherman, Bohlander, and Chruden, 1988, p. 96). Most people spend significant portions of their lives performing their jobs, so what they do and how they do it can have a major impact on their mental and physical well-being. A job also determines an individual's, and often an entire family's, standard of living.

Defining Job Analysis

A *job analysis* is "the process of obtaining information about jobs by determining what the duties, tasks, or activities of jobs are. The procedure involves undertaking a systematic investigation of jobs by following a number of predetermined steps specified in advance of the study" (Sherman, Bohlander, and Chruden, 1988, p. 101). Job analysis is sometimes called *general work analysis* (Swanson and Gradous, 1986). Its results can usually become a starting point for more detailed task or content analysis. It is performed to clarify job titles, job responsibilities, work activities, and entry qualifications for designated jobs in organizations (American Society for Training and Development, 1989a).

Defining Terms Associated with Job Analysis

Instructional designers should devote some time to familiarizing themselves with the nomenclature of job analysis; otherwise, they may become confused quickly. *Job* means simply "a group of related activities and duties" (Sherman, Bohlander, and Chruden, 1988, pp. 95–96). More than one person occupies a job. Defined another way, a job means "a group of positions which are identical with respect to their major or significant tasks" (McCormick, 1979, p. 19).

On the other hand, *position* usually does not mean the same thing as *job*. A position connotes tasks and duties performed by only one person (McCormick, 1979). For instance, an organization may employ four people in the *job* of internal auditor; however, each person is assigned different duties, so there are really four internal auditor *positions*. *Job incumbents* are persons presently sharing one job title.

The Importance of Job Analysis

Job analysis is important because it identifies what people do — or should do — and thereby provides information for selecting, appraising, compensating, training, and disciplining employees (Jackson, 1986). Indeed, job analysis helps (Werther and Davis, 1985, p. 117)

- Evaluate how environmental challenges affect individual jobs
- Eliminate unneeded job requirements that can cause discrimination in employment
- Discover job elements that help or hinder quality of work life
- Plan for future human resource requirements
- Match job applicants and job openings
- Determine training needs for new and experienced employees
- Create plans to develop employee potential
- Set realistic performance standards
- Place employees in jobs that use their skills effectively
- Compensate jobholders fairly

Without the results of job analysis, it would not be clear what activities employees should be held accountable for doing, what results they should be achieving, or how their work activities contribute to achieving organizational objectives. Job analysis can also reveal obstacles to performance that transcend the control of job incumbents and require corrective action by management.

When Should Instructional Designers Perform Job Analysis?

In most cases, instructional designers should perform job analysis only when job descriptions are nonexistent, outdated, inconsistent with information desired by decision makers, or inadequate for guiding more detailed task analysis. It should also be carried out when job descriptions are subject to dramatic future revision as a result of technological, regulatory, or other changes in the job environment. If none of these conditions exists, the time and expense necessary to perform a job analysis may be more effectively devoted to other projects. In addition, job analysis should be focused on the targeted audience for instruction, since broad-scope analysis of *all* jobs in an organization will lead instructional designers far astray from efforts of immediate, practical value for improving employee performance.

An Overview of the Steps in Performing Job Analysis

When conducting a job analysis, instructional designers should

1. Identify the jobs to be analyzed.
2. Clarify the results desired from the analysis.
3. Prepare a plan that answers these questions:
    a. Who will conduct the job analysis?
    b. What is the purpose of the analysis?
    c. How will the results be used?
    d. What sources or methods will be used to collect and analyze job information?
4. Implement the job analysis plan.
5. Analyze and use the results of the job analysis.

We now turn to a step-by-step discussion of each step.

Step One: Identifying the Jobs to Be Analyzed

Identifying the jobs to be analyzed is the first, and simplest, step in job analysis. If the job bears no title because it does not yet exist in the organization, then assign a tentative job title after consulting relevant sources from the industry and from government. A good place to begin any job analysis is with a review of *The Dictionary of Occupational Titles* (Bureau of Labor Statistics, 1977), published by the U.S. Department of Labor. *The Dictionary of Occupational Titles* lists titles and paragraph-length job descriptions for hundreds of jobs. Each job is classified according to a unique scheme indicating the skills it requires.

Step Two: Clarifying the Results Desired from the Analysis

The second step of any job analysis is clarification of the desired results. Instructional designers should focus their attention on two questions: (1) Why is the job analysis being conducted? and (2) What results are sought from it? Always begin by addressing the first question, clarifying the purpose of the investigation.

Job analysis has four possible purposes (Walker, 1980), and each implies a different approach. One purpose is to determine what people actually do in their jobs and thereby clarify *reality*. A second purpose is to determine what people believe job incumbents do in their jobs and thereby bring out *perceptions*. A third purpose is to determine what people, or their immediate supervisors, believe that job incumbents should do and thereby identify job *norms*. A fourth and final purpose is to determine what people—or their supervisors—believe job incumbents are or should be planning to do in their jobs in the future if changes in the workplace are expected to occur (Rothwell and Kazanas, 1988b). Job analysis of this kind thus focuses on *plans* or *future change*.

Unfortunately, most job analysis focuses on perceptions, since "finding out what individuals *actually do* is more time consuming and costly than finding out what individuals and managers *think they do*" (Walker, 1980, p. 147). However, instructional designers should more often focus their attention on *reality* or *plans* and *future change*. This is because instruction needs to be centered around what job incumbents actually do to perform successfully or what they should be able to do to meet future objectives of their organization.

Once the *purpose* of job analysis has been clarified, instructional designers should next decide what *results* are desired. Four are possible: (1) a *job description* "that explains the duties, working conditions, and other aspects of a specified job" (Werther and Davis, 1985, p. 124); (2) a *job specification* that "describes what the job demands of employees who do it . . . including experience, training, education, and physical and mental demands" (Werther and Davis, 1985, p. 128); (3) a *task listing* that delineates the activities performed by job incumbents; and (4) *job performance standards* that identify "objectives or targets for employee efforts" (Werther and Davis, 1985, p. 129). Hence, results may be expressed in job descriptions, job specifications, task listings (sometimes called *task inventories*), job performance standards, or all four.

The results desired from the job analysis will affect the approach used to carry out the analysis. For instance, if the aim is to prepare a job description, the instructional designer should select a job title (*What should the job be called?*), prepare a purpose statement for the job of no more than one or two sentences (*Why should the job exist?*), identify reporting relationships (*What job titles report to the job, and what job title do incumbents report to?*), and summarize major or representative job tasks (*What tasks are customarily performed by job incumbents?*). Experienced job incumbents or their supervisors are often able to prepare a job description in a few minutes.

Most organizations already have job descriptions on hand, since they are regarded as fundamental tools of good human resource management (Werther and Davis, 1985). Job descriptions are usually essential starting points for designing job-specific instruction (Bishop, 1988a), though they are rarely detailed enough to provide all the information needed by instructional designers (Swanson and Gradous, 1986).

There is no one "right" format for job descriptions. Most organizations establish their own format, and instructional designers should use that format when conducting job analysis (Swanson and Gradous, 1986). Many books are available that set forth sample job descriptions (Bruce, 1986; Bureau of Labor Statistics, 1977), and they are excellent references to consult at the beginning of a job analysis. In some organizations, decision makers may prefer that instructional designers go beyond the basics of job descriptions. In other words, they may be asked to list more than job title, purpose statement, reporting relationships, and representative tasks. They may also wish to list work standards for each task; knowledge, skills, and attitudes required to perform each task; estimated time percentages devoted by job incumbents to each task; or minimum entry requirements (*job specification*).

A *job specification* usually appears at the end of a job description. When preparing a job specification, focus attention on what people should know, do, or feel in order for them to learn—that is, train for—the job. Establish only essential, minimum entry requirements. Avoid unnecessary references to general experience or education so as to ensure that the organization engages in fair employment practices for protected labor groups (Arvey and Faley, 1988). More appropriately, list only specific skills needed by job incumbents to perform—or learn—a job. To cite a simple example, indicate that a secretary should have "a demonstrated ability to type 35 words per minute with 3 errors or less" rather than "a high school diploma."

Most job descriptions also contain a list of representative tasks called a *task listing*. Preparing such a list can be relatively simple if it is based largely on perceptions, or it can be time consuming and expensive if it is based on reality or plans. This list can be a starting point for more detailed task analysis (discussed in the next section). If the desired result of a job analysis is a detailed *task listing*—sometimes called a *task inventory*—then focus attention on detailed work results or work activities of job incumbents.

If *job performance standards* are the desired results of a job analysis, then clarify precisely *how to measure performance on each job task* and *how well each task should be carried out by an experienced job incumbent*. Although it is common for managers and workers to complain that job performance standards cannot be measured for tasks in their jobs, the fact is that standards can be established for any job (Springer, 1980). Simply examine each task for quantity, quality, or cost. The following list adapted from Jacobs (1987) suggests possible criteria:

Quality

- How well does the performance match a model?
- How superior is one performance to another based on market value or expert opinions?

Quantity

- How many items are produced in a given time?
- How timely is task completion?
- How much is produced in a given time?

Cost

- How much is the labor cost relative to what is produced?
- How much do the materials cost to achieve desired work results?
- How much are the managerial or administrative costs for achieving desired results?

Step Three: Preparing a Plan to Guide the Job Analysis

The third step is preparation of a plan to guide the investigation. That plan should address at least the following questions: (1) Who will conduct the job analysis? (2) What is the primary purpose of the analysis? (3) How will the results of the analysis be used? (4) Who is depending on the results of the analysis? and (5) What sources and/or methods should be used to collect and analyze job information?

First, decide who will conduct the job analysis. Will it be human resource professionals, external consultants, instructional designers, supervisors, or others? The answer to this question is very important, since the credibility of the job analysis is influenced by who performs it. Those perceived to have a self-interest in the results will not be credible.

Then clarify why the analysis is being conducted. Is the purpose primarily to determine what job incumbents really do? If so, then instructional designers will have to ensure that the data collected represent reality. Or is the purpose to determine what job incumbents should do in the future? If so, then it will be necessary to establish ways to forecast or scan the future. Who depends on the results (and for what reasons), and what sources of information and methods will be used?

Next, identify who is depending on the results. Is it instructional designers alone—or do others have an interest, for reasons other than instructional design, in the conclusions? If the results of the job analysis are of value to others, and not just instructional designers, then their interests must be determined at the outset so that the results will answer their questions and address their key concerns.

Finally, decide on the sources and methods that should be used to collect and analyze job information. Sources of information may include job incumbents, supervisors, those familiar with work performed by job incumbents, and others. Methods may include such standard social science data collection vehicles as written surveys, interviews, observations, work diaries, and work records. The earliest methods of job analysis, called time-and-motion studies, relied on highly detailed observation of blue-collar workers in manufacturing settings (Wren, 1979). More recently, surveys and interviews have tended to be used about as often as observation. One reason is that survey or interview results can often be obtained much more quickly than observation results—and often at substantially lower cost. A second reason has to do with the fact that the U.S. economy is moving away from blue-collar manufacturing to white-collar service jobs. Surveys and interviews are sometimes more appropriate for studying jobs requiring specialized cognitive (knowledge) and affective (feeling/attitude) skills than for those involving psychomotor (manual) skills (Zemke and Kramlinger, 1982). Consult texts on job analysis for more information on the sources and methods used to analyze jobs (Ghorpade, 1988; McCormick, 1979; Rothwell and Kazanas, 1988b).

Step Four: Implementing the Job Analysis Plan

The fourth step of job analysis is implementation. At this point, instructional designers carry out the job analysis plan, collecting information about the jobs under investigation. In many respects, the problems faced in this step resemble the problems faced in collecting data about training needs. More specifically, instructional designers should avoid creating false expectations and avoid errors in protocol during data collection.

False expectations arise when job incumbents believe that job analysis will produce results of immediate advantage to themselves. For instance, they may believe that a review of what they do will lead to a higher salary, a lofty job title, or some other advantage. Instructional designers should avoid the problems stemming from false expectations by clarifying from the beginning of the analysis precisely why it is being performed—and what will and will not happen as a result of it.

Errors in protocol stem from inappropriate interaction between the instructional designer and job incumbents or their immediate supervisors. Imagine, for instance, how a job incumbent will treat an instructional designer who shows up to perform a job analysis unannounced. To avoid that error and similar ones, instructional designers should at least (1) identify who needs to give permission for a job analysis to be conducted, (2) clarify how permissions are given, and (3) allow sufficient time for those permissions to be given.

Step Five: Analyzing and Using the Results of the Job Analysis

Instructional designers select methods for analyzing the results of the job analysis during step 3, but they carry out the analysis in step 5. As in needs assessment, this selection will depend on how the information is to be collected. The results of job analysis are expressed as job descriptions, job specifications, task listings, or job performance standards.

Summary

Job analysis is the most general form of work analysis. It lays the foundation for related, but more detailed, analysis of tasks or content. We turn next to task analysis.

Task Analysis

To design job-specific instruction, instructional designers must know in precise detail exactly what workers do, how they do it, why they do it, and what equipment or other resources they must have to perform. The results of job analysis are too general to provide this amount of detail. Consequently, task analysis is necessary as a starting point for preparing *performance objectives* to guide results to be achieved by instruction.

Defining Task Analysis

A *task analysis* is an intensive examination of how people perform work activities (American Society for Training and Development, 1985c). It can sometimes involve a critique and reexamination of work activities as well. Task analysis is carried out to (1) determine components of competent performance; (2) identify activities that may be simplified or otherwise improved; (3) determine precisely what a worker must know, do, or feel to learn a specific work activity; (4) clarify conditions (equipment and other resources) needed for competent performance; and (5) establish minimum expectations (*standards*) for how well job incumbents should perform each task appearing in their job description(s). Task analysis is not limited to any single method or technique. Indeed, as many as twenty-five different methods exist for conducting task analysis (Carlisle, 1986; Foshay, 1986).

Defining Terms Associated with Task Analysis

To understand task analysis, instructional designers should begin by familiarizing themselves with such terms as *task, subtask, element,* and *task listing.*

A *task* is "a discrete unit of work performed by an individual. It usually comprises a logical and necessary step in the performance of a job duty, and typically has an identifiable beginning and ending" (McCormick, 1979, p. 19). It is also "a set of actions or behaviors which produce a meaningful result" (Jackson, 1986, p. 68). A task does not always involve observable behavior; rather, it may also involve an unobservable mental action such as "making a correct decision." Yet a task can be clearly understood to mean "a group of related activities directed toward a goal" that "includes a mixture of decisions, perceptions, and/or physical (motor) activities required of one person." It "may be of any size or degree of complexity as well" (U.S. Air Force, 1973, p. 63). The following examples of tasks from Reddout's article "What Is a Task?" (1987, pp. 5–6) will help to clarify these points:

Introduction	Training literature is full of information on developing task-oriented training documents, such as training manuals. However, little is said about what a task is or how a trainer can identify a task.
Task Types	A task is a series of actions or behaviors which accomplishes a goal. Tasks are divided into two major types: *Cognitive tasks* are performed mentally. A cognitive behavior such as evaluating, deciding, or discriminating is not observable. These mental processes do not have a set of steps which follow a precise order. They are difficult to define and difficult to teach.
	Action tasks have a set of clearly defined steps that are observable. Action tasks have a performer and another person who is changed by the actions of the performer. Sometimes an object may be changed by the action.
Example— Cognitive Task	Select a personal computer.
	In this task, although the decision may be based upon specific criteria, the selection is made mentally. Two individuals, given the same circumstances, may follow two sets of actions and select two different computers.
Example— Action Task	Replace a burned-out bulb on an overhead projector.
	In this task, each step can be observed, and the performer must follow a particular order of actions (the new bulb cannot be put in until the old one is removed). Also, each person who performs the task follows the same set of actions to achieve the same outcome or goal.
Definition	An action task, then, is a series of actions or behaviors which:

- Involves interaction between a person (the performer) and an object or another person.
- Changes the object or person in some way.
- Accomplishes a goal.

Criteria	An action task can be further defined by applying the following criteria. An action task:

- Has a definite beginning and end.
- Is performed in relatively short periods of time.
- Can be observed.
- Can be measured.
- Is independent of other actions.

Examples of Action Tasks	

- Dial a long-distance telephone number.
- Perform a needs analysis.
- Measure and record vital signs.
- Pitch a softball.
- Build a bookcase.
- Update a computerized mailing list.

Nonexamples

- Display the main menu for a data base management system
  - Is not independent of other actions.
- Collect stamps.
  - Does not have a definite beginning and ending.
  - Is not performed in relatively short periods of time.
- Know how to fill out an expense report.
  - Cannot be observed. ("Know" is not an overt behavior.)
  - Cannot be measured. ("Know" cannot be demonstrated.)

A *subtask* is one step in a task. It "is sometimes considered the smallest step into which it is practical to subdivide any work activity without analyzing the separate motions, movements, and mental processes involved" (McCormick, 1979, pp. 19–20).

An *element* is a step-within-a-step of a task. It "consists of very specific separate motions or movements" in time-and-motion studies conducted by industrial engineers (McCormick, 1979, p. 20). An element can be detected by detailed photographic studies of manual operations. For instance, an element within the task of "shoveling coal into a furnace" is "placing a hand on the shovel."

A *task listing* means quite literally what the phrase implies: it is "a comprehensive list of tasks which must be performed by workers operating the system" (Gibbons, 1977, p. 8). The aim of a task listing is to answer this question: What do people do as they carry out their work? The result of a task listing becomes the starting point for developing a task analysis (Gibbons, 1977), since a task listing describes what people do but not how they do it. Task listings are sometimes included in job descriptions, though more detailed task listings can be developed using each major task in a job description as a starting point.

An Overview of the Steps in Performing Task Analysis

Instructional designers should begin a task analysis study in essentially the same way they begin a job analysis:

1. Identify job(s) or tasks to be analyzed.
2. Clarify the results desired from the task analysis.
3. Prepare a plan to guide the task analysis.
4. Implement the task analysis plan.
5. Analyze and use the investigation's results.

We now turn to a step-by-step discussion of this procedure.

Step One: Identifying Tasks to be Analyzed

The first step is to identify the tasks to be analyzed. Using a task listing, instructional designers identify what tasks within a job are to be analyzed. They must first decide what kinds of tasks are involved, because the nature of the tasks determines which of several approaches to task analysis should be selected (Gagne and Briggs, 1979).

There are four kinds of tasks: (1) *procedural,* (2) *process,* (3) *troubleshooting,* and (4) *mental* (Swanson and Gradous, 1986).

Procedural tasks are synonymous with *action tasks,* as described in the preceding examples from Reddout's article "What Is a Task?" They involve interactions between people and materials or machines. They are completely observable and occur in an identifiable sequence. Examples of procedures include riding a bicycle, filling an automobile's gasoline tank, or changing a light bulb.

Process tasks are partially observable, are bound to a particular process, occur within a preexisting system, and involve interactions between people and a process. Examples of processes include an organization's purchasing practices, a company's manufacturing methods, or a management information system. Processes usually lend themselves especially well to flowcharting or algorithms (Horabin and Lewis, 1978).

Troubleshooting tasks are quite similar to *process tasks* — except the flow works in reverse. If a machine or system is not functioning as it should, then human beings must *work backward from what should be to what is* to determine the problem's cause. Suppose instructional designers wish to find out why a computer will not run a program. (Computer manuals frequently contain "troubleshooting guides" to help novices figure out why these marvelous machines sometimes have trouble working for their less-than-machine-perfect owners.) To perform this troubleshooting task, instructional designers must know how the program "should" work before they can determine why it is not working. Experts are frequently able to do troubleshooting quicker than novices (Johnson, 1988).

Mental tasks are unobservable. Synonymous with cognitive tasks as described in the preceding examples from Reddout's article, they involve people-idea or people-people interactions (Swanson and Gradous, 1986). While they may occur in a predictable sequence, that sequence occurs within the mind of the performer.

Step Two: Clarifying the Desired Results

The second step of any task analysis should focus on clarifying the desired results. Always consider two key questions for that purpose: (1) Why is the analysis being conducted? and (2) What results are sought from it? To answer the first question, decide whether the purpose is to analyze how people actually perform, how they think they perform, how they should perform, or how they should perform in the future. Most task analysis combines two of these purposes, focusing both on how people actually do perform and on how they should perform.

Next, direct attention to determining what *results* are desired. How detailed does the task analysis really have to be? It makes no sense to be extremely detailed when that is unnecessary. Indeed, it makes much more sense to start out with the fewest details and add to them over time (Jackson, 1986). Jackson (1986, p. 92) advises instructional designers to "begin by getting general information about all tasks—typically inputs and outputs first, then major steps. This will help clarify relationships among tasks and ensure that the information gathered is both accurate and necessary." Results of task analysis can be expressed in terms of application of intellectual skill, cognitive strategy, verbal information, or motor skill or attitude (Gagne and Briggs, 1979). Some task analysts prefer to progress beyond simple analysis (*how is the task performed?*) in order to address performance measurements (*how well should the task be performed?*) and conditions necessary for performance (*what tools, equipment, and other resources must be available to the performer for the task to be conducted?*).

Step Three: Preparing a Plan to Guide the Task Analysis

The third step is to prepare a plan to guide the task analysis. Put in writing how the task analysis will be conducted, complete with statements of the purpose and desired results. Be sure to answer three important questions: (1) Who will conduct the task analysis? (2) Whose task performance will be examined? and (3) What approach will be used to collect and analyze task information?

Task analysis is a very time-consuming activity, and the detailed results it typically generates are not often needed by human resource professionals in the way that job analysis results usually are. Consequently, it will usually be conducted by instructional designers from inside or outside an organization, though industrial engineers are also quite capable of carrying out these investigations in blue-collar industrial settings. Instructional designers are thus the most likely to conduct—and use—task listing and analysis information.

A key issue to consider at the outset of a task analysis is the amount of time and money it will take to perform. That depends, of course, on the number of tasks to be analyzed and the detail required. If many tasks will be scrutinized or the detail required is great, one or two in-house instructional designers can rarely handle the assignment in a brief time span. For this reason, managers of instructional design projects may request contractual assistance from outside groups — vendors, local college faculty, or other instructional designers — to perform task analysis, particularly in large settings such as a nuclear power station.

When outside instructional designers are used, they should be selected with the same care as in-house staff (American Society for Training and Development, 1986e). Check their references carefully. Request samples of their work. To reduce the time it will take to orient them to the project, furnish them with examples to show the detail that is required.

It should be relatively easy to specify whose task performance will be examined. However, the sources to use in gathering task information can sometimes be debated. There are four possible sources of information about tasks: *performers, nonperformers, documents,* and *environmental features* (Jackson, 1986).

Performers are those who do the work. Much valuable information can be collected by observing what they do, asking them what they do, and examining their work results. However, there are different categories of performers — as shown below. Each category of performer furnishes a unique source of information.

Types of Performers	What They Can Tell You
Master performers	Master performers can provide information about the most efficient and effective way to perform a task. Normally, task analyses should be based on the way the most successful people perform the task.
Average performers	Information about the way average performers behave and the results they obtain can provide opportunities for improvement. A comparison of average and master performers will provide information about the extent of the gap.
Low performers	Information from low performers can be useful for making training decisions, and comparisons with average or master performers can provide information about opportunities for improvement.
The task analyst as a Performer	Analysts can also gather information by performing the tasks themselves. This can confirm information from others as well as help identify gaps in information.

Nonperformers are those who have reason to be familiar with work tasks but who do not actually perform them. They can often provide important perspectives about what results should be achieved but are not being achieved. Examples of nonperformers include supervisors, customers, subordinates, peers, resource or staff personnel, subject matter experts, and future performers. The nature of the information they provide is summarized below (Jackson, 1986, p. 89).

Types of Nonperformers	*What They Can Tell You*
Managers of performers	Managers are a good source of information about the results expected of performers. They can also provide useful information about performer characteristics, feedback and reinforcement, the performance situation, and problems they've observed with performance.
People affected by performance, such as customers, subordinates, peers, and so on	People affected by performance can provide valuable information about the consequences of behavior—its effectiveness or impact—or the value of performers' outputs.
Resource personnel: people who support or provide input to performers	Resource personnel can provide information about the performance situation and about the way in which performers access resources.
Subject matter experts: people who do not perform the task, but are knowledgeable about it	Experts may be the primary source of information for new tasks. They can also review or supplement information from performers.
Future performers: people who do not now perform the task, but are expected to do so in the future	Future performers can provide information about potential performer characteristics. By reviewing information from subject matter experts or by simulating parts of the task, they can help identify gaps in information or other problems in the task description.

Documents are references used by performers to carry out work tasks or by nonperformers to find out about those tasks. Examples of documents include procedure manuals, training manuals, and forms (Jackson, 1986). They can be valuable sources of information about how work tasks should be performed, how they should be measured, and what resources are needed for performance.

Environmental features are the conditions under which instruction is to be developed or applied. (Key features of these environments have already been described at length in Chapter Six.) In the task analysis plan, be sure to consider what approach to use in collecting and analyzing task information. Base the selection of an approach on the task to be examined, as shown in Table 7.1. If a procedural task is to be examined, then use *procedural analysis;* if a process or troubleshooting task is to be examined, then use *process and troubleshooting analysis;* if a mental task is to be examined, then use *content analysis* (Swanson and Gradous, 1986).

Steps Four and Five: Implementing the Task Analysis Plan and Analyzing and Using Results

Implementing a task analysis plan should be simple enough, even if actually conducting task analysis can be a time-consuming and tedious process. Carlisle (1986, p. 5) summarizes these steps succinctly: "First, the job or task is broken down into its component parts. Second, the relationships

Table 7.1. Summary of Approaches to Task Analysis.

Approach to task analysis	Use the approach under the following conditions	Description
Procedure analysis	Interaction between person-material or person-machine Step-by-step procedure Observable activity	List the steps in a procedure from the standpoint of a performer of it, beginning each task statement with a verb. Describe how to measure the quality of the task. Describe how to recognize cues indicating when a task should be enacted.
		Identify instances in which tasks can be more effectively or efficiently performed.
Process and trouble-shooting analysis	Interaction between person and system	Flowchart the system, showing how work should progress through it. Identify ways to improve the flow of work through the system, eliminating redundancy and unnecessary steps.
Subject matter analysis	Interactions between people-people and people-ideas	Identify the subject or topic. Investigate what experienced performers know about the topic. Investigate how people *perform* the mental (covert) activity by asking them, observing results of work activity, or other methods. Conduct a search of literature on the topic.
		Synthesize results using any one of several methods. Describe the subject/content.

Source: Adapted from Swanson, R., and Gradous, D. *Performance at Work: A Systematic Program for Analyzing Work Behavior.* New York: Wiley-Interscience, 1986.

between the parts are examined and compared with correct principles of performance. Third, the parts are restructured to form an improved job or task, and learning requirements are specified." The first step is the *task listing* component of the study. The outputs of a task listing become the basis for *task analysis,* and the outputs of a task analysis become the basis for *performance objectives* and *test items* (Dick and Carey, 1985). Of course, performance objectives provide descriptions of what learners should know, do, or feel at the end of an instructional experience.

Content Analysis

Content analysis, sometimes called *subject matter analysis,* "is intended (1) to identify and isolate single idea or skill units for instruction, (2) to act as an objective decision rule for including or excluding topics from instruction, and (3) to provide guidance to sequence topics in instruction" (Gibbons, 1977, p. 2).

When Should Instructional Designers Perform Content Analysis?

Content analysis need not follow job or task analysis. It may be performed by itself—or it may follow task analysis as a means of relating work activities and results to the knowledge necessary for individuals to perform. It is "the process of breaking large bodies of subject matter or tasks into smaller and instructionally useful units" (Gibbons, 1977, p. 2). These "instructionally useful units" may include facts, concepts, processes, procedures, and/or principles (Clark, 1986). For example, "if you make notes or prepare an outline of information for a lesson, a speech, or a paper, you list subject content" (Kemp, 1971, p. 44). Content analysis thus differs from job or task analysis because it stems from an examination of information/knowledge requirements rather than from sequences or procedures in conducting work activities or achieving work results.

Importance of Content Analysis

To perform their jobs, workers require information that they have translated into knowledge, skills, and attitudes and that they have organized in ways they can apply in a work setting. Of course, competent performance requires more than appropriate knowledge, skills, and attitudes. For instance, workers must be able to recognize the cues that signal when performance is appropriate or inappropriate. They must also be motivated to perform when they recognize the cues signaling an appropriate occasion to perform. Yet it is clear that workers will never be capable of performing competently if they lack the requisite knowledge, skills, and attitudes.

Content analysis is important, then, because it is a process of identifying the essential information that learners should translate into work-related knowledge, skills, and attitudes through planned instructional experiences. Instructional designers play an important role in organizing information in ways that will be meaningful to learners and that will help them translate information (facts, concepts, processes, procedures, principles) into work-related knowledge, skills, and attitudes.

Assumptions Underlying Content Analysis

Three key assumptions provide a theoretical foundation for content analysis. One assumption is this: "learning experiences are based on subject content" (Kemp, 1971, p. 43). In other words, learners must *know* before they can *do*. They must be familiar with a body of knowledge, skills, and attitudes associated with performance before they can perform competently.

A second assumption is that work tasks are not always the appropriate basis for instructional design because "it is not always the case that the end-purposes [objectives of instruction] reduce to a single task or set of tasks" (Gibbons, 1977, p. 4). Task analysis is not always an appropriate means of examining the components of effective performance because performance cannot always be reduced to step-by-step processes or procedures. Indeed, effective performance may on occasion depend on a learner's familiarity with facts, concepts, processes, procedures, or principles. Definitions and examples of these terms, all of which are important for understanding content analysis, appear in Table 7.2.

A third assumption underlying content analysis is related to the second: "instructional content and tasks vary across a set of categories [and] there are indeed different types of content" (Gibbons, 1977, p. 4). One implication of this statement is that "different types of content are likely to require methods of analysis suited to them individually. Hence, one type of analysis is not sufficient to handle all types of content adequately" (Gibbons, 1977, p. 4).

Instructional designers should not, of course, perform content analysis because it is intrinsically fascinating or satisfying in its own right. (Some perverse, highly technical instructional designers may find that it is!) Instead, it should be performed because it provides useful information for organizing instruction and developing objectives to guide instruction. As Kemp (1971, p. 44) explains,

Table 7.2. Content Types: Definitions and Examples.

Content	Definition	Example
Fact	An arbitrary association among concepts.	The editor of *Performance and Instruction* is Sivasailam Thiagarajan.
Concept	A category of items that share common characteristics.	Editor — A person — Responsible for articles written by others
Process	A series of steps whereby several individuals, departments, or objects accomplish a task.	How the Company collects bills. How a generator works.
Procedure	A series of steps whereby an individual completes a task.	How to log on a computer.
Principle	A predictive relationship among concepts.	Goals that are specific and difficult yield more productivity than easy or vague goals.

Source: Clark, R. "Defining the 'D' in ISD: Part 2: Task-Specific Instructional Methods." *Performance and Instruction,* 1986, *25*(3), 13. Reprinted with permission of the National Society for Performance and Instruction.

> In the pattern of the instructional design plan we should pro-
> ceed from statements of general purpose to objectives and then
> to subject content. In actual practice we often find it easier to
> begin with a statement of general purposes, follow it with a list
> of content to be taught and learned, and then backtrack to work
> on objectives, as suggested by the content. In one sense we might
> say that *"objectives are what you want content to do."* [Later] if you
> start with the content you will probably find that there is a se-
> quence of order that indicates that certain parts of the content
> must be mastered as a basis for subsequent learning.

The question is: How is this 'sequence of order' identified? The answer to
that question is the basis for content analysis.

An Overview of the Steps in Performing Content Analysis

Instructional designers should take the following steps to perform a content
analysis (Swanson and Gradous, 1986):

1. Identify the subject or topic
2. Investigate what experienced performers know about the topic
3. Investigate how people *perform* the mental (covert) activity by
    a. Asking them
    b. Observing results of work activity
    c. Using other methods
4. Conduct a literature search on the topic
5. Synthesize results using any one of several methods to develop a model
    of the subject
6. Describe the subject/content

We now turn to a step-by-step summary of each step.

Step One: Identifying the Subject or Topic

First, identify the subject or topic. Try to link it to existing databases. For
example, use the *Library of Congress Subject Index,* available in most libraries,
and see how the topic is classified by libraries. Numerous other reference
sources can be consulted to identify keywords for use in identifying subject
titles.

Step Two: Investigating What Experienced
Performers Know About the Topic

Second, investigate what experienced performers know about the topic. Use
questionnaires, interviews, observations of performers, and document re-

views. Collect background information to clarify what the subject is. Ask experienced performers to explain what the subject is, how it relates to the work, and how they would orient a new employee to the subject.

Step Three: Investigating How People Perform the Activity

Third, investigate how people *perform* the mental (covert) activity by asking them, observing results of work activity, or using other methods. Analyze what was learned about the topic from experienced performers in step 2 and then organize that information. Next try to clarify what knowledge is applied in the work setting, how it is applied, and how people organize and structure it themselves. If possible, establish categories for observation. If that is not possible, sit with performers as they work and ask them what they do as they do it (Zemke and Kramlinger, 1982).

Organize information based on problems or situations encountered in the work setting and how performers respond to them. This process is called *information processing analysis* (Gagne and Briggs, 1979). For each behavior, ask "what would a person need to know or be able to do in order to perform in this situation?" (Gagne and Briggs, 1979, p. 205).

Step Four: Conducting a Literature Search on the Topic

Fourth, conduct a search of literature on the topic. Use any of the numerous sources of information available to instructional designers. A particularly good introduction to these sources is Bard, Bell, Stephen, and Webster (1987). In addition, identify key references — organizational, occupational, governmental, industrial, or academic — during discussions with experienced performers. Other professional instructional designers may also be a valuable source of information about literature on the topic, since they may have had occasion to research the topic in the past (Bard and Loftin, 1987).

Step Five: Synthesizing Results of the Content Analysis

Fifth, synthesize results of the content analysis. Use one of several methods to develop a *synthesis model,* defined by Swanson and Gradous (1986, p. 207) as "a structure on which to organize and fit the ideas and information on any subject matter relevant to performance at work." To develop a synthesis model, instructional designers must approach the subject matter creatively, using innovative problem-solving techniques to impose organization where there may appear to be none (Ulschak, Nathanson, and Gillan, 1983; Van Gundy, 1981).

Swanson and Gradous list eight techniques to develop synthesis models: (1) *reflection,* which compresses a subject into a "metaphor, cartoon, or narrative that somehow 'says it all'" (p. 195); (2) a *two-axis matrix,* in which two ideas are juxtaposed graphically to form a series of cells, each representing a different fact, concept, process, procedure, or principle; (3) a *three-axis matrix,* in which three ideas are juxtaposed graphically to form a cube, and each cell of the cube represents a fact, concept, process, procedure, or principle; (4) a *flowchart,* which "organizes and synthesizes information that contains input-process-output items, decision points, direction of flow, documentation or preparation steps, confluence and divergence, and extraction" (p. 199); (5) an *events network,* which "will help you take into account all the activity paths and events by which work toward an organizational goal is accomplished" (p. 199); (6) *dichotomy,* which divides subject matter into two completely different parts that are then contrasted and compared; (7) *argumentation,* which is a "synthesis method aimed at resolving two or more theses, positions, or valuations of a subject matter" (p. 201); and (8) *graphic models* that organize information visually through charts, maps, and other methods.

Step Six: Describing the Subject/Content

Sixth, describe the subject/content in a way that will facilitate learning by others. *Remember that imposing organization on subject matter does not necessarily mean that the resulting arrangement will facilitate the learning of those unfamiliar with the subject (Gibbons, 1977). To organize subject matter for learning, perform an instructional analysis* that identifies what learners should know in order to demonstrate knowledge or perform a task or other activity. This topic will be treated at the beginning of the next chapter, because instructional analysis is the link between *what is to be learned* and *how instruction should be designed.*

The results of content analysis, like the results of task analysis, provide the basis for preparing performance objectives to guide development of instruction and test items (Tiemann and Markle, 1985). To emphasize this point, this principle is illustrated in Figure 7.2.

Figure 7.2. Uses for Results of Task or Content Analysis.

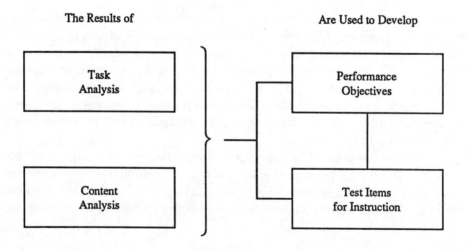

Judging Work Analysis

According to *The Standards* (1986), instructional designers should be able to evaluate work analysis studies conducted by themselves or others. The evaluation should focus on three central issues: (1) Was the procedure selected and carried out appropriately? (2) Was the analysis carried out with sufficient detail and in sufficient depth? and (3) Are the results useful for writing performance objectives to guide instruction?

Judging the Adequacy of an Analytical Method and Its Results: A Few Simple Steps

If job, task, or content analysis studies have been conducted poorly, it will be difficult — if not impossible — to design effective instruction tailored to job-related performance needs. After all, detailed analysis results in a thorough breakdown of a job, task, or subject matter area so that it can be reassembled instructionally. If the analysis is wrong, then the instruction based on it will also be wrong — and the effects on workers may be devastating to their performance and morale, not to mention the effects on the organization's productivity.

To judge whether the procedure was selected and carried out appropriately, study the plan for the work analysis to make sure it clearly sets forth each of the following:

- The purpose, goals, and objectives of the analysis.
- The analytical procedure selected.
- The reason(s) why the instructional designers chose the analytical procedure they chose.
- The constraints on time and resources that the instructional designers faced.
- The assumptions, if any, that the instructional designers made about the jobs, tasks, or content they analyzed.
- The methods used to collect and analyze data.
- The findings that resulted from the analysis.
- The background information available to instructional designer(s) as they conducted the analysis. Did they research and then apply to the analysis information about the organization's mission, goals, structure, perceived values, and specifications derived from a needs assessment/analysis? Did they apply any additional information they were able to obtain from subject matter experts and/or from documentation?

Obtain this information before evaluating the work analysis.

Second, review the documentation and clarify the constraints and resources available to carry out the analytical assignment. Then interview the instructional designers assigned to the project. Ask a few simple "acid test" questions:

What was the purpose of the analysis? What were the objectives? Was the analysis carried out primarily to: (1) Describe the job, task, or content? (2) Describe how the job or task is done or how content is used? (3) Identify ways to improve the job or task or improve content application in work performance? or (4) Identify how to instruct others on the job, task, or content?

What constraints, if any, were faced on this project? What necessary resources were not available?

How would you perform the analysis differently if you were asked to do it now?

How did the culture of the organization affect analysis? How much cooperation did you receive from members of the organization?

Base part of the evaluation of the work analysis on the answers.

Justifying Work Analysis

According to *The Standards* (1986), instructional designers should also be able to justify the work analysis conducted and the conclusions reached from it. Before, during, and after the work analysis, then, be prepared to explain and defend it against those who may have economic or political stakes in the outcomes. Detailed work analysis may sometimes seem threatening to workers and even their supervisors, and the results may have implications affecting workers' wages, salaries, and job security. For these reasons, some job incumbents and their supervisors may feel impelled to challenge job or task analysis results if they fear they may lose something valuable. These problems of acceptance can usually be averted if workers and supervisors actively participate at every stage of analysis (Rothwell and Kazanas, 1987). Greater participation will also tend to increase the likelihood that workers and supervisors will accept the results and will use them in subsequent instruction, both on and off the job. However, the greater the degree of participation and the larger the group of participants, the longer it will take to perform the analysis.

If constraints on time limit worker or supervisor participation, then be prepared to support the results of the work analysis against those who feel they may lose something. If possible, hold an "exit conference" at the end of the assignment with representatives of workers and management. Have documentation from the work analysis prepared and thoroughly organized for this conference—and do not expect to be treated cordially during the assignment. Prepare an outline to guide presentation of the results, and spell out how the investigation was conducted, who participated in it, how long it was conducted, what assumptions were made, and what the results *do not mean* as well as what they *do mean*. Find out, in advance of the assignment or the exit conference, if the results will be used in any way that may later have an effect on workers' wages or future job security. If not, say so at the beginning of the assignment and repeat it again at the end; otherwise, ask representatives of the organization to attend the conference and discuss what impact the results may have.

Conclusion

In this chapter, we defined job, task, and content analyses and briefly explained how to carry out each of them. We also offered advice to instructional designers about judging and justifying work analysis. This chapter concludes our treatment of four related forms of analysis that are conducted before performance objectives are written and instructional materials are prepared.

In the next three chapters, we turn to the process of converting information about needs, learners, work settings, and work into objectives (results) desired from instruction. In Chapter Eight we show how to write statements of performance objectives, in Chapter Nine we explain how to develop performance measurements, and in Chapter Ten we clarify how to sequence performance objectives.

PART III

Establishing
Performance Objectives
and Performance Measurements

CHAPTER EIGHT

Writing Statements
of Performance Objectives

Once work analysis has been performed, instructional designers should be ready for the next step in the instructional design process—writing statements of performance objectives. (See Figure 8.1.) Synonymous with instructional or behavioral objectives, performance objectives are necessary for one very important reason: they guide remaining steps in the instructional design process by describing precisely what the targeted learners should know, do, or feel on completion of a planned learning experience. They also communicate the results sought from the learning experience.

In a sense, performance objectives create a vision of what learners should be doing after they master the instruction. As Mager (1975, p. 5) has explained, an objective should be understood as "a description of a performance you want learners to be able to exhibit before you consider them competent. An objective describes an intended result of instruction, rather than the process of instruction itself." It thus focuses on instructional outputs—desired effects on the learners—rather than on what instructional designers should do or what activities trainers should use to effect changes in learners' work performance.

In this chapter, we will explain how to distinguish performance objectives from goals and activities, summarize how to derive performance objectives from analytical results, and describe how to write performance objectives. We will conclude with advice for instructional designers about judging and justifying performance objectives.

Distinguishing Performance Objectives from Goals and Activities

Performance objectives should not be confused with goals or activities. But what are instructional or organizational goals? What are learner or trainer activities? How do they differ from performance objectives? Let us begin the chapter by answering these questions.

Figure 8.1. A Model of Steps in the Instructional Design Process.

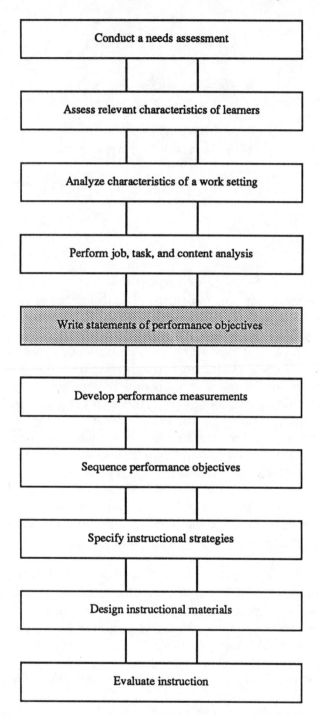

Source: Foshay, W., Silber, K., and Westgaard, O. *Instructional Design Competencies: The Standards.* Iowa City, Iowa: International Board of Standards for Training, Performance, and Instruction, 1986, p. 3. Used with permission of the publisher.

What Are Instructional/Organizational Goals?

Instructional goals are simply expressions of the general results desired from instruction. Unlike performance objectives, they are not measurable. Mager (1972) calls them *warm fuzzies* because they sound desirable (warm) but are so vague (fuzzy) that achieving them is unclear. In fact, different people may assign their own meanings or significance to them. Examples of instructional goals are easy enough to point out and include such lofty efforts as "improving customer service," "improving quality," "increasing profitability," and "increasing learner understanding." However, they are warm fuzzies, as Mager uses that term, because they do not clarify precisely what a learner must do—or how a learner should perform.

Organizational goals are results desired from an organization. Often included as part of an organization's formal mission statement, they articulate philosophy, embody management values, and imply an organization's general direction. Their achievement is rarely restricted to a specific time period. Nor do goals lend themselves, as organizational objectives do, to specific measurement methods (Rothwell and Kazanas, 1989). As expressions about an organization, their link to individual job performance is often unclear. Examples of organizational goals include "serving the community," "maintaining a safe and productive workplace for employees," and "making a reasonable return on investment." To become measurable, organizational goals must be translated into organizational objectives (Rothwell and Kazanas, 1989). To focus on individuals, organizational goals must be translated into terms that are directly related to what employees do and how well they do it.

What Are Learner/Trainer Activities?

A learner activity refers to what a learner is doing during a planned learning experience. For example, "listening to a lecture"—admittedly a rather passive activity because it implies more action by a trainer than by a learner—is a learner activity. Another example: "answering the questions at the end of a case study." Activities emphasize behaviors; in contrast, performance objectives emphasize results. A trainer activity refers to what a trainer is doing during a planned learning experience. For instance, one trainer activity is "defining terms." Other examples include lecturing, introducing a learning activity, showing a videotape, or passing out evaluations. Trainers sometimes focus on what they should do during a learning experience rather than on what learners should be able to do by the end of instruction.

How Do Performance Objectives Differ from Goals and Activities?

A performance objective is an expression of a desired result of a learning experience. It differs from a performance goal in that it is measurable and is an expression of what should be achieved. It differs from activities in that it describes desired results, not behaviors leading to results.

Any performance objective should address at least three fundamental questions: (1) What should the learner be able to do at the end of instruction? (2) How well should the learner be able to perform at the end of instruction? and (3) What conditions must exist for the learner to perform as desired?

Deriving Performance Objectives from Goal Analysis and Task or Content Analysis

Instructional designers can derive performance objectives from goal analysis, carried out with instructional/organizational goals and learner/trainer activities, or from task or content analysis results. But what is goal analysis, and how is it carried out? How are the results of task and content analysis used to write performance objectives? Let us turn to these questions next.

Defining Goal Analysis

"The function of goal analysis," as Mager (1972, p. 10) points out, "is to define the indefinable, to tangibilitate the intangible—to help us say what we mean by our important but abstract goals." It is thus a means of transforming laudable but otherwise vague desires into specific targets for learner accomplishment. Goal analysis is appropriate to use on those many occasions when instructional designers are approached by their clients to work miracles. Indeed, clients often do speak in terms of vague and ill-defined goals, and instructional designers must use methods such as performance analysis to determine what kind of performance problem exists. Goal analysis is a later step, intended to determine precisely what results are desired from an instructional design solution.

Performing Goal Analysis

To perform goal analysis, instructional designers should carry out five simple steps:

1. Identify the goal, the "warm fuzzy," and write it down. Clarify the vague goal instruction intends to achieve.
2. Write down examples of what people are saying or doing when they are behaving in a way corresponding to the goal. In short, identify behaviors associated with the goal.
3. Sort out unrelated items and polish the list developed in step 2. Eliminate duplications not clearly associated with achieving the goal.
4. Describe precisely what learners should be doing to demonstrate goal achievement. Statements of this kind become performance objectives.
5. Test the performance objectives to ensure that they are linked to the goal and, when enacted, will lead to the desired instructional results.

These five steps can help convert otherwise vague instructional or organizational goals — or learner or trainer activities — into precise performance objectives.

A simple description of the process should clarify it. Suppose a team of instructional designers has been assigned the daunting task of "improving customer service." (Clients sometimes speak vaguely when they identify perceptions of learner needs.)

First, the team members would have to make sure the aim is improving customer service, not some other goal. They would do that by analyzing the performance problem and assessing learner needs. Second — assuming a justifiable instructional need was identified — the team members would make a list of specific employee behaviors associated with effective customer service. They would ask these questions: "What will people be doing when they are serving customers effectively?" "What will they be saying?" Examples of appropriate behaviors might include answering customer phone calls quickly and courteously, approaching customers politely when they arrive in a store to look at merchandise, and identifying customers' problems or needs quickly and accurately. (These are just a few examples of behaviors associated with the goal.) Note that even these behaviors can be made more specific if the instructional designers described precisely what an employee does to "act courteously" or "identify customers' problems." And the examples just given could easily swell if the team members applied various methods of creative problem solving to identify more behaviors and worker statements associated with "improved customer service" (Ulschak, Nathanson, and Gillan, 1983; Van Gundy, 1981). Once the previous steps have been completed, the instructional designers should then eliminate duplicative behaviors from the list. Finally, team members would write performance objectives and try them out to see whether learners who achieved them would indeed demonstrate "improved customer service" as defined by the client(s).

Converting Results of Task or Content Analysis into Performance Objectives

Goal analysis is just one of two primary methods used to identify the specific results desired from instruction. The second — and perhaps more commonly used method — is conversion of task or content analysis results into performance objectives (Dick and Carey, 1985).

Recall that the results of task analysis reveal how work is, or should be, performed. As we have seen, the results of content analysis also create a logical organizational scheme for subject matter that can be used as a starting point for developing instruction. But there is quite a difference between doing the work — or organizing subject matter — and engineering instruction that will produce learners who can do the work or demonstrate the desired knowledge. For this reason, it is not enough just to analyze how the work is done or how subject matter can be logically organized. Some consideration must also be given to the related, albeit different, issue of how to produce the desired results of instruction.

Instructional designers convert the results of task or content analysis into specific performance objectives by

1. Establishing instructional purpose
2. Classifying learning tasks
3. Analyzing learning tasks

These steps are depicted in Figure 8.2.

First, instructional designers should establish purpose. Purpose means the primary reason for a planned instructional experience. There are typically four choices: (1) increasing learners' knowledge, (2) changing attitudes or feelings, (3) building skills, or (4) combining one or more of the other three choices.

Second, instructional designers should classify learning tasks by examining each work task and asking this question: What kind of instruction will be necessary to instruct people to perform this task or demonstrate this

**Figure 8.2. Steps for Converting Results of
Task or Content Analysis into Performance Objectives.**

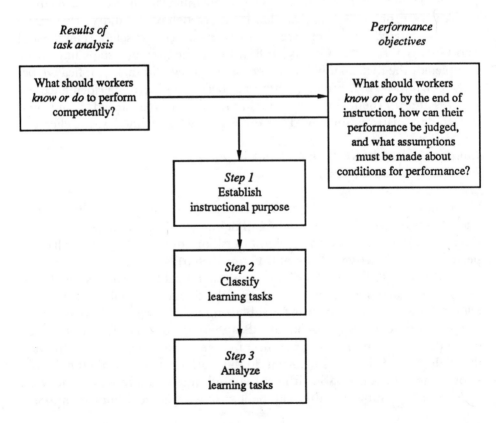

knowledge? Only four answers to this question are possible. Instruction can be designed for (1) knowledge, (2) feelings, (3) skills, or (4) some combination of the first three. Here are a few examples of ways to classify tasks:

Work Task	*Classification of Learning Tasks*
1. Explaining a procedure to others	Knowledge
2. Serving customers courteously	Feelings
3. Typing letters	Skills

Instructional designers should bear in mind that the appropriate way to carry out the instructional design process depends on the results to be achieved (Gagne, 1977a, 1977b). Classifying work tasks into learning tasks is important because it can suggest the best ways to design instruction that is intended to bring about particular results. Of course, more than one classification scheme for work and/or learning tasks/content has been devised. For example, Gagne, Briggs, and Wager (1988) distinguish between intellectual skills, cognitive skills, verbal information, motor skills, and attitude. As they define them, *intellectual skills* are equated with the ability to read, write, and compute as well as capabilities needed to perform tasks in special occupational fields. *Cognitive skills* underlie learning how to learn — that is, knowing how to get to the heart of problems. *Verbal information* is linked to summarizing or stating a principle and "is the knowledge base called upon when we execute our how-to intellectual skills" (Dick and Carey, 1985, p. 55). *Motor skill* is associated with body movement of any kind, ranging from moving a pen to using a computer keyboard. *Attitude* means a persistent set of beliefs. Since each of these learning tasks is intended to evoke a different result, each calls for different instructional strategies.

The third step is to analyze learning tasks, a process called *learning task analysis* (Gagne and Briggs, 1979). Not to be confused with work task analysis, its purpose is to identify prerequisite knowledge. A prerequisite describes what learners should know before participating in instruction. Instructional designers use three methods to identify prerequisites: (1) learning hierarchies, (2) cluster analysis, and (3) procedural analysis (Dick and Carey, 1985).

Instructional designers develop a *learning hierarchy* by repeatedly asking this question of each work task and subtask: What does a learner need to know to do that? (Davis, Alexander, and Yelon, 1974). This process is called *hierarchical analysis*. To cite a simple example: to fill an automobile's 'tank with gasoline, a learner must first know what an automobile is, what a gasoline tank is, where the gasoline tank is located, where gasoline may be purchased, how to remove the gas cap, and so on. Each task implies a learning hierarchy. Hierarchical analysis may be applied to intellectual, psychomotor, and attitudinal skills — but not to verbal information (Dick and Carey, 1985). To perform hierarchical analysis, instructional designers should simply flowchart the relationship between the work task and the required prerequisite knowledge. They then develop performance objectives from the hierarchy. For more information on hierarchical analysis, see Dick and Carey (1985).

Cluster analysis is appropriately used with verbal information or attitudes (Dick and Carey, 1985). It is particularly useful in developing performance objectives from results of content analysis and is based on categories of information. For instance, categories might include the number of letters in the alphabet (a fact) or the number of component parts in a social theory. (A social theory is a principle based on opinions of various experts.) To perform a cluster analysis, instructional designers begin by drawing a chart. They place an instructional goal at the top. They then list below it "the major categories of information that are implied by it" (Dick and Carey, 1985, p. 55). Instructional designers should try to be creative as they categorize information, but they should remember that one aim is to be as complete as possible. They must succeed in developing a scheme to organize the information. Quite often this process can economize the instructional effort (Dick and Carey, 1985).

Procedural analysis is the process of identifying what learners should know to perform one task or a series of related tasks (a procedure). It is appropriately applied to developing performance objectives for intellectual skills, motor skills, and attitudes (Dick and Carey, 1985). But it does not work with verbal information, for which no "step-by-step list of activities" can be created. To perform procedural analysis, instructional designers should first identify an instructional goal and then flowchart steps in the procedure. For each step (task) in the procedure, they should answer this question: What must the learner know, do, or feel to perform? They should then express the answer by stating precise performance objectives.

Linking Work Activities and Performance Objectives

Performance objectives must always be tied to work activities. However, they may be linked to different expressions of work activities — for instance, as work tasks are presently performed or as they could be more efficiently and effectively performed at present or in the future. Performance objectives can also be linked to subject matter as related to job performance. When learners achieve performance objectives by the end of a planned learning experience, they should be able to perform in the application environment — or at least be familiar with the verbal information on which work performance depends. Instructional designers generally direct their attention to demonstrating learner change by the end of instruction, not on the learner's return to the application environment.

To demonstrate achievement of performance objectives in the application environment rather than merely at the end of instruction, they would probably have to devise more than one type of performance objective. Indeed,

Briggs (1977a) has identified four types of performance objectives. Each reflects a different time span. But instructional designers have seldom expressed performance objectives in terms of on-the-job changes; rather, the traditional focus has been on end-of-instruction changes. On-the-job change requires instructional designers to consider more than just what learners will be able to do: it also requires consideration of what the organization and the learners' supervisors must do to support the learner's application of knowledge, skills, and attitudes.

Stating Objectives in Performance Terms

According to *The Standards* (1986, p. 52), instructional designers should be able to "state an objective in performance terms that reflects the intent of instruction." They should be able to classify the type of performance objectives that must be written and then state performance objectives directly or indirectly linked to work requirements. The objectives should clarify, in measurable terms, what learners should be able to do at the end of instruction, how well they should be able to do it, and what conditions have to exist or equipment has to be available for them to exhibit the performance. To write performance objectives, however, instructional designers must have "a task/concept analysis and a learner analysis" (*The Standards*, 1986, p. 52).

Classifying Performance Objectives

Instructional designers begin the process of stating performance objectives by identifying the kinds of objectives that must be written. Referring to the task classification prepared earlier in the instructional design process, they should clarify whether each objective will focus on knowledge, skills, or attitudes.

The most commonly used classification scheme for performance objectives was first described in 1956. That year, Bloom and his colleagues published a *Taxonomy of Educational Objectives* and defined three domains of learning—knowledge, attitudes, and skills. Objectives focused on increasing learner knowledge are called *cognitive objectives;* objectives focused on changing learners' attitudes are called *affective objectives;* and objectives focused on building skills are called *psychomotor objectives. Knowledge,* as we defined it in Chapter One, means "facts and information essential to performing a job or task"; *skills* involve the "ability to behave in ways associated with successful job performance"; and *attitudes* are "feelings about performance that are voiced to other people".

Each "domain" of learning consists of increasingly complicated levels, as shown in Figures 8.3 to 8.5. Instructional designers begin classifying performance objectives by identifying the level of the domain that they are trying to reach. When they have done that for the end results desired from a planned learning experience, they are ready to begin writing performance objectives.

Figure 8.3. Levels of Objectives in the Cognitive Domain.

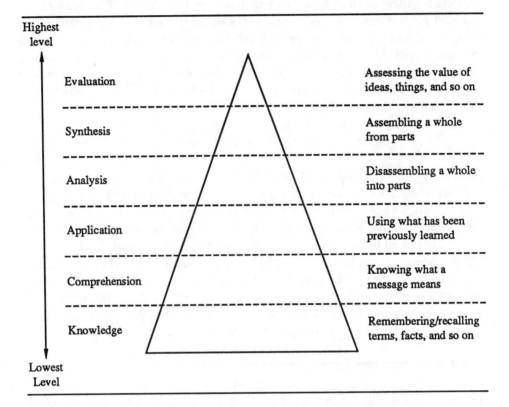

Source: Rothwell, W., and Kazanas, H. *Strategic Human Resource Development.* ©1989, p. 204. Reprinted by permission of Prentice-Hall, Inc., Englewood Cliffs, N.J.

Describing Parts of Performance Objectives

Performance objectives make tangible a vision of what learners should know, do, or feel at the end of a planned instructional experience. They should contain statements about at least two of the following three components (Mager, 1975):

1. Performance
2. Criterion
3. Condition

Other components could also be included in performance objectives, "such as a description of the students for which the objective is intended or a description of the instructional procedure by which the objective will be accomplished" (Mager, 1975, p. 21).

The *performance* component of an objective describes "what a learner will be doing when demonstrating mastery of the objective" at the end of the planned instructional experience (Mager, 1975, p. 48). It is an activity

Figure 8.4. Levels of Objectives in the Affective Domain.

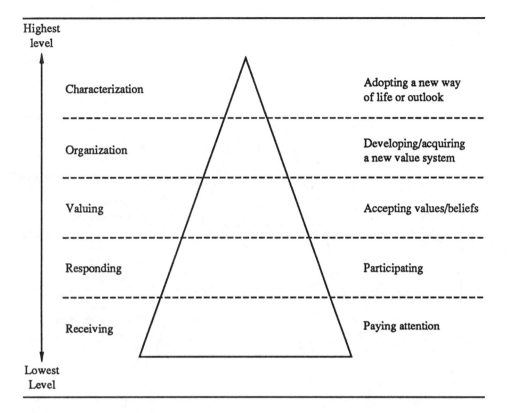

Highest level

Characterization — Adopting a new way of life or outlook

Organization — Developing/acquiring a new value system

Valuing — Accepting values/beliefs

Responding — Participating

Receiving — Paying attention

Lowest Level

Source: Rothwell, W., and Kazanas, H. *Strategic Human Resource Development.* ©1989, p. 205. Reprinted by permission of Prentice-Hall, Inc., Englewood Cliffs, N.J.

or behavior to be learned during instruction and demonstrated afterward. A statement of performance always begins with a verb, and the choice of verb is typically linked to the type of task to be learned. Lists of verbs associated with cognitive, affective, and psychomotor performance are provided in Tables 8.1 to 8.3.

The *criterion* component of an objective describes "how well the learner must perform in order to be considered acceptable" (Mager, 1975, p. 21). It must be measurable. Measures may be expressed by quantity, quality, or cost. Criteria may be derived from past work practices, present performance needs, future organizational plans, academic and government research, and other sources. They should be tied to historical performance standards or future organizational plans (Rothwell and Kazanas, 1989; Springer, 1980).

There are two different kinds of criteria: process and product (Blank, 1982). A process criterion describes how well the learner should perform the task; a product criterion describes the product of the task. Examples of process criteria include "following company procedures"; "conforming to the organization's safety practices"; and "within ten minutes." Product criteria

Figure 8.5. Levels of Objectives in the Psychomotor Domain.

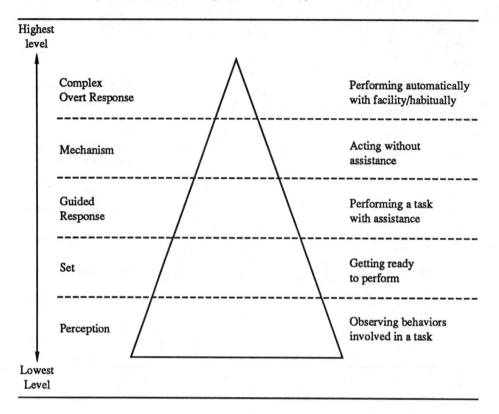

Source: Rothwell, W., and Kazanas, H. *Strategic Human Resource Development.* ©1989, p. 206. Reprinted by permission of Prentice-Hall, Inc., Englewood Cliffs, N.J.

include any of the following: "to the client's satisfaction"; "with fewer than three errors"; and "ready for sale." To establish criteria, instructional designers should ask questions such as the following:

How has competent work performance historically been identified through measurable means?

How well must the work task associated with this performance objective be performed for the organization to meet its present competitive needs?

How can these organizational needs be expressed as measurable results to be achieved?

How well must the work task be performed in the future to help the organization achieve its Strategic Business Plans?

How can performance be measured?

What will the consequences of task performance be?

In some cases, there will be a difference between *existing* and *possible* criteria. In other words, workers can simply perform better than they have

Table 8.1. Verbs Associated with Objectives in the Cognitive Domain.

I. Knowledge Recall information		*II. Comprehension* Interpret information in one's own words		*III. Application* Apply knowledge or generalize it to a new situation	
arrange	name	classify	recognize	apply	operate
define	order	describe	report	choose	practice
duplicate	recognize	discuss	restate	demonstrate	prepare
label	recall	explain	review	dramatize	schedule
list	relate	express	select	employ	sketch
match	repeat	identify	sort	illustrate	solve
memorize	reproduce	indicate	tell	interpret	use
		locate	translate		

IV. Analysis Break down knowledge into parts and whole relationship		*V. Synthesis* Bring together parts of knowledge to form a whole and build relationships for new situations		*VI. Evaluation* Make judgments on basis of given criteria	
analyze	differentiate	arrange	manage	appraise	judge
appraise	discriminate	assemble	organize	argue	predict
calculate	distinguish	collect	plan	assess	rate
categorize	examine	compose	prepare	attack	score
compare	experiment	construct	propose	choose	select
contrast	inventory	create	set up	compare	support
criticize	question	design	synthesize	estimate	value
diagram	test	formulate	write	evaluate	

Source: from *The Instructional Design Process* by J. Kemp, p. 84. Copyright © 1985 by Harper & Row, Publishers, Inc. Reprinted by permission of HarperCollins Publishers.

Table 8.2. Verbs Associated with Objectives in the Affective Domain.

I. Receiving Paying attention	*II. Responding* Minimal participation	*III. Valuing* Internalizing preferences
Listen to	Reply	Attain
Perceive	Answer	Assume
Be alert to	Follow along	Support
Show tolerance of	Approve	Participate
	Obey	Continue

IV. Organization Development of a value system	*V. Characterization* Practice of a total philosophy of life
Organize	Believe
Select	Practice
Judge	Continue to
Decide	Carry out
Identify with	

Source: from *The Instructional Design Process* by J. Kemp, p. 82. Copyright © 1985 by Harper & Row, Publishers, Inc. Reprinted by permission of HarperCollins Publishers.

Table 8.3. Verbs Associated with Objectives in the Psychomotor Domain.

I. Reflexes Involuntary movement	II. Fundamental Movements Simple movements	III. Perception Response to stimuli
Stiffen	Crawl	Turn
Extend	Walk	Bend
Flex	Run	Balance
Stretch	Reach	Catch
IV. Physical Abilities Developed psychomotor movement	V. Skilled Movements Advanced learned movement	VI. Nondiscursive Most advanced learned movement
Move heavy objects	Play instrument	Dancing
Make quick motions	Use a hand tool	Changes in expression
Stop and restart movement		

Source: from *The Instructional Design Process* by J. Kemp, pp. 80–81. Copyright © 1985 by Harper & Row, Publishers, Inc. Reprinted by permission of HarperCollins Publishers.

been performing. One way that instructional designers can gauge the possibility for productivity improvement is to subtract the difference between the work output of the highest and lowest performers. This difference is called the *productivity improvement potential* or PIP (Gilbert, 1978). It too can serve as the basis for criteria in performance objectives.

The *condition* component of a performance objective "describes the important conditions (if any) under which the performance is to occur" (Mager, 1975, p. 21). Conditions may include "situations in which performance is necessary" or special equipment or other resources with which performers must be furnished before they can perform. Condition statements usually begin with the word "given," as in the following phrase: "given a ruler, the learner will be able to measure inches." In this context, "given" means "the learner is provided with some equipment, resources, or information with which to function and cannot perform competently without them."

Writing Performance Objectives

To write performance objectives, instructional designers should begin with the following sentence or some variation of it: "On completion of instruction, learners should be able to . . . ." They should then list the performance objectives, beginning each phrase with a verb. The portion of the objective that begins with the verb is the performance component. It is usually followed by statements about criterion and condition. Of course, criterion addresses this question: How well should the performance be done? It should always be measurable. The condition component addresses the following question: What equipment or other resources are necessary for the performance to be demonstrated by the learner? Some instructional designers may find this process easier if they use a worksheet like that shown in Exhibit 8.1.

Exhibit 8.1. A Worksheet for Preparing Instructional Objectives.

Directions: Use this worksheet as a job aid whenever you draft performance objectives. In column 1 below, write a description of the work task or subject matter topic on which the objective is to be based. Then, moving across the worksheet, complete columns 2 to 4.

Work task or subject matter topic	Performance objectives On completion of instruction, learners should be able to . . .		
Column 1	Column 2	Column 3	Column 4
Begin with a verb.	*Performance* Begin with a verb and answer this question: What will the learner know or do?	*Criterion* Describe how well the learner should know or be able to do the performance.	*Condition* Begin with "given" or "when" and describe the conditions that must exist for the learner to perform.

Avoiding Common Mistakes in Writing Performance Objectives

Writing performance objectives is more difficult than it may appear at first blush. Some mistakes are relatively common. They are worth describing so they can be avoided:

1. Avoid making objectives long-winded. Try to make them as concise as possible.
2. Do not use vague language. Words and phrases such as "understand," "demonstrate familiarity with," or "know" should usually be avoided because they are vague.
3. Try to avoid descriptions of criteria that are linked to instructor (or supervisor) satisfaction, as in the phrase "will perform to the satisfaction of the instructor." The reason: performance objectives of this kind lead to arbitrary differences in assessment of learner achievement.
4. Avoid lengthy "laundry lists" of required equipment and other resources when describing the conditions necessary for performance. List only the equipment and other resources that would not be obvious to a reasonable person.

Judging Performance Objectives

According to *The Standards* (1986), instructional designers should be able to evaluate the performance objectives written by themselves or others. In this process, they should be able to judge the accuracy, comprehensiveness, and appropriateness of the objectives. One of the easiest ways to evaluate performance objectives is to use a worksheet like that shown in Exhibit 8.2. Examine each objective with the aid of the worksheet and revise objective(s) whenever a no is checked.

Explaining Performance Objectives

According to *The Standards* (1986), instructional designers should be able to explain why they have written performance objectives the way they have. Indeed, as in all steps of the instructional design process, instructional designers are accountable to their colleagues and to clients for what they do. This accountability is particularly important for identifying the results sought from instruction.

Once performance objectives have been written, instructional designers should be prepared to answer the following questions about them:

1. Who will be expected to achieve them?
2. What do the objectives mean?
3. When should they be achieved
4. Where will they apply?
5. Why are they necessary?

To answer the question "Who will be expected to achieve the performance objectives?," instructional designers should be sure to clarify their targeted learners. In addition, they should be sure to determine precisely what those learners should already feel, know, or do before they enter the instruction. In short, prerequisites must be clarified.

To answer the question "What do the performance objectives mean?," instructional designers should clarify the targeted results of instruction. They should be able to explain the objectives in the everyday language of the workplace. Objectives should become touchstones, so to speak, to determine whether the end results sought by instructional designers match those expected by learners and clients.

To answer the question "When should the performance objectives be achieved?," instructional designers need to explain to others that the focus of performance objectives is always on *results* — that is, on what learners can do on completion of the instructional experience. Instructional designers should also emphasize that they do not necessarily assume that the performance objectives can be applied in the work setting — and they should be prepared to explain why they make that assumption. If possible, instructional designers should enlist management support to examine the application environment and create support for application of instruction when learners return to their work settings.

Exhibit 8.2. A Worksheet for Judging Performance Objectives.

Directions: Use this worksheet to judge performance objectives written by yourself or others. For each objective, consider each question appearing in the left column below. Mark a check (✔) for the appropriate response to each question in the center column. Then make notes to yourself for revision in the right column. If you answer yes to all questions, the objective meets all required criteria and it will not need to be revised. If you answer no to any question, the objective does not meet all required criteria. It should be revised.

     Make copies of this worksheet as necessary, depending on the number of objectives that you will review.

Question	Response		Notes for Revision
	Yes	*No*	
Does the objective . . .	(✔)	(✔)	
1. Describe observable behaviors?	( )	( )	
2. Describe measurable behaviors?	( )	( )	
3. Match behaviors in the task?	( )	( )	
4. Describe or imply conditions . . .			
a. affecting the job, task, or content to be taught?	( )	( )	
b. in terms of information provided to the performer?	( )	( )	
c. in terms of the situation of performance?	( )	( )	
d. by means of which information is provided?	( )	( )	
e. in terms of tools available?	( )	( )	
5. Describe or imply criteria that			
a. are observable?	( )	( )	
b. require performance in the same sequence as the task being taught?	( )	( )	
c. require performance to the level of precision appropriate to the learner?	( )	( )	
d. require performance to the level of the ultimate requirements of the task specification?	( )	( )	
6. Represent at least one task or relevant subject matter topic?	( )	( )	

To answer the question "Where will the performance objectives apply?," instructional designers should emphasize that the focus is on the instructional setting. They should continue to build support from management to create an application environment in which learners can apply what they learned.

To answer the question "Why are performance objectives necessary?," several points should be brought out. Instructional designers need to emphasize that they establish accountability for learners, draw learner attention to the expected results of instruction, provide indicators to the learners' supervisors about the benefits resulting from instruction, and establish targeted results for the instructional design process.

These explanations about performance objectives should be discussed with the client after goal analysis or task/content analysis has been performed but before preparation of test items or instruction itself. They provide the client with an early indication of the results that will be produced by instruction. If the client disagrees with these results, then the concerns should be addressed before additional time is devoted to the project. If instructional designers progress farther without client agreement and support, they will have wasted substantial time and work.

Conclusion

In this chapter, we explained how to write performance objectives. In the next chapter, we turn to a related subject: developing performance measurements.

CHAPTER NINE

Developing
Performance Measurements

Instructional designers should develop performance measurements during—
or immediately following—preparation of performance objectives. In this
chapter, we consider the development of performance measurements, the
next step in the instructional design process. (See Figure 9.1.) We will define
performance measurements, explain their importance, and provide advice
to instructional designers about developing them, judging them, and explaining them.

What Are Performance Measurements?

Performance measurements are various means established by instructional
designers of monitoring learner achievement. Paper-and-pencil tests are
perhaps the most common. Test items are developed directly from performance objectives before instructional materials are prepared (Dick and Carey,
1985). In this way, accountability for results is built into instruction from
early in the process.

  However, paper-and-pencil testing is not the only way to assess learner
achievement. Other methods may also be used. For instance, trainees can
be observed on the job as they perform the tasks they have learned (*The Standards,* 1986, p. 56).

Why Are Performance Measurements Important?

Performance measurements become benchmarks that, along with performance objectives (discussed in the previous chapter), provide guidance in
the preparation of instructional programs. They help answer an age-old question about every instructional experience: "What should be taught?" (Egan,
1978, p. 72). They are thus important for two major reasons. First, they

Figure 9.1. A Model of Steps in the Instructional Design Process.

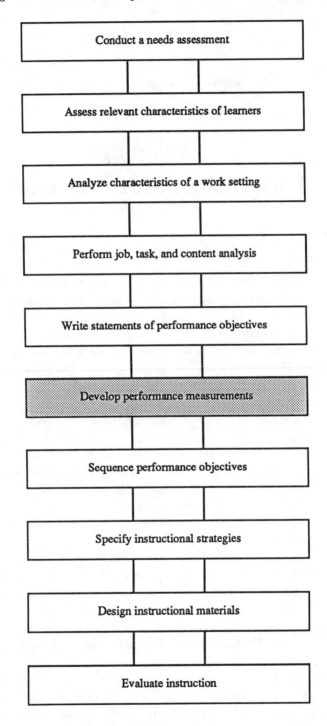

Source: Foshay, W., Silber, K., and Westgaard, O. *Instructional Design Competencies: The Standards.* Iowa City, Iowa: International Board of Standards for Training, Performance, and Instruction, 1986, p. 3. Used with permission of the publisher.

ensure economical choice of instructional content. Indeed, establishing performance measurements is part of the preliminary work, to be completed before instructional materials are developed, to help "determine what content should be included or omitted, as well as to identify the end result of the training—the goals to be met in terms of an acceptable success level for the trainee" (*The Standards*, 1986, p. 56). Second, performance measurements provide a basis for learner accountability to ensure that learner progress toward predetermined performance goals can be monitored during and after instruction.

Developing Performance Measurements

According to *The Standards* (1986, p. 57), the competency study on which this book is based, instructional designers should be capable of developing "criterion-referenced achievement tests, questionnaires (surveys), interviews, observations, simulations, performance checklists, or product checklists." The performance measures should be written clearly and correspond to performance objectives, rely on appropriate methods of measuring learning outcomes, comply with time and instructional constraints, and meet requirements for validity and reliability (*The Standards*, 1986, p. 57). Instructional designers should be able to develop performance measurements when "given appropriate information on learner characteristics, setting resources and constraints, statements of performance objectives, and needs assessment/analysis or evaluation plan, if applicable" (*The Standards*, 1986, p. 57).

Stated more simply, instructional designers should be able to answer two basic questions before they prepare instructional materials: (1) What should be measured? and (2) How should it be measured? To answer the first question, instructional designers should determine the purpose of the measurement and focus on appropriate methods of measuring instruction. To answer the second question, they should be able to design appropriate instruments—and write appropriate items for the instruments—to achieve the intended purpose.

Deciding on the Purpose

Once performance objectives have been written based on job requirements, instructional designers should decide

- What purpose will guide their performance measurement efforts
- What performance measurement methods should be used to assess learners' progress
- How performance should be measured

Instructional designers should always begin by clarifying their purpose(s) for measuring performance. There are four possible purposes (Kirkpatrick, 1975, 1987, 1988; Rae, 1986):

1. *Participant reaction.* How much do participants *enjoy* what they are learning? How much do they *enjoy* the instructional methods used?
2. *Participant learning.* How well are participants meeting performance objectives? How well have they learned?
3. *On-the-job performance change.* How much change is evident on the job based on what participants have learned? How well has the learning transferred from the instructional stage to the work performance environment?
4. *Organizational impact.* How has the organization been affected by the results of an instructional epxerience?

These purposes are summarized in Table 9.1.

Determining Sources of Information

After determining the purpose of performance measurement, instructional designers should next determine the source(s) of information that will be used in measurement. There are three major sources of information. Performance objectives are the first. They should provide clues about what to measure because, as explained in Chapter Eight, each objective needs to contain a *measurable criterion* for assessment. To measure performance, then, instructional designers should simply consider how well learners have met the criterion set forth in each objective. Each objective should be directly tied to satisfying job-related learning needs. Hence, the process of measuring objectives provides information about how well learning needs are being met by instruction.

Learner (worker) performance is the second source of information. Since instruction is — or should be — intended to improve individual performance on the job, information about what to measure should result from analysis of worker responsibilities, work standards, historical patterns of experienced workers' performance problems on the job, and forecasts of likely future job changes. Using job descriptions, performance appraisal data, work standards, and other information, instructional designers should be able to develop performance measures linked directly to successful job performance (Rae, 1986).

Stakeholder preferences are the third source of information. *Stakeholders* are people having a vested interest in instructional outcomes. Consider, for instance, what top managers and other interested parties want to know about instruction or its results. Quite often, instructional designers find that two key questions merit special consideration when measuring instruction or its results: (1) Who wants to know? and (2) What do they want to know? (Brandenburg and Smith, 1986). A third question that may be addressed is Why do they want to know?

Some instructional designers find it helpful to consult a menu of general questions about performance measures when deciding what to measure. Rae (1986, pp. 9–10) has developed such a menu, shown below.

Table 9.1. Purposes of Performance Measurement.

Purpose	Description	Advantages	Disadvantages	Examples	Guidelines for Development
Participant reaction	Measure student feelings about a program/course	Easy to administer Provides immediate feedback on instructors, facilities, and program design	Subjective Provides no measurement of learning, transfer of skills, or benefit to the organization	"Happiness reports" Informal student/instructor interview Group discussion	Design a form which can be easily tabulated Ask questions which provide information about what you need to know: instructor effectiveness, facility quality, relevance of program content, etc. Allow for anonymity and opportunity to provide additional comments
Participant learning	Measure the amount of learning that has occurred in a proram/course	Provides objective data on the effectiveness of the training	Requires skill in test construction Provides no measurement of skills or benefit to the organization	Written pre/post tests Skills laboratories Role plays Simulations Projects or presentations Oral examinations	Design an instrument which will provide quantitative data Include pre and post level of skill/knowledge in design Tie evaluation items directly to program learning objectives
On-the-job performance change	Measure the transfer of training	Data can be collected before students leave the training program Provides objective data on impact to job situation	Requires task analysis skills to construct and is time consuming to administer Can be a "politically" sensitive issue	Performance checklists Performance appraisals Critical incident analysis Self-appraisal	Base measurement instrument on systematic task analysis of job Consider the use of a variety of persons to conduct the evaluation Inform participants of evaluation process

Organizational impact	Measure impact of training on the organization	Provides objective data for cost-benefit analysis and organizational support	Requires high level of evaluation design skills; requires collection of data over a period of time
			Requires knowledge of organization needs and goals
				Employee suggestions
				Manufacturing indices
				  – Cost
				  – Scrap
				  – Schedule compliance
				  – Quality
				  – Employee donations
				Quality-of-worklife surveys
				Union grievances
				Absenteeism rates
				Accident rates
				Customer complaints
					Involve all necessary levels of organization
					Gain commitment to allow access to organization indices and records
					Use organization business plans and mission statements to identify organizational needs

Source: U.S. Department of Labor and U.S. Department of Education. *The Bottom Line: Basic Skills in the Workplace.* Washington, D.C.: U.S. Department of Labor and U.S. Department of Education, 1988, pp. 38–39.

Issue	*Questions*
Content of instruction	Is it relevant and in step with the instructional needs? Is it up to date?
Method of instruction	Were the methods used the most appropriate ones for the subject? Were the methods used the most appropriate for the learning styles of the participants?
Amount of learning	What was the material of the course? Was it new to the learner? Was it useful, although not new to the learner, as confirmation or revision material?
Instructor skills	Did the instructor have the necessary attitude and skill to present the material in a way which encouraged learning?
Length and place of instruction	Given the material essential to learning, was the learning event of the appropriate length and pace? Were some aspects [of instruction] laboured and others skimped?
Objectives	Did the instruction satisfy its declared objectives? Was the learner given the opportunity to try to satisfy any personal objectives? Was this need welcomed? Were personal objectives actually satisfied?
Omissions	Were any essential aspects omitted from the learning event? Was any material included which was not essential to the learning?
Learning transfer	How much of the learning is likely to be put into action on return to work? If it is to be a limited amount only or none, why is this? What factors will deter or assist the transfer of learning?
Accommodation	If course accommodation is within the control of the instructor, or is relevant to the type of instructional event, he may wish to ask whether the hotel/conference centre/training centre was suitable. Was the accommodation acceptable? Were the meals satisfactory?
Relevance	Was this course/seminar/conference/workshop/tutorial/coaching assignment/project/etc. the most appropriate means of presenting a learning opportunity?
Application of learning	Which aspects of your work now include elements which are a direct result of the learning event? Which new aspects of work have you introduced as a result of your learning? Which aspects of your previous work have you replaced or modified as a result of the learning? Which aspects of your learning have you not applied? Why not?

Efficiency	How much more efficient and/or effective are you in your work as a result of the instructional experience? Why/why not?
Hindsight	With the passage of time and attempts to apply the learning, are there any amendments you would wish to make to your immediate outcome validation answers?

Select appropriate source(s) of information based on learner characteristics, setting resources and constraints, statements of performance objectives, and needs assessment/analysis or evaluation plan.

Deciding How to Measure

When deciding how to measure performance, instructional designers should apply the same criteria that Newstrom and Lilyquist (1979) have suggested in selecting a data collection method for needs assessment. The following issues may thus warrant consideration:

1. *Learner involvement.* How much learner involvement is desired or feasible?
2. *Management involvement.* How much management involvement is desired or feasible?
3. *Time required.* How much time is available for measurement?
4. *Cost.* How much is the organization willing to spend to measure performance?
5. *Relevant quantifiable data.* How important is it for instructional designers to devise quantifiable measurements that are directly linked to on-the-job performance?

Different methods of measuring performance earn high, moderate, or low ratings on each of these criteria. For this reason, it is usually necessary to identify priorities—that is, which one is the most important, second most important, and so on.

An Overview of Steps in Preparing Instruments

Having decided on a purpose (what is to be measured) and a measurement method (how it will be measured), instructional designers are then ready to begin developing measurement instruments. Instruments may be classified into three general types: (1) questionnaires, interview guides or schedules, observation forms, simulations, and checklists, (2) criterion-referenced tests, and (3) others. There are ten basic steps to be taken during the preparation of a measurement instrument:

1. Clarifying the purpose of measurement and selecting a type of instrument
2. Giving the instrument a descriptive title
3. Conducting background research

4. Drafting or modifying items
5. Sequencing—or reviewing the sequence of—items
6. Trying out the instrument on a small-group representative of the learner population
7. Revising the instrument based on the small-group tryout
8. Testing the instrument on a larger group
9. Using the instrument—but establishing a means of tracking experience with it
10. Revising the instrument—or specific items—periodically

These steps are summarized in the following paragraphs.

Step One: Clarifying the Purpose of Measurement and Selecting a Type of Instrument

Instructional designers should start developing performance measurements by thinking through exactly *why* they are measuring instruction and, more important, *what results* they wish to achieve. Performance objectives are one starting point, since one purpose of measurement should usually be to determine how well learners have met instructional objectives by the end of the instructional experience. Instructional designers should ask themselves, among other questions, this one: "How can I find out whether these results are being achieved during the instructional experience and whether they were achieved following the instructional experience?" At this point they can select or prepare an instrument well suited to helping answer this question.

Step Two: Giving the Instrument a Descriptive Title

If performance will be measured using an instrument developed by someone else, instructional designers should consider the title to see if it accurately describes what they wish to measure. On the other hand, if the instrument will be tailor-made, the title should be chosen with great care. The reason: by selecting a title, instructional designers focus their thinking on exactly what will be measured.

Step Three: Conducting Background Research

Instructional designers can often save themselves considerable time and effort by locating previously prepared instruments. One way to do that is to network with other instructional designers to find out whether they have developed instruments for similar purposes (Bard and Loftin, 1987). In addition, instructional designers can sometimes successfully track down elusive instruments or research studies by using specialized reference guides (Bard, Bell, Stephen, and Webster, 1987; Peters, 1985). Tests in print can be located through Buros (1938–1985), Mitchell (1983), or the impressive library of the Educational Testing Service in Princeton, New Jersey, which maintains a collection of 10,000 tests.

Background research on instrumentation will rarely be a complete waste of time. Even when instructional designers are unable to locate instruments that measure exactly what they want, they may still be able to locate examples that will stimulate new ideas about item layout or item sequence.

When previously prepared instruments are found, instructional designers should decide whether to use them as they are or modify them to meet special needs. If previously prepared instruments can be easily modified, instructional designers can reduce the time and effort necessary to prepare and validate an instrument. But if efforts to locate instruments or research are to no avail, then it will be necessary to prepare a tailor-made instrument. Begin instrument development by addressing several important questions: (1) Who will be measured? (2) Who will conduct the measurement? (3) What will be measured? (4) When will the measurement occur? (5) Where will the measurement be conducted? and (6) How will the measurement be conducted?

Step Four: Drafting or Modifying Items

Relying on instructional objectives or other sources as a starting point, instructional designers should next decide what questions they need to ask to measure the change(s) wrought by the instructional experience. If a previously prepared instrument was located, each item must be reviewed to ensure that it is appropriate. On the other hand, drafting original items or questions for interviews, questionnaires, observation forms, simulations, or checklists is a highly creative activity. Generate items or questions using focus groups or other creative methods (Morgan, 1988; Van Gundy, 1981).

When drafting items, instructional designers should be sure to consider item format. *Item format* refers to the way performance is measured. Questionnaires or interview guides, for instance, may rely on open-ended items, closed-ended items, or some combination. *Open-ended* items produce qualitative or essay responses. The question "What do you feel you have learned in this instructional experience?" is an open-ended item. *Closed-ended* items produce quantifiable response. Respondents asked to "rate how much you feel you learned during this instructional experience on a scale from 1 to 5, with 1 representing 'very little' and 5 representing 'very much,'" are answering a closed-ended item. An instrument relies on a *combination* when it contains both open-ended and closed-ended items.

Open-ended items are frequently used in conducting exploratory measurement studies (Marshall and Rossman, 1989). While the information they yield is difficult to quantify and analyze, they may also be used to establish response categories for closed-ended instruments (Isaac and Michael, 1984). In contrast, closed-ended items are frequently utilized in analytical measurement studies. Though the information they produce is easily quantified and analyzed, it can sometimes be misleading if respondents are not given appropriate response categories. When that happens, respondents will select an approximation of what they believe and reply accordingly. Item format has a different, though related, meaning for observation forms, simulations, or checklists. These instruments are usually designed around behaviors (*observable actions*) associated with the instructional objectives or competent on-the-job performance. Instructional designers may prepare these instruments to count the frequencies of a behavior ("How often did the learner do something?"), assess the quality of a behavior ("How well did the learner perform?"), or both. The instrument user may exercise considerable flexibility in identifying what behavior to count or assess. Alternatively, the user may not exercise flexibility in identifying or assessing behaviors, because categories are predefined or methods of assessment have been provided on the instrument itself.

Item format has yet another meaning for tests. Indeed, developing criterion-referenced tests poses a challenge somewhat different from developing questionnaires, interviews, simulations, or other measurement instruments. Test preparation is an entire field of its own (American Telephone and Telegraph Company, 1987b; Denova, 1979). When developing criterion-referenced tests, "the verb component of the instructional objective indicates the form that a test item should take" (Kemp, 1985, p. 161). Examples of behaviors specified in instructional objectives and appropriately matched test item formats are shown in Table 9.2.

Step Five: Sequencing—or Reviewing the Sequence of—Items

One choice is to sequence items in a logical order based on work tasks. Another choice is to sequence items according to a learning hierarchy.

Step Six: Trying Out the Instrument on a Small-Group Representative of the Learner Population

Sometimes called *instrument pretesting*, this step should not be confused with learner pretesting. If possible, instructional designers should select a sample of people representative of the learner population to participate in the instrument pretest and ask for their help in identifying wording that is unclear or is otherwise inappropriate. Instructional designers should explain the instrument items to the group rather than ask them to answer the questions. Their responses should be noted for use during the next step.

Step Seven: Revising the Instrument Based on the Small-Group Tryout

If a complete revision is necessary—which should rarely be the case—another small group should be selected for the purpose of a second instrument pretest.

Otherwise, instructional designers should revise items, based on their notes from the previous step, to improve clarity.

Step Eight: Testing the Instrument on a Larger Group

The next step is a field test of the instrument on a larger group under conditions resembling, as closely as possible, those in which the instrument will later be used. The results of the field test should be noted.

Table 9.2. Behaviors Specified in
Instructional Objectives and Corresponding Test Items.

Type of test item	Brief description of test-item format	Behavior (verb specified in the instructional objective)
1. **Essay** (*Example:* "What are the chief advantages and disadvantages of the essay format as a test item?")	A type of test item requiring a learner to respond in essay format. This type of item is appropriate for assessing higher levels of cognition—such as analysis, synthesis, and evaluation.	Construct Define Develop Discuss Generate Locate Solve State
2. **Fill-in-the-blank** (*Example:* "The _____ - in-the-blank is a type of test item.")	A type of test item requiring the learner to fill in the blank with an appropriate word or phrase. Scoring can be objective because the required response is quite specific—often only one word is correct.	Construct Define Identify Locate Solve State
3. **Completion** (*Example:* "A type of test item that requires the completion of a sentence is called the _____.")	A type of test item that closely resembles the fill-in-the-blank type, except that the learner is asked to complete a sentence stem.	Construct Define Develop Discuss Generate Identify Locate Solve State
4. **Multiple-choice** (*Example:* "A type of test item requiring the learner to choose from more than one possible answer is the (a) multiple-choice; (b) essay; (c) completion.")	Kemp (1985, p. 162) calls multiple-choice "the most useful and versatile type of objective testing." Learners must choose between three and five options or alternatives as the answer to a question.	Discriminate Identify Locate Select Solve
5. **True-False** (*Example:* "A true-false test item is less versatile than a multiple-choice one.") (True-False)	A type of test item in which learners are asked to determine whether a statement is true or false.	Discriminate Locate Select Solve

Table 9.2. Behaviors Specified in
Instructional Objectives and Corresponding Test Items, Cont'd.

Type of test item	Brief description of test-item format	Behavior (verb specified in the instructional objective)
6. **Matching** (*See the example below.*)	A type of test item in which learners are asked to match up items in one column with items in another column.	Discriminate Locate Select

For each item in column 1 below, select a corresponding item in column 2 by placing the number of the item before the item in column 1. Use items only once.

Column 1	Column 2
_____ 1. Essay	1. A type of test item in which learners have only two right answers
_____ 2. Multiple-choice	2. A type of test item in which learners have between three and five alternatives
_____ 3. True-false	3. A test item requiring a narrative response

7. **Project** (*Example:* "Write an essay question to describe ten steps in preparing an assessment instrument.")	A type of test in which learners are asked to demonstrate the ability to perform a task they have (presumably) learned through participation in an instructional experience.	Construct Develop Generate Locate Solve

Step Nine: Using the Instrument—But Establishing a Means of Tracking Experience with It

Instructional designers should use the instrument but should also establish a way of tracking future experience with it. The results need to be monitored over time. If tests are administered, instructional designers should periodically conduct item analysis to determine what questions the learners are missing and how often they are missing them. If questionnaires or interviews are used to measure performance, instructional designers need to note the response patterns they receive to determine whether specific questions are yielding useful answers. If instructional designers are using structured observation, they should periodically review the categories they initially created.

Step Ten: Revising the Instrument—or Specific Items—Periodically

As performance measurements are made using instruments, instructional designers gain experience. They can take advantage of that experience by periodically revising the instrument, or specific items on it. Of course, revisions should also be made whenever changes are made to performance objectives or when new performance objectives are added. As Rowntree (1977, p. 84) notes, "some assessment goals can be specified in advance, more or less precisely; others emerge. . . . We are not always totally aware of what assessment constructs we are exercising." In this context, Rowntree borrows the term *assessment construct* from Kelly (1955) to mean an explicit or implicit goal of instruction.

Other Methods of Measuring Performance

Apart from questionnaires, interviews, simulations, and checklists, other methods may be used to measure participant reactions, participant learning, on-the-job performance change, or organizational impact. However, not every method is appropriate for every purpose. These methods—note that we do not call them *items* or *instruments*—include advisory committees, external assessment centers, attitude surveys, group discussions, exit interviews, and performance appraisals.

An *advisory committee* is a group consisting of stakeholders in instructional experiences (Kruger, 1983; Rothwell and Kazanas, 1989; "Win New Allies . . . ," 1982). A committee may be established as standing (permanent and formal) or ad hoc (temporary and informal). One way to use an advisory committee is to ask its members to observe an instructional experience and assess how well they feel its objectives are achieved. Another way is to direct results of participant tests or other measures to committee members for interpretation.

An *external assessment center* is a process of measuring individual knowledge and skills. It is an extended simulation of job or group work. It could be used—though it would admittedly be expensive to do so—to determine what measurable change resulted from an instructional experience (Uretsky, 1989/1990).

An *attitude survey* is usually intended to assess individual perceptions about working conditions, co-workers, work tasks, and other issues. It could be used to determine people's perceptions of what changes or how much change resulted from instructional experiences.

A *group discussion* is simply a meeting. It could be used to identify relevant measurement issues and/or assess a group's perceptions about what changes or how much change occurred as a result of an instructional experience.

An *exit interview* is a meeting with an employee just prior to the individual's departure from an organization, department, or work unit. In some cases, exit interviews may be combined with questionnaires mailed to terminating employees some time after they leave the organization. Exit interviews may be used to identify relevant measurement issues and/or assess an individual's perceptions about what changes or how much change occurred as a result of an instructional experience.

A *performance appraisal* is an assessment of an individual's job-related activities and results over a predetermined time frame. It could be used to document a supervisor's perceptions of what changes or how much change occurred as a result of an individual's participation in an instructional experience.

For More Information

For more information about performance measurement, consult the following sources: the American Society for Training and Development (1986h, 1987b), Fink and Kosecoff (1985), Guba and Lincoln (1981), Lineberry and Bullock (1980), Mager (1973), Marshall and Weinstein (1982), Morris, Fitz-Gibbon, and Lindheim (1987), and Pfeiffer and Ballew (1988a).

Judging Performance Measurements

Instructional designers should be able to judge performance measurements they or their colleagues have developed when they are "given a performance measure . . . and appropriate information on learner characteristics, setting resources and constraints, statements of performance objectives, and needs assessment/analysis or evaluation plan (as applicable)" (*The Standards*, 1986, p. 58).

As in the case of performance objectives, instructional designers may find it useful to rely on a worksheet when judging performance measures (see Exhibit 9.1). Every time an answer of no is given, instructional designers should reexamine the performance measurements and, when necessary, revise them.

Justifying Performance Measurements

Instructional designers should also be able to explain their reasons for developing performance measurements and instruments as they did. As in most instructional design activities, they should consider themselves accountable for what they do. Consequently, they should be prepared to answer questions posed by other stakeholders. These questions include all those posed in *The Standards* (1986, p. 57):

1. Why was the performance measurement method selected?
2. What are the relevant advantages and disadvantages of the performance measurement method that was selected?
3. Who should care about the results of the performance measurements?
4. Why should they care?
5. Why are the results of the performance measurements important?
6. How can the results of the performance measurements be used?

Exhibit 9.1. A Worksheet for Judging Performance Measurements.

Directions: Use this worksheet to judge a performance measurement you or others have prepared.

First complete Part I to ensure that you have everything you need to judge a performance measurement properly. For each question in the left column, place a check (✔) in the center column to indicate an answer. If you are missing something necessary for proper judgment, make notes to yourself in the right column.

Second, complete Part II to judge each performance measurement. For each question appearing in the left column below, place a check (✔) in the center column. Each performance measurement should lend itself to a yes response. If you answer yes to all questions, the performance measurement should meet all required criteria. It should not need to be revised. If you must check no, make notes for revision in the right column. Use N/A (for "not applicable") when the performance measurement does not lend itself to the conditions set forth in the question.

Make copies of this worksheet as necessary, depending on the number of performance measurements you will review.

Part I. Conditions

Question	Response			Notes for Revision
	Yes	No	N/A	
Do you have available . . .	(✔)	(✔)	(✔)	
1. A performance measure?	( )	( )	( )	
2. Appropriate information on				
a. Learner characteristics?	( )	( )	( )	
b. Setting resources and constraints?	( )	( )	( )	
c. Statements of performance objectives?	( )	( )	( )	
d. Needs assessment/ analysis or evaluation plan (as applicable)?	( )	( )	( )	

Part II. Judgments of Performance Measurements

Question	Response			Notes for Revision
	Yes	No	N/A	
Does the performance measurement . . .	(✔)	(✔)	(✔)	
1. Show a one-to-one correspondence with the conditions being measured (when the instrument is designed to measure learning outcomes)?	( )	( )	( )	
2. Show a one-to-one correspondence with performance of the learning outcomes being measured (when the instrument is designed to measure learning outcomes)?	( )	( )	( )	

Exhibit 9.1. A Worksheet for Judging Performance Measurements, Cont'd.

Question	Response			Notes for Revision
	Yes	No	N/A	
Does the performance measurement . . .	(✔)	(✔)	(✔)	
3. Use item types appropriate to objectives and the requirements of the performance environment?	( )	( )	( )	
4. Use development time efficiently, considering course length and project parameters?	( )	( )	( )	
5. Use respondent time efficiently, considering course length and project parameters?	( )	( )	( )	
6. Have acceptable reliability?	( )	( )	( )	
7. Have acceptable validity?	( )	( )	( )	
8. Show acceptable item-writing style	( )	( )	( )	

7. How does the performance measurement
    a. Show a one-to-one correspondence with the performance objectives?
    b. Use item types appropriate to the performance objectives?
    c. Use time efficiently?
8. How well does the performance measurement
    a. Prove to have acceptable reliability?
    b. Prove to have acceptable validity?
    c. Show clear, acceptable item-writing style?

Conclusion

As we noted at the beginning of this chapter, instructional designers should develop performance measurements during—or immediately following—preparation of performance objectives. In the chapter, we defined performance measurements, explained their importance, and provided advice about developing them, judging them, and explaining them. In the next chapter, we turn to sequencing performance objectives.

CHAPTER TEN

Sequencing Performance Objectives

Sequencing instruction should occur after work tasks have been analyzed, performance objectives have been written, and performance measurements have been developed. As the next step in the instructional design process following the development of performance measurements (see Figure 10.1), it ensures that workers are introduced systematically to what they must know or do to perform competently. The reasons for sequencing performance objectives are explained in *The Standards* (1986, p. 60):

> After a set of objectives has been written, the instructional designer must put them in the sequence in which they will be taught to trainees. There are a number of approaches to sequencing objectives (for example, simple to complex, part to whole, bottom to top of a hierarchy, and the reverse of each of these), each of which works well for different types of trainees and content.
>
> Based on the previous steps in the process, the instructional designer must select a sequence for the objectives that is most appropriate for a particular course, the trainee population, and the organizational setting.

The resulting sequence of objectives becomes the basis for an *instructional outline,* sometimes called an *instructional syllabus* (Dick and Carey, 1985). It is a blueprint for choosing an instructional strategy and selecting, modifying, or preparing instructional materials. In this chapter, we will describe approaches to sequencing performance objectives and offer simple advice to instructional designers about judging and justifying sequencing decisions.

Defining Key Terms

Sequence connotes the order in which learners are introduced, through planned instruction, to information and tasks essential to job performance. An in-

Figure 10.1. A Model of Steps in the Instructional Design Process.

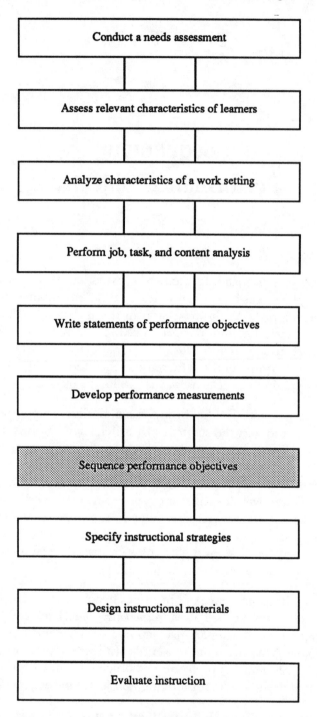

Source: Foshay, W., Silber, K., and Westgaard, O. *Instructional Design Competencies: The Standards.* Iowa City, Iowa: International Board of Standards for Training, Performance, and Instruction, 1986, p. 3. Used with permission of the publisher.

structional sequence ranges on a continuum from *inflexible* (a fixed sequence that never varies across learners) to *flexible* (a varying sequence that is influenced by each learner's background, desired learning outcomes, and conditions in the learning environment).

Rules for sequencing instruction provide guidance for instructional designs. Some methods of sequencing instruction are simply more appropriate than others, depending on the performance objectives, the learner, and the learning environment. When these methods are clearly spelled out so that an instructional designer knows how to sequence performance objectives when furnished with information about the objectives, the learners, and the learning environment, the result is *a rule for sequencing instruction*.

The Importance of Sequencing

To find out about instructional sequencing, try an experiment. Ask several questions of the next five or six employed people you meet:

1. How were you first introduced to your job? Did you receive planned training — or were you forced to struggle to learn on your own, as best you could?
2. How clearly were you informed of performance expectations at the time you began your job? Did your supervisor explain to you, early on, what you should be able to do after you were trained? If you received planned on-the-job training, were you told how long the training period would last? how your progress would be assessed? how the training was organized — that is, sequenced — to help you acquire job-related information or build desired job skills?
3. How do you feel employees should be introduced to work activities? Is there an ideal way to organize information or build skills? How does this ideal match up to your experiences?

Instructional designers who carry out this experiment will no doubt hear some very interesting answers to these questions. The people who respond will probably say that they received minimal on-the-job training, that most learning had to be done on their own, and that nobody clarified what they should be able to do on completion of their job training. Most people are left to learn their jobs as best they can — through the "sink or swim method" — and few are happy about that (Rothwell and Kazanas, 1990a). In those rare cases when planned on-the-job training is available, it is often sequenced around problems as they arise on the job (Rothwell and Kazanas, 1990b).

However, effective instruction is rarely sequenced around the (sometimes random) order in which problems arise on learners' jobs. Nor does it necessarily match up to a convenient schedule for using equipment or trainer time. It should instead be sequenced so learners will be systematically introduced to work activities in ways appropriate to the performance objectives, the learners themselves, and the situations or conditions in which they must learn.

Approaches to Sequencing

There are at least nine approaches to sequencing performance objectives:

1. Chronological sequencing
2. Topical sequencing
3. Whole-to-part sequencing
4. Part-to-whole sequencing
5. Known-to-unknown sequencing
6. Unknown-to-known sequencing
7. Step-by-step sequencing
8. Part-to-part-to-part sequencing
9. General-to-specific sequencing

Let us describe each one.

Chronological Sequencing

When performance objectives are sequenced *chronologically,* "facts and ideas are arranged in a time sequence so that the presentation of later events is preceded by discussion of earlier ones. This is the [typical] organization followed in history courses — and frequently in literature courses, literary selections being arranged in time sequence" (Smith, Stanley, and Shores, 1957, p. 233). Many academic experts who write college textbooks favor a chronological approach, beginning with the history of their discipline. Instruction is then sequenced from past to present to future.

Topical Sequencing

When performance objectives are sequenced *topically,* learners are immediately immersed in the middle of a topical problem or issue. For example, today's newspaper headline may be of topical significance to a given performance objective, and it could be used as a starting point for instruction. Learners are then led back in time to see how the problem originated. They may sometimes be led forward to see what will happen if the problem is not solved. This sequencing method is sometimes called *in medias res,* a Latin phrase meaning that instruction begins "in the middle of things."

Whole-to-Part Sequencing

When performance objectives are sequenced from *whole to part,* learners are first presented with a complete model or a description of the full complexities of a physical object (such as an automobile engine or the world globe), abstraction (such as steps in a model of instructional design), or work duty (such as "writing a letter"). Instruction is then organized around *parts* of the whole. For instance, learners are then led through each part of an automobile engine, each nation on a world globe, each step in a model of the instructional design process, or each task comprising the work duty.

This approach to sequencing was first advocated by Ausubel (1962), building on the work of Gestalt learning theorists (Sredl and Rothwell, 1987). Learners should be presented with an overarching logic to govern what they should know (Pucel, 1989). In this way, they can see how each part relates to a larger conceptual system.

Part-to-Whole Sequencing

When performance objectives are sequenced from *part to whole,* learners are introduced to each part of a larger object, abstraction, or work duty. By the end of instruction, they should be able to conceptualize the entire object or abstraction or perform the entire duty. For example, learners could be oriented to an organization by visiting, investigating, and charting work activities in each department. They should eventually be able to describe the activities of each organizational part and thus (presumably) the entire organization.

Known-to-Unknown Sequencing

When performance objectives are sequenced from *known to unknown,* learners are introduced to what they already know and are gradually led into what they do not know. Herbart (1898) was among the first to advocate this approach to sequencing desired results of instruction, arguing that learners bring their experience to bear on what they learn. Consequently, he concluded, it is essential for instruction to build on what the learner already knows.

Suppose, for example, that it is necessary to train a novice on how to make an overhead transparency on a copy machine. A trainer wishing to save time would first pose two questions: (1) Does the novice already know what an overhead transparency is? and (2) Does the novice already know how to make paper photocopies? If the answer to either question is no, instruction will have to begin by providing this essential *prerequisite information.* But if the answer to both questions is yes, the trainer can begin by explaining that transparencies are simply placed in the paper tray of a photocopier and an original sheet is copied. The result: an overhead transparency. In this way, the trainer has sequenced instruction from what the learner already knows about transparencies and photocopying to what the learner does not know about producing transparencies.

Unknown-to-Known Sequencing

When performance objectives are sequenced from *unknown to known,* learners are *deliberately* disoriented at the outset of instruction. In short, instructional designers deliberately set out to "put the learners in over their heads." This approach dramatizes how little they really know about a subject or the performance of a task or work duty with which they already feel smugly familiar.

The aim of this approach is to motivate learners for a subsequent learning task. It gives them an uncomfortable experience that leads them to question their own knowledge, thereby demonstrating to them that they need to learn more. Perhaps the most obvious example is military boot camp, in which new recruits undergo an initial upending experience that clearly dramatizes how little they really know about their own physical and mental limitations.

Step-by-Step Sequencing

When performance objectives are sequenced *step by step,* learners are introduced to a task or work duty through either of two methods. The first method is based on the steps of the task or work duty itself. Instructional designers begin by analyzing *how* the task or duty is performed. They then sequence instruction around each step in the task — or each task comprising a work duty.

The second method is based on the knowledge that learners must already possess or the skills they must have mastered to be capable of learning the procedure. Instructional designers analyze *how* people learn the skill or process information. This analysis is conducted using techniques such as *information processing analysis, information mapping,* or *learning hierarchy analysis.* Performance objectives are then sequencing around each step ("chunk of knowledge" or "specific skill") that learners must possess in order to be able to master a task or work duty. On occasion, training is not necessary for step-by-step learning to occur. Learners may be coached through a task by means of a job aid, such as a checklist or step-by-step description of a procedure. Alternatively, they may be coached through a task with a decision tool such as a flowchart or diagram.

Part-to-Part-to-Part Sequencing

When performance objectives are sequenced *part to part to part,* learners are treated to a relatively shallow introduction to a topic, move on to another topic that is also treated superficially, move on to a third topic that is treated superficially, eventually return to the original topic for more in-depth exposure, and so on. This is the so-called *spiral curriculum* popularized by Bruner (1966). The aim, as Romiszowski (1981, p. 282) notes, is to ensure that "on the first time round the spiral, [*the learner is introduced to*] all of the first topic that will be required as prerequisites of the content planned for the 'first time round' for all the other topics." As Romiszowski further explains: "Similarly, the 'first time round' for these other topics must include all the prerequisites for the 'second time round' of the earlier topics in the sequence. This gives an added dimension of difficulty which does not exist in the planning of the sequence of a linear curriculum, as in that case one treats the internal sequence of each topic as more or less independent of other topics once the topics themselves have been sequenced."

General-to-Specific Sequencing

When performance objectives are sequenced from *general to specific,* all learners are introduced to the same foundation of knowledge of the same skills. Later, however, each learner specializes. This method of sequencing is sometimes called the pyramidal or core structure method. It is "something like an apple which you can bite at here and there, not necessarily eating all of it, but with a core that must be swallowed whole by everyone" (Romiszowski, 1981, p. 283).

Other Approaches to Sequencing

Other sequencing methods may, at times, be appropriate. The nine described in this section are not intended to be exhaustive. Readers interested in other approaches should refer to American Telephone and Telegraph Company (1987f) and Romiszowski (1981) for additional information.

Making Decisions About Sequencing Performance Objectives

According to *The Standards* (1986), instructional designers should be able to make decisions about sequencing performance objectives so as to identify and apply a sequencing approach that is appropriate for the learners and learning situation. Unfortunately, there are few "absolute certainties" when facing these decisions. Each situation may dictate its own rules. We have provided a flowchart in Figure 10.2 to aid instructional designers in making decisions about sequencing performance objectives.

Judging the Sequencing of Performance Objectives

As the authors of *The Standards* (1986) point out, instructional designers should be able to judge the sequencing decisions they and others have made about performance objectives. Such judgments can be made when instructional designers are furnished with "statements of performance objectives, statements of learner/trainee characteristics, analysis of job, task, or content, results of a needs assessment/analysis, results of a setting analysis, and the sequencing rules" (*The Standards,* 1986, p. 63).

Figure 10.2. Rules for Sequencing Performance Objectives:
A Flowchart to Aid Decision Making by Instructional Designers.

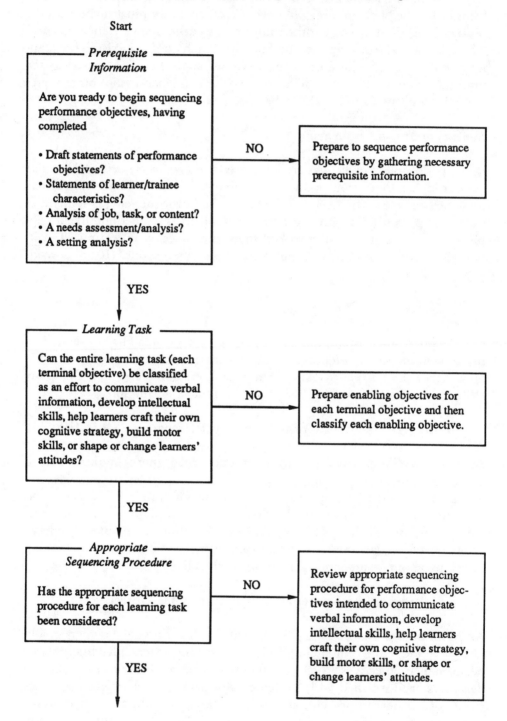

Start

Prerequisite Information

Are you ready to begin sequencing performance objectives, having completed

- Draft statements of performance objectives?
- Statements of learner/trainee characteristics?
- Analysis of job, task, or content?
- A needs assessment/analysis?
- A setting analysis?

NO → Prepare to sequence performance objectives by gathering necessary prerequisite information.

YES ↓

Learning Task

Can the entire learning task (each terminal objective) be classified as an effort to communicate verbal information, develop intellectual skills, help learners craft their own cognitive strategy, build motor skills, or shape or change learners' attitudes?

NO → Prepare enabling objectives for each terminal objective and then classify each enabling objective.

YES ↓

Appropriate Sequencing Procedure

Has the appropriate sequencing procedure for each learning task been considered?

NO → Review appropriate sequencing procedure for performance objectives intended to communicate verbal information, develop intellectual skills, help learners craft their own cognitive strategy, build motor skills, or shape or change learners' attitudes.

YES ↓

Figure 10.2. Rules for Sequencing Performance Objectives:
A Flowchart to Aid Decision Making by Instructional Designers, Cont'd.

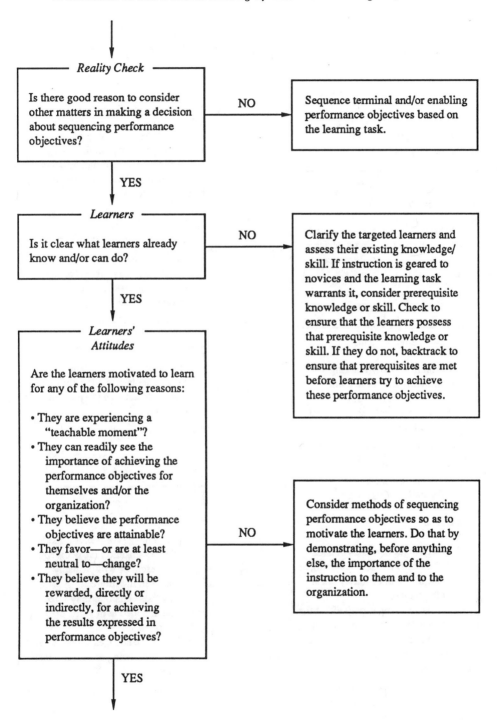

Figure 10.2. Rules for Sequencing Performance Objectives:
A Flowchart to Aid Decision Making by Instructional Designers, Cont'd.

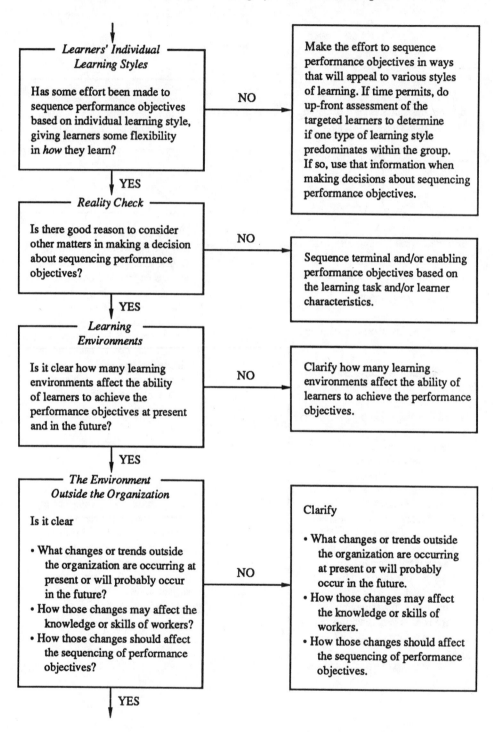

Figure 10.2. Rules for Sequencing Performance Objectives:
A Flowchart to Aid Decision Making by Instructional Designers, Cont'd.

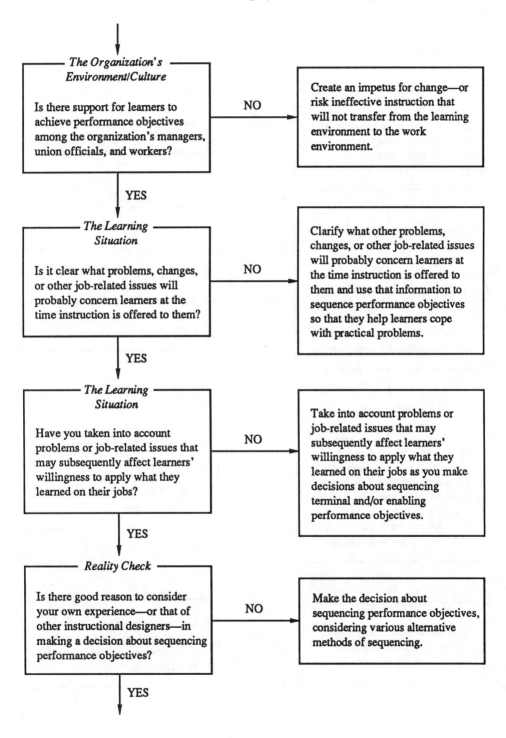

Figure 10.2. Rules for Sequencing Performance Objectives:
A Flowchart to Aid Decision Making by Instructional Designers, Cont'd.

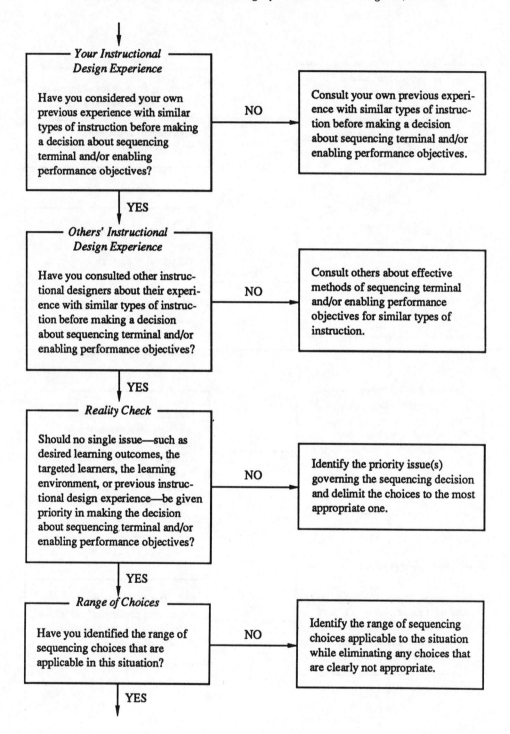

Figure 10.2. Rules for Sequencing Performance Objectives:
A Flowchart to Aid Decision Making by Instructional Designers, Cont'd.

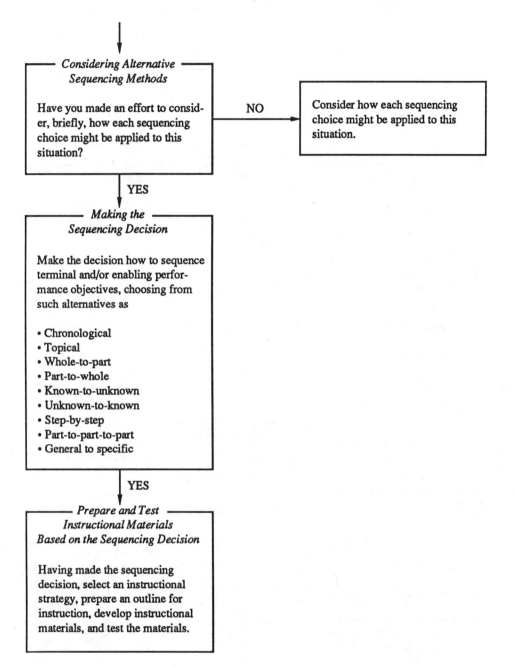

Exhibit 10.1. A Worksheet for Judging the Sequencing of Performance Objectives.

Directions: Use this worksheet to judge the sequencing of performance objectives.

First complete Part I to ensure that you have everything you need to judge the sequencing. For each question appearing in the left column, place a check ($\checkmark$) in the center column to indicate an answer. If you are missing something, make notes to yourself in the right column.

Second, complete Part II to judge the sequencing decisions that have been made. For each question appearing in the left column below, place a check ($\checkmark$) in the center column. You should be able to answer each question with a yes. If you must answer no to an item, (1) review the sequencing decision, and (2) be ready and able to state a rationale for it.

Make copies of this worksheet as necessary.

Part I. Conditions				
Question	*Response*			*Notes for Revision*
Do you have available . . .	*Yes* ($\checkmark$)	*No* ($\checkmark$)	*N/A* ($\checkmark$)	
1. Statements of performance objectives?	( )	( )	( )	
2. Statements of learner characteristics?	( )	( )	( )	
3. Results of job, task, and/or content analysis?	( )	( )	( )	
4. Results of needs assessment/analysis?	( )	( )	( )	
5. Results of a setting analysis?	( )	( )	( )	

Part II. Decisions				
Question	*Response*			*Notes for Revision*
In making the decision to sequence performance objectives, did you consider . . .	*Yes* ($\checkmark$)	*No* ($\checkmark$)	*N/A* ($\checkmark$)	
6. The nature of the performance objectives?	( )	( )	( )	
7. The learners?	( )	( )	( )	
8. The learning environment?	( )	( )	( )	
9. Your experience—or the experience of other instructional designers—with similar types of instruction?	( )	( )	( )	
10. Alternative methods of sequencing performance objectives?	( )	( )	( )	

In earlier chapters, we have pointed out the value of using a worksheet as an aid in judging work performed by instructional designers or their colleagues. A worksheet of the same kind can be helpful on these occasions as well. (Such a worksheet is shown in Exhibit 10.1.) Every time instructional designers must answer no to an item on the worksheet, they should go back and reexamine the sequence of performance objectives.

Justifying the Sequencing of Performance Objectives

As the final topic of this chapter, as in others, we turn to justification. Instructional designers should be able to explain, when asked, why they decide on sequencing performance objectives in a certain way but not in others. More specifically, instructional designers should be prepared to answer the following questions as the need arises:

1. Why were performance objectives for instruction sequenced as they were?
2. What are the relative advantages and disadvantages of the approach to sequencing performance objectives that was selected?
3. Who should care about the decisions made about sequencing performance objectives?
4. Why should they care about sequencing?

Answer the foregoing questions as a starting point for justifying the decisions made about sequencing performance objectives.

Conclusion

In this chapter, we described approaches to sequencing objectives and offered advice to instructional designers about judging and justifying sequencing decisions. This chapter was the last of three related chapters on performance objectives. Taken together, they have focused on the steps in the instructional design process that lay the foundation for planned learning experiences. In the next chapter, we turn to specifying instructional strategies, the process of planning learning experiences.

PART IV

Delivering
the Instruction Effectively

CHAPTER ELEVEN

Specifying
Instructional Strategies

Having written and sequenced performance objectives, instructional designers are ready to plan "a set of events external to the learner which are designed to support the internal processes of learning" (Gagne and Briggs, 1979, p. 155; Gagne, 1977c). They should begin by asking this question: How can the desired results of instruction be achieved?

The answer is through instructional strategy, which is the next step in the instructional design process. (See Figure 11.1). While *instructional strategy* sometimes refers to the various methods, techniques, and devices for instructing, the term is used here to mean *strategies for instructing others—that is, how to go about the instructional process*. Methods, techniques, and devices for instructing are described in the next chapter.

In this chapter, we will define instructional strategy. We will also distinguish between two kinds of strategy (macroinstructional and microinstructional strategy), between instructional strategy and instructional tactics, and between instructional strategy and learning strategy. Finally, we will describe how to conceptualize instructional strategy, choose strategy and tactics, choose media and delivery methods, and judge and justify strategy once chosen.

Defining Instructional Strategy

In the most general sense, an *instructional strategy* is perhaps best understood as an overall plan governing instructional content (*what will be taught?*) and process (*how will it be taught?*). Any strategy consists of "a set of decisions that result in a plan, method, or series of activities aimed at obtaining a specific goal. This definition is derived from its historical use as a term that represents an overall plan, for instance, to win a game" (Jonassen, Grabinger, and Harris, 1990, p. 31)—or to gain competitive advantage over business rivals (Rothwell and Kazanas, 1989).

Figure 11.1. A Model of Steps in the Instructional Design Process.

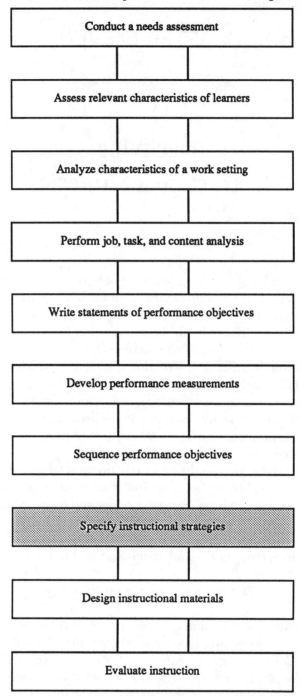

Source: Foshay, W., Silber, K., and Westgaard, O. *Instructional Design Competencies: The Standards.* Iowa City, Iowa: International Board of Standards for Training, Performance, and Instruction, 1986, p. 3. Used with permission of the publisher.

An instructional strategy is no different. It is a plan for systematically exposing learners to experiences that will help them acquire verbal information, establish cognitive strategy, or develop intellectual skills, motor skills, or new attitudes. Instructional strategy should grow out of an analysis of the work tasks that learners are being instructed to perform and from the corresponding performance objectives established to achieve those desired results (Martinetz, 1988). An instructional strategy is also "a translation of a philosophical or theoretical position regarding instruction into a statement of the way in which instruction should be carried out in specific circumstances" (Romiszowski, 1981, p. 292).

An instructional strategy is thus "like a blueprint; it shows what must be done" to achieve the desired outcomes of instruction (Jonassen, Grabinger, and Harris, 1990, p. 32). Once an instructional strategy has been decided on, it becomes "a product that can be used (1) as a prescription to develop instructional materials, (2) as a set of criteria to evaluate existing materials, (3) as a set of criteria and a prescription to revise existing materials, or (4) as a framework from which class lecture notes, interactive group exercises, and homework assignments can be planned" (Dick and Carey, 1985, p. 140). Instructional strategy should usually be described in writing, though not in the detail typical of final instructional materials comprising a module, unit, or lesson. It should be prepared *before* instructional materials are designed—or selected from other sources—and should spell out (1) what methods, materials, devices, settings, and people will be needed to transmit the instructional message, (2) what media will be used, (3) the physical location in which learners will receive instruction, and (4) the methods of integrating these elements (*The Standards,* 1986, p. 65).

The aim of establishing an instructional strategy is, quite simply, "to think through the entire lesson before developing or selecting any instruction" (Dick and Carey, 1985, p. 141). It helps instructional designers conceptualize, before they begin time-consuming and expensive preparation or selection of instructional materials, what must be done to facilitate learning.

Distinguishing Between Two Kinds of Instructional Strategy

There are two kinds of instructional strategy. A *macroinstructional strategy* is an overall plan governing a discrete learning experience—such as a course or module. It is the way instructional designers plan to help learners achieve terminal performance objectives. On the other hand, a *microinstructional strategy* is a specific plan governing each part of the learning experience—such as a unit or lesson within a course or module. It is the way instructional designers plan to help learners achieve performance objectives. Macroinstructional strategy should typically be specified first.

Distinguishing Between Instructional Strategy and Instructional Tactics

An *instructional tactic* is related to, but more specific than, an instructional strategy. It is any instructional activity undertaken to facilitate a strategy. While much has been written about instructional strategy (for example, Merrill, 1983; Gagne and Briggs, 1979; Van Patten, Chao, and Reigeluth, 1986), relatively little has been written about instructional tactics (Jonassen, Grabinger, and Harris, 1990). But all grand instructional strategies are enacted through simple instructional tactics, just as any long-term strategy for winning a game is realized through many short-term plays or activities.

Distinguishing Between Instructional Strategy and Learning Strategy

Learning strategy should not be confused with instructional strategy. A learning strategy is any "mental behavior in which learners engage that enables them to store, retrieve, organize, and comprehend information more effectively" (Jonassen, Grabinger, and Harris, 1990, p. 33). It "represents 'learning-to-learn' phenomena" and is controlled by the learner rather than orchestrated by an instructor (Jonassen, Grabinger, and Harris, 1990, p. 33). A simple example of learning strategy is the use of flash cards to improve rote memorization. Learners may also underline key passages in written material, take notes during oral presentations, or ask questions of their instructor. Each is an example of learning strategy; each is controlled by the learner and not by an instructor. Much has been written about learning strategies (Paris, Lipson, and Wixson, 1983; Snowman, 1986; Tessmer and Jonassen, 1988), and no doubt planned learning experiences could be enhanced if learners were advised about strategies *they* could use to learn more efficiently and effectively. But this chapter focuses on *instructional* strategies.

Conceptualizing Instructional Strategy

There are two ways to think about instructional strategy. The first stems from the philosophy of the instructional designer about learning and instructing; the second stems from events of instruction and conditions of learning. Each way provides some guidance when instructional designers find it necessary to identify the range of available instructional strategies.

Instructional Strategy Based on Philosophy of Learning and Instructing

Instructional designers have fought contentious battles, stemming from contrasting philosophical views, about the nature of learning and instructing. Two theoretical positions about learning and instructing seem to represent major anchor points on a philosophical continuum of instructional strategies (Romiszowski, 1981). Some instructional designers believe that all learning can be described best as resulting from a process of *reception*. This view leads to *expositive instructional strategies*. But other instructional designers believe that all learning is best described as resulting from a process of learner *discovery*. This view leads to *experiential instructional strategies* (Romiszowski, 1981).

To the behaviorist adherents of *reception learning*, learning centers around the communication process. Learning occurs through exposure to environmental variables outside the learner; instructing is a process of manipulating those variables to achieve predetermined ends. Learning occurs as people receive, understand, apply, and act on information directed to them by others. Learners are thus passive recipients of instructional messages; instructors or instructional designers are active transmitters of those messages; and instruction itself is synonymous with the message. When instructional designers believe that learning occurs through this communication process, they select an *expositive instructional strategy* (Romiszowski, 1981). Most traditional educators favor this approach. It is a four-step process in which the instructor should (1) present information to (passive) learners, (2) test learners on their recall or understanding of the message, (3) present opportunities for learners to practice or apply the message, and (4) present opportunities for learners to generalize what they have learned to real situations or problems (Romiszowski, 1981, p. 293).

At the other anchor point on the continuum is a different philosophy about learning and instructing. To the phenomenological adherents of *discovery learning*, learning is intensely personal. Set in the intimate mental world of the learner, it results not so much from manipulation of environmental variables outside the learner as from the learner's own internalized insight, reflection, and experience. When instructional designers believe that learning occurs through this experience-oriented process, they favor a *discovery strategy* for instruction (Romiszowski, 1981). This approach is often associated with the adult learning movement (Knowles, 1980, 1984). It is a four-step process in which the instructional designer will (1) structure opportunities for learners to receive important experiences and observe or reflect on them, (2) question the learners about the experiences and observe learner reactions, (3) help learners think about the general principles and significant emotional experiences they have experienced, and (4) structure opportunities for learners to apply what they have learned to actual situations and problems (Romiszowski, 1981, p. 294).

While expositive and discovery instructional strategies constitute more or less opposite anchor points on a continuum, there are many points in between. Instructional designers are thus free to select from numerous methods that are appropriate to achieve the desired outcomes of an instructional experience. Romiszowski's summary of these methods is given below (p. 180).

Strategy	*Description*
Impromptu discovery	Unplanned learning: no instruction was involved directly (e.g., free use of a library/resource center).
Free exploratory discovery	Broad learning goals are fixed; otherwise the learner is free to choose how to achieve the desired outcomes.
Guided discovery	Objectives are fixed; learner is guided as to appropriate methods, conclusion.
Adaptively programmed discovery	Guidance and feedback is given individually.
Intrinsically programmed discovery	Guidance and feedback according to a pre-planned programme, based on the "typical" student.
Inductive exposition	The trainer "talks through" the discovery process.
Deductive exposition	Lectures.
Drill and practice	Rote reception learning: instruction demonstrates what to do and provides practice. No conceptual understanding needs to be involved.

Instructional Strategy Based on Events of Instruction

Another way to think of instructional strategy is based on the events of instruction and the conditions of learning, not on the philosophy of the instructional designer. In this sense, instructional strategy is rooted in assumptions about what does — or should — happen during any planned learning experience and about what type of learning the instruction is intended to facilitate. In other words, different instructional strategies are required to help learners acquire verbal information, establish cognitive strategy, develop intellectual skills, build motor skills, or appreciate new attitudes (Gagne and Briggs, 1979).

To select instructional strategy, then, instructional designers start by examining performance objectives in order to determine what type of learning is to be facilitated. They should choose instructional strategy based on the type of learning. For example, if learners are to acquire verbal information, it will be necessary to discover a way to make that information meaningful to them. The instructional designer may adopt a strategy of fitting isolated information, like definitions, into some pattern — such as rhymes, mnemonics, or acronyms — that will be meaningful to learners and will improve their retention. If learners are to be aided in establishing a cognitive strategy or in changing their attitudes, they should be led through a process of discovery using the discovery strategies listed earlier. If learners are to develop intellectual or motor skills, expositive strategies are often appropriate.

Once the overall instructional strategy has been selected, instructional designers should focus attention on each event of instruction. "The events of instruction," note Gagne and Briggs (1979, p. 155), "are designed to make it possible for learners to proceed from 'where they are' to the achievement of the capability identified as the target objective." *Events of instruction constitute what should be done in a planned learning experience: instructional strategy, a closely related notion, constitutes how they will or should be done.* To plan instructional strategy for a learning experience, instructional designers begin by identifying each step in a learning experience. Then, bearing in mind the type of learning being planned, they pose the simple question "How can that be done?"

Authorities on instructional design have devised many schemes for describing the events of instruction. Pucel (1989), for example, has identified eight key instructional events based on a combination of his own independent research and the research of Ausubel (1962), Chase and Chi (1980), and Herbart (1898). To apply the results of their research, instructional designers should

1. State the performance objective(s) for the learning experience so as to clarify
   a. What is to be learned
   b. How the learner can demonstrate the desired performance
   c. How performance will be judged
2. Explain the importance of the learning experience
3. Provide crucial background information that the learner must have to achieve the performance objectives ("tell" the learner what to do and why)
4. Demonstrate the behavior ("show" the learner)
5. Guide practice (ask the learner to "do" it or apply it)
6. Allow for unguided practice (ask the learner to "do" it or apply it without benefit of extensive instructor feedback)
7. Evaluate the learner's performance and knowledge base ("follow up" with the learner)
8. Provide feedback and direction for future learning

Possibly more widely known than these eight steps are the nine key instructional events identified by Gagne and Briggs (1979) and summarized here:

1. Capture the attention of the learner
2. Describe to learners what performance objective(s) are to be achieved
3. Help learners recall prerequisite learning
4. Present instruction to facilitate the learners' achievement of the performance objectives
5. Guide the learners through the material so they begin to meet the objectives
6. Prompt the performance desired from the instruction so learners meet the objectives
7. Give the learners feedback — and make suggestions for improvement as appropriate — so learners sense how well they are beginning to meet the objectives

8. Evaluate how well learners are beginning to achieve the objectives
9. Work toward helping the learners retain what they have learned and apply it

The appropriate instructional strategy for each event depends on the desired results. Hence, types of instruction aimed at helping learners acquire verbal information, establish cognitive strategy, or develop intellectual skills, motor skills, or new attitudes will require its own appropriate strategy within the planned learning experience. Those strategies are summarized in Table 11.1.

Choosing Instructional Strategy and Tactics

For instruction to be effective, instructional designers should be able to choose among many instructional strategies and tactics.

Choosing an Appropriate Instructional Strategy

Although authorities on reception and discovery learning have usually been interpreted as favoring a single instructional strategy for every learning situation, there really is no one universally appropriate strategy. For the most part, the authorities have been misinterpreted (Romiszowski, 1981). Any instructional strategy can actually be used to achieve any performance objective. Likewise, any instructional strategy can be used to carry out any instructional event. However, no one instructional strategy works uniformly well under all conditions. To choose the appropriate strategy, consider the learners, the desired learning outcomes, the learning and working environments, and constraints on the instructional design process.

If learners are inexperienced, instruction based on an expositive strategy is usually the most efficient approach. Exposition leads learners through a subject at a uniform rate, with the pace set more by the instructor than by the learner. On the other hand, learners who are already experienced will often rebel against an expositive strategy (Knowles, 1984). They often prefer a process of discovery that makes full use of their own experiences — and allows them to become involved in, and committed to, learning.

The desired learning outcomes should also influence choice of instructional strategy. For example, learners should not be asked to acquire verbal information in precisely the same way that they are led to develop a cognitive strategy, intellectual skills, motor skills, or new attitudes (Gagne and Briggs, 1979). Learning experiences are of different kinds, and a different instructional strategy is appropriate for each kind.

The learning and working environments also influence the appropriate choice of instructional strategy. If the two environments are the same, as is the case with on-the-job training, an expositive strategy is usually most

Table 11.1. Instructional Events and the Conditions of Learning
They Imply for Five Types of Learned Capabilities.

Event	Intellectual Skill	Capability Cognitive Strategy	Information
1. Capture the attention of the learner	Introduce a change in stimulus		
2. Describe to learners what performance objectives are to be achieved	Describe the performance to be achieved and give an example	Inform learners of the kind of solution that is expected	Describe what question is to be answered
3. Help learners recall prerequisite learning	Encourage learners to recall subordinate concepts and rules	Encourage learners to recall related strategies and intellectual skills	Encourage learners to recall the context of the information
4. Present instruction to facilitate the learners' achievement of performance objectives	Give examples of concepts or rules to be learned	Give unique problems to be solved	Give the information in the form of propositions
5. Guide the learners through the material so they begin to meet the objectives	Give cues to the learners	Hint at solutions	Link to a broader context
6. Prompt the performance	Have the learners apply the performance	Request solution	Have the learners provide information or other examples
7. Give feedback to the learners	Affirm that the rule or concept has been applied correctly	Affirm that the solution to the problem is correct	Affirm that information has been stated correctly
8. Evaluate how well the learners are beginning to achieve the objectives	Learner demonstrates application of concept or rule	Learner originates a novel solution	Learner restates information in paraphrased form
9. Work toward helping the learners retain what they have learned and apply it	Review the material periodically with learners, giving them various examples	Give the learners opportunities to grapple with different solutions	Link the material to other information

**Table 11.1. Instructional Events and the Conditions of Learning
They Imply for Five Types of Learned Capabilities, Cont'd.**

Event	Capability	
	Attitude	*Motor Skill*
1. Capture the attention of the learner	Introduce a change in stimulus	
2. Describe to learners what performance objectives are to be achieved	Give an example of what action is called for	Demonstrate the expected performance
3. Help learners recall prerequisite learning	Encourage learners to recall information and other relevant skills	Help learners remember what to do
4. Present instruction to facilitate the learners' achievement of performance objectives	Give learners a choice in their actions	Give learners what they need to perform—such as appropriate tools, equipment, or other resources
5. Guide the learners through the material so they begin to meet the objectives	Give learners the opportunity to observe the model or choice of what to do	Give learners the chance to practice and the chance to receive feedback about their performance
6. Prompt the performance	Have the learners describe what they would do in real or simulated situations	Have the learners demonstrate performance
7. Give feedback to the learners	Give the learners reinforcement based on their choice	Give learners feedback on what they chose
8. Evaluate how well the learners are beginning to achieve the objectives	Learners choose the desired course of action as appropriate	Learners are capable of demonstrating the skill/performance
9. Work toward helping the learners retain what they have learned and apply it	Give learners new opportunities to choose the desired course of action	Encourage learners to practice

Source: Adapted from Gagne, R., and Briggs, L. *Principles of Instructional Design.* (2nd ed.) Troy, Mo.: Holt, Rinehart & Winston, 1979, p. 166.

efficient; however, if they differ, a discovery strategy usually works best. Generally, the closer the relationship between conditions in the learning and working environments, the greater the likelihood that learners will be able to apply on the job what they learn during instruction (Baldwin and Ford, 1988).

Finally, constraints on the instructional design process should also be considered during selection of strategy. Of primary consideration are time and control factors. A discovery strategy simply requires more delivery than an expositive strategy. Learners must be led to reach their own discoveries. That takes time, since individuals learn at different rates. However, greater control is possible with an expositive strategy in which the instructor transmits the same information to all learners. There may be differences in how that information is received and interpreted. But an expositive strategy usually leads to greater control over outcomes than a discovery strategy in which learners reach their own independent conclusions about their experiences.

Choosing Appropriate Instructional Tactics

Tactics are the way instructional strategies are implemented. They are the detailed approaches and activities used by an instructional designer to accomplish a strategy. In this respect, they bear the same relationship to instructional strategy as daily operational tactics bear to corporate strategy. Just as a corporate strategy of growth is achieved through such tactics as increasing sales, decreasing expenses, increasing market share, or a combination of all these, so too can instructional strategies of reception or discovery learning be achieved through various methods (tactics).

The choice of instructional tactics has often been more art than science. Instructional designers should first identify the results they wish to achieve through instruction and then plot out how they will achieve those results. The process of choosing tactics has usually been left to instructional designers' creativity and imagination, whether they are working as individuals or on a team. Through systematic study of the events of instruction and writings about them, Jonassen, Grabinger, and Harris (1990, pp. 34–38) have identified five key instructional strategies and a range of instructional tactics for each strategy. Their research results are presented in Table 11.2. (Note that the list can be used effectively as a laundry list of tactics.)

Choosing Media and Delivery Methods

The variety of available media and delivery methods may present unique problems to instructional designers. The choice should be made carefully and be based on the medium used.

Choosing Media

To plan to achieve performance objectives, instructional designers should also choose a medium, or media, after selecting an instructional strategy. The term *medium* just means *the way an instructional message is communicated to the learner.* Media thus include "the materials, devices, and people through which information is delivered" (*The Standards*, 1986, p. 65). Although the term *media* has not always been used consistently by instructional designers (Gagne and Briggs, 1979), examples are easy enough to identify: books, programmed texts, computers, slide/tape, videotape, and film.

A *media selection model*, sometimes called just a *media model*, is a decision-making aid. It is intended to guide selection of instructional media according to their instructional and cost effectiveness. Many media selection models

Table 11.2. Instructional Strategies and Tactics.

1. **Contextualizing instruction**[a]

   1.1   Gaining the attention of the learner

       1.1.1   arouse learner with novelty, uncertainty, surprise
       1.1.2   pose question to learner
       1.1.3   learner poses question to be answered by lesson

   1.2   Relate the goals of instruction to the learner's needs

       1.2.1   explain purpose or relevance of content
       1.2.2   present goals for learners to select
       1.2.3   ask learners to select own goals
       1.2.4   have learner pose questions to answer

   1.3   State the outcomes of instruction

       1.3.1   describe required performance
       1.3.2   describe criteria for standard performance
       1.3.3   learner establishes criteria for standard performance

   1.4   Present advance organizers

       1.4.1   verbal expository: establish context for content
       1.4.2   verbal comparative: relate to content familiar to learner
       1.4.3   oral expository: establish context for instruction
       1.4.4   oral comparative: relate to content familiar to learner
       1.4.5   pictorial: show maps, globes, pictures, tables

   1.5   Present structured overviews and organizers

       1.5.1   outlines of content: verbal (see also 1.4.1, 1.4.2)
       1.5.2   outlines of content: oral (see also 1.4.3, 1.4.4)
       1.5.3   graphic organizers/overviews
       1.5.4   combinations of verbal, oral, and pictorial overviews

   1.6   Adapt context of instruction

       1.6.1   content adapted to learner preferences (different situations)
       1.6.2   content adapted to prior knowledge

2. **Present and cue lesson content**

   2.1   Vary lesson unit size

       2.1.1   large chunks
       2.1.2   small chunks

   2.2   Present vocabulary

       2.2.1   present new terms plus definitions
       2.2.2   student looks up list of new terms
       2.2.3   present attributes of rule definition, concept, principle
       2.2.4   paraphrase definitions, present synonyms
       2.2.5   present definitions
       2.2.6   derive definitions from synonym list

   2.3   Provide examples

       2.3.1   prototypical examples
       2.3.2   matched example/non-example pairs
       2.3.3   divergent examples
       2.3.4   close-in non-examples
       2.3.5   vary the number of examples
       2.3.6   model appropriate behavior

Table 11.2. Instructional Strategies and Tactics, Cont'd.

2.4   Use cuing systems

    2.4.1   provide graphic cues: lines, colors, boxes, arrows, highlighting
    2.4.2   provide oral cues: oral direction
    2.4.3   provide auditory cues: stimulus change (e.g., music, sound effects, voice change)
    2.4.4   provide type style cues: font changes, uppercase, type size, headings, hierarchical numbering system, indentation
    2.4.5   present special information in windows

2.5   Advise learner

    2.5.1   instructional support needed: number of examples, number of practice items, tools, materials, resources
    2.5.2   learning strategies to use

3.   **Activating learner processing of instruction**

3.1   Elicit learner activities

    3.1.1   review prerequisite skills or knowledge
    3.1.2   learner selects information sources
    3.1.3   learner selects study methods
    3.1.4   learner estimates task difficulty and time
    3.1.5   learner monitors comprehension
    3.1.6   learner relates questions to objectives
    3.1.7   learner recalls elaborations
    3.1.8   learner evaluates meaningfulness of information

3.2   Elicit recall strategies

    3.2.1   underline relevant material
    3.2.2   rehearse/repeat/re-read
    3.2.3   use mnemonic strategies
    3.2.4   cloze reading activities
    3.2.5   identification with location (loci method)
    3.2.6   create summaries: hierarchical titles
    3.2.7   create summaries: prose
    3.2.8   create summaries: diagrammatic/symbolic (math)
    3.2.9   create summaries: mind maps

3.3   Facilitate learner elaborations

    3.3.1   imaging (creating images)
    3.3.2   inferring from information
    3.3.3   generating analogies
    3.3.4   creating story lines: narrative description of information

3.4   Help learners integrate new knowledge

    3.4.1   paraphrase content
    3.4.2   use metaphors and learner generated metaphors
    3.4.3   generating examples
    3.4.4   note-taking

3.5   Help learners organize information

    3.5.1   analysis of key ideas
    3.5.2   create content outline
    3.5.3   categorize elements
    3.5.4   pattern note techniques
    3.5.5   construct concept map
    3.5.6   construct graphic organizers

Table 11.2. Instructional Strategies and Tactics, Cont'd.

4. **Assessing learning**

    4.1 Provide feedback after practice

         4.1.1 confirmatory, knowledge of correct response
         4.1.2 corrective and remedial
         4.1.3 informative feedback
         4.1.4 analytical feedback
         4.1.5 enrichment feedback
         4.1.6 self-generated feedback

    4.2 Provide practice

         4.2.1 massed practice session
         4.2.2 distributed practice session
         4.2.3 overlearning
         4.2.4 apply in real world or simulated situation (near transfer)
         4.2.5 change context or circumstances (far from transfer)
         4.2.6 vary the number of practice items

    4.3 Testing learning

         4.3.1 pretest for prior knowledge
         4.3.2 pretest for prerequisite knowledge or skills
         4.3.3 pretest for endpoint knowledge or skills
         4.3.4 embedded questions throughout instruction
         4.3.5 objective referenced performance
         4.3.6 normative referenced performance
         4.3.7 incidental information, not objective referenced

5. **Sequencing instructional events**

    5.1 Sequence instruction in logical order

         5.1.1 deductive sequence
         5.1.2 inductive sequence
         5.1.3 inductive sequence with practice

    5.2 Sequence instruction in learning prerequisite order

         5.2.1 hierarchical, prerequisite sequence
         5.2.2 easy-to-difficult
         5.2.3 concrete-to-abstract

    5.3 Sequence instruction in procedural order

         5.3.1 procedural, job sequence
         5.3.2 information processing sequence (path sequencing)
         5.3.3 algorithmic presentation
         5.3.4 procedural elaboration

    5.4 Sequence instruction according to content organization

         5.4.1 general-to-detailed (progressive differentiation)
         5.4.2 conceptual elaboration
         5.4.3 theoretical elaboration

    5.5 Sequence instruction according to story structure

         5.5.1 narrative sequence

ªKey steps of instruction are in bold print; tactics are underlined.

Source: Jonassen, D., Grabinger, S., and Harris, N. "Analyzing and Selecting Instructional Strategies and Tactics." *Performance Improvement Quarterly,* 1990, *3*(2), 34–38. Reprinted with permission of the National Society for Performance and Instruction.

have been devised to help instructional designers (see American Telephone and Telegraph Company, 1987a; Anderson, 1983).

The Range of Media

Instructional media range from simple to complex. This distinction can be understood in two ways. First, a medium that does not require much advance preparation can be considered simple, while one requiring much preparation can be considered complex. For example, direct experience — possibly occurring on the job — is simple because it does not require much preparation. Second, a medium that appeals to only one sense can be considered simple; a medium appealing to more than one sense can be considered complex. The fewer the senses to which instruction is designed to appeal, the less need there is to be concerned about the effects on each sense — and how media can appeal to the learners' senses *in combination*.

The classification scheme below proceeds from simple to complex media, in the same way that the system devised originally by Dale (1969) did. The simplest media are placed at the bottom of the media "cone"; more complex media are placed at the top. This scheme is based on a list by Kemp (1985).

Media	*Examples*
Combinations of media	Interactive video Multi-image and sound computer-based training Multi-image/videotape Multi-image/audiotape Microfiche/audiotape Filmstrip/audiotape Slides/audiotape Print/videotape Print/audiotape
Projected motion pictures	Videotape Film
Projected still pictures	Computer programs (displayed) Overhead transparencies Filmstrips Slides
Audio recordings	Compact disc recordings Audiocassette recordings
Nonprojected materials	Job aids Photographs Diagrams Charts Graphs Flipchart Chalkboard Print materials

Tangible objects	Models Objects/devices/ equipment Instructors/speakers

How do instructional designers decide just which medium is best to achieve performance objectives? Unfortunately, there is no one right answer to this question. Substantial research has been conducted over the years to determine which media are most appropriate for achieving desired instructional outcomes and supporting instructional strategy. But that research has not led to firm conclusions. Any medium can be used to achieve any performance objective. But not all media should be used in precisely the same ways (Kemp, 1985).

Media selection decisions may improve in the future as artificial intelligence and expert systems are applied to the instructional design process (Gayeski, 1990). At present, however, the best approach to media selection is to make a primary media selection decision for an entire learning experience first. Then make secondary media selection decisions for each part of the experience. Do that by asking a series of questions and noting the answers (Kemp, 1985).

When making a media selection decision, ask these questions first: What are the desired outcomes of instruction? Do they provide clues about what medium or media to choose? For example, suppose that instruction is being prepared so that learners "will be able to troubleshoot problems with a diesel engine when given diagnostic instruments and a diesel engine." Given that performance objective, what medium is appropriate? In this example, the performance objective itself specifies that the learner will be "given diagnostic instruments and a diesel engine." That phrase suggests that learners will be using tangible objects (as identified on the media classification scheme presented above). The objects may, however, range from *real* to *simulated* objects. The same principle applies to other performance objectives. Consult them first to determine whether they *imply* the appropriate medium (or media) to use during the planned learning experience.

When making a media selection decision, ask this question second: What constraints on time, equipment, staff skills, and costs affect this planned learning experience? Consider the following questions about constraints:

Question	*Implication(s) for Media Selection*
How much *time* is available to plan and test instruction?	The less the time available for planning and/or testing instruction, the greater the propriety of choosing media toward the bottom of the classification scheme presented earlier.

What *equipment* is available to use in designing and/or delivering instruction?

When equipment for instructional design and/or delivery is not available, choose media at the bottom of the preceding classification scheme.

Other things being equal, choose media for which equipment is available (Wong and Raulerson, 1974).

For what media can instructional designers in one organization prepare instruction? Do *staff skills* lend themselves better to some media than to others?

Choose media for which staff can design and/or develop instruction.

Choose media for which competent external consultant support can be identified, when that support is possible and is instructionally justifiable.

How much is an organization willing to spend on the design and development of instruction?

When an organization is unwilling to authorize significant expenditures to meet an instructional need, choose media that are closer to the bottom of the classification scheme shown earlier. The more complex the media selection, the greater the cost of designing instruction.

When making a media selection decision, ask this question third: How will the instruction be delivered? While that question cannot be answered until a delivery method has been chosen (see the next section), instructional designers should bear in mind that some media are more appropriate than others for particular audiences (Ellington, 1985). Overhead transparencies, for example, are frequently used in group presentations but are not very effective for individualized instruction.

When making a media selection decision, a fourth and final question to ask is this: How often will this planned learning experience have to be revised in the future? Obviously, it does not make much sense to invest large sums in a medium that will be difficult to revise. Yet that can happen to those who opt for video-based programs, when their organizations have no video production facilities. An expensive consultant is hired, the video is prepared and edited, and it is outdated by the time it is shown. Some media — print materials, slide shows, and overhead transparencies — are relatively easy to revise. Other media — such as video or computer-based instruction — are not that easy to revise, and the equipment necessary to make the revisions is often expensive and difficult to use.

Selecting Delivery Modes

To plan performance objectives, instructional designers should also choose a delivery mode. A *delivery mode* means the choice made about the conditions under which instruction is to be offered. Not to be confused with media or instructional strategy, delivery mode is synonymous with the situation that confronts learners as they learn.

The range of delivery modes is not great. There are only four basic choices (Ellington, 1985):

1. *Mass instruction* involving many learners
2. *Group instruction* involving fewer learners
3. *Individualized instruction* involving only one learner at a time
4. *Direct experience* involving real-time learning, such as informal on-the-job training

Make a selection of delivery mode based on the performance objectives to be achieved. (See Figure 11.2.) If many people share the same instructional need, select mass instruction (Laird, 1985). It is appropriate, for instance, when everyone in the same organization should receive the same instruction. If only some people—such as employees in one work unit—require instruction, select group instruction. It is often appropriate for introducing new work methods or new technology. If only one person experiences an instructional need, select individualized instruction. If the need is a minor one—not really enough of a "chunk" of information to warrant preparation of a planned learning experience—then rely on such direct experiential methods as supervisory coaching or on-the-job training to supply learners with what they need to perform competently (Halson, 1990; Rothwell and Kazanas, 1990a, 1990b).

Once the delivery mode for the entire learning experience has been selected on the basis of terminal performance objectives, reconsider media selection for each enabling objective (Ellington, 1985).

Allowing for Constraints on Choice of Delivery Mode

Instructional designers rarely enjoy complete freedom to choose whatever delivery mode they wish. They face the same constraints when choosing delivery mode that they face when choosing media. Limitations of time, equipment, staff skills, and costs can and often do affect choice of delivery mode. In addition, managers—and sometimes the learners themselves—will make their preferences about delivery modes known. For instance, middle managers in some organizational cultures dislike mass instruction delivered during working hours because it removes workers from the production process and results in too much lost production time. They may require that mass instruction be delivered after hours or on weekends—thus reducing the chances

Figure 11.2. Algorithm for Selection of Instructional Mode.

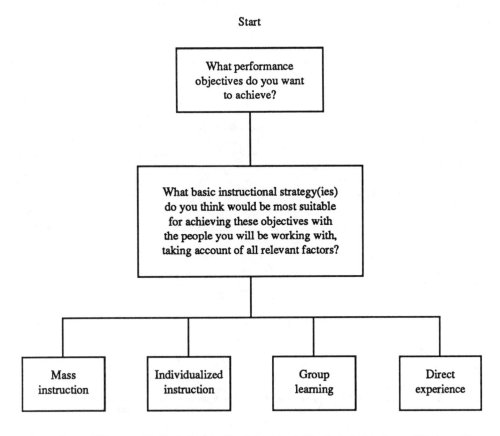

Source: Ellington, H. *Producing Teaching Materials: A Handbook for Teachers and Trainers.* New York: Nichols, 1985, p. 28. Used by permission of the publisher.

that all workers can participate in it. Likewise, some learners prefer individualized instruction because they have a storehouse of unpleasant memories from their formal schooling about classroom learning situations. When choosing delivery mode, then, be sure to consider *constraints* and *management/worker preferences.*

Judging Instructional Strategy

According to *The Standards* (1986), instructional designers should be able to judge instructional strategies specified by themselves and their colleagues. Instructional designers should be able to evaluate how appropriate the strategy is. They should consider the following questions among others (*The Standards,* 1986, p. 67):

How sound is the instructional strategy, considering the learners' characteristics?

How sound is the instructional strategy, considering the performance objectives?

**Exhibit 11.1. A Worksheet for Judging the Appropriateness
of a Specified Instructional Strategy.**

Directions: Use this worksheet to judge the appropriateness of an instructional strategy specified by yourself or other instructional designers.

First complete Part I to ensure that you have everything you need to judge the instructional strategy. For each question appearing in the left column, place a check (✔) in the center column to indicate an answer. If you are missing something, make notes to yourself in the right column.

Second, complete Part II to judge the appropriateness of the instructional strategy that has been selected. For each question appearing in the left column below, place a check (✔) in the center column. You should be able to answer each question with a yes. If you must answer no to any item, (1) review the choice of instructional strategy in light of that answer, and (2) be ready to furnish justification for it.

Make copies of this worksheet as necessary.

Part I. Conditions			
Question	*Response*		*Notes for revision*
Do you have available a description of . . .	*Yes* (✔)	*No* (✔) *N/A* (✔)	
1. Learner characteristics?	( )	( ) ( )	
2. Setting resources/ constraints?	( )	( ) ( )	
3. Desired learning outcomes in a sequence of instruction?	( )	( ) ( )	

Part II. Judging the Appropriateness of a Specified Instructional Strategy			
			~~Notes for revision~~
Question	*Response*		
	Yes	*No* *N/A*	
In judging the appropriateness of a specified instructional strategy, do you find evidence that each of the following issues has been considered during the process of specifying instructional strategy?	(✔)	(✔) (✔)	
4. The instructional strategy based on the instructional designer's philosophical views of learning and instructing?	( )	( ) ( )	
5. The instructional strategy based on conditions of learning?	( )	( ) ( )	
6. The instructional strategy based on events of instruction?	( )	( ) ( )	

Exhibit 11.1. A Worksheet for Judging the Appropriateness
of a Specified Instructional Strategy, Cont'd.

---

7. Appropriate media for the
    planned learning experience?   ( ) ( ) ( )

8. Appropriate delivery mode
    for the planned learning   ( ) ( ) ( )
    experience?

9. Other issues as necessary?   ( ) ( ) ( )

How congruent is the instructional strategy with setting resources and
constraints?
How clearly does the instructional strategy describe the techniques,
media, and settings?

Instructional designers may find it useful to rely on a worksheet, like that
shown in Exhibit 11.1, when they are called on to judge a specified instructional strategy. Every time an answer of no must be given, the instructional
designer should reexamine the instructional strategy.

Justifying Instructional Strategy

Instructional designers should be able to justify the instructional strategy
they have chosen. As in most instructional design activities, they should be
held accountable by other stakeholders for what they do. Instructional designers should thus be prepared to answer questions such as the following:

1. Why was an instructional strategy chosen?
2. What assumptions guided the choice of strategy? More specifically, what
    did instructional designers assume about the nature of learning and in-
    struction?
3. Who should care about the instructional strategy?
4. Why should stakeholders care about the instructional strategy?

Conclusion

In this chapter, we defined instructional strategy. We also distinguished between two kinds of strategy (macroinstructional and microinstructional
strategy), between instructional strategy and instructional tactics, and between
instructional strategy and learning strategy. Finally, we described how to
conceptualize instructional strategy, choose strategy and tactics, choose media
and delivery methods, and judge and justify strategy once chosen. In the
next chapter, we turn to designing instructional materials.

CHAPTER TWELVE

Designing
Instructional Materials

All the previous steps in the instructional design process culminate in instructional materials that will help learners achieve desired performance objectives. (See Figure 12.1.) In this chapter, we focus on selecting, modifying, or designing instructional materials and offer advice to instructional designers about judging and justifying instructional materials they or others have prepared.

An Overview of Steps in Designing Instructional Materials

Instructional designers take several steps to select, modify, or design instructional materials:

1. Preparing a working outline
2. Conducting research
3. Examining existing instructional materials
4. Arranging or modifying existing materials
5. Preparing tailor-made instructional materials
6. Selecting or preparing learning activities

We will describe these steps in the following sections of this chapter.

Step One: Preparing a Working Outline

Preparing a *working outline,* sometimes called a *syllabus,* is the first step in designing instructional materials. A working outline summarizes the contents of the planned learning experience. This outline is based on the instructional strategy and on measurable, sequenced performance objectives that were written previously. An outline is useful because it reminds instruc-

Figure 12.1. A Model of Steps in the Instructional Design Process.

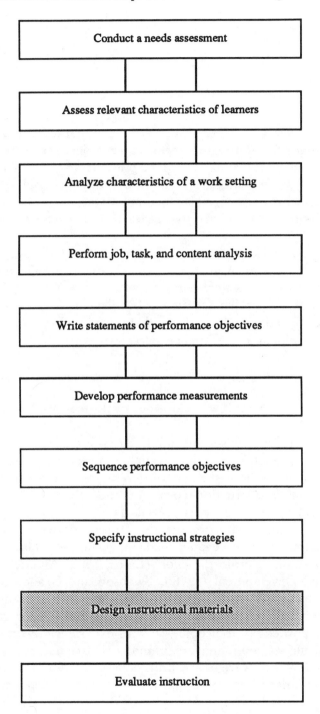

Source: Foshay, W., Silber, K., and Westgaard, O. *Instructional Design Competencies: The Standards.* Iowa City, Iowa: International Board of Standards for Training, Performance, and Instruction, 1986, p. 3. Used with permission of the publisher.

tional designers what they are doing—and helps them plan how to address each objective.

Recall from Chapter Eleven that all planned learning experiences should consist of certain clearly identifiable instructional events. For example, according to Gagne and Briggs (1979), instructional designers should

1. Gain the learners' attention for the learning event
2. Inform learners of the performance objective(s) to be achieved
3. Stimulate recall of prerequisite learning so that learners have a frame of reference for addressing performance objectives
4. Present the stimulus material to help learners achieve the objective(s)
5. Provide "learning guidance" with the stimulus material so that learners begin to achieve the performance objectives
6. Elicit desired performance so that learners achieve the desired performance objectives
7. Provide feedback so that learners have a sense of how well they are progressing toward achievement of performance objectives—and can make corrections as necessary
8. Assess learner performance toward achievement of the objectives
9. Enhance retention and transfer so that learners will remember what they learned and can apply it when necessary

These events of instruction are reflected in the working outline.

Step Two: Conducting Research

Conducting research, the second step in designing instructional materials, is carried out to identify materials available inside or outside an organization. Suffice it to say that the cost of developing tailor-made materials is usually formidable. Instructional designers should not waste precious time, staff, and money preparing these materials if they can be obtained from other sources inside or outside the organization. It is possible to estimate the time needed to design and validate tailor-made instruction—and forecast the financial benefits resulting from the effort (Laird, 1985; American Society for Training and Development, 1988d; Swanson and Gradous, 1988). (See Figure 12.2 for an algorithm to help decide whether to use existing materials.)

Begin research for instructional materials inside an organization by identifying knowledgeable people—such as experienced workers, supervisors, union officials, top managers, human resource managers, or trainers. Ask them if they are aware of any unit, department, or division that might have had a past need (perhaps for on-the-job training purposes) for instructional materials like those necessary to meet the performance objectives.

Describing the materials carefully, ask the knowledgeable people three questions:

Figure 12.2. An Algorithm for Deciding
Whether to Produce Your Own Instructional Materials.

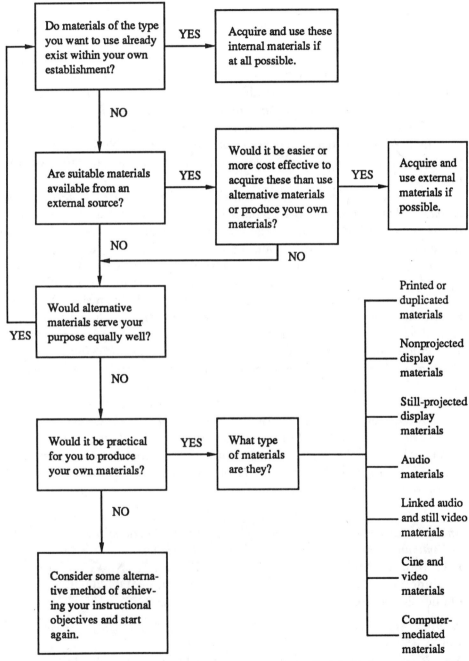

Source: Ellington, H. *Producing Teaching Materials: A Handbook for Teachers and Trainers.* New York: Nichols, 1985, p. 32. Used by permission of the publisher.

1. *Have you ever seen any procedure manuals, checklists, descriptive booklets, or training manuals on [subject name]?* By asking this question, instructional designers may uncover instructional materials already available within the organization. These may be suitable for immediate use or may lend themselves to modification. Procedure manuals and checklists are the most common materials used to support on-the-job training (Rothwell and Kazanas, 1990b). They provide a solid foundation on which to base instruction, particularly if they are current and have already been field-tested. Additionally, they have built-in credibility with operating management, especially if they have been used successfully.

2. *Who do you know in this organization who is especially knowledgeable about this subject?* Use this question to link up with in-house experts who may be aware of instructional materials already available inside the organization. Focus attention on employees who perform training at the operating level.

3. *What department might have needed, in the past, to do special training on the subject?* This question may help pinpoint the best places to look for materials in the organization. In some organizations, operating managers have authority to purchase their own training materials. Hence, useful instructional materials may be squirreled away somewhere, perhaps gathering dust, and they could be used or modified to meet other needs in the organization.

Even when instructional materials are not available inside an organization, instructional designers may still be able to transform existing work-related materials into instructional materials with minimal effort. For a practical guidebook that describes how to do that, see Drew, Mikulecky, and Pershing (1988). While this guidebook focuses on *literacy* instruction, the principles it is based on are appropriate to other topics.

Begin research for materials outside the organization in a different way. First, network with instructional designers in other organizations (Bard and Loftin, 1987). Find them by attending local, regional, and national meetings of organizations frequented by instructional designers. (The addresses and phone numbers of several such organizations appear below.)

American Association for Adult and Continuing Education
1112 16th St. N.W., Suite 420
Washington, DC 20036
Phone: 202-463-6333

American Management Association
135 W. 50th St.
New York, NY 10020
Phone: 212-903-8234

American Educational Research Association
1230 17th St. N.W.
Washington, DC 20036
Phone: 202-223-9485

American Psychological Association
1200 17th St. N.W.
Washington, DC 20036
Phone: 202-955-7600

*American Society for Healthcare
    Education and Training (ASHET)*
840 N. Lake Shore Drive
Chicago, IL 60611
Phone: 312-280-6113

*American Society for Training and
    Development (ASTD)*
1640 King Street
P.O. Box 1443
Alexandria, VA 22313
Phone: 703-683-8100

*Association for the Development of
    Computer-Based Instructional
    Systems (ADCIS)*
409 Miller Hall
Western Washington University
Bellingham, WA
Phone: 206-676-2860

*Association for Educational
    Communications and
    Technology (AECT)*
1126 16th St. N.W.
Washington, DC 20036
Phone: 202-466-4780

Association of CBT Professionals
600 Radnor Drive
Roselle, IL 60172
Phone: 312-893-8670

Interactive Video Industry Association
1900 L Street, Suite 500
Washington, DC 20036
Phone: 202-872-8845

*International Federation of Training
    and Development Associations
    (IFTDO)*
Institute of Management
    Education
7 Westbourne Road
Southport PR 8-2HZ
England

International Tape/Disc Association
505 8th Avenue,
Floor 12A
New York, NY 10018
Phone: 212-643-0620

*International Teleconferencing
    Association*
1299 Woodside Drive
McLean, VA 22102
Phone: 703-556-6115

*National Society for Performance and
    Instruction (NSPI)*
1126 16th St. N.W.
Suite 102
Washington, DC 20036
Phone: 202-861-0777

*National Society of Sales Training
    Executives*
203 East 3rd St.
Sanford, FL 32771
Phone: 305-322-3364

*Society for Accelerative Learning and
    Teaching (SALT)*
Box 1216
Welch Station
Ames, IA 50010
Phone: 515-292-3911

Society for Applied Learning
   Technology (SALT)
50 Culpeper St.
Warrenton, VA 22186
Phone: 703-347-0555

Society for Technical Communication
   (STC)
815 15th St., Suite 400
Washington, DC 20005
Phone: 202-737-0035

Society for Intercultural Education,
   Training, and Research (SIETAR)
1505 22nd St. N.W.
Washington, DC 20037
Phone: 202-296-4710

Training Media Association
198 Thomas Johnson Dr.
Suite 206
Frederick, MD 21701
Phone: 301-662-4268

Contact colleagues through these organizations to determine whether they have previously had occasion to design — or select — similar instructional materials. Ask to see their materials. Bear in mind, however, that some organizations consider their instructional materials proprietary, so be sure to comply with any organizational protocols that must be observed. If it is not possible to examine materials, then at least ask how they were prepared, focusing on the process(es) used rather than the product(s) developed. Most instructional designers will share that information, even if they cannot share actual work products. (The favor may have to be reciprocated someday, of course.)

Searching print and computer-based references is another way to find existing instructional materials outside an organization. While few references will lead directly to instructional materials, many books and articles will be useful in designing them. In some cases, instructional designers may even be lucky enough to find off-the-shelf instructional materials. Numerous references can be invaluable in conducting such searches. Some are listed below. Others are listed in Bard, Bell, Stephen, and Webster (1987).

Print Sources

American Society for Training and Development. *American Society for Training and Development Training Video Directory.* 2 vols. Baltimore, Md.: American Society for Training and Development Press, 1990.

Association for Media-Based Continuing Education for Engineers. *Catalog of AMCEE Videotape Courses.* Atlanta, Ga.: Association for Media-Based Continuing Education for Engineers, 1990.

Bowker. *Audio Video Marketplace: A Multimedia Guide.* New York, N.Y.: Bowker, 1990.

Bowker. *Educational Film Locator.* New York, N.Y.: Bowker, 1986.

Gale Research. *Training Directory for Business and Industry 1989–1990.* Detroit, Mich.: Gale Research, 1989.

Gale Research. *Videos for Business and Training*. Detroit, Mich.: Gale Research, 1989.

Nadler, L., Nadler, Z., and Fetteroll, T. *The Trainer's Resource 1989: A Comprehensive Guide to Packaged Training Programs*. Amherst, Mass.: Human Resource Development Press, 1989.

Computer-Based Sources

A-V Online [a source for nonprint instructional material].

    Contact: Access Innovations
              P.O. Box 40130
              Albuquerque, NM 87196
              Phone: 1-800-421-8711

Business Periodicals Index [a source for locating business periodicals].

    Contact: Wilsonline
              H. W. Wilson Co.
              950 University Avenue
              Bronx, NY 10452
              Phone: 212-588-8400

Education Index [a source for locating articles on education].

    Contact: Wilsonline
              H. W. Wilson Co.
              950 University Avenue
              Bronx, NY 10452
              Phone: 212-588-8400

Educational Resources Information Center (ERIC) [a source for locating educational information including some off-the-shelf instructional materials].

    Contact: ERIC Processing and Reference Facility
              4833 Rugby Avenue, Suite 301
              Bethesda, MD 20814
              Phone: 301-656-9723

Step Three: Examining Existing Instructional Materials

Evaluating existing instructional materials is the third step in the process of designing instructional materials. When debating whether to use existing instructional materials, be sure they are consistent with the instructional strategy and performance objectives established for the planned learning experience. (Do not expect to use existing materials without making at least *minor* modifications.) Sometimes it is helpful to compare existing materials to a list of criteria on an evaluation checklist. Such checklists have been printed in Gardner (1987), Heinich, Molenda, and Russell (1985), and Lerch (1985). When using such a checklist, think about these questions: (1) Can the existing instructional materials be used as they are, with minimal revisions? (2) What revisions, if any, must be made? (3) Are the performance objectives to be met by learners so unique as to prevent use of anything except tailor-made materials?

Step Four: Arranging or Modifying Existing Materials

Arranging or modifying existing materials is the fourth step in the process of designing instructional materials. When existing instructional materials are appropriate to use, it may be necessary to secure copyright permissions and arrange or modify the materials in ways appropriate for satisfying the objectives.

Securing Copyright Permissions

Copyright permissions must be secured for existing instructional materials whenever a copyright notice appears on the title page, or on a footer, of instructional materials. It is unethical for an instructional designer to do otherwise (McLagan, 1989). (For an example of a copyright notice, see the reverse of this book's title page.) As a rule of thumb, assume that any material purchased from a vendor or borrowed from another organization is copyrighted. Most government documents are not copyrighted.

To request permission to use the material, write directly to the copyright holder. Be sure to state where the material will be used (in-house only?), how much will be used (the entire document or only part of it?), and how it will be used (in-house training only? will the material be adapted in any way?). Also indicate how soon it will be used (is there an urgent need for a response?), how many copies are to be made (will all participants in training be given a copy?), who will receive the copies (who are the learners?), why the material is needed (training only? promotional use?), and how often future requests will be made (how many times will the material be used each year?). Be prepared to pay a fee for the privilege of using the material (Kemp and Dayton, 1985; Kemp and Smellie, 1989).

Arranging Instructional Materials

Even when existing instructional materials can be found to meet the needs of targeted learners, take care to arrange the materials suitable for the intended use. Do not assume that materials designed by other professionals will always be letter-perfect or suitable for specialized purposes. Be sure to modify the material, even if only cosmetically, so (1) it appears tailor-made to the industry and organization in which it will be used, and (2) it matches up *exactly* to the performance objectives established for the learning experience.

Begin by making the most obvious changes. Revise titles and case-study settings so they match up to the organization and learners. (Be sure that changes to be made to copyrighted material are noted in the permission request.) Proceed to major changes, if they must be made. It is often helpful to record each change on a *point sheet*. The point sheet, a lined document resembling a page of footnotes, becomes a guiding document to help a team of instructional designers tackle revision. Finally, arrange the materials so their format matches up to any special requirements favored by the organization in which they will be used.

Step Five: Preparing Tailor-Made Instructional Materials

Preparing tailor-made instructional materials is the fifth step in the process of designing instructional materials. This step should be carried out only when it is not possible to use or modify existing materials from inside or outside the organization. When approaching the task of designing tailor-made instructional materials, think in terms of developing a complete instructional package.

Traditional Components of an Instructional Package

Sometimes called a *learning package* (Blank, 1982), an *instructional package* contains all the materials necessary to tell learners what they need to know, show them what to do or how to use that information, allow them to practice what they have learned, and follow up with learners to give them feedback on how well they have learned. A complete instructional package traditionally has four distinct components (Dick and Carey, 1985):

1. *Learner directions or guidesheets* are instructions for learners. They explain how to use the instructional package. They sometimes take the form of a student manual and are particularly important for individualized instruction. They are usually unnecessary when instruction is delivered in a group setting, since the instructor can provide learner directions orally. However, most instructors do want to provide group participants with an organized manual, and that manual is a method of providing directions to learners.

2. *Instructional materials* contain the actual contents of instruction — including text, visual aids, and handouts. They provide learners with the information they need to achieve the performance objectives.

3. *Tests* are student evaluation tools. The term *test* is used in a broad sense. Types of tests include preinstructional assessments (*pretests*) to determine what learners know before they participate in planned learning experiences. Other types include self-check and instructor-check activities during instruction to determine how well learners are achieving enabling performance objectives (*progress tests*) and postinstructional assessments to determine how well learners have achieved the terminal performance objectives

by the end of the planned learning experience (*posttests*). Further examples include job-based assessments (*on-the-job performance tests*) to determine how well learners are applying on the job what they learned in the instructional setting.

4. *Instructor directions or guidesheets* are the instructors' counterparts of *learner directions* or *guidesheets*. They are procedural guides to aid instructors in delivering instruction — or supporting learners as they individually apply themselves to planned learning tasks. Examples range from one-page instructor guidesheets or content and procedure outlines or lesson plans to voluminous trainers' guides, trainers' manuals, or tutors' guides.

Differences of Opinion About Components of an Instructional Package

Authorities on instructional design sometimes differ in their opinions about what should be included in an instructional package. One reason for this difference of opinion is that authorities on instructional design do not agree uniformly on one philosophy of learning and instructing (Reigeluth, 1987). The instructional designers' underlying philosophies can have a major impact on how instruction is prepared, as numerous concrete examples of widely diverse lesson plan formats clearly show (Collins, 1987; Gropper, 1987; Keller and Kopp, 1987). Another reason is that considerable flexibility exists in preparing instruction. Indeed, instructional materials should be prepared so that they are consistent with the type of learning, learners, and setting in which they will be used.

Preparing Instructional Materials for Individualized Use

In most cases, instructional designers should prepare materials for individualized use first and then modify them, as necessary, for group use (Dick and Carey, 1985). One reason to take this approach is that instruction designed for individualized use, with minimal instructor guidance, can save valuable instructor time. This time can then be devoted to those learners needing special help. A second reason: since group-paced instruction drags along at the pace of the slowest learner, it "actually *prevents* the majority of students from reaching a high level of mastery" (Blank, 1982, p. 194). A third reason to begin with learner-centered, individually paced instruction is that it usually requires more complete learner instructions than group-paced instruction, making modification for group use relatively simple. A fourth reason is that individualized instruction encourages learners to accept responsibility for their own instruction. This is not always true in group settings, in which learners play passive roles while an instructor plays an active role as transmitter of information.

How Should Instructional Materials Be Prepared and Formatted

Once instructional designers have decided what components of an instructional package should be used, they are ready to prepare and format the material.

Preparing instructional materials is the process by which a sketchy working outline is transformed into finished learner directions or guidesheets, instructional materials, tests, and instructor directions or guidesheets. This process is a highly creative one. On occasion, it can often be made more efficient and effective by techniques such as *detailed outlining* or *storyboarding* (Kemp, 1985).

Detailed outlining is a step following preparation of a working outline or syllabus. A detailed outline summarizes the content of the planned learning experience — or series of related learning experiences — based on the instructional strategy and media that were selected earlier. Detailed outlining literally "adds details" to the simple working outline. Examples of such details might include visual aids, instructional material (handouts, text for the learner), and directions to the instructor and/or the learner. In this way, instructional materials are prepared directly from the working outline and are linked directly to performance objectives. At the end of this process, then, the working outline has been converted into a detailed outline and, from that, into even more detailed learner directions or guidesheets, instructional materials, tests, and instructor directions or guidesheets.

Storyboarding is a different method of preparing instructional materials. A *storyboard* is a visual representation, such as a series of pictures of major frames in a videotape accompanied by the script text and musical score to go with them. However, storyboarding is not limited solely to visual media, though it is frequently associated with them. To create a storyboard: (1) find a large blank wall that can serve as the backdrop for the storyboard; (2) fasten a picture of each step in a designated instructional experience to the wall; and (3) develop accompanying learner directions/guidesheets, instructional materials, tests, and instructor directions/guidesheets for each picture. Each step in the instructional experience must be represented visually in some way, although index cards bearing text may serve this purpose as well as pictures or murals. Instructional materials are then created to support each step. The value of the storyboard is that it helps organize instructional design efforts, whether they are performed individually or on a team. It also tracks what must be done in every step of the planned learning experience.

Format means the print or audiovisual layout of instructional material in a given medium. Choosing format means making decisions about how the instructional message — and instructor or learner directions and tests — will be organized and presented. Much has been written in recent years about the crucial importance of effective formatting techniques in facilitating learning (for example, Duffy, 1985; Fleming and Levie, 1978; Gerlach and Ely, 1980; Hartley, 1981, 1985), and instructional designers should at least be cognizant of what has been written on this subject.

Formatting learner directions/guidesheets or student manuals is often of greatest concern when instruction is designed for individual use (Blank, 1982), since learners depend on this part of an instructional package to tell them what to do to progress through the learning experience.

To prepare learner directions, some instructional designers like to start out by thinking of themselves as "novices" who are approaching the subject for the first time. This mindset is helpful because it forces them to view the material as the least experienced learner will see it. They then ask themselves this question: What step-by-step guidance do the learners — *and* instructors — need to approach the planned learning experience through which the instructional package is intended to guide them?

Begin the learner directions or guidesheet with a few carefully chosen, one-phrase or one-sentence descriptions of the purpose of the learning experience and its performance objectives. Other topics that should be covered include the importance of the learning experience to the learner, its relationship (if any) to other planned learning experiences or work tasks, prerequisites required, and necessary equipment or supplies. List, step by step, precisely what a learner must *do* to proceed through the instructional materials and tests. Once that is done, go back and list precisely what the instructor or tutor should *do* to prompt the learner through each step and place that information on an instructor (or tutor's) guidesheet. When finished, the directions should be so clear that they could guide anybody, without a need to ask further questions about how to proceed, through the entire planned learning experience. (A portion of a representative learner guidesheet appears in Exhibit 12.1.)

Student manuals tend to be formatted in two ways. One way is to set up the format so that the manual consists of many individualized learner guidesheets, each focusing on one lesson within a series of related learning experiences. The manual begins with a program description, a statement of program purpose, terminal performance objectives, relationships between lessons (organization of the series), equipment and supplies needed to complete instruction, and self-check activities or tests to assess student progress.

A second way to set up the format is to gear it toward participants in instructor-centered, group-paced instruction. In this format, the manual should also describe the program's purpose, terminal performance objectives, and organization. In addition, it should contain highlights of the program contents, handouts, activities, tests, space for notes, and other material. Both formats can be used on or off the job. One advantage of giving participants a student manual in off-the-job instruction is that they can take it back to the job with them and use it as a job aid. (For this reason, some instructional designers prefer to use three-ring notebooks for the manuals to make the task of revising material that much easier for them — and the task of adding or revising material on the job that much easier for learners.) For more information on formats for student manuals, see American Telephone and Telegraph Company (1987c). More specific advice can also be found in Hartley (1985) and Ribler (1983).

Instructional materials have no one "right" format; rather, there are many possibilities. Examples may include lesson plans, audio or video scripts, and print-based or computer-based frames of programmed instruction. The choice

Exhibit 12.1. A Portion of a Representative Learner Guidesheet.

SAMPLE 6-3	LEARNING GUIDE	E-02

AUTOMOTIVE MECHANICS

AVTI
ANY VO-TECH INSTITUTE
1234 MASTERY LANE
ANYTOWN, U.S.A. 98765

TASK: Repair exhaust pipe, muffler, and tail pipe

INTRODUCTION:

Since the exhaust pipe, muffler, and tail pipe are on the underside of the car, they take a terrific beating. If you can spot exhaust system parts that are corroded, cracked, or broken, you may save the customer more costly and inconvenient repairs later. Often, the exhaust pipe, muffler, or tail pipe must be replaced. If not replaced properly by the mechanic, the exhaust system may rattle or may leak deadly exhaust gases into the passenger compartment, causing sickness or even death.

TERMINAL PERFORMANCE OBJECTIVE
To Demonstrate Your Mastery of This Task, Do the Following:

GIVEN: Automobiles needing exhaust system repair and access to tools, equipment, and replacement parts.

YOU WILL: Remove and replace defective exhaust system components.

HOW WELL: Written test and performance test must be completed with 100% mastery.

ENABLING OBJECTIVES
This Learning Guide Is Divided into Several Parts to Help You:

(1) Describe function of and inspect exhaust system components.

(2) Remove and replace tail pipe.

(3) Remove and replace muffler.

(4) Remove and replace exhaust pipe.

School	Dept.	Prog.	Duty	Task	Preqt.	Avg.Hrs.		Dates Revised	
AVTI	Ind.	7291	E	02	E-01	36			

© Date AVTI

(right margin, vertical text): Program 7291 Task E-02: Replace exhaust pipe, muffler, and tail pipe.

Exhibit 12.1. A Portion of a Representative Learner Guidesheet, Cont'd.

AVTI	Follow the LEARNING STEPS listed below:	Task E-02
EO (1)	Describe function of and inspect exhaust system components.	

✓ 1. Read pages 171–174 in *Modern Auto Repair* describing the function of exhaust system components.

✓ 2. Read Instruction Sheet 1, enclosed, describing what to look for when inspecting the exhaust system.

✓ 3. See if you can describe parts of the exhaust system and determine which parts need replacing by completing Self-Check 1, enclosed.

EO (2)	Remove and replace tail pipe.

✓ 1. View slides 1–32 in slide-tape E-02, showing how to remove and replace tail pipe on automobile, all the way through.

✓ 2. While viewing slides 1–32 again, remove and replace the tail pipe from vehicle assigned by instructor.

_____ 3. Check your work using Self-Check 2, enclosed.

_____ 4. Have instructor check your work before going any further.

EO (3)	Remove and replace muffler.

_____ 1. View slides 33–50, showing how to remove and replace muffler, all the way through.

_____ 2. While viewing slides 33–50 again, remove and replace muffler on vehicle assigned by instructor.

_____ 3. Check your work using Self-Check 3, enclosed.

_____ 4. Have instructor check your work before going any further.

EO (4)	Remove and replace exhaust pipe.

_____ 1. While viewing slides 51–64, remove and replace muffler on assigned vehicle.

_____ 2. Check your work using Self-Check 4 enclosed, then have instructor check your work.

_____ 3. Now, practice replacing muffler, tail pipe, and exhaust pipe on customer's car assigned by shop foreman.

_____ 4. Have instructor check your work.

_____ 5. When you are ready, take the Written Test for Task E-02.

_____ 6. When ready, take the Performance Test for Task E-02. | Program 7291 |

Exhibit 12.1. A Portion of a Representative Learner Guidesheet, Cont'd.

AVTI	INSTRUCTION SHEET 1	Task E-02

Listed below are the steps to inspect the exhaust system. Make these checks both with and without the engine running. *Caution:* Exhaust system components are *hot!*

1. Identify vehicle—match car with work order—read it twice.

2. Raise vehicle on lift—be sure to follow rules for raising cars on lift. Review learning guide B-04 if needed.

3. Locate and inspect *muffler*. You will need to replace muffler if you find any of the following:

   a. Holes or cracks in body of muffler

   b. Breaks in either end of muffler where end is attached to body of muffler

   c. Excessive rust or corrosion

   d. Large dents or areas weakened by rust

   e. Loose, broken, or missing muffler clamps (check both ends—tighten or replace as needed)

4. Inspect the *exhaust pipe*. You will need to repair or replace if you find:

   a. Loose or missing nuts holding exhaust pipe to manifold (tighten)

   b. Missing or broken gasket (replace)

   c. Leaks in manifold/exhaust pipe connection. Feel for leaks with your hand (*caution:* exhaust pipe and manifold are hot!)

   d. Cracks or holes or split seams in pipe (replace)

   e. Loose connections at manifold or muffler (tighten)

   f. Dents or kinks that restrict flow of exhaust gases (replace)

5. Inspect *tail pipe.* You will need to repair or replace if you find:

   a. Loose connections (tighten)

   b. Cracks, holds, or split seams (replace)

   c. Dents or kinks (replace)

   d. Broken or frayed support brackets (replace brackets)

	Program 7291

of format depends on the purpose of instruction, who will use the instructional materials and why, how and where they are to be used, and what medium will be used for delivery of the instructional message.

   Instructor directions or *guidesheets* frequently take the form of *lesson plans,* detailed outlines intended to guide instructors through group or individualized instructional activities (American Society for Training and Development, 1989b, 1989e; Torrence, 1987). A *lesson* is "the level at which instruction is designed in detail" (Gagne and Briggs, 1979, p. 197). Focusing on what instructors should do to facilitate a single planned learning experience — such as a class or tutorial session — lesson plans are essential to establishing the link between learners' achievement of desired performance objectives and instructors' activities intended to foster that achievement. There is no one standardized format for a lesson plan. Many are acceptable. However, institutions may establish policies of their own on appropriate lesson plan format. A portion of a representative lesson plan appears in Exhibit 12.2.

   A lesson plan should usually be developed directly from an outline describing instructional content. It should reflect previous decisions made

Exhibit 12.2. A Portion of a Representative Lesson Plan.

(This lesson plan format is designed for group delivery.)

Suggested Procedures	*Notes for the Instructor*
	Welcome the participants to the Workshop on Employee Incentive Programs.
Display Visual 1.	Describe the purpose of the workshop:

> *Purpose of the workshop*
>
> To review methods of increasing employee involvement by tying rewards to work methods and results.
>
> —————— Visual 1 ——————

Display Visual 2.	Describe the terminal performance objectives of the workshop:

> *Objectives of the workshop*
>
> When you complete this workshop, you should be able to
>
> 1. Define the term *Employee Incentive Program.*
>
> —————— Visual 2 ——————

about instructional strategy, media, and sequence of performance objectives. It should be organized in several distinct parts, reflecting necessary instructional events for learning and the directions necessary for an instructor to facilitate the planned learning experience (Gagne and Briggs, 1979). The necessary instructional events become a guide for the parts of the lesson. Lesson plans should also specify the instructional resources, supplies, equipment, facilities, and other support materials needed for the planned learning experience. In this way, instructors — who may not be the same as the instructional designer(s) who prepared the material — know what to do and how to do it.

Scripts are similar to lesson plans in that they can be used to establish the link between learners' achievement of desired performance objectives and instructors' activities intended to foster that achievement. They may be word-for-word texts of what an instructor will say to learners in a group, what a tutor will say to learners individually, or what will be said in electronically based presentations on videotapes, films, slide/tape shows, or audiocassettes. Like lesson plans, effective instructional scripts should be organized into distinct parts reflecting the events of instruction. If instruction is presented in an electronic medium, the script should also provide directions for camera and background music (American Society for Training and Development, 1986c, 1987f).

Formatting instructor directions/guidesheets or trainers' guides is of greatest concern when instruction is designed for group use (Blank, 1982), since trainers depend on this part of an instructional package to tell them how to facilitate a planned learning experience.

Any learning package requires some directions to let instructors or tutors know what support they should provide to learners. For learning packages geared to individualized use, simplified instructor directions are usually adequate. These directions should describe the purpose of the package, the performance objectives, the structure of the learning experience, the resources, equipment, and facilities necesary for the experience, and (most important) an overview of what learners must *do* to use the package. Instructor directions may be particularly useful when they identify the most common problems encountered by learners during their individualized experiences — and tips to guide instructors in responding to those problems.

Trainers' guides are usually necessary for group-oriented classroom instruction. They may take any number of formats and range from simple two-page brochures or outlines to three-ring notebooks filled with detailed lesson plans and everything else a trainer needs to deliver a classroom presentation (American Society for Training and Development, 1988b). Detailed trainers' guides, such as those published for workshops, typically contain more than one lesson. One excellent approach to formatting trainers' guides is to purchase and review several examples of them. The following (Rothwell, 1990, Preface) is an overview of the parts of such a guide.

Section	Contents
Overview	Performance objectives
	Module outline
	Transparency master list
	Handout master list
	Suggested training time
Introduction	Description of needs assessment
	Needs assessment questionnaire
	Training materials and aids
	Delivery preparation checklist
	Description of follow-up procedures
	Questionnaire for follow-up
Related Materials	A list of books, articles, videotapes, and other aids to be used in delivering the workshop
Trainer's Lesson Plan for the Workshop	Lesson outline (points to be covered during the training session)
	Instructional notes (directions and information for the trainer)
Transparency Masters	Master copies of overhead transparencies from which transparencies can be made
Handout Masters	Master copies of all handouts for the workshop

Research on trainers' guides has shown that, under certain conditions at least, an outline format can be just as effective as a detailed format (McLinden, Cummings, and Bond, 1990). A *detailed format* is one in which an "instructor is provided with a picture of an overhead transparency, questions to ask, scripted statements to make, and directions as to when a discussion should be generated and what it should cover" (McLinden, Cummings, and Bond, 1990, p. 3). In contrast, an *outline format* is defined as one in which the instructor is "provided necessary content and sequence; however, scripted presentations, directions, and cues are kept to a minimum" (McLinden, Cummings, and Bond, 1990, p. 3). The outline format saves substantial time and expense in materials preparation. But it presupposes that the content of instruction is nontechnical and that the instructors are prepared and highly experienced and expert in their subject matter (McLinden, Cummings, and Bond, 1990).

Tests should be formatted on the basis of learner assessment methods that have been chosen. While most novice instructional designers associate testing with paper-and-pencil instruments, there are really numerous ways to test knowledge, skills, and attitudes (American Telephone and Telegraph Company, 1987b). Testing may occur through one-on-one questioning of learners, one-on-one demonstrations of ability during or after instruction, or questionnaires to assess changes in learner attitudes. In short, considerable creativity should be exercised when formatting tests. One reason: the word *test* itself makes some representatives of management, union, or workers very nervous, since they wonder how test results will be used in subsequent personnel decision making.

Step Six: Selecting or Preparing Learning Activities

The sixth step in designing instructional materials is selecting or preparing learning activities. Materials selected from other sources will usually have learning activities included; tailor-made instructional materials will require selecting or preparing activities. Learners should be given the opportunity to discover or demonstrate what they have learned, and activities are intended for that purpose.

Selecting Existing Learning Activities

It is possible to select existing learning activities from external sources for use in otherwise tailor-made instructional materials. These activities must, of course, support achievement of predefined performance objectives, and the instructional designer must comply with any copyright requirements. There are numerous sources of existing learning activities on many topics — for example, Bond (1986), Christopher and Smith (1987), Mill (1980), Newstrom and Scannell (1980), Pfeiffer and Jones (1972–1990), and Wasserman (1987).

Preparing Individual Learning Activities

There are two general categories of learning activities: *individual* and *group*. Individual learning activities are geared to individualized instruction and informal learning. Compared to the wealth of writings available on group learning activities, relatively little has been written about preparing individual learning activities on — or off — the job. There are, however, some sources to which instructional designers may refer when they undertake the task of preparing individual learning activities or helping people structure their own learning projects (Gross, 1982, 1977; Houle, 1961; Knowles, 1975; Tough, 1979).

Almost any experience can be transformed into an individualized learning activity, provided that (1) outcomes are specified in advance, (2) the outcomes can be compared to preestablished performance objectives, and (3) the experience meets certain requirements from the standpoint of the learner and/or the instructor. It should furnish the learner with new information or skills, give the learner an opportunity to observe others applying a skill, allow a learner the opportunity to demonstrate knowledge or skill, or afford an instructor a chance to assess how well the learner has acquired information or skills. Examples of individualized learning activities may include the following:

- Reading a book
- Interviewing others
- Reviewing documents
- Addressing a group on a new topic
- Finding a problem
- Researching a subject
- Watching a videotape
- Observing others
- Demonstrating a skill
- Performing a new job
- Starting something new
- Solving a problem

Numerous others are possible (McCall, 1988; McCauley, 1986). Even off the job, informal life experiences as community volunteer, civic or church leader, parent or spouse can become learning experiences and may serve job-related instructional purposes (Lombardo and Eichinger, 1989; Pedler, 1983; Revans, 1983).

To prepare individual learning activities, first decide how much instructor involvement will be necessary *during* the learning experience. If instructor involvement is necessary, supplement learner materials with instructor directions/guidesheets or "tutoraids" so that learners can be provided with instructor help as needed. For instance, instructor directions of some kind are important to support learners progressing through planned learning experiences in off-the-job, in-house learning centers (Reynolds, 1985).

On the other hand, if instructor support is unnecessary, then use contract learning to guide individualized learning experiences. *Contract learning* is defined as "an alternative way of structuring a learning experience: it replaces a content plan with a process plan. Instead of specifying how a body of content will be transmitted (content plan), it specifies how a body of content will be acquired by the learner (process plan)" (Knowles, 1986, pp. 39–40). To be effective, according to Knowles (1986, p. 38), a learning contract should specify

1.   The knowledge, skills, attitudes, and values to be acquired by the learner (learning objectives)
2.   How these objectives are to be accomplished (learning resources and strategies)
3.   The target date for their accomplishment
4.   What evidence will be presented to demonstrate that the objectives have been accomplished
5.   How this evidence will be judged or validated

Preparing Group Learning Activities

Group learning activities are perhaps most frequently associated with experiential instructional methods in classroom settings. While results of research studies on the relative effectiveness of group learning activities in classroom instruction have proved largely inconclusive (Carroll, Paine, and Ivancevich, 1972; Newstrom, 1980), it appears that some group learning activities are better suited than others for meeting specific types of performance objectives. Indeed, the choice of what learning activity to use should stem from the match between the performance objective and the activity (Laird, 1985).

Numerous group learning activities can be identified. In fact, one enterprising author has catalogued and described over 350 (Huczynski, 1983). Research conducted by Lakewood Publications suggests that some are presently used more often than others in organizational settings (Gordon, 1990). Laird (1985) points out that some group learning activities are superior to others for giving learners the chance to become involved in, and thus committed to, the learning process.

In the following paragraphs, we will provide brief descriptions of many common group learning activities, simple guidelines for developing them, notes about conditions when they are appropriate to use, and sources of additional information about them.

A *panel discussion* is an assembly of knowledgeable people who meet with learners to deliver short presentations or answer questions about issues with which the panelists are familiar. A panel discussion is appropriate for helping learners with verbal information; it is inappropriate for providing instruction on cognitive strategies or for changing attitudes.

To prepare a panel discussion, identify knowledgeable people who can speak on the issue and thus contribute toward achievement of the predefined performance objectives. Provide the panelists with a list of questions—or else ask the participants to do so. Then identify an individual who can serve as panel leader to introduce panelists, pose questions to them, and keep the discussion on track (Laird, 1985).

A *case study* is a narrative description of a situation in which learners are asked to identify or solve a problem. It is particularly appropriate for instruction focused on cognitive strategy. Much has been written about it. See, for example, American Society for Training and Development (1987b), Fidel (1984), Kirrane (1989), Pfeiffer and Ballew (1988a), and Smith (1987).

To prepare a case study, first identify its purpose, the performance objectives it is intended to support, and the targeted learners. Then conduct some research inside and outside the organization. Try to find existing case studies that have already been prepared and field-tested by others. Look for those in books and articles (Pensyl, 1985). If existing case studies cannot be located, then interview experienced workers in the organization to find examples of real situations demonstrating problems pertinent to the planned learning experience — and supportive of its performance objectives. Use the interview guide appearing in Exhibit 12.3 to help structure questions that will produce the skeletal basis for a case study.

Exhibit 12.3. An Interview Guide for Collecting Case-Study Information.

Directions to the Instructional Designer: Use the questions appearing on this interview guide to help you collect information for a case study. First, find one or more experienced workers from the targeted job class for which instruction is to be designed. (Supervisors may also be used.) Then explain what kind of situation you are looking for — and why. When you find respondents who can think of example(s), ask the following questions. Finally, write up the case study and ask one or more respondents to review it for accuracy. Use disguised names, job titles, locations, and other facts. Add questions at the end of the case, if you wish.

---

1.   What was the background of the situation? Where and when did it occur? Who was involved? Why was it important?

---

2.   What happened? (*"Tell me the story."*)

---

3.   What caused the situation — or problem(s) in the situation — so far as you know? (*Describe the cause.*)

---

4.   What were the consequences of the situation for the people in it? the work unit? the department? the organization? (*Describe the consequences.*)

---

5.   What conclusions can be drawn from the situation? What should be learned from it? If it happened again, how would you handle it? Why?

As a last resort, prepare a fictitious case to serve the intended purpose. Use settings and characters compatible with the organization in which the instruction will be delivered. Then present the draft case to supervisors and workers for their review. Revise it according to their suggestions so as to make it as realistic as possible. Occasionally, this approach will help the reviewers remember actual situations suitable for case-study treatment. Actual situations may then be substituted for the fictitious ones. ("Actual situations," when labeled as such, tend to have great credibility with learners. It is important, however, to conceal names so as to avoid embarrassing individuals.)

An *action maze* is "a printed description of an incident, for analysis, followed by a list of alternative actions" (Malasky, 1984, p. 9.3). As learners make suggestions about what actions to take, they are directed further in the action maze to find out the consequences of their decisions. This approach is particularly effective for training people how to troubleshoot problems and make decisions. For more information on this approach, see Laird (1985) and Malasky (1984).

To construct an action maze, begin the same way you would in preparing a case study. First, identify the purpose. Second, clarify how the action maze will help learners achieve performance objectives, providing them with new information or affording them an opportunity to try out their skills and receive feedback about what they know or do. Third, select a situation requiring a series of decisions to reach a conclusion, such as a procedure consisting of related tasks. Fourth, write up each step of the procedure to a *decision point* in which learners must choose what to do. Fifth, give participants two, three, or four choices only. Sixth, prepare a separate sheet describing what happened as a result of that decision and leading the learners to another decision point. Seventh, complete enough sheets to reflect the entire procedure, with or without "detours" made by novices. Eighth, request experienced workers to progress through the action maze to test how "realistic" it is. Ninth, revise the action maze based on the suggestions offered by experienced workers.

An *in-basket exercise* "is a variation of a case study. Each participant is provided with an in-basket, including correspondence, reports, memos, and phone messages, some of which may be important to the case or process under study, and some of which may be extraneous" (Malasky, 1984, p. 9.13). It is a timed exercise intended to discover how well each participant can manage details and withstand stress. Use an in-basket exercise only for "office skills" and supervisory practices. Do not use it for technical training focusing on use of heavy equipment or application of shop-floor procedures. For more information, see Laird (1985) and Malasky (1984).

To prepare an in-basket exercise, begin in the same way that a case study is prepared. Identify the purpose. Then clarify how the exercise will help learners achieve performance objectives. Select—or create—actual memos, letters, or phone messages that require decision making and priority setting. Train experienced workers to observe participants and evaluate the quality of their decisions, providing feedback and coaching after the activity is completed.

A *roleplay* is a dramatic representation of a real situation. It is an umbrella term for a whole range of similar group-oriented experiential activities. A roleplay "permits learners to re-enact situations which they face on the job, or which they will face in the future, or which they perceive to be job-like" (Laird, 1985, p. 154). This group learning activity is particularly useful for helping participants demonstrate and practice what they have learned (Malasky, 1984). However, participants sometimes find roleplays artificial and have trouble feeling and acting as they say they would on the job. For more information on roleplays, see American Society for Training and Development (1984a), Ellington (1985), Malasky (1984), Pfeiffer and Ballew (1988c), Van Ments (1983), and Wohlking and Gill (1980).

Prepare a roleplay by writing a case study and then adding character descriptions to the case. Be sure to spell out exactly what learners should *do* during the roleplay. Use the framework for a roleplay presented in Exhibit 12.4 as the basis for preparing one. Simply fill in the blanks with information obtained from interviews with experienced workers. As in preparing case studies, base your roleplays on actual situations confronted by workers, if possible. If that is not possible, then imagine realistic but fictitious situations.

Exhibit 12.4. A Framework for Preparing a Roleplay.

Introduction   Use this roleplay to help you _____

_____ .

Purpose of the roleplay	To do _____ .
Objectives of the roleplay	At the end of this roleplay, you should be able to:
Time required for the roleplay	Spend _____ minutes on this roleplay.
Number of people required for the roleplay	This roleplay is intended for groups of _____ .
Equipment/seating required for the roleplay	To enact this roleplay properly, you will need a room with the following configuration and number of chairs:
Procedures	
Step 1	Assemble in groups of _____ for how long?
Step 2	Choose someone to play the part of each character. (Note how long that will take.)
Step 3	Read a description of the situation.
Step 4	Carry out the roleplay. (Indicate how long that will take.)
Step 5	Prepare for discussion. (Indicate how long that will take.)
Step 6	Ask participants to draw conclusions from what they learned and indicate how they will apply on their jobs what they have learned.

A *simulation* is an artificial representation of real conditions. It may be computerized, using videodisc technology (DeBloois, 1982), or it may be prepared in print form (Thiagarajan and Stolovich, 1978). It should be used to assess previous learning or demonstrate technical ability (Malasky, 1984). Simulations are advantageous because they provide hands-on experience and are engaging to participants in a planned learning experience. But they do have disadvantages. Among them: (1) they are usually expensive to develop, and (2) they require an instructor to play the role of facilitator or evaluator (Malasky, 1984). For more information about them, see Greenblatt and Duke (1981) and Pfeiffer and Ballew (1988a).

Prepare a simulation by preparing a case study and then creating detailed descriptions of characters in the simulation. Be sure to spell out the purpose and objectives first. Then set the parameters of the simulation — how long it will last, where the simulation is to be conducted, who will do what, and when the simulation should end. Allow participants a measure of freedom so that this extended "roleplay" feels "realistic." Test out the simulation before using it to make sure it works. Revise it so that it has reasonably predictable outcomes that are pertinent to achieving the performance objectives of the learning experience.

The *critical incident technique* (CIT), sometimes called an *incident process,* is the production of a very brief narrative description of a problem or situation. Often compared to the case-study method, this CIT is appropriate for developing learners' troubleshooting, decision-making, and questioning skills (Malasky, 1984). It has been used in assessing needs as well as in delivering instruction (Johnson, 1983). For more information about the CIT, see Flanagan (1949, 1954) and Pigors and Pigors (1980, 1987).

To prepare a critical incident description, interview experienced job incumbents performing the same work as the targeted trainees. Ask them to identify the most common — or the most important (*critical*) — problem situations (*incidents*) that they have heard about or experienced in the past. Then ask (1) how the situation was handled, (2) what results were obtained, (3) how the situation should be handled in the future if it should come up again, and (4) what results should be obtained by using the recommended solution. From this information, create one- or two-sentence critical incidents based on real situations. Use the interview guide appearing in Exhibit 12.5 to help gather critical information.

Another approach to preparing descriptions of critical incidents is to ask experienced job incumbents or their supervisors to keep performance logs in order to identify common or serious problem situations encountered during the course of work. Use the performance log to identify how often specific problem situations are actually encountered by job incumbents and obtain detailed advice on how to handle them from exemplary job incumbents or their supervisors. Be sure to find out (1) the circumstances of the

Exhibit 12.5. An Interview Guide for Gathering Information on Critical Incidents.

Directions to the Instructional Designer: The questions appearing on this interview guide are intended to help you gather information about critical incidents for use in preparing experiential activities for instruction.

First, find one or more experienced workers — or supervisors of those workers — from the targeted group of trainees. Second, ask them the questions that follow. Third, use the results of a series of these interviews to prepare critical incident activities for the targeted trainees. If you wish, prepare a second sheet showing the answers or recommended solutions for each critical incident. Ask the trainees to work on the incidents individually or in a small group.

---

1. Think back to a time when you faced a difficult problem on the job, perhaps the most difficult situation you had ever faced. (*Describe, briefly, the nature of that situation.*)

---

2. What did you do in that situation? What solution or approach did you use? (*Describe it briefly.*)

---

3. What happened as a result of your solution or approach? (*Describe the results.*)

---

4. Suppose this situation arose again. What would you do now? Why? (*Describe a recommended solution and reasons for suggesting it.*)

---

5. What results would you expect from using the solution or the approach you suggested in response to question 4? (*Describe what you would expect the consequences of your action to be.*)

Figure 12.3. A Flowchart for Judging the Accuracy, Completeness, and Appropriateness of Selected Instructional Materials.

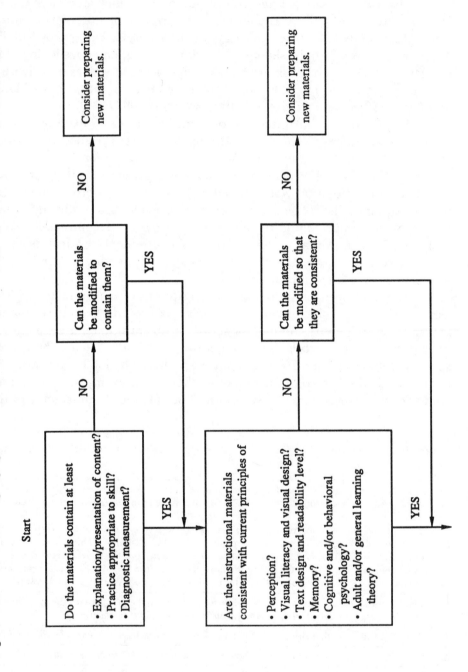

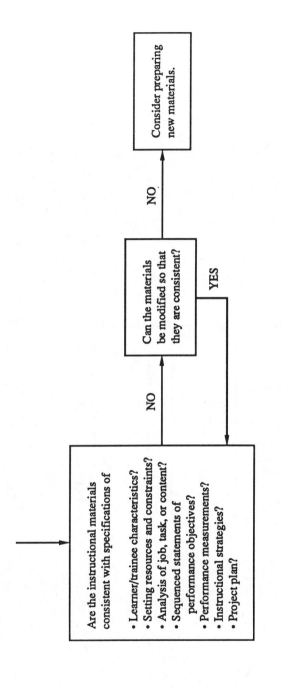

Figure 12.3. A Flowchart for Judging the Accuracy, Completeness, and Appropriateness of Selected Instructional Materials, Cont'd.

Are the instructional materials
consistent with specifications of

• Learner/trainee characteristics?
• Setting resources and constraints?
• Analysis of job, task, or content?
• Sequenced statements of
  performance objectives?
• Performance measurements?
• Instructional strategies?
• Project plan?

NO

Can the materials
be modified so that
they are consistent?

YES

NO

Consider preparing
new materials.

Figure 12.4. A Flowchart for Judging the Accuracy, Completeness, and Appropriateness of Prepared Instructional Materials.

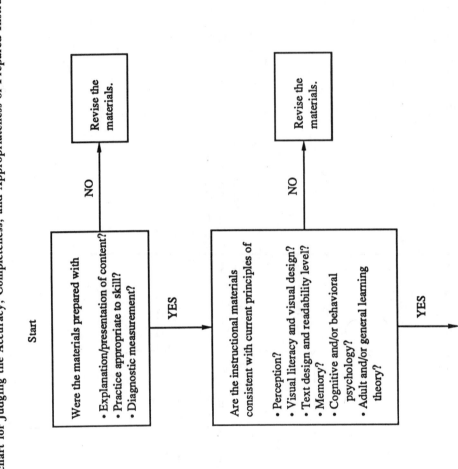

Start

Were the materials prepared with

- Explanation/presentation of content?
- Practice appropriate to skill?
- Diagnostic measurement?

NO → Revise the materials.

YES

Are the instructional materials consistent with current principles of

- Perception?
- Visual literacy and visual design?
- Text design and readability level?
- Memory?
- Cognitive and/or behavioral psychology?
- Adult and/or general learning theory?

NO → Revise the materials.

YES

Figure 12.4. A Flowchart for Judging the Accuracy, Completeness, and Appropriateness of Prepared Instructional Materials, Cont'd.

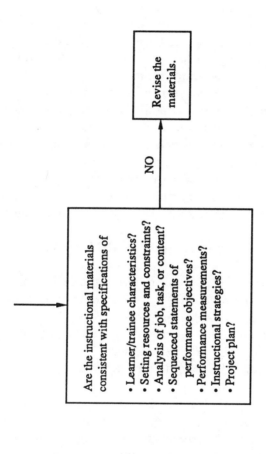

Are the instructional materials
consistent with specifications of

• Learner/trainee characteristics?
• Setting resources and constraints?
• Analysis of job, task, or content?
• Sequenced statements of
  performance objectives?
• Performance measurements?
• Instructional strategies?
• Project plan?

NO

Revise the
materials.

problem, (2) how the situations are handled, (3) what happens as a result of that solution, (4) how the situation should be handled in the future if it should come up again, and (5) what results should be obtained by using the recommended solution.

Judging Instructional Materials

Instructional designers should be able to evaluate instructional materials they or others have selected, modified, or prepared. As noted in *The Standards* (1986, p. 71), their judgments should be guided by three chief considerations. First, do the instructional materials contain explanations of the content, afford an opportunity for learners to practice the skill being learned, and provide measures of accomplishment? Second, are the instructional materials consistent with current principles of perception, visual literacy and visual design, text design and readability level, memory, cognitive and/or behavioral psychology, and adult and/or general learning theory? Third, do the materials conform to learner characteristics, setting constraints, results of work analysis, sequenced performance objectives, performance measurements, and instructional strategies? Instructional designers may rely on flowcharts as decision aids when they must judge instructional materials. Sample flowcharts appear in Figures 12.3 and 12.4. Consult them as necessary.

Justifying Instructional Materials

Instructional designers should be able to justify the decisions they make about selecting, modifying, or preparing instructional materials to others. As in most steps of the instructional design process, then, they should be prepared to explain what they have done to other stakeholders, such as operating managers and supervisors and targeted learners.

More specifically, they should be prepared to answer questions such as the following:

1. Why was the decision made to use instructional materials selected from inside or outside the organization?
2. Why was the decision made to modify existing instructional materials?
3. Why was the decision made to prepare tailor-made instructional materials?
4. What is the estimated difference in cost between investigating existing instructional materials (and possibly modifying them to meet present needs) and preparing tailor-made materials?

Instructional designers should be prepared to answer these questions after selecting, modifying, or preparing instructional materials. If they cannot do so, they may have to make further revisions.

Conclusion

In this chapter, we described how to select, modify, or design instructional materials. We also offered simple advice on judging and justifying instructional materials. In the next chapter, we will focus on the last step in the instructional design process that was introduced in Chapter Four—that is, formative evaluation.

CHAPTER THIRTEEN

Evaluating Instruction

"A basic belief of instructional design," write the authors of *The Standards* (1986, p. 73), "is that instruction is not considered complete or released until it has been demonstrated that trainees can indeed learn from the materials." Concerned with helping *form*ulate instruction, this step in the instructional design process calls for *formative evaluation*. Usually distinguished from *summative evaluation*, which helps *summa*rize results of instruction (Bloom, Hastings, and Madaus, 1971), formative evaluation is conducted *before* instructional materials are delivered to a majority of the targeted learners. Summative evaluation—a topic that is not treated in this book—is conducted *after* instructional materials have been used with targeted trainees and results have been measured.

Formative evaluation is the final step in the model of the instructional design process we introduced in Chapter Four. (See Figure 13.1.) In this chapter, we begin by clarifying assumptions about formative evaluation and defining key terms associated with it. We turn next to a case study that dramatizes issues in developing a formative evaluation plan. We then describe the steps in developing a formative evaluation plan and approaches to implementing the plan. We conclude the chapter by offering some advice to instructional designers about judging and justifying formative evaluations.

Assumptions About Formative Evaluation

Instructional designers make three fundamental assumptions when evaluating instructional materials and methods.

First, they view evaluation as primarily a formative process. This assumption rests on the belief that instructional materials and methods should be evaluated—and revised—prior to widespread use to increase their instructional effectiveness. In this way, it is hoped, learner confusion will be minimized.

Figure 13.1. A Model of Steps in the Instructional Design Process.

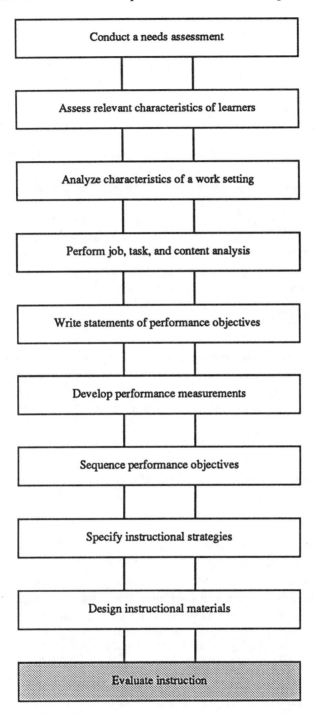

```
┌─────────────────────────────────────────┐
│        Conduct a needs assessment        │
└─────────────────────────────────────────┘

┌─────────────────────────────────────────┐
│  Assess relevant characteristics of learners │
└─────────────────────────────────────────┘

┌─────────────────────────────────────────┐
│   Analyze characteristics of a work setting  │
└─────────────────────────────────────────┘

┌─────────────────────────────────────────┐
│   Perform job, task, and content analysis    │
└─────────────────────────────────────────┘

┌─────────────────────────────────────────┐
│  Write statements of performance objectives  │
└─────────────────────────────────────────┘

┌─────────────────────────────────────────┐
│     Develop performance measurements     │
└─────────────────────────────────────────┘

┌─────────────────────────────────────────┐
│      Sequence performance objectives      │
└─────────────────────────────────────────┘

┌─────────────────────────────────────────┐
│      Specify instructional strategies      │
└─────────────────────────────────────────┘

┌─────────────────────────────────────────┐
│       Design instructional materials       │
└─────────────────────────────────────────┘

┌─────────────────────────────────────────┐
│           Evaluate instruction            │
└─────────────────────────────────────────┘
```

Source: Foshay, W., Silber, K., and Westgaard, O. *Instructional Design Competencies: The Standards.* Iowa City, Iowa: International Board of Standards for Training, Performance, and Instruction, 1986, p. 3. Used with permission of the publisher.

Second, instructional designers assume that evaluation means "the process of placing value on something" (Sredl and Rothwell, 1987). Evaluation is not completely objective and empirical; rather, it rests heavily on *human* judgment and *human* decisions. Human judgment, in turn, reflects the individual values of instructional designers and the groups they serve.

Third, instructional designers expect to collect and analyze data as part of the evaluation process. To determine how well instructional materials and methods work, instructional designers must try them out. It is then possible, based on actual experience with learners, to make useful revisions to the materials.

Defining Terms Associated with Formative Evaluation

Before undertaking a formative evaluation, instructional designers should take the time to familiarize themselves with at least two key terms: *formative product evaluation* and *formative process evaluation*. However, instructional designers should also minimize the use of this special terminology. Operating managers or clients will only be confused by it.

Formative Product Evaluation

The term *formative product evaluation* means "the appraisal of instructional sequences and materials during their stages of formulation and development. The major purpose of formative product evaluation is to provide both descriptive and judgmental information regarding the worthiness of an instructional experience" (Lawson, 1974, p. 5). *Descriptive information* "defines or characterizes the adequacy or inadequacy of various instructional components" (Lawson, 1974, p. 5). In contrast, *judgmental information* is "employed to determine the learning or instructional implications of descriptive data; that is, the appropriateness or value of highly delineated learning goals" (Lawson, 1974, p. 5).

Formative Process Evaluation

Related to *formative product evaluation, formative process evaluation* means the appraisal of instructional methods — that is, how planned learning experiences are delivered or facilitated. Like product evaluation, it too provides both descriptive and judgmental information about planned learning experiences.

Developing a Formative Evaluation Plan: A Case Study

Read the following case study, which is intended to dramatize key issues involved in developing a formative evaluation plan. Make notes as you read the case. Then read the section on developing a formative evaluation plan that follows the case.

Joan Richter has just completed a draft instructional materials package for a preretirement workshop. An experienced instructional designer,

she has applied the instructional systems design model to technical training, but (until now) she has not applied it to "soft skills" instruction. Joan's
preretirement package is intended for group-focused, instructor-led delivery. The learners will be employees of her client organization, and they will
be screened so that only people within three years of retirement will participate in the workshop. The purpose of the workshop is to prepare learners
emotionally for approaching retirement.

Joan has completed a thorough needs assessment. She has clarified
the problems that will be addressed by the workshop, prepared measurable
and sequenced performance objectives, and crafted tailor-made instructional
materials using relevant information about the learners and the setting. She
is now ready to plan a formative evaluation.

Using a simple worksheet she constructed to help her remember what
should be included in a formative evaluation plan, Joan formulates that plan.
In this process she determines her workshop's purpose, objectives, audience,
and subjects. She also assesses the information needs of the intended au-
dience(s) of the evaluation, considers proper protocol, describes the popula-
tion(s) to be studied, selects her subjects, ponders other variables of importance, formulates a design for the study, and formulates a corresponding
management plan to guide the study. She makes sure that her formative
evaluation plan includes the following:

- A statement of purpose
- A description of data collection plans
- A description of procedures for analyzing data that are appro-
  priate for them and the constraints imposed by the situation
- Decision rules that will guide revisions based on the data
- A description of the expected results consistent with the data
  collection techniques chosen and specified analysis plans
- Time estimates for implementation of the evaluation plan
- Plans for communicating results to appropriate decision
  makers [*The Standards,* 1986, p. 74]

Joan is now ready to implement her formative evaluation plan.

Developing a Formative Evaluation Plan

As the case study dramatizes, instructional designers should develop a formative evaluation plan that focuses attention on the instructional materials.
There are seven steps in the process of developing a formative evaluation
plan. We will describe them in the following sections.

Step One: Determining Purpose, Objectives, Audience, and Subjects

The first step of formative evaluation is to determine the purpose, objectives, audience, and subjects of the formative evaluation. Begin by clarifying

the purpose. Answer the question, "Why is this evaluation being conducted?" How much is the focus solely on the quality of the instructional materials or methods, and how much is it on other issues such as the following (Kirkpatrick, 1975):

1. How much will the targeted trainees enjoy the instructional materials, content, or methods?
2. How much will the participants *learn*?
3. How much *impact* will the learning experience have on the participants' job performance?
4. How much *impact* will the planned learning experience have on the organization?

As part of the first step, clarify the desired results of the formative evaluation. For each purpose identified, establish measurable objectives for the evalation. In this way, instructional designers help themselves and others assess the results against planned intentions.

In addition, be sure to consider who wants the evaluation and why. Is it being conducted primarily for the benefit of instructional designers, key decision makers (top managers), immediate supervisors of the targeted learners, union representatives, or some combination of all these groups? Always clarify *who* will review the results of the formative evaluation and *what information they need* from it (Brandenburg and Smith, 1986).

Identify who will participate in the formative evaluation. Will the evaluation be focused on representative targeted learners only, or will it also focus on learners with special needs or low abilities? subject matter specialists? representatives of the supervisors of targeted trainees? their managers? top managers? There are reasons to target formative evaluation to each group of subjects, depending on the purpose and objectives of the evaluation.

Step Two: Assessing Information Needs

The second step in conducting formative evaluation is to assess the information needs of the targeted audiences. Precisely what information is sought from the results of the formative evaluation? In most cases, the targeted audiences will provide important clues about information needs:

*   *Instructional designers* will usually be interested in how they can revise instructional materials or delivery methods to make them more effective for learners.
*   *Key decision makers* will usually be interested in how well the materials meet previously identified instructional needs and solve performance problems. They may also want to assess how much and what kind of financial or managerial support is necessary to ensure instructional success or on-the-job application of what was learned.

- *The immediate supervisors of targeted learners* will usually be interested in familiarizing themselves with the instructional content so they can hold learners accountable on their jobs for applying what they learned.
- *Union representatives* may be concerned about how much the instruction increases productivity and thereby provides justification for future wage demands.
- *Representatives of the targeted learners* may be interested in how "easy" or "difficult" the instructional materials are and how "test" results will be used.

In addition, consider the extent to which each group might be interested in determining how well instructional materials and methods present the content, allow participants to apply what they learn, measure accomplishment, and demonstrate learner achievement of performance objectives.

Step Three: Considering Proper Protocol

The third step in conducting a formative evaluation is to consider and observe proper protocol. Several questions about the protocol of conducting formative evaluation should be considered:

> How much do the targeted audiences expect to be consulted about a formative evaluation *before, during,* and *after* it is conducted?
> What permissions are necessary to carry out the study?
> Whose permissions are necessary?
> What formal or informal steps are necessary to secure the necessary permissions to conduct a formative evaluation, select subjects, collect data, and feed back results?

Protocol is affected by five key factors: (1) the decision makers' experience with formative evaluation, (2) labels, (3) timing, (4) participation, and (5) method of evaluation.

The decision makers' experience with formative evaluation is the first factor influencing protocol. If the decision makers have had no experience with formative evaluation, instructional designers should take special care to lay the foundation for it by describing to the key stakeholders what it is and why it is necessary. If decision makers have had experience with formative evaluation, determine what mistakes (if any) were made in previous evaluative efforts. Make it a point to avoid repeating them. Common mistakes may include forgetting to secure the right permissions, forgetting to feed back to decision makers information about evaluation results, and forgetting to use the results in a visible way to demonstrate that the evaluation was worth the time and effort.

Labels are a second factor affecting protocol. Avoid using the imposing term *formative evaluation* with anyone other than instructional designers, since it may only create confusion. Try less formidable and more descriptive labels such as *walkthroughs, rehearsals, tryouts,* or *executive previews.*

Timing is a third factor affecting protocol. Is it better to conduct a formative evaluation at certain times in the month or year than at other times, due to predictable work cycles or work schedules? Make sure that formative evaluations will not be carried out at times when they conflict with peak workloads or other events that may make it difficult for key stakeholders to approve or participate.

The participation of key stakeholders is a fourth factor affecting protocol. How essential is it to obtain permission from a few key individuals before conducting a formative evaluation? If so, who are they? How is their permission secured? How much time should be allowed for obtaining the necessary permissions?

The method of evaluation is the fifth and final factor affecting protocol. Given the organization's culture, should some instruments, methods of data collection, or analysis be used instead of others?

Instructional designers should never underestimate the importance of protocol (House, 1973). If protocol is forgotten, instructional designers can lose support for the instructional effort before it begins. Remember: any instructional experience is a change effort, and formative evaluation, like needs assessment, offers a valuable opportunity to build support for change. But if proper protocol is violated, it will militate against success. The audiences will focus attention on the violation, not instructional materials or methods.

Step Four: Describing the Population to Be Studied and Selecting the Subjects

The fourth step in conducting formative evaluation is to describe the population for study and to select participants.

Always describe from the outset the population to be studied. In most cases, of course, instructional materials and/or methods should be tried out with a sample, usually chosen at random, from the targeted group of learners. But take care to *precisely* clarify the kind of learners the materials will be tried out with. Should participants in formative evaluation be chosen, for any reason, on the basis of any specialized situation-related characteristics, decision-related characteristics, or learner-related characteristics, as those terms were described in Chapter Five?

There may be occasions when it is appropriate to try out instructional materials or methods with such specialized populations as exemplars (the top performers), veterans (the most experienced), problem performers (the lowest performers), novices (the least experienced), high-potential workers (those with great, but as yet unrealized, performance capabilities), or disabled workers. Formative evaluations conducted with each group will yield specialized information about how to adapt instructional materials to unique needs.

Once the learners have been identified, select a random sample. Use automated human resource information systems for that chore, if possible.

If a specialized population is sought for the study, other methods of selecting a sample may be substituted. These could include announcements to employees or supervisors, word-of-mouth contact with supervisors, or appeals to unique representatives. If specialized methods of selecting participants for formative evaluation must be used, be sure to consider the protocol involved in contacting possible participants, securing their cooperation, securing permission from their immediate supervisors and/or union representatives, and securing approval for any time off the job that may be necessary.

Step Five: Identifying Other Variables of Importance

The fifth step in conducting a formative evaluation is to identify other variables of importance. Ask these questions to identify the variables:

1. What setting(s) should be used for the formative evaluation?
2. What specific program issues are particularly worth pretesting before widespread delivery of instruction?
3. How much should the formative evaluation focus solely on instructional issues, and how much (if at all) should it focus on such other important but noninstructional issues as equipment needs, staff needs, financial resources required, facilities needs, and noninstructional needs of participants?
4. What *positive* but postinstructional outcomes of the planned learning experience can be anticipated? What *negative* postinstructional outcomes can be anticipated?
5. What estimates should be made about expected costs of the instructional program?
6. How accurate are the prerequisites previously identified?

Step Six: Formulating a Study Design

The sixth step in conducting a formative evaluation is to formulate an evaluation design. At this point, the central question is this: How should the formative evaluation be conducted?

An *evaluation design* is comparable in many respects to a *research design* (Campbell and Stanley, 1966), except that its purpose is to judge instructional materials and methods rather than make new discoveries. An evaluation design is thus the "plan of attack," the approach to be used in carrying out the evaluation. In formulating a design, be sure to (1) define key terms; (2) clarify the purpose and objectives of the evaluation; (3) provide a logical structure or series of procedures for assessing instructional materials and methods; (4) identify the evaluation's methodologies — such as survey(s), trial runs/rehearsals, and interviews; (5) identify population(s) to be studied and means by which representative subjects will be selected; and (6) summarize key standards by which the instructional materials/methods will be judged.

For practical guidance in clarifying issues of evaluation design, consult specialized publications such as American Society for Training and Development (1986d) and American Telephone and Telegraph Company (1987d).

Step Seven: Formulating a Management Plan to Guide the Study

The seventh and final step in conducting a formative evaluation is to formulate a management plan, a detailed schedule of procedures, events, or tasks to be completed in order to implement the evaluation design. A management plan should specify due dates and descriptions of the tangible products resulting from the evaluation. It should also clarify in detail how information will be collected, analyzed, and interpreted in the evaluation.

The importance of a management plan should be obvious. When a team is conducting a formative evaluation, the efforts of team members must be coordinated. A management plan helps avoid the frustration that results when team members are unsure of what must be done, who will perform each step, and where and when the steps will be performed.

There are essentially two ways to establish a management plan. One way is to prepare a complete list of the tasks to be performed, preferably in the sequence they are to be performed in. This list should be as complete and as detailed as possible, since this task-by-task management plan becomes the basis for dividing up the work of instructional designers, establishing timetables and deadlines, holding staff members responsible for their segments of project work, and (later) assessing individual and team effort.

A second way is to describe the final work product of the project and the final conditions existing on project completion. What should the final project report contain? Who will read it? What will happen as a result of it? How much and what kind of support will exist in the organization to facilitate successful introduction of instruction? Ask team members to explore these and similar questions before the formative evaluation plan is finalized, using their answers to organize the steps to achieve the final results.

Four Major Approaches to Conducting Formative Evaluation

Four major approaches may be used to conduct formative evaluations. Each has its own unique advantages and disadvantages. These approaches may be used separately or in combination. They are as follows:

1.   Expert reviews
2.   Management or executive rehearsals
3.   Individualized pretests and pilot tests
4.   Group pretests and pilot tests

We will describe each approach briefly below.

Expert Reviews

There are two kinds of expert reviews: (1) those focusing on the content of instruction, and (2) those focusing on delivery methods. Most instructional designers associate expert reviews with content evaluation.

Expert reviews focusing on content are, by definition, conducted by subject matter experts (SMEs), individuals whose education or experience on the instructional content cannot be disputed. Expert reviews ensure that the instructional package, often prepared by instructional design experts (IDEs) who may not be versed in the specialized subject matter, is consistent with current or desired work methods or state-of-the-art thinking on the subject matter. A key advantage of the expert review is that it ensures that materials are current, accurate, and credible. On the other hand, expert reviews may be difficult and expensive to conduct if "experts" on the subject matter cannot be located easily.

Begin an expert review by identifying "experts" from inside or outside the organization. Do that by accessing automated human resource information systems (skill inventories), contacting key management personnel, or conducting surveys. Identify experts outside the organization by asking colleagues, accessing automated sources such as the American Society for Training and Development's Membership Information Services, or compiling a bibliography of recent printed works on the subject and then contacting authors.

Once the experts have been identified, prepare a list of specific questions for them to address about the instructional materials. Use open-ended questions like those appearing in Exhibit 13.1. To ensure that the experts address every key question you want considered, use a highly structured checklist like that appearing in Exhibit 13.2. Expert reviews are rarely conducted in group settings; rather, each expert prepares an independent review. The results are then compiled and used by instructional designers to revise instructional materials.

Expert reviews that focus on delivery methods are sometimes more difficult to conduct than expert reviews focusing on content. The reason: "experts" on "delivery methods" are not that easy to find. One good approach is to ask "fresh" instructional designers, those who have not previously worked on the project, to review instructional materials for the delivery methods that are used. For each problematic issue the reviewers identify, ask them to note its location in the instructional materials and suggest revisions. Another good approach is to ask experienced instructors/tutors to review an instructional package. If the package is designed for group-paced, instructor-led delivery, offer a "dress rehearsal" and invite experienced instructors to evaluate it (Braskamp, Brandenburg, and Ory, 1984; Moos and Trickett, 1974). If the package is designed for individualized, learner-paced delivery, ask an experienced "tutor" to try out the material.

**Exhibit 13.1. A Worksheet on Instructional
Materials/Methods for Expert Reviewers.**

Directions for Reviewers: Use this worksheet to record your comments about the strengths and weaknesses of the instructional package with which you have been provided. (You should also have received information about the performance problem to be addressed and relevant information regarding the organization in which the instruction must operate.) For each question appearing in the left column below, provide an answer in the right column. When you are finished, return the completed worksheet to _____ at _____

(Name)　　　　　　　　　　　　　　　　　(Address)

_____ by _____ .

(Date)

Your comments will be helpful in revising, and thereby improving, the instructional package prior to widespread use. Attach more paper, if necessary.

Questions	*Answers*
1. How clearly do the instructional materials state the desired outcomes of instruction? (*Consider the instructional objectives for completeness, sequence, and priority.*)	
2. How well do the materials appear to match learner/trainee characteristics? (*Consider the clarity with which those characteristics are described and/or used.*)	
3. How well are the instructional materials based on the instructional objectives? (*Consider the match between objectives and materials.*)	
4. How complete and up to date is the content of the instructional package? (*Consider whether the instructional package is adequate for delivery in an individualized or group format and whether it reflects the latest thinking on the topic.*)	
5. How well are learners given opportunities to be informed of content, practice or apply what they learn, and receive feedback on how well they practiced or applied what they learned? (*Consider the sequence of instructional events within each part of the instructional package.*)	
6. What other issues did you notice that should be considered during revision?	

Management or Executive Rehearsals

Management or executive rehearsals are different from expert reviews. They build support by involving key stakeholders in preparation, and review, of instructional materials prior to widespread delivery. In a management rehearsal, an experienced instructor describes to supervisors and managers of the targeted trainees — or even to top managers — what content is covered by the instructional materials and how they are to be delivered. No attempt

Exhibit 13.2. A Checklist About Instructional
Materials/Methods for Expert Reviewers.

Directions for Reviewers: Use this checklist to review the instructional package with which you have been provided. For each question appearing in the left column below, check (✔) yes, no, or not applicable in the center column. If you check no, attach separate sheets to describe the problem and possible ways to revise the materials to address that problem. (Along with the instructional package, you should have also received information about the performance problem to be addressed and relevant information regarding the organization in which the instruction will be used.) When you are finished, return the completed checklist to _____

(Name)

at _____ by _____ .

(Address)   (Date)

By completing this checklist, you will help identify the means by which the instructional package can be improved prior to widespread delivery to the targeted learner.

		Response	
	Yes	*No*	*Not Applicable*
Question	*(✔)*	*(✔)*	*(✔)*
1. Do the instructional materials clearly state the desired outcomes of instruction?	( )	( )	( )
2. Do the instructional materials appear to match learner/trainee characteristics?	( )	( )	( )
3. Are the instructional materials clearly based on the instructional objectives?	( )	( )	( )
4. Is the content of the instructional package			
a. Complete?	( )	( )	( )
b. Up to date?	( )	( )	( )
5. Are learners given adequate opportunities to			
a. Receive information about the content?	( )	( )	( )
b. Practice or apply what they learn?	( )	( )	( )
c. Receive feedback on how well they practiced or applied what they learned?	( )	( )	( )
6. Are there other issues you noticed that should be considered during revision?	( )	( )	( )

If yes, describe:

is made to "train" the participants in the rehearsal; rather, the focus is on familiarizing them with its contents so that they can hold their employees accountable for on-the-job application. Rehearsals are advantageous for building management support for job-related application. However, they are problematic when key managers insist on presenting instruction consistent with their own idiosyncratic preferences rather than with current job methods or thinking on the subject.

To conduct a management or executive rehearsal, begin by identifying and inviting key managers to a short (thirty-minute to one-hour) "overview" of the materials. Some instructional designers prefer to limit invitations to specific job categories, such as top managers or middle managers. Others prefer to offer several different kinds of rehearsals.

Be sure to prepare a special agenda for the rehearsal. Make it a point to cover at least (1) the purpose of the instructional materials, (2) the performance objectives, (3) a description of targeted trainees, (4) evidence of need, (5) an overview of the instructional materials, (6) steps taken so far to improve the instruction, and (7) steps that members of this audience can take to encourage application of the learning in the workplace. Ask a colleague to attend the rehearsals to take notes about suggested revisions that stem from the discussions with participants.

Individualized Pretests and Pilot Tests

Individualized pretests, conducted on-site or off-site, constitute another approach to formative evaluation. Frequently recommended as a starting point for trying out and improving draft instructional materials, they focus on learners — rather than "experts'" or "managers'" — responses to instructional materials and methods (Dick and Carey, 1985). Most appropriate for individualized instructional materials, they are useful because they yield valuable information about how well the materials will work with the targeted learners. However, pretests and pilot tests do have their drawbacks: (1) they can be time consuming, and (2) they require learners' time away from work and may thus pose difficulties for supervisors and co-workers in today's lean-staffed, right-sized organizations.

Individualized pretests are intensive "tryouts" of instructional materials by one learner. They are conducted to find out just how well one participant fares with the instructional materials. A pretest is usually held in a "nonthreatening" or "off-the-job" environment, such as in a corporate training classroom or learning center. Instructional designers should meet with one person who is chosen randomly from a sample of the target population. That person should preferably be a lower-than-average performer, since average or better-than-average performers may succeed with instructional materials despite their poor quality (Lawson, 1974). Begin the session by explaining that the purpose of the pretest is not to "train" the participant but, instead, to test the material. Then deliver the material one-on-one. Each time the participant encounters difficulty, encourage the person to stop and point it out. Note these instances for future revision. Typically, instructional designers should direct their attention to the following issues: (1) How much does the participant like the material? (2) How much does the participant learn (as measured by tests)? (3) What concerns, if any, does the participant express about applying what he or she has learned on the job? Use the notes from this pretest to revise the instructional materials.

The individualized pilot test is another approach to formative evaluation. It is usually conducted after the pretest, focusing on participants' reactions to instructional materials in a setting comparable to that in which the instruction is to be delivered. Like pretests, pilot tests provide instructional designers with valuable information about how well the instructional materials work with representatives from the group of targeted trainees. However, their drawbacks are similar to those for pretests: (1) they can be time consuming, and (2) they require learners' time away from work.

Conduct a pilot test in a field setting, one resembling the environment in which the instructional materials are intended to be used. Proceed exactly as in a pretest: (1) select one person at random from a sample of the target population; (2) begin by explaining that the purpose of the pilot test is not to "train" the participant but, instead, to test the material; (3) progress through the material with the participant in a one-on-one delivery method; (4) note each instance in which the participant encounters difficulty with the material; (5) focus attention on how much the participant likes the material, how much the participant learns as measured by tests, and what concerns, if any, the participant expresses about applying on the job what he or she has learned; and (6) use the notes from the pilot test to revise instructional materials prior to widespread use.

Group Pretests and Pilot Tests

Group pretests resemble individualized pretests but are used to try out group-paced, instructor-led instructional materials. Their purpose is to find out just how well a randomly selected group of participants from the targeted trainees fares with the instructional materials. Held in a "safe" or "off-the-job" environment, such as in a corporate training classroom or learning center, the group pretest is handled precisely the same way as an individualized pretest.

A group pilot test resembles an individualized pilot test but is delivered to a group of learners from the targeted trainee group, not to one person at a time. Typically the next step following a group pretest, it focuses on participants' reactions to instructional materials in a field setting, just like its individualized counterpart. Administer attitude surveys to the learners about the experience — scales for developing such surveys can be found in Mahler (1974), Robinson and Shaver (1969), and Shaw and Wright (1967) — as well as paper-and-pencil or demonstrations tests to measure learning (Dick and Carey, 1985).

Using Approaches to Formative Evaluation

Each approach to formative evaluation is appropriate under certain conditions. Use an expert review to double-check the instructional content and recommended delivery methods. Use a management or executive rehearsal to build support for instruction, familiarize key stakeholders with its contents, and establish a basis for holding learners accountable on the job for what they learned off the job. Use individualized pretests and pilot tests to gain experience with, and improve, individualized instructional materials prior to widespread delivery; use group pretests and pilot tests to serve the same purpose in group-paced, instructor-led learning experiences.

Providing Feedback from Formative Evaluation

One final issue to consider when conducting formative evaluation is how to provide feedback to key stakeholders about the study and its results. Generally speaking, the shorter the report, the better. One good format is to prepare a formal report with an attached, and much shorter, executive summary.

The report should usually describe the study's purpose, key objectives, limitations, and any special issues to be addressed. It should also describe the study methodology (including methods of sample selection) and instruments prepared and used during the study, and should summarize the results. Include copies of the instructional materials that were reviewed, or at least summaries of them. Then describe the study's results, including descriptions of how well learners liked the material, how much they learned as measured by tests, what barriers to on-the-job application of the instruction they identified, and what revisions will be made to the materials (Morris, Fitz-Gibbon, and Freeman, 1987).

An executive summary should summarize the study's key results first and then briefly describe the study's background, purpose and objectives, and sample selection. It should be limited to no more than three pages— and it should preferably be one or two pages.

Formative product evaluation results are rarely presented to management, since their primary purpose is to guide instructional designers in the process of improving instructional materials. However, instructional designers can feed back the results of formative evaluation to management as a way of encouraging management to hold employees accountable on the job for what they learned.

Judging Formative Evaluations

According to *The Standards* (1986, p. 77), instructional designers should be able to "judge the appropriateness, comprehensiveness, and adequacy of statements of the evaluation plan" prepared by themselves or other designers. They should base their judgments on the contents of the plan, its implementation, and the revisions subsequently made to instructional materials. As in judging other steps of the instructional design process, a checklist (like the one shown in Exhibit 13.3) can be a useful decision aid.

Justifying Formative Evaluations

According to *The Standards* (1986), instructional designers should be able to justify the formative evaluations they conduct. As in other steps of the instructional design process, they should be accountable to other stakeholders—

Exhibit 13.3. A Checklist for Judging the Appropriateness, Comprehensiveness, and Adequacy of Statements of the Evaluation Plan and Revision Specifications.

Directions: After preparing a written evaluation plan and revision specifications for instructional materials, do a quality check by completing the following checklist. Answer each question appearing in the left column below by checking (✔) an appropriate response in the middle column. If necessary, make notes for revising materials in the right column.

Question	Response		Notes for Revision
	Yes	*No*	
Does the . . .	(✔)	(✔)	

1. Evaluation plan include

a.	A clear statement of purpose that is appropriate to the given situation?	( ) ( )	
b.	Data collection plans that are consistent with the purpose of the evaluation and the instruction and that are appropriate for the given situation?	( ) ( )	
c.	Data collection procedures that yield data as reliable and as valid as possible under the constraints imposed by the given situation?	( ) ( )	
d.	Plans that reflect the relative importance of different objectives within the instruction being evaluated?	( ) ( )	
e.	Plans for the analysis of the data that are appropriate for the type of data collected and the constraints imposed by the situation?	( ) ( )	
f.	Decision rules that will guide revisions based on the data?	( ) ( )	
g.	A description of the expected results consistent with the data collection techniques chosen and the specified analysis plans?	( ) ( )	
h.	Time estimates for the implementation of the evaluation plan that are realistic and appropriate for the given situation?	( ) ( )	
i.	Plans for communicating results to appropriate decision makers that are effective, efficient, consistent with the types of data collected, and congruent with the particulars of the given situation?	( ) ( )	

Exhibit 13.3. A Checklist for Judging the Appropriateness, Comprehensiveness, and Adequacy of Statements of the Evaluation Plan and Revision Specifications, Cont'd.

Question	Response		Notes for Revision
	Yes	No	
Does the . . .	(✔)	(✔)	
2. Specifications for revision:			
a. Directly reflect the data?	( )	( )	
b. Appear in the order recommended for implementation?	( )	( )	
c. Contain specific instructions for implementation?	( )	( )	

such as operating managers, learners, and other designers — and should be prepared to answer questions posed about formative evaluation by key stakeholders. Four questions are perhaps most often posed.

Question One: "Why Is It Necessary to Conduct Formative Evaluation?"

To answer this question, be prepared to provide — and stand behind — the purpose(s) of the formative evaluation. Try to anticipate, if possible, any objections to the purpose(s) that may be raised. Have responses prepared for on-the-spot justification.

Question Two: "What Valuable, Measurable Results Will Stem from the Study?"

Be sure to clarify the performance objectives of instruction for the benefit of the audience(s). Explain the value of the formative evaluation results in terms of their relationship to the performance objectives.

Question Three: "How Much Will the Study Cost?"

Be prepared to justify the formative evaluation on the basis of costs and benefits. Be sure to prepare a budget for the evaluation following preparation of the management plan to guide it. But go a step further: prepare to discuss why *each* step in the formative evaluation is necessary. And be ready to point out that, without formative evaluation, instructional delivery may be pointless because the learners may waste valuable time with untested materials.

Question Four: "How Soon Will the Evaluation Be Completed?"

Use the task-by-task estimates provided in the management plan to prepare a realistic time frame for study completion. Be prepared to say when the instructional materials will be ready to deliver *following* the evaluation.

In short, be prepared to justify every step taken in planning the formative evaluation, carrying it out, and taking actions based on it.

Conclusion

The final step in the model of the instructional design process we unveiled in Chapter Four, formative evaluation provides a means by which to improve instructional materials before they are released for widespread use. In this chapter, we clarified assumptions about formative evaluation, defined key terms associated with it, provided a case study to dramatize important issues in developing a formative evaluation plan, described the steps in developing a formative evaluation plan and approaches to implementing the plan, and offered advice about judging and justifying formative evaluations.

In the remaining chapters of this book, we turn to competencies linked to managing and communicating about instructional design projects. In the next chapter, we focus on the instructional management system that is essential to "get trainees to the training, get them started in the right place, track them through the program, keep records of their test scores for each course (and for all the courses they have taken), and provide some diagnostic information for trainees having difficulty" (*The Standards,* 1986, p. 79).

PART V

Managing
Instructional Design Projects
Successfully

CHAPTER FOURTEEN

Designing
the Instructional Management
System

"Merely having good training is not enough," note the authors of *The Standards* (1986, p. 79), since "there must be a logistical support system." An effective logistical support system, known as an *instructional management system,* ensures that

- Entrance into the instruction is quick and easy.
- Learners entering instruction are diagnosed as to their readiness.
- Learners are directed to appropriate sections with a minimum of time and effort.
- Each step, section, or experience within the instruction is provided with transitions and references.
- Each instructional element is easily identified.
- Competence is documented so that management and learners know precisely what is required.
- The learner's exit from the instruction is diagnostic of future needs.
- Recordkeeping is adequate for both individual and organizational purposes.

But how are these requirements of an effective instructional management system put in place? In this chapter, we answer that question for each requirement listed above. We begin with a brief case study to dramatize key issues and then address each requirement. Finally, we offer advice to instructional designers about judging and justifying instructional management systems.

Designing an Instructional Management System: A Case Study

Georganna Smithson is an instructional designer employed by a private vendor under contract to a small manufacturing firm. Smithson's client has recently established a series of planned instructional experiences using the model of instructional systems design described in this book. It is now time to design an instructional management system.

Smithson reads this chapter and prepares a worksheet (see Exhibit 14.1) to help her structure her thinking. She uses the worksheet as an agenda in a meeting with representatives of client management and other instructional designers on her team. They find that, by answering the questions posed on the worksheet, they are able to meet the minimum criteria for effective instructional management systems.

Ensuring That Entrance into Instruction Is Quick and Easy

By following the steps in the model of the instructional design process, instructional designers should have ensured that the instruction is useful and can have a demonstrated impact on improving employee performance. But

Exhibit 14.1. A Worksheet on the Instructional Management System.

Directions: Use this worksheet to help you, your client, and other instructional designers on your team structure your thinking. For each criterion for an effective instructional management system described in the left column below, jot down some ideas in the right column about how you can meet the criterion. There are no right or wrong answers in any absolute sense, though some answers may be more right or wrong, depending on the organization.

Criteria for effective instructional management systems	*What ideas do you have about how to meet the criteria?*
1. Entrance into instruction should be quick and easy.	
2. Entering learners should be diagnosed as to their readiness for the instruction.	
3. Learners should be directed to appropriate sections of instruction with minimum time and effort.	
4. Each step, section, or experience within the instruction should be provided with transitions and references.	
5. Each instructional element should be easily identified in terms of both content and purpose.	
6. Competence should be documented in such a way that both management and learners know precisely what is required, when, and the standards applicable.	
7. Exit from the instruction should be well documented and diagnostic of future needs.	
8. Recordkeeping should be adequate for both individual and organizational purposes.	

practicality is not enough: the targeted learners must be attracted to the instruction and participation must be made as convenient as possible for them. In other words, instructional designers must be able to *market* their products and services. To that end, they should start by paying keen attention to four key issues (McCarthy, 1978):

1. Place
2. Promotion
3. Product
4. Price

Each provides clues to the appropriate marketing of instruction (American Society for Training and Development, 1986f).

Place

To make it easy for targeted participants to enter instruction, instructional designers should consider this question: *How can instruction be delivered at a location, or locations, convenient to the targeted learners?* To answer that question, first identify the geographical locations of the learners by doing some rudimentary market research. Are most of the learners grouped closely together in one work location? several identifiable work locations? Are they spread all over the map?

Next decide how to make the instruction available *conveniently*. There are, of course, a range of options. For instance, group-oriented, instructor-led, or individually oriented, learner-directed instruction can be offered in one or more locations: (1) on-site at key work locations where prospective participants are centralized, (2) off-site at key work locations, (3) on-site at key locations that are geographically positioned between other locations, (4) off-site at key locations that are geographically positioned near other locations, and (5) on a regional basis.

Remember one important principle: *the more delivery formats in which instruction is made available, the greater the likelihood that the broadest audience will be attracted.* There are at least two reasons why this is true. First, learners differ in their learning styles and preferences and therefore differ in the formats—group oriented or individually oriented—that they prefer (Kolb, 1984; Smith, 1982). Second, individual learners face different constraints on their time, both on and off the job. Some have time to progress through instruction on the job—and prefer to do so. Some have time to progress through instruction off the job—and prefer that. However, others have no time to progress through instruction on or off the job or have no desire to do it at all. By making instruction available in multiple delivery formats, instructional designers increase the likelihood that the unique constraints each targeted learner must cope with are minimized.

Promotion

To make it easy for targeted participants to enter instruction, consider promotion next. Promotion, of course, means communicating with targeted participants so they are aware that the right kind of instruction to meet their
needs is available at a convenient location and at a reasonable cost. To consider promotion, pose this question: *How can participants be alerted to the avail-
ability of instruction in ways that will attract them?* To answer this question, begin by identifying the learning need(s). For instance: (1) What exactly is
the need? Is the aim to correct past performance deficiencies, address present
performance problems, or avert future problems? Are people being initially
trained, retrained, or educated for future advancement? How might the participants view the need—that is, "What's in it for me?" (2) How important
is the need? Is it particularly keen for everyone in the organization or only
for workers in specific departments or work units? (3) How much time is
available to meet the need? Is time an important issue? Are there good reasons, from the standpoint of individuals or the organization, that instruction be delivered before, during, or after some planned change effort—such
as the introduction of new equipment, work methods, new leaders, or new
products and services? When these questions about time have been answered,
consider how the targeted participants can best be reached. For instance,
what methods might work best: personal selling? organizational selling? sales
promotion methods? a blend of two or more promotion methods?

    Personal selling is direct, face-to-face contact between instructional de-
signers—or other representatives of a human resource development department—and prospective learners or their immediate supervisors. Quite expensive since it usually involves travel to identifiable work locations of targeted
learners, personal selling is appropriate when immediate feedback from the
targeted learners about instruction must be secured.

    As in all promotion, there are essentially three basic steps to personal
selling (McCarthy, 1978). First, secure the willingness of learners to participate in the instruction by pointing out to them—and their immediate supervisors—the advantages of participation. Second, help learners through the
enrollment process by coaching them on how to complete any necessary
forms. Make sure they actually enroll. Third, support them so that they
do participate. Continue to stress the advantages of participation to them
before, during, and after the planned learning experiences.

    Organizational selling is geared to large groups of people in the organi-
zation. Less expensive than personal selling, it relies on advertising devices
like instructional catalogues, brochures, newsletter articles, bulletin board
notices, announcements by supervisors, specially prepared newsletters is-
sued by the human resource development department, and other methods.
Appropriate for reaching large groups of learners in the shortest time, it is
particularly useful when the targeted participants are geographically scattered.

    Sales promotion methods are, for the most part, much neglected in instructional marketing. McCarthy (1978, p. 404) defines them as "those promotional activities, other than personal selling, advertising, and publicity, that encourage consumer purchasing and dealer effectiveness, such as displays, shows and expositions, demonstrations, and other nonrecurring promotional efforts." They are akin to organizational selling in that they secure much attention very quickly.

To carry out sales promotion methods for marketing instruction, consider sponsoring "information fairs" about instruction in-house, one-time "walkthroughs" of instruction for groups within the organization, and give-away items such as mugs, thermos bottles, matchboxes, and pens (Rothwell and Brandenburg, 1990b). If they will not work, try a small-scale lottery. Use give-away items and lotteries as vehicles to advertise instruction. While some instructional designers might dub give-aways or lotteries as "hokey," realize that they can, and do, work!

Product

To attract targeted participants, always consider the *product*. By *product*, of course, we do not mean instruction by itself. Rather, we are referring to the capacity of instruction to help learners rectify past performance problems, meet present job performance requirements, prepare for future job needs, and prepare for increasing responsibility and advancement. In other words, product refers to everything having to do with an instructional experience. This includes the opportunity provided to employees and their supervisors during sign-up to discuss each employee's future and the organization's goals, the social experience of group instruction, the challenge of individualized instruction, and the valuable feedback that postinstructional evaluation provides to individuals.

Pose this question when considering product: *How can instruction be packaged in a way that will appeal to the needs of learners and the organization?* Consider that question relative to the types of learners who may participate in instruction.

Recall that individual learners can be classified into three basic types (Houle, 1961; Knowles, 1984): (1) *the goal-oriented,* who use instruction to satisfy an immediate need; (2) *the activity-oriented,* who use instruction to find social support while they struggle with problems; and (3) *the learning-oriented,* who seek instructional experiences for their own sake. Each category of individual learner provides clues about how to market instruction, since each suggests what learners seek from it.

Supervisors of targeted learners may be classified as learners are. Goal-oriented supervisors use instruction instrumentally as a tool to help them prepare their people for present or future change or cope with past change. Activity-oriented supervisors use instructions as a reward, a way of giving their people a "break" for work well done. While instructional designers may strongly reject activity-oriented motives, be aware that they do exist. This should be considered when marketing instruction. Learning-oriented supervisors encourage their employees to participate in instructional experiences for the sake of learning itself, to give them a chance to familiarize themselves with new ideas.

Learners and supervisors are thus prospective instructional consumers whose needs and wants must be satisfied if they are to be attracted to instruction and participate in it willingly. Instructional designers face the challenge of appealing to all types of learners and supervisors. To that end, the following questions must be addressed to market instruction: (1) How does instruction meet a demonstrable need of the organization and/or learners? (2) What opportunities for social support and/or networking will the instructional experience open up to participants? (3) How does the instructional experience furnish new ideas to learners, even those who may feel they are familiar with the subject matter?

Price

It has been said that "nothing in life is free," so the *price* of instruction is always an issue in marketing it. Even when instruction is "free" to all learners, there are organizational costs associated with instructor time, learner time, facilities, equipment, and supplies. When considering price, pose this question: *How can instruction be priced at a level that will attract participation?* To address this question, identify possible competitors — that is, organizations that offer comparable instruction. Locate competitors by scanning the catalogues of local colleges and vocational schools and by accessing such computerized data bases as the American Society for Training and Development's TRAINET or the Seminar Information Service (SIS) to identify seminars offered by profit-making vendors. Then compare the content of offerings and their prices to in-house experiences. If in-house price and/or content compares favorably to competitors, publicize that fact in marketing efforts. Let prospective participants research the differences themselves, if they wish. In fact, help them do so to demonstrate that the price of in-house instruction compares favorably to other sources.

Ensuring That Learners Entering Instruction Are Diagnosed for Their Readiness

Once learners have been enrolled, turn attention to diagnosing their readiness for instruction. Diagnose learner readiness by making sure that they have satisfied prerequisites and that they are motivated to learn.

Have Learners Satisfied Prerequisites?

For an instructional management system to work effectively, there must be a means in place to assess how well learners have satisfied the necessary prerequisites *before* they participate in instruction. One way to do that is to screen learners during formal enrollment. Use an enrollment form or application blank and ask learners to document how they have met the prerequisites. Prerequisites may include minimum levels of education, experience, or past training. Learners may also be required to provide testimonials from knowledgeable people to attest that prerequisites have been met.

Another way to screen for prerequisites is to administer proficiency examinations to learners. These examinations are used to measure the learners' mastery of prerequisites. Examinations may be administered by paper-and-pencil or by demonstrations of performance (American Society for Training and Development, 1989f).

How Motivated Are the Learners?

It is folly to ignore learners' willingness to participate in instruction, since there is a direct and undeniable relationship between learner motivation and achievement (Brown, 1989). The trouble is that assessing and influencing learner motivation is by no means quick or easy (Wlodkowski, 1985). However, several approaches can be used. These approaches can be classified by timing. Some may be used before the instructional experience, some may be used during the experience, and some may be used after it.

Before the experience, simply ask the learners how interested they are in participating in the instruction and what they hope to gain through participation. Do that by including a question on training applications or enrollment forms. As an alternative, send them an attitude questionnaire to complete and return before they begin instruction. (An example of such a questionnaire appears in Exhibit 14.2.) Use the results to assess the level of learner motivation and to determine methods by which to increase it.

During the instructional experience, ask learners what they hope to gain from the instructional experience and then, as instruction is presented, tie each major point to learner interests (Knowles, 1980). Alternatively, ask learners how much the key points are useful to them—and why they are. These approaches will help to crystallize the value of the instruction to the learners.

After the instructional experience, ask learners whether their interest in the subject has increased, and how they can apply what they learned on their jobs. Use their responses to assess the learners' motivation. If the instructional experience is subsequently repeated, describe to learners how previous individuals or groups of learners reacted to the instruction, perceived its value, and subsequently applied it to their jobs. Use these testimonials, then, to motivate learners by stressing the value of instruction to them.

Ensuring That Learners Are Directed to an Appropriate Section with Minimum Time and Effort

If learners have demonstrated sufficient mastery of the subject matter, they may have to complete only a portion of it. A *section* is part of an instructional

Exhibit 14.2. A Survey Questionnaire to Assess Learner Motivation.

Directions to Participants: You are enrolled in instruction on (*topic description*). As part of your preparation, please complete the questionnaire that follows. Read each statement in the left column and then circle a number appearing in the right column that best summarizes your feelings. Use this scale:

1 = Strongly disagree
2 = Disagree
3 = Neutral
4 = Agree
5 = Strongly agree

When you finish, please return the completed questionnaire to _____
                                                                        (name)
at _____ by _____ .
                          (address)   (date)
Thank you for your cooperation!

Question	Response				
	Strongly Disagree 1	Disagree 2	Neutral 3	Agree 4	Strongly Agree 5
1. I am highly enthusiastic about participating in this instructional experience.	1	2	3	4	5
2. Based on my past experience, I am sure the instructor or tutor will help increase my interest in this subject.	1	2	3	4	5
3. I find that I enjoy participating in any instructional experience just for the sake of learning something new.	1	2	3	4	5
4. I once experienced a job-related problem that is associated with the subject of this instruction.	1	2	3	4	5
5. I am now experiencing a job-related problem that is associated with the subject of this instruction.	1	2	3	4	5
6. I soon expect to be experiencing a problem, on or off the job, that is related to the subject of this instruction.	1	2	3	4	5
7. Whenever I attend instruction, I find that I learn more from other participants than from the instructor or handouts.	1	2	3	4	5
8. I really find it helpful to discuss job-related problems I face with other people.	1	2	3	4	5
9. Whenever I attend instruction, I always have a clear sense of what I "need."	1	2	3	4	5
10. Whenever I attend instruction, I ask questions until my need for help on a problem is satisfied.	1	2	3	4	5

---

11. If I don't learn anything else, the one thing I *do* want to learn when I participate in this instructional experience is (*fill in the blank*): _____

Exhibit 14.2. A Survey Questionnaire to Assess Learner Motivation, Cont'd.

---

12. The one thing that really interferes with my learning is (*fill in the blank*): _____

Thank you for your cooperation!

(Please send the completed questionnaire to _____

at _____ by _____ .)

---

experience — either one unit or lesson. Use instructional flowcharts, decision charts, advanced organizers, enabling objectives, proficiency examinations, or a combination of these methods to direct learners to appropriate sections of an instructional experience, depending on their level of subject mastery.

An *instructional flowchart* illustrates the flow of lessons or topics in an instructional experience. It is frequently used by advocates of Gestalt learning theory to provide learners with an overview of an entire instructional experience before they proceed sequentially through individual parts (Sredl and Rothwell, 1987). An example of such a flowchart appears in Figure 14.1.

A *decision chart* presents prospective learners with an array of choices for entering instruction, based on their demonstrated proficiency. It allows the learner to decide quickly where to begin instruction. An example of such a decision chart appears in Table 14.1.

An *advanced organizer* can be understood as a narrative summary or overview of instruction, although other interpretations are possible (Ausubel, 1962). By giving learners advanced organizers for *each* unit or lesson, they can draw their own conclusions about whether they need to proceed through it.

Figure 14.1. An Example of a Simplified Instructional Flowchart.

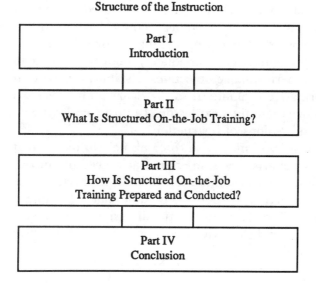

Structure of the Instruction

Table 14.1. An Example of a Simplified Decision Chart.

	If you already know, or have demonstrated proficiency with, the following	THEN	Move on to this part
1.	Familiarity with the difference between structured and unstructured on-the-job training (lesson 1)		Lesson 2
2.	Knowledge of the four steps in structured on-the-job training (lesson 2)		Lesson 3
3.	How to "tell" learners (lesson 3)		Lesson 4
4.	How to "show" learners (lesson 4)		Lesson 5
5.	How to ask learners to "do" the task to demonstrate competency with it (lesson 5)		Lesson 6
6.	How to "follow up" with learners, providing them with feedback on how well they perform (lesson 6)		Lesson 7
7.	How to demonstrate all four steps of structured on-the-job training (lesson 7)		Skip the entire instructional experience

An *enabling objective* is, of course, directly related to a terminal (or end-of-instruction) performance objective. It *enables* the learner to master part of a terminal objective. Learners, or instructors, may use enabling objectives to guide entry to instruction. Learners who have demonstrated mastery of some, but not all, enabling objectives may be channeled to begin instruction at the point they need to through successful completion of proficiency examinations or other methods.

Proficiency examinations are pretests, often administered prior to instructional entry, that assess a learner's level of knowledge, skill, or ability and that are specifically intended to channel a learner through instruction to begin at an appropriate point. They are frequently used at the outset of computer-based or text-based programmed instructional lessons, though they may also be used at the outset of group-paced, instructor-led instruction. Administer the proficiency examination immediately following the statement of each lesson's terminal performance objectives. Establish an arbitrary cutoff score, based on formative evaluation, so that learners who achieve all items correctly can move on to the next lesson. In this way, learners can be directed to appropriate sections of instruction.

Of course, you may wish to combine two or more approaches—instructional flowcharts, decision charts, advanced organizers, enabling objectives, or proficiency examinations—to direct learners to appropriate sections of an instructional experience. While that will require expenditure of more up-front effort for an instructional designer, it is likely to ensure that learners will, in fact, be effectively channeled to the point at which they should begin instruction.

Ensuring That Each Step, Section, or Experience Within the Instruction Is Provided with Transitions and References

Instructional designers should ensure that each step, section, or experience within instruction is provided with transitions and references. A *transition* is a link from past to future learning.

Appropriate transitions depend, for the most part, on how performance objectives have been sequenced. Recall that performance objectives may be sequenced in several ways. Some sequencing possibilities and corresponding transitions are listed below.

Sequencing	*Appropriate Transitions*
Chronologically	Use time as the basis for transitions. Clarify when each task, step, or procedure should occur.
Topically	Simply explain how one topic relates to another.
Whole-to-part	Remind learners of the whole (model, procedure) before proceeding to a description of each individual part.
Part-to-whole	Remind learners of previous parts before proceeding into descriptions of subsequent parts.
Known-to-unknown	Use learner knowledge and skill in building-block fashion.
Unknown-to-known	Begin with an upending or unsettling experience, using it to stimulate learner interest in a search for solutions.
Step-by-step	Remind learners of the last step before proceeding to a description of each subsequent step.
Part-to-part-to-part	Relate each part to other parts.
General-to-specific	Begin with a very general description, moving to specialized parts based on learner interests.

Instructional sequence may thus provide important clues about appropriate transitions.

A *reference* is a link to materials outside those of the instructional experience. For instance, learners may be furnished with up-to-date bibliographies of books, articles, videotapes, and other material in case they wish to pursue learning on their own. Be sure to clarify whether the materials are available through the organization, or whether learners must seek out the materials on their own time or at their own expense.

Ensuring That Each Instructional Element Is Easily Identified

Be sure to identify each part of instruction, clarifying its purpose (*why is it there?*) and its content (*what does the instruction cover?*). If the instruction is to be delivered in print media, use headings effectively to identify each instructional element. If instruction is delivered in other media, be sure to clarify purpose and summarize content briefly *before* presenting it to learners.

Ensuring That Competence Is Documented

Be sure to document that learners have successfully completed the instruction. Do that by testing them and then keeping records of the test scores. Alternatively, instructional designers may wish to have designated subject matter experts, line managers, or union officials question or observe the learners' performance and then document in writing that the learners have reached a predefined, acceptable level of competence based on performance measures.

Ensuring That the Learner's Exit from Instruction Is Diagnostic of Future Needs

Instructional designers should make an effort to ensure that each learner's completion of instruction is recognized and used diagnostically in assessing future needs.

First, establish some means by which to recognize or reward learners for successful completion of instructional experiences. For example, prepare training certificates—or, if the budget allows, elaborate engraved plaques—for each learner. Issue them routinely in a "graduation ceremony" on completion of instruction. In this way, learners feel encouraged—and they may display the certificates or plaques, thereby providing free promotion for the instruction.

In addition, diagnose future learner needs. Plan to do that at the time learners complete each instructional experience. More specifically, determine whether a future need will exist for each learner, depending on expected changes in organizational strategy, job requirements, or technology. One method: perform a strategic needs assessment at the *end* of the instructional experience (Rothwell, 1984; Rothwell and Kazanas, 1989). Another method: ask learners to have a follow-up discussion with their supervisors about the value of the instruction for their careers (American Society for Training and Development, 1985e).

Ensuring That Recordkeeping Is Adequate for Individuals and the Organization

Without information about the individual instructional needs of each learner in the organization, much time and effort can be wasted. After all, learners may be routinely scheduled to participate in instruction that is unnecessary for them.

There are several ways of keeping records of individual participation in instructional experiences. One is through personnel records or human resource information systems. In some organizations, managers prefer to keep all records — job application, information about salary, training, off-the-job education, performance appraisal, disciplinary notices, and others — together in one place.

Personnel records are usually paper files. Historically, organizations have retained extensive paper files on employees. Indeed, the government-prompted necessity for keeping these files was one of the earliest factors that led organizations to establish human resource management departments (Eilbirt, 1959). However, not all organizations keep personnel records of employee participation in off-the-job or on-the-job training, off-the-job educational courses, and conferences.

Human resource information systems are developed to systematically collect, store, maintain, retrieve, and validate data needed by an organization about its human resources. They typically include information about employee security, recruiting, education/training, human resource planning, employee skills, employment records, benefits, wages and salaries, labor relations, medical concerns, and safety (Milkovich and Glueck, 1985). They may, therefore, be used to retain records about employee completion of instruction. Unfortunately, one of the authors of this book had an opportunity to view, firsthand, the two best-selling, state-of-the-art human resource information systems currently available off the shelf for mainframe use (and costing, at this writing, more than $100,000 each). Neither is adequate for keeping extensive employee training records.

Skill inventories are systematic lists of employee skills in organizational settings. They customarily provide information about individuals' work experiences, educational attainment, proficiency in foreign languages, performance appraisal ratings, employment dates, and other information. Although they have been frequently used, they are by no means easy to develop or maintain (Rothwell and Kazanas, 1988b; Walker, 1980). They can be used to keep records of employee participation in instructional experiences (Gould, 1986).

Training record systems may be maintained separate from, or as part of, personnel files, human resource information systems, or skill inventories. Dosher (1987) distinguishes between three parts of a comprehensive record-keeping system. The first part, the training center, provides course and cost data and class equipment requirements, class rosters, and enrollment status by class. The second part, the student center, provides information for prospective trainees. It gives them the ability to search for available courses, obtain information on specific courses, enroll in instruction, check on their enrollment status, change their enrollment status, or even review the evaluations of courses. The third part, the data bases, "provide student data from personnel files and receive financial and student enrollment data" (Dosher, 1987, p. 82).

Various formats can be used to maintain instructional records. At minimum, most organizations will want to have one system to keep employee

**Exhibit 14.3. A Checklist for Judging the Appropriateness,
Comprehensiveness, and Adequacy of the Instructional
Management System.**

Directions: Judge the appropriateness, comprehensiveness, and adequacy of an instructional management system using this checklist. Answer each question appearing in the left column below by checking (✓) an appropriate response in the middle column. If necessary, make notes in the right column on any aspect of the instructional management system that, in your opinion, deserves improvement.

Question	*Response*		*Notes for Revision*
Does the organization have in place an instructional management system that ensures that . . .	*Yes* (✓)	*No* (✓)	
1. Entrance into the instruction is quick and easy?	( )	( )	
2. Entering learners are diagnosed as to their readiness for the instruction?	( )	( )	
3. Learners are directed to appropriate sections with a minimum of time and effort?	( )	( )	
4. Each step, section, or experience within the instruction is provided with transitions and references?	( )	( )	
5. Each instructional element is easily identified in terms of both content and purpose?	( )	( )	
6. Competence is documented in such a way that both management and learners know precisely what is required, when, and the standards applicable?	( )	( )	
7. Exit from the instruction is well documented and diagnostic of future needs?	( )	( )	
8. Recordkeeping is adequate for both individual and organizational purposes?	( )	( )	

information and a separate system to keep course/instructor information. Of course, they should be integrated such that a user can find a direct relationship between attendance in various courses and individual employees.

In some organizations, there may be reasons to tie together personnel records, skill inventories, and training record systems — and thus to use a combination of the approaches mentioned above. Instructional designers must lay the foundation for recordkeeping by systematically analyzing intended *uses* for records on employee participation in instruction.

Judging an Instructional Management System

According to *The Standards* (1986, p. 81), instructional designers should be able to "judge the appropriateness, comprehensiveness, and adequacy of a selection of an instructional management system." This judgment should be based on how well the system meets the criteria for an effective instructional management system described previously in this chapter.

Instructional designers may find it helpful to use a checklist as a decision aid on those occasions when they must judge the appropriateness, comprehensiveness, and adequacy of an instructional management system. An example of such a checklist appears in Exhibit 14.3.

Justifying an Instructional Management System

According to *The Standards* (1986, p. 82), instructional designers should be able to justify decisions they have made when constructing or judging an instructional management system. To that end, they should be prepared to explain to other people — such as other instructional designers, operating managers, or learners — why the instructional management system was established as it was. For this reason, instructional designers should keep notes about what they have done, and why, so that they can justify their decisions to others when necessary.

Conclusion

In this chapter, we began with a brief case study to dramatize issues associated with instructional management systems. We then described how to address each key requirement for an effective system. Finally, we offered a few words of advice about judging and justifying such a system. In the next chapter, we turn to a related subject — planning and monitoring instructional design projects.

CHAPTER FIFTEEN

Planning and Monitoring
Instructional Design Projects

According to *The Standards* (1986, p. 83), "instructional design projects are complex undertakings. Even the simplest ones involve one instructional designer, one subject matter expert, and one production person. Complex projects involve large teams of instructional designers, several subject matter experts at different locations, complex production and delivery systems (like interactive videodisc) and teams of production specialists." It is therefore important to develop a plan as a basis for monitoring the progress of each project.

In this chapter, we will describe how to develop a project management plan for an instructional design project, beginning with a brief discussion about the background of project planning. We will then describe key issues to consider when planning and monitoring projects. We will conclude the chapter with a few words about judging and justifying project plans.

The Background of Project Planning

Project management as it is known today first emerged in the aerospace industry (Glueck and Jauch, 1984). It was introduced as an efficient and effective way to assemble, in a short time, a team of people whose combined knowledge and expertise matched up to unique situational and technical demands posed by a given work assignment (Cleland, 1964). Since that time, project management has been widely used whenever it has been necessary to assemble groups of technical or professional employees — such as groups of medical doctors, lawyers, engineers, accountants, or combinations of all these.

Differences Between Project Management and Traditional Management

Project management differs in key respects from traditional management, which is typified by a *line and staff organization*. In a traditional organizational structure, *line managers* exert direct authority over people. They are action-takers, responsible for getting the work out. They issue orders, make decisions, and allocate rewards. A production manager in manufacturing exemplifies line management. *Staff managers,* on the other hand, support and advise line managers. In the simplest sense, they are idea-makers and are responsible for seeing to it that decisions made by line managers are well advised. They do not have the authority to issue orders, make decisions, or allocate rewards; rather, their social power stems from expert knowledge of their specialty (French and Raven, 1959). A human resource manager exemplifies staff management. Conflict frequently arises between line and staff managers, particularly because staff managers have historically tended to be younger, less experienced, and better educated than their line management counterparts (Dalton, 1969).

Unique Challenges Posed by Project Management

Project management poses unique challenges unlike those encountered in traditional line and staff organizations.

First, project members are assembled on the basis of their ability to grapple with a temporary problem or complete a unique work assignment. Team members may not have worked with each other before — and may never work with each other again. The team leader must be skillful in facilitating group dynamics and teambuilding, helping members of the group proceed quickly through the forming and storming stages in which all groups progress (American Society for Training and Development, 1987e; Gibson, Ivancevich, and Donnelly, 1985).

Second, project managers lack the long-term authority over people that is effectively wielded by supervisors in line and staff organizations. They are only temporary bosses. Hence, project managers must be very skillful in negotiating with people and influencing them (Hodgetts, 1968; Wilemon and Cicero, 1970).

Third, project managers exercise greater control and enjoy greater flexibility over their work assignments than most traditional managers do. As the workload necessitates, they can add or subtract team members, sharing expertise with other project managers. That is usually difficult in line and staff organizations.

Project planning and managing thus poses its own challenges and frustrations. Its unique strengths make it well suited to the demands of instructional design work, in which it is usually necessary to pair up experts in instructional design with experts in subject matter and instructional media production.

For more information on project management, consult Frame (1987) and Hennessy and Hennessy (1989).

Key Features of Project Planning and Controlling

All projects share certain common features: they must be planned, scheduled, and controlled. Figure 15.1 illustrates key project tasks, means of accomplishing tasks, and timing of tasks.

As part of project planning, instructional designers must also prepare a timeline or chart and a budget, establish a control system to monitor the time of instructional designers and track project accomplishments, establish methods for allocating funds, and plan equipment and facility requirements. Each activity deserves closer consideration.

Preparing a Timeline

When developing a project management plan, instructional designers should be able to prepare "some form of timeline or chart which includes key development milestones, and interim and final deadlines" (*The Standards*, 1986, p. 84). Such timelines or charts serve several purposes.

First, they focus attention on identifying procedures—and specific tasks and subtasks within procedures—that are to be performed during the project. Second, they help allocate responsibilities by identifying *who* is to do *what*

Figure 15.1. Planning, Scheduling, and Controlling Instructional Design Projects.

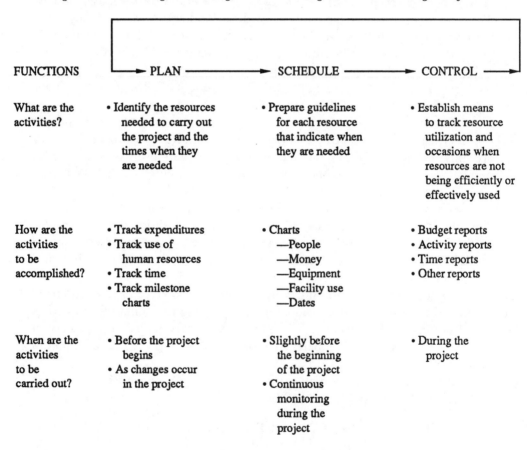

FUNCTIONS	PLAN →	SCHEDULE →	CONTROL →
What are the activities?	• Identify the resources needed to carry out the project and the times when they are needed	• Prepare guidelines for each resource that indicate when they are needed	• Establish means to track resource utilization and occasions when resources are not being efficiently or effectively used
How are the activities to be accomplished?	• Track expenditures • Track use of human resources • Track time • Track milestone charts	• Charts —People —Money —Equipment —Facility use —Dates	• Budget reports • Activity reports • Time reports • Other reports
When are the activities to be carried out?	• Before the project begins • As changes occur in the project	• Slightly before the beginning of the project • Continuous monitoring during the project	• During the project

Source: Adapted from Gaither, N. *Production and Operations Management: A Problem-Solving and Decision-Making Approach.* Hinsdale, Ill.: Dryden Press, 1980, p. 311.

by *when*. Third, they provide the basis for controlling project time, budgeting money, and estimating staffing requirements. Fourth, they minimize the work needed to complete the project successfully, since they allow the project manager to identify efficient ways to cut corners while achieving effective results. Fifth, they provide a basis for estimating project duration. Hence, preparation of a project timeline or chart requires members of an instructional design team to think through project activities before they begin.

Instructional design work usually involves separate teams working on different, but related, projects. However, there are different types of projects. Each requires an appropriate timeline or chart, designed especially for the project. For example, *performance analysis* is one kind of instructional design project. Described at length in Chapter Two, performance analysis clarifies what the performance problem is and what alternative performance improvement strategies can be used to address the problem. In carrying out a performance analysis project, a team of instructional designers conducts a background investigation. That means they clarify what is happening, identify what should be happening, assess the difference, consider the importance of that difference, identify possible causes of the problem, identify possible performance improvement strategies, and select a strategy. Other steps may be added (Rothwell and Kazanas, 1988b).

The second type of project is *needs assessment,* described at length in Chapter Four. Sometimes it is conducted by the same team that conducted the initial performance analysis. But since needs assessment is often a massive undertaking and is crucial for providing information about the instruction necessary to address a performance problem, it is more often carried out by a team different from the one conducting the initial performance analysis. As a result, needs assessment becomes a separate project in which the following questions should be addressed:

1. What results are desired from the needs assessment?
2. Whose needs are to be assessed?
3. What methods will be used to select a representative group of people from the target audience?
4. By what means will information be collected?
5. What management approvals are necessary to collect that information?
6. How will the information collected during the needs assessment be analyzed?
7. How will instructional needs be identified from results of data collection and analysis?

Some needs assessment projects may encompass assessments of relevant characteristics of learners (Chapter Five), analysis of relevant characteristics of the work setting (Chapter Six), and job, task, or content analysis (Chapter Seven).

The third project type takes up where needs assessment leaves off. Called *preinstructional planning* and described in Chapters Eight to Eleven, such projects have a fourfold purpose: (1) preparation of performance objectives, (2) development of performance measurements, (3) sequencing of performance objectives, and (4) specification of instructional strategies.

The fourth type of project takes up where preinstructional planning leaves off. It involves the *preparation of instructional materials*. Members of an instructional design team work together, using the blueprints prepared in earlier steps, to create the materials that will help narrow or close an identified performance gap. The steps in this type of project were described in Chapter Twelve.

The fifth type of project is *formative evaluation*. It may be combined with the design of an instructional management system, though that may be a sixth type of project in its own right. The steps in these projects are outlined in Chapters Thirteen and Fourteen.

To prepare a timeline or chart, instructional designers must first clarify the scope of the project. In other words, what results or tangible products ("deliverables") must the project produce? Next, identify questions or issues to be addressed by the project. Arrange them in a logical order. Then ask team members to think through *how* the questions are to be answered. In other words, what procedures—and tasks or subtasks within the procedures— must be carried out to answer the questions or address the issues? Next, estimate the number of staff members and types of expertise they must possess to carry out the procedures. Allocate the workload (procedures, tasks, and subtasks) and assign responsibility to individuals on the team, describing *who* must do *what* by *when*.

When these steps have been carried out, instructional designers have established the basis for a timeline or chart that will set forth, in a visual format, *who* does *what* by *when*. Though it may be subject to eventual revision, it provides the basis for estimating project requirements and establishing direction for conducting the project.

Over the years, several different techniques have been suggested for preparing project timelines or charts. They include scheduling and control charts, the critical path method, and the program evaluation and review technique. Although they deserve more attention than we will devote to them here, instructional designers should have some awareness of what these techniques are and how they can be used in planning, scheduling, and controlling instructional design projects.

Scheduling and control charts are commonly used in instructional design work, as they are in manufacturing (Gaither, 1980). A variation of the original chart prepared at the beginning of this century by Henry Gantt (Wren, 1979), the chart is formatted with project activities along the left margin, dates along the top, and bars representing timelines. By consulting the one-page chart, which is updated during the project as progress on activities is made, members of an instructional design team can receive simple and instant feedback about their progress.

The critical path method (CPM) was developed by Remington Rand in 1957. It is appropriate for complex instructional design projects in which timely completion of each procedure, task, or subtask is imperative. Since it is relatively expensive to use, CPM should be reserved for those occasions when it is really justified by the costs involved or by the importance of retaining client goodwill. Like scheduling and control charts, CPM allows for continual updating as a project unfolds. Also like scheduling and control charts, CPM requires a complete list of project activities (procedures, tasks, and even subtasks). Unlike scheduling and control charts, however, CPM requires instructional designers to describe the interrelationships between activities carefully. The time necessary for each activity must be specified. Using a CPM chart, members of an instructional design team identify what tasks must be performed in what sequence. Moreover, it is possible to identify the most *efficient* methods of conducting tasks.

The program evaluation and review technique (PERT) closely resembles CPM. Indeed, PERT and CPM are frequently confused. The chief difference is that CPM requires only *one* time estimate per activity; PERT, on the other hand, requires *three*. According to Gaither (1980, p. 336), "the ability to make probabilistic statements about project path durations is the only material difference between CPM and PERT." In other words, PERT relies on probabilistic estimates of each activity's duration; CPM relies on a single estimate. In all other respects, PERT and CPM are identical. Both are valuable tools for planning, scheduling, and controlling instructional design projects. For more information on these subjects, see Brennan (1968), Lockyear (1969), Morris (1967), and West and Levy (1977).

Budgeting Projects

When developing a project management plan for an instructional design project, instructional designers should not only be able to devise some form of timeline or chart but should also be able to prepare a budget that considers project expenses. "A budget," writes Sweeney and Wisner (1975, p. 4),

> is the key part of the entire planning and control system [of many organizations]—a system with built-in feedback that permits management to monitor, control, and direct activities of an organization. In other words, a budget enables the management of an organization to plan for and keep close tabs on the amount of profit it makes. Essentially, a budget is a plan for the short-term future (generally one year) expressed in numbers. . . . It is a statement of intention to act over a definite period of time—and it is agreed to by the people involved before the budgeting period starts.

Most organizations have some budgeting process. Budgets are tools for translating organizational plans into action. In business firms, organizational budgets are usually based on, and constrained by, projections of sales and production levels. In governmental agencies, on the other hand, budgets are based on (and constrained by) projections of tax and other revenues.

Budgeting for instructional design projects, however, poses a somewhat different challenge than is typically encountered by managers who budget for long-term, continuing operations.

First of all, instructional design projects are usually one of a kind. As a consequence, they do not provide a historical record of activities. By way of contrast, a production manager in a manufacturing firm may enjoy the luxury of many years' past budgets, providing valuable clues about (1) what to budget for, (2) how much to budget based on expected levels of production activity, and (3) what areas in the production budget have been most difficult to estimate. Instructional designers rarely enjoy the luxury of an extended project history.

Second, instructional design projects are temporary. Although they can and often do spill across annual budgeting cycles, they do come to an eventual conclusion. In this respect, they differ from (for example) departmental budgeting in line and staff organizations. Project budgets stem directly from detailed descriptions of planned project activities. In other words, instructional designers must first have very detailed descriptions of what they plan to do before they can prepare a budget of what resources are needed to do it! This detailed description should at least set forth the expected project duration, project tasks, staffing requirements, staff travel, equipment needs, facility needs, and other resources necessary for conducting the project. Project budgets should also provide estimates of how much financial support will be needed to enact the project plan and when that support will be needed. For this reason, instructional designers must think through, before the project begins, how much money will be required to obtain the necessary resources and when that money is likely to be expended.

Third, budgets for instructional design projects require as much — if not more — control than is typical for departmental budgets. After all, budgets are only useful if there is a reliable way to keep track of spending, linking budgeted estimates (*plans*) with expended dollars and project oucomes (*results*). It is thus important to establish a budgeting control system that keeps track of expenditures and ties them to budget estimates originally made through an *audit* or *paper trail*. In this way, instructional designers can see how well the budgeted estimates eventually compare to expended funds and project results.

How is a project budget developed? First, learn the budgeting system and budgeting cycle of the client organization. Budgeting systems and cycles are not all the same! How does the budgeting process work in the organization? What special forms, if any, are used in the budgeting process? What special charts of accounts — providing ready-to-go budget categories — already exist? What key dates must be met to submit a budget in your organization? How do decision makers want to handle *project budgets* relative to the *human resource development department's budget?* What special audit requirements are tied to organizational budgets? What other special requirements—such as governmental recordkeeping—must be established and maintained for the budget?

When these difficult questions have been answered, then prepare a detailed project plan that describes what procedures, tasks, and subtasks will be performed and what resources will be needed to perform them. Use this plan as the basis for the budget. Above all, be sure to estimate how many staff members will be needed at different stages of the project, how long they will be needed, and how much they will cost to maintain by way of salary, benefits, and equipment. (The expenses for staff are usually the most costly ones!) If there is reason to do it, budget for *each step* of a project separately.

In some organizations, there is an overall budget for the human resource development department—but separate budgets for each instructional design project. There may, in fact, be other budget centers as well. For a new instructional designer, the relationship between the department budget and specific project budgets may be difficult to understand.

Probably the best way to integrate project and departmental budgets is to use a bottom-up approach to the budgeting process. Instructional designers budget separately for each project, based on their project plans, and then submit them to become part of the human resource development department budget. For more information on budgeting for instructional design projects, see Head (1985), Hennessy and Hennessy (1989), Laird (1985), and Warren (1979).

Monitoring the Time of Instructional Designers

Instructional design projects are often successful to the extent that they are completed on a timely basis. For this reason, when a project plan is developed, instructional designers need a system to track the time and timeliness of instructional designers on a project team.

One effective way to track the time of instructional designers is to develop a chart at the outset of a project and update it on a regular basis as milestones are achieved. For instance, a *scheduling and control chart* can be prepared with activities listed along the left margin, dates along the top, and bars representing timelines. Each bar is then color coded to indicate which instructional designer on a team is primarily responsible for that task or activity. If posted in a prominent location, the chart provides feedback to all team members about project progress. Color coding can also designate individual responsibility on a PERT or CPM chart.

Another effective way to track time is to request regular (usually weekly) progress reports from each instructional designer. These reports may be submitted in a simple memo format—or the project leader can supply team members with a simple standardized format to save time (see Exhibit 15.1). Reports can uncover short-term or intermediate-term problems, allowing the project leader to intervene when help is needed. Particularly useful for

Exhibit 15.1. A Standardized Format for a Progress Report.

Progress Report

Name _____ /Date _____
Location _____ Project # _____

1. Duties and Activities. (*Describe briefly what activities you have been assigned and pertinent deadlines.*)

2. Progress. (*Describe briefly how much progress you have made over the past week. Cite specifics.*)

3. Problems. (*Describe any special problems you are encountering on the project.*)

helping to manage different teams operating at geographically scattered locations, they provide documentation of progress that can later contribute valuable information for project performance appraisals of each team member.

A third way to track the time of instructional designers is to conduct regular weekly meetings with all team members. These meetings provide opportunities for sharing information across the team—and lack of information *can* cause problems when team members are working on different activities simultaneously. Most staff meetings are held with groups of no more than twelve people. The project leader opens the meeting with a project summary and any news affecting the entire project team. Groups or individuals assigned to different activities then report briefly on their status, explaining how they are progressing relative to deadlines, what special problems they have encountered, and how they are coping with those problems. Meetings usually conclude after in-depth discussion of special problems affecting individuals or the entire project team.

Tracking Project Accomplishments

Just as instructional design projects are often successful only when they are completed on a timely basis, instructional design work is often successful in an organization only when instructional designers can track—and publicize—project successes. Small change efforts tend to build an impetus for larger, and more successful, efforts (Beer, 1969). For this reason, be sure to establish a means of tracking project accomplishments.

There are two ways to do that: success cases and documented change.

A *success case* is a description of something that worked out well. For instructional designers, it is an anecdote that captures the essence of a project and describes a successful result (Brinkerhoff, 1983). Despite everything that has been said about the weight placed on profits in business and industry, human nature is such that telling a story about a success often has more emotional—and persuasive—impact on listeners than pages of financial reports. People have a natural interest in others, and a success case is a way to tell a story in the context of an instructional project.

Set out to collect success cases during each instructional design project.

Ask team members to keep their eyes peeled for individuals whose scores on pretests and posttests are phenomenal; appeal to participants during instruction to report any successes they subsequently experience when they apply on the job what they learned in instruction. Classify these cases as individual or departmental successes. Then report them when there is a need to build, or keep, support for an instructional project in the organization — or when attracting members of the targeted audience to participate in instruction.

If facts and figures are preferable to emotionally appealing success stories, track instructional design project accomplishments by documenting measurable change resulting from them. *Documented change* can be arrived at in several ways, perhaps in a way consistent with Kirkpatrick's (1975) hierarchy of evaluation.

Document participant reaction by collecting information about participant attitudes, perhaps through an attitude survey, before the instructional experience. Then administer an identical attitude survey as a participant reaction questionnaire following the instructional experience. Compare the differences. Use the results to demonstrate attitudinal change among participants (Henerson, Morris, and Fitz-Gibbon, 1987).

Document learning by administering pretests and posttests. Compare the results. Use them to demonstrate changes in knowledge or skills of participants, being sure to comply with standard statistical requirements for data analysis (Herman, Morris, and Fitz-Gibbon, 1987). Document postinstructional results by tracking the turnover and relative career success of participants. If possible, compare participants over an extended time period to a comparable control group of individuals who, for one reason or another, did not participate in the instruction (Miller and Barnett, 1986). Use positive results to make the case that participation in instruction benefits individuals and the organization.

Establishing and Using Methods to Reallocate Funds

When developing a project plan, be sure to establish "some procedure for reallocating funds (within project constraints) to resolve discrepancies between actual and planned project performance to meet project commitments" (*The Standards,* 1986, p. 84). For instance, match the project budget to deadlines. If deadlines are not reached, or are reached sooner than expected, be prepared to compensate by making adjustments to the budget. Establish a regular schedule to review the budget and expenses compared to project deadlines. Find out, too, what procedures are used in the organization to justify *budget variances,* differences between planned and actual expenditures.

Planning and Monitoring Equipment and Facility Requirements

Consider equipment and facility requirements as a plan for an instructional design project is prepared. Each project necessitates specialized planning for equipment and facilities. For instance, during a performance analysis, members of an instructional design team will typically need desks, chairs, lights, and telephones. They may also need access to computer equipment. Although there is a temptation for the management of a client organization to supply whatever spare space and equipment may already be available, the project leader should see to it that necessary equipment and facilities are requested before they are needed and are available at the time they are needed.

To plan equipment and facilities, begin with a master scheduling and control chart for the project. For each activity listed on the chart, estimate equipment and facility needs. Be sure to consider, of course, *what* will be needed, *how much* will be needed, and *when* it will be needed. Then allow time for the equipment and facility requests to be reviewed, approved, and acted on.

Establish a sign-up system for allocating equipment and/or facilities, since they may face conflicting demands. Make sure that the project leader resolves conflicting demands as they arise. Monitor equipment and facilities against the master scheduling and control chart. Each time a piece of equipment or a facility is used, ask instructional designers to track it. Then review equipment and facility use periodically. For more information about planning for equipment and facilities, consult standard references on the topic (Kemp and Smellie, 1989; Sener, 1987).

Judging a Project Plan

According to *The Standards* (1986, p. 86), instructional designers should be able to "judge the appropriateness and comprehensiveness of the project plan." This judgment should be based on whether the plan includes

- A timeline or chart
- A budget
- A control system to monitor time and track project accomplishments
- Methods for allocating funds
- Descriptions of equipment and facility requirements

Judge the appropriateness and comprehensiveness of a project plan by using a checklist as a decision aid. An example of such a checklist appears in Exhibit 15.2.

Justifying a Project Plan

According to *The Standards* (1986, p. 87), instructional designers should be able to "state a rationale for a project plan, exceptions reported, or the judgments made." In other words, instructional designers should be prepared to explain to colleagues on the instructional design team and managers what elements have been included in the project plan, what elements have been

Exhibit 15.2. A Checklist for Judging the Appropriateness
and Comprehensiveness of a Project Plan.

Directions: Judge the appropriateness and comprehensiveness of a project plan using this check-list. Answer each question appearing in the left column below by checking (✔) an appropriate response in the middle column. If necessary, make notes in the right column on any aspect of the project plan that, in your opinion, deserves improvement.

Question	*Response*		*Notes for Revision*
	Yes	*No*	
Does the project plan include . . .	(✔)	(✔)	
1. Some form of timeline or chart that includes key development milestones and interim and final deadlines?	( )	( )	
2. A budget that	( )	( )	
a. Considers project expenses?	( )	( )	
b. Considers the total amount available for the project?	( )	( )	
c. Is broken down into generally acceptable budget categories?	( )	( )	
3. Some system that keeps track (weekly) of the			
a. Designer's time?	( )	( )	
b. Budgets?	( )	( )	
c. Timelines?	( )	( )	
4. Some mechanism for identifying discrepancies between the project plan and actual progress?	( )	( )	
5. Some procedure for reallocating funds (within project constraints) to resolve discrepancies between actual and planned project performance to meet project commitments?	( )	( )	
6. Equipment requirements?	( )	( )	
7. Facility requirements?	( )	( )	

omitted, and the reasoning underlying the choices made. As always, instructional designers should be prepared to address challenges to their judgment by others. Be prepared, then, to answer each of the following questions:

How was project time planned and monitored?
How was the budget prepared, and what variances resulted?

How was the control system established to monitor time and track
   project accomplishments?
How were funds allocated?
How was equipment planned? How were facility requirements
   planned?

Be prepared to answer — and justify the answers — to each of these questions.

Conclusion

In this chapter, we described key issues to consider when planning and monitoring instructional design projects. We concluded the chapter with a few words about judging and justifying project plans. Now we turn to the first of three related chapters on the importance of communication in instructional design.

CHAPTER SIXTEEN

Communicating Effectively

According to *The Standards* (1986, p. 88), instructional designers should be able to "communicate effectively in written, oral, or visual forms." That means they should be able to read, write, speak, listen, and express themselves effectively with visual aids. Effective communication is essential to success in the field of instructional design, as it is in many other areas of human endeavor. One work sampling study of 136 managers revealed that they spent between 74 and 87 percent of their work days communicating (Hinrichs, 1964). In that study, top managers spent an average of 62 percent of their time listening and speaking, 8 percent of their time on the telephone, 13 percent of their time writing, and 12 percent of their time reading. In contrast, supervisors and middle managers devoted about 48 percent of their time to listening and speaking, 8 percent to the telephone, 17 percent to writing, and 9 percent to reading. Instructional designers probably devote even more time than managers to listening, speaking, writing, and reading.

Unfortunately, few people—whether high school or college graduates— bring to their jobs the polished communication skills expected by many managers today. As evidence of a gap between management expectations and job incumbent communication skills, consider that a 1977 survey of human resource executives revealed that recent college graduates experience the most trouble in making their writing concise, clarifying what they mean, engineering a message to accomplish its intended purpose, and spelling properly (Allred and Clark, 1980). When the Center for Public Resources conducted a survey of 1,000 randomly selected employers in 1982, they found that 50 percent of their respondents were experiencing problems with the writing skills of their college-educated managerial and supervisory employees (Center for Public Resources, 1983). This finding was sustained in a 1990 survey conducted by *Business Month*. When asked "among managers, where do you see the most serious shortcomings?", fully 47 percent of *Business Month*'s respondents, selected by convenience sample, answered that "writing memos or reports" was the most serious shortcoming ("A Poor Report Card," 1990, p. 9). Other problems were also cited: 32 percent noted that managers experienced difficulties in "solving complex problems," 31 percent pointed to "communicating with superiors" as a problem area, and 21 percent noted that managers have trouble "analyzing statistical data" ("A Poor Report Card," 1990, p. 9). Asked what to do about these problems, several employers offered creative solutions: "pray," quipped one; "move to Switzerland," offered another.

Instructional designers are not immune to criticism about their communication skills. This chapter briefly reviews principles of effective communication as they apply to instructional design. Its purpose is to provide useful information to sharpen and improve communication skills.

Using Effective Visual Communication

Instructional designers should be able to "communicate effectively in visual form so that cues are used well and consistently; key attributes are highlighted in a visualization; irrelevant attributes are minimized; all concrete concepts are selected; and some abstract concepts may be selected" (*The Standards*, 1986, p. 89).

The Power of Visual Communication

Of all modes of communication, visual communication may be the most powerful. In describing the efficiency of visual communication, Peoples (1988, p. 66) writes: "Of the total inventory of knowledge you have in your head, 75 percent came to you visually, 13 percent through hearing, and a sum total of 12 percent through smell, taste, and touch. In fact, if I show you a pictorial presentation of a key point and say nothing, the comprehension and retention will be 3½ times greater than if I just say the words without a picture. And if I do both — give you the words and the picture — the comprehension and retention will be six times greater than just saying the words." The sense of sight can thus lead to significantly increased learner comprehension and retention. As Wileman (1980, p. 16) points out, visualization is a powerful communication tool for three major reasons: (1) a visual message can be attention-getting, (2) a visual message can be efficient, and (3) a visual message can be effective. Instructional designers should thus be skilled in using techniques of effective visual communication so they can take full advantage of its power to increase learner comprehension and retention (American Society for Training and Development, 1984b).

Appropriate Uses of Visualization in Communication

According to Wileman (1980), visual messages can be appropriate for presenting or reinforcing any of the following kinds of information:

1. *Concrete facts* (such as the types of energy particles in elementary physics)
2. *Directions* (such as steps in preparing spaghetti)
3. *Processes* (such as steps in conducting Strategic Business Planning)
4. *Bits of data* (such as the age distribution of the U.S. population)
5. *Comparative data* (such as the relative temperature averages between Miami and Chicago)
6. *Data recorded over time* (such as the average annual rainfall in New Zealand)
7. *Organizational structure* (such as reporting relationships at IBM)
8. *Places* (such as a map of Washington, D.C.)
9. *Chronologies* (such as the history of industrial training)
10. *A generalization* (such as the rate of return on investments in human capital)
11. *A theory* (such as Einstein's theory of relativity)
12. *Feelings or attitudes* (such as sadness, love).

Each occasion imposes its own demands on the instructional designer, prompting a different type of visual representation.

Identifying Types of Visual Images

Wileman (1980) identifies seven types of visual images, ranging from the purely verbal to the purely visual (see Figure 16.1). At the lowest level (*Type I*), the visual image is simply a representation of the printed word. At the highest level (*Type VII*), information is conveyed through pictorial or graphic symbol, is highly abstract, and is purely visual. For Wileman, the choice of appropriate visual imagery is not absolute; rather, it depends on the occasion.

Using Cues

A *cue* is a signal for action. In visual communication, a cue is a signal to the viewer that an object, represented on a visual, is worthy of special note (Wileman, 1980). Suppose, for example, that a visual shows a group of people representing all age categories, but an arrow is drawn to a small child in the group. That arrow is a cue, since it draws attention to one person in the picture. To "cue" the significance of a visually depicted object to a viewer, use various techniques. One technique is to superimpose writing on the object itself. Other methods of adding emphasis also work. These can include using colors, decorations, or symbols such as stars or arrows.

Highlighting Key Attributes in a Visualization and Minimizing Irrelevant Attributes

An *attribute* is an essential quality or feature. Since the visual medium does not lend itself well to verbal discourse, instructional designers should be able

Figure 16.1. Types of Verbal/Visual Image Relationships.

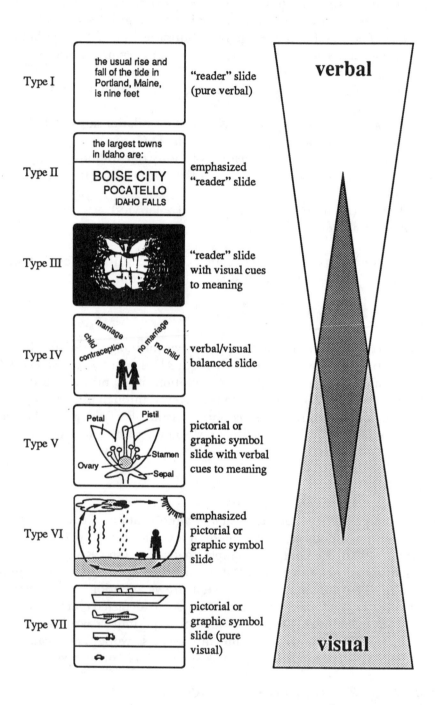

Source: Wileman, R. *Exercises in Visual Thinking.* New York: ©Hastings House, 1980, p. 34. Used by permission of the publisher.

to highlight key attributes of a message for visual representation. As evidence of the importance of selectivity in the visual medium consider that many audiovisual experts recommend including no more than twenty-four words on an overhead transparency or a still slide (Wileman, 1980). The reason: more information than that will diminish the value of such a Type I visual representation, simply confusing the viewer with too many stimuli.

Develop images and visual reinforcements by starting with the instructional materials. Identify key ideas for presentation or reinforcement. Use three criteria by which to judge:

1. Is the idea essential to achieving performance objectives?
2. Does the occasion lend itself to visual representation because an idea can be effectively presented visually?
3. Is the idea important enough, relative to other ideas presented in the instructional materials, to warrant special reinforcement through visual representation?

If all three questions can be answered yes, use visual representation; if the answer to any question is no, devote attention to highlighting other ideas visually.

Selecting Concrete Concepts for Visualization

A *concrete concept* is usually equated with phenomena found in everyday life. There are three kinds: (1) plans and organization charts, (2) maps, and (3) chronologies (Wileman, 1980). Each lends itself to *concrete representation,* "an attempt to be literal and realistic in the presentation of information" (Wileman, 1980, p. 12).

Concrete concepts can be illustrated in several ways. For instance, each step in a plan may be conveyed through graphic images associated with time or activities. As an example, a timeline running through a year may show symbols representing four seasons. (Examples of symbols might include snow for winter, birds and flowers for spring, falling leaves for fall, and a hot sun for summer.) Organization charts lend themselves easily to visual representation through lines and boxes, representing positions of authority and reporting relationships. Maps may be presented three-dimensionally, proportionally, or by other means. Chronologies, like steps in a plan, may be conveyed through graphic images.

Select concrete concepts for visualization by examining instructional materials. Highlight plans, reporting relationships, maps, or chronologies. Then decide, based on the relative importance of the concepts, whether they warrant visual presentation or reinforcement. If they do, decide what kind of visual representation to use.

Selecting Abstract Concepts for Visualization

An *abstract concept* is the same as an *invisible concept*. It is equated with complex or highly abstract phenomena. There are three kinds: (1) generalizations, (2) theories, and (3) feelings and attitudes (Wileman, 1980). A *generalization* is "a conclusion or 'truth' underlying a field of inquiry" (Wileman, 1980, p. 12). A *theory* is "a verified or conjectured formulation about an underlying artistic or scientific principle" (Wileman, 1980, p. 12). *Feelings and attitudes* are expressions of subjective emotions, not as easily depicted visually as tangible facts. Each does not lend itself easily to *concrete representation*, since no visual object is closely associated with the concept (Wileman, 1980).

If an abstract concept must be visually represented, seize the chance to exercise considerable creativity. Abstract concepts usually require visualization through pictorial or graphic symbols, sometimes highly abstract ones. Use essentially the same approach to select abstract concepts for visualization that would be used to select concrete concepts for visualization. Begin by examining instructional materials, identifying abstract concepts. Highlight generalizations, theories or feelings, and attitudes. Then, based on the relative importance of the concepts, decide whether they warrant visual representation. If so, use graphic or pictorial displays for this purpose.

Using Effective Oral Communication

According to *The Standards* (1986, p. 89), instructional designers should be able to "communicate effectively in oral form so they use correct grammar, use an appropriate understandability level, use acceptable organization, use an acceptable presentation format, answer questions posed by others, and use rules or standards of conduct accepted as appropriate by an authentic source."

Principles of Effective Oral Communication

Perhaps the first principle of effective oral communication is the use of correct grammar. The English word *grammar* is derived from the Greek word for "letters," *grammatikos*. *The American Heritage Dictionary* (1982, p. 571) defines grammar as "a normative or prescriptive system of rules setting forth the current standard of usage for pedagogical or reference purposes." Appropriate use of grammar is expected in everyday conversation and in formal group presentations. When grammar is used inappropriately, however, speakers lose credibility. Indeed, an audience may discount the speakers' message simply because its presentation is faulty. The reasoning, fair or unfair as it might be, is that speakers who cannot use appropriate grammar probably also have faulty thinking or a flawed message. Use of appropriate grammar is important for establishing and maintaining credibility.

Spoken language is rarely scrutinized for grammatical correctness in the same way that written language often is. One reason is that spoken language is fleeting; written language is enduring. The receiver of a spoken message also has less time to subject the message to scrutiny. In addition, spoken language relies in part on the speaker's body language and tone of voice to establish meaning. In written language, the words stand alone and must convey the message.

Grammatical problems do occur in speech, however. They are likely to occur when speakers engage in heated debate and thus make statements without thinking about them carefully first, make use of convoluted sentence structure in an effort to impress others, or for some other reason utilize nonstandard syntax.

Use the following tips to help improve grammar while speaking. First, think through what will be said before saying it. If unsure of subject-verb agreement or pronunciation, then recast the sentence so as to avoid using a problematic construction. Second, use simple sentences. Avoid trying to impress listeners. Simply say what should be said. There is elegance in simplicity. Third, become familiar with books on English usage. Purchase at least one good dictionary, a thesaurus, and a book on specialized usage. For usage, the classic book is Fowler's *Modern English Usage* (1965).

Using an Appropriate Understandability Level

To make oral communication understandable, always plan the presentation. Make the effort to do that even when the occasion is informal and the presentation will be made to just one other person or to a small group. Decide whether the aim is to inform or persuade. Whenever preparing to speak, perform an *audience analysis audit* (Morrisey and Sechrest, 1987). As Morrisey and Sechrest (1987) point out, an audit should include a review of the objectives for the presentation, the speaker's relationship to the audience, the length of that relationship with the audience, the audience's vocabulary level, and the willingness of the audience to accept the ideas that will be presented. As part of the audit, analyze specific members of the audience to whom the presentation will be addressed. Classify their knowledge of the subject, their opinions, any reasons why they may have a special interest in the subject, and any attention-getting techniques — such as stories, demonstrations, or statistical information — that may make a favorable impression. Base the presentation on the results of that analysis.

Using Acceptable Organization

Organizing conversation, whether it is formal or informal, is very much like sequencing performance objectives. In fact, the very same principles of organization may be applied in both cases. An oral presentation may thus be organized based on time or topic. It may also flow from whole to part, part to whole, known to unknown, unknown to known, step by step, part to part to part, or general to specific. (We will not describe these organizing principles here, since they were described at length in Chapter Ten.)

The important point is to choose the organization of the presentation based on the objectives (*what results are to be achieved?*), the audience (*what do they think of the desired results?*), and the subject matter (*what is the subject, and what does the audience know about it?*). In the broadest sense, any conversation may be classified as informative or persuasive. An informative presentation is geared to instructing an audience. It begins with background information and then moves into topical, timely, or detailed descriptions. A persuasive presentation is intended to convince an audience that an idea or belief has value. The presentation is usually organized in such a way that audience interests are described first, followed by a description of an idea that will satisfy those interests.

Using an Acceptable Presentation Format

Presentation format refers to the way messages are delivered to an audience. In oral communication, presentation format may include one-on-one (dyadic) meetings, small-group meetings, and large-group meetings. Choose a presentation format based on the communication climate, situation, expectations of others, and expectations of the presenter.

Communication climate is "a composite of human behaviors, perceptions of events, responses of employees to one another, expectations, interpersonal conflicts, and opportunities for growth in the organization. . . . " (Pace, 1983, p. 124). It is thus related to perceptions of organizational members about "how they are free to act or behave" and "what seems responsible in how others act or behave" (Goldhaber, Dennis, Richetto, and Wiio, 1979). In using communication climate to choose presentation format, consider these questions adapted from Waters, Roach, and Batlis (1974):

1. How are important messages typically presented in the organization?
2. How are important decisions typically made?
3. How is technology used in the organization's communication processes?
4. How do lower-level members of the organization influence decision making at the top?

The answers to these questions should provide useful clues about what presentation format is appropriate for a given occasion.

Situation means the relative willingness of the organization to accept change. Situations range from highly favorable to highly unfavorable. The more unfavorable the situation, the greater the likelihood that the presentation format will have to be highly persuasive; the more favorable the situation, the greater the likelihood that the presentation format should be informative.

Expectations of others are influenced, to a great extent, by organizational climate and culture. Consider: How have instructional designers presented their ideas in the past? How do others expect them to present their ideas now?

Expectations of presenters are also influenced by organizational climate, culture, and expectations of others. Consider: How do instructional designers feel they should present their ideas? Why? Choose the presentation format based on answers to these questions.

Answering Questions Posed by Others

Be prepared to field questions posed by others. Indeed, it should be possible to anticipate the questions others will pose, based on an advance analysis of audience members' self-interests. Fielding questions may be viewed as a process, and answers to questions may be arranged in a taxonomy of difficulty loosely adapted from the Bloom (1956) taxonomy of educational objectives. The taxonomy of answer categories is as follows (Sanders, 1966, p. 3):

1. *Memory.* Be prepared to answer questions requiring listeners to recall information.
2. *Translation.* Be prepared to answer questions in such a way as to change existing information into something new.
3. *Interpretation.* Be prepared to answer questions so as to help listeners discover relationships between facts, generalizations, values, and skills.
4. *Application.* Be prepared to answer questions so as to lead listeners to solve a problem requiring identification of an issue and selection and use of appropriate generalizations and skills.
5. *Analysis.* Be prepared to answer questions so as to help listeners solve a problem in light of conscious knowledge of parts and forms of thinking.
6. *Synthesis.* Be prepared to answer questions requiring original thought and insight.
7. *Evaluation.* Be prepared to answer questions requiring judgments of what is good and bad, right or wrong, according to predefined standards.

Use a worksheet like the one shown in Exhibit 16.1 to help anticipate questions that may be posed by others and to choose the types of answers appropriate to the occasion.

Using Rules or Standards of Conduct Accepted as Appropriate by an Authentic Source

There are two sets of rules and standards of conduct that should be considered when planning and delivering oral messages.

The first set is organizational, having to do with the organization's

Exhibit 16.1. A Worksheet for Assessing Appropriate Answers to Questions.

Directions: Use this simple worksheet to help you anticipate questions that you may be asked by others and to formulate appropriate answers to them. Assume, for purposes of this worksheet, that you have prepared a presentation and that you intend to give it to one or more people. In the first part of the worksheet, summarize your audience analysis. In the second part, describe the questions you fully expect to be asked by your audience, based on your analysis of their interests. In the third part, consider the taxonomy of answers and select one answer category appropriate for addressing the concerns of your audience.

Part I: Audience Analysis

1. *Describe the results of your audience analysis.* Consider: What is your relationship to your audience? How is the audience likely to receive your message? What does the audience know about the subject? What are their opinions on the subject likely to be? What interest will the audience have in the subject? How important is the subject likely to be to the audience, considering members' present problems and concerns? In what ways have you tried to secure and retain their attention during the presentation?

Part II: Questions Expected from the Audience

2. *List the questions you expect from the audience about your presentation.* What are they likely to want to know more about, considering their self-interests?

Part III: Answer Categories

3. *Select answer categories for each question listed in response to Part II.* Recall that the answer categories are as follows: (1) memory, (2) translation, (3) interpretation, (4) application, (5) analysis, (6) synthesis, and (7) evaluation.

rules, standards of conduct, and protocol. How do people communicate orally in the organization? The answer to that question depends, of course, on culture—"the way we do things around here"—and on individual preferences. Be sure to ask others how people communicate. Is it necessary to make an appointment with someone, or does an "open door policy" make it possible for instructional designers to meet with people informally and on the spur of the moment? What are the expectations of decision makers in the organization about appropriate ways to conduct oral communication? Is anything in particular (such as profane language) not permitted?

If instructional designers have occasion to communicate orally—particularly if they must make formal presentations—they may wish to polish their oral communication skills. Books on public speaking are available through professional societies, libraries, and bookstores. Obtain one and study it carefully (for instance, see American Society for Training and Development, 1986g, 1988a).

To learn more, observe effective speakers in action. Note their techniques closely. What do they *do?* Practice those techniques. Instructional designers who desire eventual promotion should be aware that special competencies ("platform skills") are expected of classroom instructors, whose positions are sometimes a rung up on the career ladder above instructional designers. As described by another competency study sponsored by the International Board of Standards for Training, Performance, and Instruction (Foshay, Silber, and Westgaard, 1988), instructors should at least be able to

1. Analyze course materials and learner information
2. Assure preparation of the instructional site
3. Establish and maintain instructor credibility
4. Manage the learning environment
5. Demonstrate effective communication skills
6. Demonstrate effective presentation skills
7. Demonstrate effective questioning skills and techniques
8. Respond appropriately to learners' needs for clarification or feedback
9. Provide positive reinforcement and motivational incentives
10. Use instructional methods appropriately
11. Use media effectively
12. Evaluate learner performance
13. Evaluate delivery of instruction
14. Report evaluation information

To improve communication skill, perhaps in anticipation of becoming an instructor, instructional designers should examine each competency described above. Then they should rate themselves on them, identifying strengths and weaknesses. They should ask their supervisors, and perhaps their professional peers as well, to do the same. Finally, they should solicit opinions about how they may overcome identified weaknesses through formal or informal learning.

Using Effective Written Communication

According to *The Standards* (1986, p. 89), instructional designers should be able to "communicate effectively in written form so that in written communication they use correct grammar, use an appropriate understandability level, use acceptable organization, use an acceptable presentation format, answer questions posed by others, and use rules or standards of conduct accepted as appropriate by an authentic source."

Principles of Effective Written Communication

The key grammatical "rules" for effective written communication with which instructional designers should be familiar are summarized succinctly in Strunk and White (1979). Instructional designers may use the worksheet appearing in Exhibit 16.2 to assess examples of their writing against the grammatical rules offered by Strunk and White. If they identify a discrepancy between what they have written and a "rule" of grammar, they should review the appropriate section in Strunk and White (1979) or discuss the discrepancy with a more seasoned instructional designer whose writing is considered clear and concise by others. Training on writing can also help improve writing skills (see American Society for Training and Development, 1986b; Felker, Redish, and Peterson, 1985).

**Exhibit 16.2. A Worksheet for Assessing
Your Writing for Grammatical Correctness.**

Directions: Select an example of your writing. Compare it to the rules stated below. You should be able to answer every question by checking (✔) yes. If you must check no, then review your writing for grammatical correctness. If you do not understand the question, then read the section in Strunk and White (1979) to understand it.

	Questions	*Yes*	*No*
	Have you . . .	(✔)	(✔)
1.	Formed the possessive singular of nouns by adding 's?	( )	( )
2.	Used a comma, in a series of three or more terms, after each term except the last?	( )	( )
3.	Enclosed parenthetical expressions between commas?	( )	( )
4.	Placed a comma before a conjunction introducing an independent clause?	( )	( )
5.	Taken care not to join independent clauses by a comma?	( )	( )
6.	Avoided breaking sentences in two?	( )	( )
7.	Used colons appropriately to introduce		
	a. A list of particulars?	( )	( )
	b. An appositive?	( )	( )
	c. An amplification?	( )	( )
	d. An illustrative quotation?	( )	( )
8.	Used a dash to set off an abrupt break and to announce a long appositive or summary?	( )	( )
9.	Used the number of the subject to determine the number of the verb?	( )	( )
10.	Used the proper case of each pronoun?	( )	( )
11.	Made sure that each participial phrase at the beginning of a sentence refers to the grammatical subject?	( )	( )
12.	Chosen a suitable design for your composition and held to it?	( )	( )
13.	Made the paragraph the clear unit of composition?	( )	( )
14.	Used the active, rather than passive, voice?	( )	( )
15.	Made an effort to state ideas positively?	( )	( )
16.	Used definite, specific, and concrete language?	( )	( )
17.	Omitted needless words?	( )	( )
18.	Avoided instances in which there are successions of loose sentences without clear logical connections between them?	( )	( )
19.	Expressed coordinate ideas in similar form?	( )	( )
20.	Kept related words together?	( )	( )
21.	Used a consistent tense?	( )	( )

Source: Used with the permission of Macmillan Publishing Company. *The Elements of Style.* (3rd ed.) by W. Strunk, Jr., and E. White. Copyright © 1979 by Macmillan Publishing Company.

Using an Appropriate Understandability Level

Instructional designers should gear their messages to their readers' level, using language that is likely to be understood. However, they should remember that the message is more likely to be read when it is *easy* to read, short and succinct, answers all the key questions of importance to the reader, makes clear what action (if any) is required by the reader, and has been revised several times for clarity.

First, make the message easy to read. Readers are more likely to understand written communication best when it does not use many multi-syllabic words, lengthy sentence structure, or passive constructions in which nobody ever takes any action. Unfortunately, we have found that it is far easier to get people to criticize the writing of others than to view their own writing with a critical eye.

One tool may be useful for this purpose—the *readability formula*. A readability formula measures the relative difficulty of writing, often expressing it in the form of a "grade-level" equivalent. Although such a formula does not help a writer detect grammatical errors, it may improve the ease with which readers can comprehend a written message. However, the evidence to prove that is admittedly problematic (Duffy, 1985). More than 100 such formulas exist (Klare, 1979; Torrence and Torrence, 1987).

Perhaps the most popular readability formula is the Gunning Fog Index (Gunning, 1952). To apply the Gunning Fog Index: (1) select three passages of 100 words each; (2) count 100 words from each passage; (3) count the number of sentences in each passage; (4) divide the number of sentences by 100 to determine average sentence length; (5) count the words of three or more syllables, excluding capitalized words and verbs ending in -*ing* or -*ed;* (6) add average sentence length and number of three-syllable words; and (7) multiply the sum of (6) by 0.4 to obtain a *grade-level equivalent* (Drew, Mikulecky, and Pershing, 1988). The theory is that the lower the grade-level equivalent, the easier the material should be to read.

Second, make the message short and succinct. Some managers routinely place any memo or report longer than one or two pages at the bottom of their in-baskets, where the document remains to collect dust for some time. Bear that expectation for brevity in mind whenever writing to learners or to managers. Long written messages often receive the same treatment as bottles cast in the ocean!

Third, answer key questions of significance to the reader. It is just as important to conduct an audience analysis audit before writing as it is to do so before speaking. Try to anticipate the questions that the readers will want to have answered. Be sure to answer them. One way to measure the effectiveness of written communication is surprisingly simple: count the number of people who have to ask questions after reading the message. Less effective messages produce many people who have to ask follow-up questions.

Fourth, make clear what action is required from the reader. Always ask this question: "Is it clear to the reader what he or she must *do* after reading this correspondence or this memo?" Be sure to ask for that action in the final paragraph, if not before. If no action is required, ponder whether a written message is warranted at all.

Fifth, be willing to revise the writing for clarity. Some people who seldom write have the impression that revision is a sign of weakness — or mental inefficiency. That is just not true. Effective writers prepare a draft, then (if time allows) they lay it aside for awhile. When they return to it, they are able to revise it for clarity with a fresh eye. Revision often economizes writing, making it more powerful and succinct.

Using Acceptable Organization

Many instructional design projects culminate in a letter, report, memo, instructional text, or script. As in speaking, writing should be organized based on objectives (*what results are to be achieved?*), the audience (*what do they think of those desired results?*), and the subject matter (*what is the subject, and what does the audience know about it?*). There are no simple and clearcut rules.

When organizing written communication, be sure to grapple with at least one major issue: Should sufficient detail be provided to answer all the questions that might be posed by interested readers, or should brevity be the guiding factor? Unfortunately, the answer to this question is not always clear.

But it is possible to strike a balance. Do that by providing both completeness *and* brevity. How is that possible? First, write a complete report of the project; second, write a very brief executive summary addressing key points. Apply other rules to preparation of instructional materials themselves (Carter, 1985).

Organize the report chronologically, reflecting the progress of the project itself. First, describe the background, explaining why the project was initiated and how its objectives were clarified. Second, describe the investigation, detailing how the problem was researched. Third, summarize results of the investigation. Fourth, make recommendations for action, supporting them by appropriate estimates of costs and benefits. A fifth but optional section can address possible difficulties that may arise in implementing the recommendations, suggesting steps that can be taken to minimize problems that may stem from taking action (Morris, Fitz-Gibbon, and Freeman, 1987).

Reverse this order in an executive summary. First, make recommendations for corrective action. Second, summarize results of the investigation so that the reasons for taking action are clear. Third, describe briefly how the investigation was conducted. Fourth, remind readers why the project was initiated. Keep the executive summary as short as possible — one or two pages is usually the right length. Refer interested readers of the summary to details in the report — or offer to make an oral presentation to them.

Using an Acceptable Presentation Format

Should a letter, memo, formal report, E-Mail (computer-mail) message, or some combination of them be written to present the results of the project to management? Choose the presentation format based on the same three questions that guided the organization: (1) What results are to be achieved? (2) What do they think of those desired results? (3) What is the subject, and what does the audience know about it?

Follow some simple guidelines. In most cases, it is a good idea to use a letter or memo to make a short proposal, express a simple idea, or summarize and follow up on meetings. Memos are particularly useful for making simple and noncontroversial progress reports or expressing a simple idea for broad distribution to others. Write a formal report when describing the results of an in-depth investigation. Use E-Mail for short, timely messages that do not require immediate answers, such as those that may be obtained by telephone or personal visit.

Answering Questions Posed by Others

Use a written message when there is good reason to prompt others to reflect on a problem or issue before giving an answer or directions. Written messages may also help instructional designers crystallize their own thinking. The process of composing written language demands thought and reflection; spoken language, spontaneous as it is, does not require the same degree of thoughtful consideration and planning. Likewise, the process of reading prompts people to reflect on a problem or idea in a way that they may not when a message is communicated orally.

Using Rules or Standards of Conduct Accepted as Appropriate by an Authentic Source

Refer to a definitive source such as a dictionary, thesaurus, and usage manual whenever there is an occasion to write. Remember that the writer's credibility depends as much on *how* a message is written as on *what* is written. Spelling errors, word usage problems, typographical errors, and grammatical faults will detract from the writer's credibility, leading others to question the quality of the message — and the writer's competence. On occasion, instructional designers may wish to ask colleagues to read what they have written before they send it to its intended audience. In this way they can "test" its effects (Duffy, 1985).

Conclusion

In this chapter, we briefly reviewed principles of effective communication as they apply to instructional design. In the next chapter, we turn to another topic that is also related to effective communication — successful interpersonal skills.

CHAPTER SEVENTEEN

Interacting with Others

Instructional design is not a solitary pursuit. Instead, it requires relations with many different people—such as training managers, managers of operating departments, subject matter experts, media production people, and trainees. When designing instruction, interaction with others is "frequently difficult because the process may require others, or organizations as a whole, to think and act in ways that are different from those to which they are accustomed" (*The Standards,* 1986, p. 90).

Yet interpersonal skills are crucial to success in the instructional design field. In this chapter, we will describe how instructional designers should establish rapport, state the purpose of an interaction, ask questions, provide explanations, listen actively, deal with friction, handle resistance to change, keep people on track, secure commitment, and select appropriate behaviors for effective interpersonal interaction.

Establishing Rapport

According to *The Standards* (1986, p. 92), instructional designers should be able to "establish rapport with individuals and groups." *The American Heritage Dictionary* (1982, p. 1,026) defines *rapport* as a "relationship, especially one of mutual trust or emotional affinity." Hence, "establishing rapport" means "creating a trusting relationship with another person or group of people." It is perhaps best understood as synonymous with what Schoonover (1988, p. 23) calls *interaction,* defined as "the set of interpersonal skills that produces trust between people."

Several years ago, Kirkpatrick (1978, p. 46) described the key conditions of rapport as follows: (1) "There is mutual respect between sender and receiver; (2) Friendly relationships exist between sender and receiver; (3) The sender encourages questions and feedback from the receiver; (4) The receiver doesn't hesitate to say, 'I don't understand'; (5) When [the] sender says 'Do you have any questions?', the receiver feels free to ask questions without fear of being embarrassed or ridiculed; (6) The sender is willing to accept responsibility for the receiver's understanding or lack of understanding; and (7) The sender compliments [the] receiver for understanding and blames self if the receiver misunderstands." To these conditions we can add several listed in *The Standards* (1986, p. 92): (1) "the dialogue should continue as long as the instructional designer wants, (2) information is not withheld from or by the instructional designer, (3) false assumptions about the instructional designer are not made, and (4) information given to the instructional designer is not changed to meet the individual's or group's assumptions about what kind of person the instructional designer is."

But how are these conditions established? The instructional designer's affiliation is the first consideration in creating and maintaining rapport. Conditions for establishing rapport differ, depending on whether you are an instructional designer working as an internal or external consultant. Insiders, working as internal consultants, are employed by the same organization as their potential clients. They have usually established a reputation by which group members may predict their behavior. On the other hand, outsiders, working as external consultants or simply vendors, are not employed by the same organization.

Instructional designers who work within organizations sometimes enjoy an advantage over outsiders in that they may have more understanding of the organization's culture as well as the key beliefs and values of its leaders. They can thus have unique insight into the causes and ramifications of a problem. Yet they may also experience difficulties in initiating contact with others, since insiders are so familiar that their expertise may not be fully appreciated, they may lack authority within the organization's chain of command, or they may have experienced past problems with others so that their ability to help is compromised.

Instructional designers working as external consultants, on the other hand, may not have interacted with members of the client organization's management before. They may thus lack social ties to the clientele. Members of the organization have had no experience—as they may have had with insiders—by which to predict the instructional designer's behavior or assess how they interact with others. Yet instructional designers who work as external consultants do enjoy certain advantages: they are (sometimes) accorded expert status in a way that insiders rarely are; they might enjoy a special reporting relationship with top managers; and they might be able to look at a problem with a fresh perspective, one that is not colored by in-house politics or organizational traditions and culture.

Lippitt and Lippitt (1978, p. 10) point out that "the outsider generally has a more difficult time than the insider in taking the initiative because of the problem of credible entry from the outside." Outsiders must establish, to the satisfaction of their clientele, that they are trustworthy, knowledgeable, and diligent. By trustworthy, we mean that instructional designers must demonstrate that they are not mere pawns of top managers. By knowledgeable, we mean that they must demonstrate enough knowledge about the organization, industry, and problem that they are viewed as credible. By diligent, we mean that instructional designers must be perceived by insiders as capable of researching problems in all their complexity and as capable of following up or implementing the solutions they propose. To establish rapport when working as an outsider, instructional designers must demonstrate thoughtfulness, a willingness to listen to what others have to say, and the ability to function within the norms of the organization's culture.

The situation is the second issue affecting interaction. Instructional designers typically initiate relationships with potential clients under two possible sets of circumstances. In the first situation, help is requested by a prospective client, and instructional designers are asked to research a problem, assess needs, or otherwise investigate and take appropriate action. In this situation, they do not initiate the relationship. They are asked for help, and they meet with a representative or group of representatives from the organization requesting that help. In the second situation, instructional designers request help from others. In this situation, then, they initiate the interaction and the relationship. Others are asked for information or for permission to obtain information.

Both situations may be encountered in the same instructional design project. For instance, top managers or key middle managers may request assistance to analyze a performance problem or design instruction. In the process of conducting performance analysis, the instructional designer may also need to initiate contact with others in the organization to obtain information.

The basic steps in establishing and maintaining rapport are outlined in Table 17.1. Study that table carefully.

Stating the Purpose of an Interaction

According to *The Standards* (1986, p. 93), instructional designers should be able to "state the purpose or agenda of the interaction so that the individual or group understands it and finds it acceptable." *Purpose* simply means the reason for an interaction with another person. *Agenda,* on the other hand, refers to the sequence of events that will occur during an interaction.

When deciding how to state the purpose or agenda of an interaction, instructional designers should always ask themselves three questions: (1) Have good relations already been established with the individual or group with whom interaction is necessary? (2) Is the nature of the interaction structured or unstructured? (3) How much authority do instructional designers have to enforce cooperation from others? These questions, based on Fiedler's contingency theory of leadership, can provide practical guidance about how to state the purpose or agenda of an interpersonal interaction (Fiedler, 1967; Fiedler and Chemers, 1974). While Fiedler's views on leadership have not escaped criticism (Graen, Orrin, and Alvares, 1971; Kelly, (1980), they

Table 17.1. A Model for Selecting Techniques to Establish
and Maintain Rapport in Instructional Design Projects.

| Situation | Affiliation | |
	Insider	Outsider
Request Initiated by Others	*Before initial meeting* Ask for advance information about the problem. Research the in-house politics of the problem, if possible. Research the person who requested assistance, if possible. Dress to make a good first impression. Prepare some questions in advance.	*Before initial meeting* Ask for advance information about the organization, problem. Find out what you can. Dress to make a good impression. Prepare some questions in advance. Prepare biosketch and list of references who can provide information about your skills/abilities.
	During initial meeting Allow the initiator of the meeting to set agenda. Take notes. Demonstrate attending skills. Ask "how can I help?". Determine purpose of meeting, nature of help required. Clarify your reporting relationship. Ask key questions. Clarify next steps.	*During initial meeting* Allow the initiator of the meeting to set agenda. Take notes. Ask "how can I help?". Determine purpose of meeting, nature of help required. Clarify your reporting relationship. Ask key questions. Clarify next steps.
	After initial meeting Follow up, summarizing help requested and next steps.	*After initial meeting* Follow up, summarizing help requested and next steps.
	In subsequent interaction Demonstrate thoughtfulness, keeping others informed.	*In subsequent interaction* Demonstrate thoughtfulness, keeping others informed.
Request Initiated by Instructional Designer	*Before initial meeting* Clarify protocol for contacting people and follow it. Make advance contact, clarifying nature of request. Try to arrange for another person in the organization to contact the individual, requesting his or her cooperation (when appropriate). Dress to make a good first impression. Prepare questions in advance. Prepare an agenda for the meeting in advance.	*Before initial meeting* Clarify protocol for contacting people and follow it. Make advance contact, clarifying nature of request and who has approved the meeting. Ask your "contact" in the organization to help arrange the meeting, when appropriate, to help lay the groundwork for cooperation and show evidence that the request for information has been approved by key managers in the organization. Dress to make a good first impression. Prepare questions in advance. Prepare an agenda for the meeting in advance.

Table 17.1. A Model for Selecting Techniques to Establish
and Maintain Rapport in Instructional Design Projects, Cont'd.

| Situation | *Affiliation* | |
	Insider	*Outsider*
	During initial meeting	*During initial meeting*
	Run the meeting.	Run the meeting.
	Begin the meeting with small talk to set the individual at ease.	Begin the meeting with small talk to set the individual at ease.
	Clarify who you are, where you come from, what you want, why you want it, how the information you request will be used, and who will see the results of any investigation you conduct.	Clarify who you are, where you come from, what you want, why you want it, how the information requested will be used, and who will see the results of any investigation you will conduct.
	Establish your own credibility.	Establish your own credibility.
	Listen thoughtfully.	Listen thoughtfully.
	Make your request specific and (if possible) show how providing information could benefit the individual to whom the request is being made.	Make your request specific and (if possible) show how providing information could benefit the individual of whom the request is being made.
	Encourage participation by the individual who will provide the information.	Encourage participation by the individual who will provide the information.
	Clarify next steps.	Clarify next steps.
	After initial meeting	*After initial meeting*
	Thank the individual for his or her time and effort.	Thank the individual for his or her time and effort.
	Summarize the meeting and next steps.	Summarize the meeting and next steps.
	In subsequent interaction	*In subsequent interaction*
	Remain thoughtful and considerate of others' viewpoints and feelings.	Remain thoughtful and considerate of others' viewpoints and feelings.

are quite practical and can be applied in specific situations as instructional designers confront situations while performing their work.

Relations Between Instructional Designer and Individual or Group Members

How well have instructional designers been able to establish and maintain good rapport with the clients? How much trust, respect, and confidence exists in this relationship?

When little or no rapport has been successfully established between instructional designers and others within the organization — an unfortunate situation that does happen—instructional designers should work on improving their interaction. They can do that by spending more time with others or by giving them opportunities to participate in the process of collecting or interpreting information (Fiedler, 1972; Rothwell and Kazanas, 1987).

Nature of the Interaction

What is the nature of the interaction? In other words, how easily can instructional designers explain to others the tasks to be performed during their project? How clearcut is the range of possible strategies that can be used to identify or address performance problems? How easily can instructional design decisions be justified? When the nature of the activities to be performed in the interaction is easily understood, the range of possible strategies is limited, and instructional designers can justify their actions and decisions without too much difficulty, the situation is *structured*. On the other hand, when activities are difficult to explain, the range of solutions is not limited, and instructional designers find it difficult to justify their actions and decisions, the situation is *unstructured*.

When the situation is structured, instructional designers should find interaction easy enough. They need only explain their reasons (purposes) and describe what steps they must take to collect information or find a solution. On the other hand, unstructured situations are more difficult. In those cases, they should try to find an "idea champion" from the organization to help reassure those who may be concerned about the project and to function as a liaison with others. To reduce the likelihood of misunderstandings that could destroy rapport, instructional designers should take pains to brief managers at the outset of the project about their need for information, the steps in the project, and key assumptions underlying those steps.

Instructional Designers' Position Power

Position power refers to the ability, perceived or real, to exact obedience from others. When instructional designers begin an assignment with full support from top managers and easy access to them, their position power is said to be *high;* when they begin an assignment without full support from top managers or without access to them, their position power is said to be *low*.

When position power is high, ask that a top manager or sponsor send out a memo to solicit support and cooperation during data collection. (Instructional designers may have to draft the memo themselves for the top manager's initials.) That should provide an adequate introduction to those who must be contacted within the organization. When position power is low, base information requests on the problem itself. Explain why the information is needed and how it can help solve the problem or prepare instruction. In other words, point out the problem, state what information needs have to be met to solve it, and ask others pointedly for their cooperation.

Asking Questions

According to *The Standards* (1986, p. 94), instructional designers should be able to "ask questions of individuals or groups so that they (1) gather all the information that is required for their purpose; (2) gather the information accurately; (3) phrase and sequence questions so the individual or groups provide the information they have." Of course, questions are powerful tools for data gathering (Amidon and Hough, 1967). They can shed new light on perceptions of problems, people, or events (Antaki, 1988). Instructional designers may use questions to collect information about existing performance problems, identify performance criteria or managerial expectations, pinpoint causes of performance problems, and determine the significance of those problems. They can also use questions to consider possible solutions to address those problems, select one or more solutions, anticipate problems that may stem from implementing solutions, establish goals for learners, test learners' knowledge, manage classroom instruction, and for other purposes (Leeds, 1988; Sanders, 1966; Schoonover, 1988).

Questions may be categorized in two ways. First, they may be open or closed. Second, they can be externally or internally focused.

Open questions invite people to talk; closed questions tend to shut off or redirect responses. Open questions begin with words like *who, what, when, where, why,* and *how.* Instructional designers may ask open questions such as these: When did you first notice this performance problem? Who is affected by the problem? Where is it most and least evident? Open questions can also begin with such words as *could* or *would,* as in the question "could you tell me a little more about . . . ?" As a matter of fact, questions beginning with *could* tend to prompt the most talking and offer the least clues about what the interviewer is looking for by way of an answer (Ivey and Gluckstern, 1982, p. 33). Use open questions to explore and investigate problems, probe what others have said, and prompt creative thinking by learners.

On the other hand, closed questions begin with such words as *is, are, was, were, do, did, have,* and *has.* Instructional designers can ask closed questions such as these: Is that an accurate description? Was that always the work standard? Do you have ideas about the cause of the problem? Have you taken steps to investigate this problem in greater depth? Use closed questions to guide a conversation, verifying information or tactfully shutting off further talk.

Externally focused questions are directed to conditions in the outside world; internally focused questions are directed to conditions in the inside (mental) world. Externally focused questions are appropriate for collecting objective or factual information. Examples include any of the following questions: How would you describe the performance problem your organization is experiencing? When was it first noticed? In what locations is it most

apparent? Use externally focused questions to collect descriptive information. On the other hand, internally focused questions are appropriate for
assessing attitudes, opinions, beliefs, and perceptions. Examples include any
of the following: How do you feel about this problem? What do you think
others feel about this problem? What is your perception of this problem's
cause or causes? Use internally focused questions to collect interpretive information.

Providing Explanations

According to *The Standards* (1986, p. 95), instructional designers should be
able to "explain information to individuals or groups so that the presentation of information is done clearly, accurately, and so the individuals or
groups can act on it appropriately." *Explanation* is simply a description of
facts, conclusions, decisions, judgments, or actions. It includes clarification
and paraphrase, responses to feelings and emotions, summarization, and
justification (Ivey and Gluckstern, 1982). A good explanation anticipates,
and addresses, questions of interest to the prospective audience.

Before taking action, instructional designers should always ask themselves "who should know about it?" Use the answer to identify those who
deserve explanation. Then try to anticipate what they will need or want to
know about it. Plan an explanation to provide them with information they
will view as important.

Listening Actively

According to *The Standards* (1986, p. 96), instructional designers should be
able to "listen to individuals or groups so that they gather sufficient information for the purpose, the individuals or groups feel listened to, and the
individuals or groups continue to provide information for as long as you
want them to." Instructional designers should, of course, distinguish projects
appropriate for instructional design from those that are not, conduct needs
assessment, and carry out many other activities. Listening may require at
least 48 percent of project time. However, when people are not trained to
listen, their listening efficiency can dip as low as 25 percent of a complete
message (Nichols, 1957). Part of the problem is that most people speak at
a rate of about 125 words per minute, yet an average listener is capable of
thinking at a rate of about 400 words per minute. Hence, there is a significant amount of extra time that can be wasted as one person listens to
another. It is easy to fall into the trap of listening passively or spending time
planning what to say next rather than hearing what others are saying. However, listening should be an active endeavor, one in which the listener devotes as much attention to the *feeling* (emotional) components as to the *content* (meaning) components of the message.

There are several keys to active listening. First, instructional designers should focus on what is being said on more than one level. In other words, they should ask themselves not only "what does the speaker *mean*?" but also "what does the speaker *feel* about the subject at hand?" Body language, tone of voice, and any other clues to meaning and feeling should be noted.

Second, instructional designers should *work* at listening. They should ask questions, show interest, and use body language that encourages rather than discourages speakers. The key is to remain self-conscious, aware of how a listener's actions influence speakers, while simultaneously focusing attention on a speaker's content and feelings. For additional information about effective listening, see American Society for Training and Development (1988c).

Dealing with Friction

According to *The Standards* (1986, p. 97), instructional designers should be able to "deal with friction among members of the group in a way that facilitates, or at least does not impede, attaining the purpose of the interaction by either (1) controlling the friction, or (2) recognizing when it is out of control and minimizing the damage by 'cutting the losses and running.'" *Friction* is synonymous with conflict, and conflict is perhaps best understood simply as any situation in which individuals disagree (Baker and Morgan, 1989).

How Does Friction Arise?

Friction arises whenever individuals or groups disagree about philosophy, values, goals, measurement methods, and results. It also stems from differences in personal styles, communication problems, competition, association, interdependence, expectations, and change. As Hensey (1983, p. 52) points out, "conflict is often a result of changes, actual or perceived, and conflict is a very legitimate way of managing change, though not the only way. Planning, collaboration, problem-solving, and co-existence are some other ways of dealing with change."

How Does Friction Arise in Instructional Design Projects?

Whenever people work together, undergo change, or experience interdependence, the potential for friction exists. Of course, instructional design projects tend to have all these elements: instructional designers work with colleagues, operating managers, media production people, learners, learners' supervisors, and others. Naturally, change and learning are synonymous (Sredl and Rothwell, 1987), and instructional design projects typically require interdependence among team members. Very real differences of opinion can arise about instructional design projects. Moreover, personality conflicts can arise between members of an instructional design team and between instructional designers and operating managers.

How Should Friction Be Managed?

Before attempting to manage friction, instructional designers should first clarify their assumptions about it. Second, they should try to determine its cause. They should then apply one of many available approaches to manage it.

The starting point for managing conflict is to clarify assumptions about it. Many people tend to view any disagreement as something to be avoided. "Conflict," as Baker and Morgan (1989, p. 151) point out, "is often viewed negatively, although it is neither good nor bad in itself. If properly handled, conflict can become a positive source of energy and creativity; if mishandled, it can become dysfunctional, draining energy and reducing both personal and organizational effectiveness."

Each instructional designer should begin by clarifying his or her own views about friction. If that is difficult, then they should think back to the last time in which they observed, or were a party to, a disagreement. It could have been a disagreement with a supervisor, co-worker, team member, or even a spouse. What feelings did it evoke? How was the conflict handled? Were any of the following ineffective conflict resolution strategies used to cope with it?

> *Moralizing* ("my way is right!")
> *Submitting* ("I'll give up just to keep the peace, even though I still think this is wrong")
> *Denying* ("maybe we don't disagree after all")
> *Coercing* ("you better do it my way or else")
> *Bribing* ("if you do it my way this time, I'll see to it you get your way on something else")

Reflect on past actions in conflict situations, at work or at some other location. Determine what assumptions were made about the conflict. Was it handled as though it was best avoided? If so, rethink how it was handled, realizing that conflict is a natural part of social life and can be a stimulus for new ideas.

The second step in managing conflict is to identify its cause(s). To that end, apply essentially the same techniques used in performance analysis. Never be misled by symptoms alone. Of course, symptoms of conflict may include arguments between people, name calling, malicious gossip, the formation of cliques among team members, and (when friction is at its worst) absenteeism, turnover, or even sabotage. These problems result from more than simple "personality conflicts" and may reflect much deeper causes stemming from differing philosophies, values, goals, or work methods. Consider:

When did the conflict first appear? What are its consequences? Who is involved? Is it a difference between individuals or groups? What do the conflicting parties believe the cause(s) of the conflict to be? Probe for answers, just as you would do in performance analysis.

The third step in managing conflict is to apply a conflict resolution approach. Use collaboration, which means "attempting to work with other persons to find some solution which fully satisfies the concerns of both" (Thomas and Kilmann, 1983, p. 58). If conflict exists between two people, use *interpersonal peacemaking* techniques to help them resolve destructive differences (McEwan, 1989; Walton, 1969). If the conflict is between two groups of people, use *teambuilding* techniques to mediate the dispute and build esprit de corps (Dyer, 1977). Alternatives to teambuilding may also be used in group settings (Guest, 1986).

Handling Resistance to Change

According to *The Standards* (1986, p. 98), instructional designers should be able to "deal with resistance from an individual or group in a way that indicates recognition of the existence of resistance, manages or controls the resistance, or minimizes the damage by 'cutting losses and running.'" Each step in the instructional design process implies change. As human resource professionals, instructional designers should understand their roles as change agents (London, 1988). Here are some questions worth pondering:

Step in Instructional Design	*Change Issue*
1. Determining projects appropriate for instructional design	1. Is change warranted to address a performance problem?
2. Conducting a needs assessment	2. What kind of individual change is appropriate? What should people know, do, or feel that is different from what they presently know, do, or feel?
3. Assessing relevant characteristics of learners	3. What learner characteristics can affect the intended change effort?
4. Analyzing characteristics of a work setting	4. What characteristics of the setting(s) can affect the intended change effort?

5. Performing job, task, and/or content analysis

5. What characteristics of the job, task, or subject should be a focus of change with prospective learners?

6. Writing statements of performance objectives

6. What results are desired from a change effort?

7. Developing performance measurements

7. How will individual change be assessed?

8. Sequencing performance objectives

8. In what order should changes in individual knowledge, skills, or attitudes be introduced?

9. Specifying instructional strategies

9. What are the best ways to introduce change?

10. Designing instructional materials

10. What materials can help introduce or guide the change effort?

11. Evaluating instruction

11. How can change efforts be assessed, particularly before widespread implementation?

12. Designing the instructional management system

12. How can the change effort be supported?

13. Planning and monitoring instructional design projects

13. How can efforts to introduce change be effectively managed among the change agents themselves?

14. Communicating effectively

14. How can effective communication facilitate a change effort?

15. Interacting with others

15. How can effective interpersonal communication facilitate the change effort?

16. Promoting the use of instructional design

16. How can this approach to identifying the need for change — and to designing and implementing it — be passed on to others?

How Do People React to Change?

There are essentially three possible reactions to change among learners, their immediate superiors, and others with whom instructional designers must interact: individuals may resist it, favor it, or remain neutral to it (Kirkpatrick, 1985). However, most managers, like most instructional designers, probably find resistance to change the most noticeable reaction, if only because it appears to stymie success in a way that the other reactions do not (Odiorne, 1981).

Why Do People Resist Change?

Before instructional designers can deal effectively with resistance to change, they should make an attempt to understand its causes. Kirkpatrick (1985) has enumerated most of the reasons why people resist change. One reason is that they fear they will lose security, money, pride, satisfaction, friends and contacts, freedom, responsibility, authority, good working conditions, or status. A second reason is that they see no need for change. They are comfortable with the way things are and do not experience a deep need to depart from the known into the realm of the unknown. A third reason is that they perceive that change will produce more harmful than useful consequences. Other reasons for resisting change are easily identifiable: people lack respect for those making the change, feel the change has been introduced in an objectionable manner, and experience negative attitudes about the organization (or people running it). They may also feel powerless, dislike criticism of existing conditions implicit when the need for change is identified, sense that the change will place additional burdens on them, and anticipate that additional effort will be required of them to cope with the change. They might feel, too, that the change is poorly timed, wish to challenge authority, dislike receiving information about the change from secondhand sources, and dislike their own lack of input in the change process.

Of course, people can also welcome change. They may do so for reasons that are exactly the reverse of those producing resistance (Kirkpatrick, 1985). For instance, people may favor change when they feel it will lead to increased security, money, pride, satisfaction, friends and contacts, freedom, responsibility, authority, better working conditions, or status. Likewise, they may be experiencing a problem that change could solve. In addition, they may be restless with the way things are and experience a deep personal need to depart from existing conditions. They may also perceive that change will produce consequences leading to benefits that outweigh their costs. Finally, they may welcome change because they have deep respect for those making it, feel the change has been introduced in an exemplary manner, or experience strong loyalty and commitment to the organization (or people running it). They might also feel that the change makes them more powerful, like the criticism of existing conditions implicit when the need for change is identified, and sense that the change will reduce the burdens and stress placed on them. In addition, they might feel that the change is well timed, wish to support authority, and like the opportunity for input in the change process that they may be afforded.

How Should Instructional Designers Deal with Resistance to Change?

Adopt different strategies for dealing with resistance to change, depending on the stage of the change effort and the source(s) of resistance. Each stage of the change effort implies a different role for the instructional designer (Dormant, 1986). During the earliest stages in which the need for change is being recognized, adopt the role of *advertiser of the need for change.* Once the need for change has been recognized, plan on serving as a *counselor* to help decision makers decide on appropriate performance improvement strategies, depending on the cause(s) of the problems which change is intended to rectify. Once decision makers have fixed on a course of action, be prepared to function as *demonstrator* of that action, helping conceptualize what to do and how to do it. As the change process unfolds, be prepared to function as *instructor* and *technical assistant* to show others appropriate ways to act to facilitate implementation of change.

Each source of resistance should be considered when planning the change effort. Like anyone involved in a change effort (Kirkpatrick, 1985; Odiorne, 1981), instructional designers should try to identify individuals or groups likely to resist change. They should also plan specific strategies to anticipate and head off each source of resistance (Connor and Lake, 1988).

Keeping People on Track

According to *The Standards* (1986, p. 99), instructional designers should be able to "keep an individual or group on track so that the interaction returns quickly to its purpose and the individual or group does not feel slighted." They should be able to enact this performance when "an individual or group wanders from the purpose of the interaction." Keeping people on track thus means achieving desired results from interactions with others while being spared distractions of peripheral interest or concern.

Why Do People Lose Track of Purpose?

Any interaction between people can lose focus. Individuals are driven by different wants, needs, and goals. Moreover, they often have different priorities. A meeting expressly called to address instructional needs can turn into a platform for a handful of vocal participants to launch into a tirade against the organization's selection, promotion, pay, or retirement practices! Likewise, an individual who is being interviewed about training needs may offer advice about what—or who—to believe in the organization! These sometimes frustrating (and sometimes amusing) mismatches between the goals and outcomes of an interaction occur because some issues weigh more heavily than others on the minds of the participants. Without exercising control and exerting influence over interactions with others, instructional designers may find themselves wasting valuable time and effort — or struggling to establish priorities among a myriad of competing interests.

How Should People Be Guided Back on Track?

Instructional designers may use several approaches in exercising control over interactions. But first they should clarify in their own minds what results they seek from a meeting, interview, or discussion. When an interaction will be lengthy and formalized — as is often the case with meetings or interviews — instructional designers should prepare an agenda or list of questions in advance. They should then send it to the participants as a place to start discussion and as a control mechanism in case others turn to tangential issues.

Second, instructional designers should restate the purpose of the meeting or discussion when others begin to wander off the topic. In one meeting, for example, a participant wanted to discuss the organization's pay practices rather than employees' instructional needs. (The latter topic was the reason for the meeting.) The instructional designer noted that "what you have said is most interesting and possibly true. However, I am neither qualified to judge or knowledgeable enough on the subject to respond. Could we turn back for now to the subject of instructional needs?" That remark brought a prompt apology from the wanderer — and renewed attention to the subject of the meeting from other participants.

Third, if all else fails, an instructional designer should begin speaking at the same time as the individual who has wandered off the topic. While that may seem rude and socially unacceptable, it can turn a discussion back on track. The trick is to *keep talking,* even when the inclination is not to do so. Other people will usually stop to listen, and at that point the discussion can be guided back to the subject.

Fourth, use periodic feedback to keep people on track (Schein, 1969). End each meeting or discussion by asking participants "how well did we stay on the subject of the meeting, and how well did we interact as a group?" This is an approach borrowed from *process consultation,* defined by Schein (1969, p. 9) as "a set of activities . . . which helps the client to perceive, understand, and act upon process events which occur in the client's environment."

Securing Commitment

According to *The Standards* (1986, p. 100), instructional designers should be able to "obtain commitment from an individual or group so that the commitment facilitates [the project's] goals, both parties feel the commitment is binding, both parties are willing to follow through on it, and both parties feel there is value in it." Obtaining commitment simply means that people support the instructional design project. They are thus willing to provide information, resources, facilities, and their own time to ensure that the project's goals are achieved.

Why Is Commitment Important?

Instructional designers, by virtue of the work they perform, must work with — and often through — others. If they are unable to secure cooperation and commitment, they will probably waste much time, effort, and organizational resources as they analyze performance problems, conduct needs assessment, and carry out other steps in the instructional design process. Hence, commitment from key decision makers and other affected groups and individuals is essential to project success.

How Is Commitment Obtained?

Obtain and maintain commitment to an instructional design project by practicing empathy about the project, communicating with individuals or groups affected by the project, and encouraging participation in the project by those affected by it. These are also three key methods for managing change (Kirkpatrick, 1985).

Practicing empathy means looking at a project, problem or issue from another person's viewpoint. It is an appreciation of the viewpoints and feelings of other. To practice empathy, instructional designers must first have some information about the individual or group with which they must interact. For instance, in preparing to deal with individuals, instructional designers may find it useful to learn about their education, experience, outside hobbies and activities, and other issues (Kirkpatrick, 1985). Instructional designers might also find it useful to know what others think about instructional design projects generally, the present project specifically, the organization, their prospects within the organization, and any other matters that could affect their support of the project. In this way, it is possible to bring out hidden agendas and address individual concerns at the project's outset.

Communicating means "creating understanding" (Kirkpatrick, 1985, p. 118). To obtain and maintain commitment to an instructional design project, be sure to identify who will be affected by it, select appropriate timing to communicate about it, pick appropriate methods of communicating, and establish methods by which to obtain feedback (Kirkpatrick, 1985).

Encouraging participation means "getting involvement from those concerned with and affected by change" (Kirkpatrick, 1985, p. 133). It is the third and final key to obtaining and maintaining commitment to an instructional design project.

Since the late 1940s, numerous authors have emphasized the crucial importance of participative decision making in planning, implementing, and sustaining change (Coch and French, 1948; Likert, 1967; Marrow, 1972; Myers, 1970). Subsequent research has even demonstrated that participation is of critical importance in instructional design efforts in particular (Rothwell and Kazanas, 1987). Surprisingly, corporate planners and instructional designers alike feel that Strategic Business Planning activities, typically carried out by top managers only, are more open to participation than most instructional design efforts!

To obtain commitment, instructional designers should begin by identifying those affected by the instructional design process. They should then use the following techniques to encourage participation in this process (Kirkpatrick, 1985, p. 144):

1. Ask for input before and during each step of the project.
2. Consider and evaluate the input received.
3. Give credit to those who contributed useful ideas.
4. Thank those who contributed ideas that were not used and explain why they were not used.

Participation may be solicited during each step of the instructional design process. Indeed, there are good reasons for instructional designers to encourage participation by others even after instruction has been designed: different groups may be involved, and members of those groups may have their own ideas about present and future instruction.

Selecting for Effective Interpersonal Interaction

According to *The Standards* (1986, p. 101), instructional designers should be able to "select and tailor appropriate behaviors for specific interactions with other people." While it is important for instructional designers to establish rapport, state the purpose of an interaction, ask questions, provide explanations, listen actively, deal with friction, handle resistance to change, keep people on track, and secure commitment, it is equally important to be able to select appropriate behaviors for effective interpersonal interaction.

When to Establish Rapport

Establishing rapport is usually associated with the beginning of a relationship; maintaining rapport, on the other hand, is associated with preserving a relationship. Establishing rapport is frequently an issue when you have been contacted for help and are meeting, for the first time, with a prospective client or clients. The need to maintain rapport will continue as long as instructional designers meet new people in the organization while seeking information, present results of investigations such as performance analyses or needs assessments, and work on subsequent instructional design steps.

When to State the Purpose of an Interaction

State the purpose of—or establish an agenda for—each interpersonal interaction at the outset. Repeat the purpose or remind people of the agenda whenever it appears that the interaction may shift to unrelated topics.

When to Ask Questions

Ask questions to collect information or exercise control over interactions with others. Remember that open questions are suitable for exploring opinions and collecting information. Closed questions are appropriate for controlling interactions and closing off discussion.

When to Provide Explanations

Try to avoid misunderstandings with others by providing explanations and justifications of actions taken and decisions made.

When to Listen Actively

Listen actively to hear what others say and how they feel. In this way, instructional designers can collect the maximum amount of information about the subject under investigation *and* about those from whom the information is collected.

When to Deal with Friction

Use conflict resolution techniques to deal with friction whenever it appears to threaten the objectives of the instructional design project. Remember that conflict can be both constructive and destructive. Encourage issue-oriented conflict leading to creative solutions; discourage—and work to alleviate—destructive, unproductive conflict.

When to Deal with Resistance

Realize that some people will resist change, some will welcome it, and some will not care about it. Try to identify, in advance, who is likely to resist change because of their fear of real (or perceived) loss of security, money, pride, satisfaction, friends and contacts, freedom, responsibility, authority, good working conditions, status, or for other reasons. Then try to mount convincing arguments in favor of the change. Allow others the opportunity to participate in the instructional design project, since participation builds ownership and reduces resistance.

When to Keep People on Track

Take steps to keep people on track when they attempt to deviate from the stated purpose of an interaction.

When to Secure Commitment

Take steps to secure and maintain commitment during all steps in an instructional design project.

Judging Interactions with Others

According to *The Standards* (1986, p. 102), instructional designers should be able to "judge the appropriateness and effectiveness of behaviors used in specific interactions with other people." Use a checklist as a decision aid when it becomes necessary to make such judgments. An example of such a checklist appears in Exhibit 17.1.

Justifying Behaviors Used in Interactions with Others

According to *The Standards* (1986, p. 103), instructional designers should also be able to justify "the selection and tailoring of appropriate behaviors for specific interactions with other people." This justification should include: "(a) An explanation of the logic of the plan for the selection and tailoring of appropriate behaviors for that interaction; (b) A plan for dealing with, rather than avoiding, friction or resistance; (c) An explanation of how well the selection and tailoring worked; (d) An explanation of any deviations from the plan during the actual interaction; (e) A description of the instructional designer's perception of the effectiveness of the interaction; and (f) An explanation of any specific behaviors asked about."

In other words, instructional designers should be prepared to explain their actions and behaviors and able to justify why they acted as they did. Realize that not everyone involved with the project may be trusting, share the natural enthusiasm of the designer, understand what is being done, or appreciate why it should be done. As a result, they may become anxious about the designer's methods, behaviors, credentials — and whatever else they can become anxious about. As agents of change, instructional designers do occasionally feel that they are placed squarely in the role of lightning rod for controversy. Be patient enough with the clients — and others with whom interaction is necessary — to explain the need for each step in the instructional design process. Plan to state those reasons at each step of a project and on each occasion when interaction with others is necessary.

Conclusion

In this chapter, we described how instructional designers establish rapport, state the purposes of an interaction, ask questions, provide explanations, listen

Exhibit 17.1. A Checklist for Judging the Appropriateness and Effectiveness of Behaviors Used in Specific Interactions with Other People.

Directions: Use this checklist to judge the appropriateness and effectiveness of the behaviors used on a project by instructional designers. Answer each question appearing in the left column below by circling an appropriate numeral in the center column. Use the following scale in the center column:

1 = Needs substantial improvement
2 = Needs some improvement
3 = Adequate
4 = Better than adequate
5 = Excellent

In the right column, make notes about project behaviors that instructional designers could improve.

Behavior	How Well Is the Behavior Exhibited on the Project by Instructional Designers?					Notes for Improvement
How well do instructional designers . . .	Needs . . . 1	2	Adequate 3	4	Excellent 5	
1. Establish rapport with individuals and groups?	1	2	3	4	5	
2. State the purpose and/or agenda of each interaction?	1	2	3	4	5	
3. Ask questions of individuals or groups?	1	2	3	4	5	
4. Explain information to individuals or groups?	1	2	3	4	5	
5. Listen to individuals or groups?	1	2	3	4	5	
6. Deal with friction among members of a group?	1	2	3	4	5	
7. Deal with resistance from an individual or group?	1	2	3	4	5	
8. Keep an individual or group on track?	1	2	3	4	5	
9. Obtain commitment from an individual or group?	1	2	3	4	5	
10. Select and tailor appropriate behaviors for specific interactions with other people?	1	2	3	4	5	

actively, deal with friction, handle resistance to change, keep people on track, secure commitment, and select appropriate behaviors for effective interpersonal interaction. Such day-to-day behaviors are critical to the success of each instructional design project. However, instructional designers also have an obligation to promote the use of instructional design over the long term, extending beyond a single project. That is the topic of the next chapter.

CHAPTER EIGHTEEN

Promoting the Use
of Instructional Design

"Not everyone believes that the rigorous instructional design process described in the preceding competencies is the best way to develop training," write the authors of *The Standards* (1986, p. 104). "Many do not even know instructional design exists. Many know just enough to misapply it. Many do not agree all this fuss is necessary. And, many do not want to go through all the work it requires. Part of an instructional designer's role is to talk to these people about the advantages of instructional design, and to change both individual attitudes and corporate policies toward the use of some form of systematic approach to instructional design as the official training methodology of the organization." In doing so, they should promote the use of instructional design and the application of the instructional design model described in this book.

We begin this chapter with a brief case study to dramatize important issues in promoting instructional design. We then turn to describing ways to make others aware of instructional design. We conclude the chapter with a few words of advice about justifying these promotional efforts.

Promoting the Use of Instructional Design: A Case Study

George McDonald is the Director of Human Resource Development for a large insurance company. He was hired not long ago to establish formal training in a 100-year-old company that has never before offered it to employees. An experienced specialist who is quite familiar with current professional approaches to instructional design, George wants to introduce a performance-based approach as he establishes his new human resource development department.

George reports to an Advisory Committee that was created shortly before he was hired. Its purpose is to provide advice about the direction of human resource development activities in the organization. The committee consists of representatives from first-line supervision, middle management, and top management. George has decided that, if he can inform and persuade members of that committee to support adoption of a rigorous approach to instructional design from the outset, it will be much easier for him to implement it as the organization's instructional efforts grow in number.

George prepares a short (two-page) white paper on the topic of instructional design for the next meeting of the Advisory Committee. At the meeting, he makes a brief presentation on the white paper, with the dual goals of informing and persuading his listeners to support the introduction of a rigorous instructional design process. George is fully aware that, as a newcomer to the organization, he is accorded a certain amount of license to introduce whatever innovations he feels appropriate. He takes advantage of that license with committee members to ensure that this innovation is adopted. He is even successful in soliciting their support for persuading others in the organization to adopt the approach.

Making Others Aware of Instructional Design

As the case study has illustrated, instructional designers who set out to promote a rigorous and systematic approach to instructional design should begin by targeting key decision makers. After all, they are the ones who should be informed of the importance of such an approach. Moreover, decision makers should be the target of goals and a strategy formulated to guide the promotion effort. Of course, the promotional strategy chosen should be attuned to the organization's and the human resource development department's stage in adopting the instructional design model.

In one sense at least, every organization can be viewed as composed of different market segments or interest groups. As in classifying learners, individuals in any organization may be segmented on the basis of their experience, education, job responsibilities, level within the organizational hierarchy, and other characteristics (Richey, 1986). In each organizational market segment there are opinion leaders who are regularly consulted by others for their ideas about issues affecting the organization. Some opinion leaders are positioned in management, some are positioned in unions, and some informal opinion leaders are affiliated with neither one. Opinion leaders wield considerable social power arising from their positions, extraordinary knowledge of the work, personal charisma, or other characteristics (French and Raven, 1959).

As a first step in making others aware of instructional design, identify key market segments in the organization. Then identify opinion leaders for each market segment. Target such key decision makers and opinion leaders as colleagues in the human resource development department, professional or organizational superiors, line managers, union representatives, and others. Finally, for each organizational market segment, ask three questions:

1. What special interests exist in this group that might lead its members to explore—and perhaps support—a rigorous, professional approach to instructional design?
2. How might the members of this group benefit from a rigorous approach to instructional design?
3. What would opinion leaders in this group need to know to be persuaded to support such an approach?

Use the answers to these questions in establishing goals for promoting a professional approach to instructional design in an organization.

Establishing Goals

Make a list of goals for promoting a professional approach to instructional design for each organizational market segment. Goals may vary. For instance, instructional designers may choose any or all of the following goals:

1. Inform opinion leaders of the advantages of a professional approach to instructional design.
2. Answer any questions or address any concerns that opinion leaders may have about the application of the instructional design model in an organization.
3. Persuade opinion leaders that a rigorous and systematic approach to instructional design can produce results superior to less rigorous approaches. (Such benefits may include reduced training time, reduced long-term costs, increased production, decreased scrap rates, or improved customer service.)
4. Prompt opinion leaders to back the application of a rigorous and systematic approach to instructional design by the organization or the human resource development department, perhaps supplanting an existing but less rigorous approach.
5. Convince decision makers to reconsider an earlier rejection of a systematic approach to instructional design.

When opinion leaders are not sophisticated, instructional designers will usually want to establish goals in more or less the order listed above. First, inform opinion leaders about the options; then convince them that a professional approach to instructional design deserves to be adopted. Other goals may, of course, be established. For instance, some instructional designers may wish to convince decision makers to commit resources to experimentation with instructional design.

Selecting a Promotional Strategy

Once instructional designers know what goals to seek from their promotional efforts, they will be well positioned to decide how to accomplish them. Each goal implies possible promotional strategies. For instance:

Goal	*Possible Promotional Strategies*
1. Inform opinion leaders about professional approaches to instructional design.	Route articles about instructional design to opinion leaders.
	Decribe instructional design in management, professional, and technical training sponsored by the organization.
	Take advantage of "windows of opportunity" by describing what to do when decision makers ask for help to address immediate performance problems confronting them.
	Invite outside speakers to address managers about instructional design.
	Write articles on instructional design for in-company publications.
	Write articles about instructional design for professional journals in the field and then route the articles to key opinion leaders in the organization.
	Build support informally for rigorous approaches to instructional design by discussing the issue with opinion leaders who may be possible supporters. (Try members of a training advisory committee first.)
	Describe how a rigorous approach to instructional design can help implement the organization's Strategic Business Plan.
2. Persuade opinion leaders that the benefits of a rigorous, systematic approach to instructional design outweigh its costs.	Gather testimonials from colleagues in other organizations.
	Collect information about the application of rigorous approaches to instructional design by key competitors.

	Prepare a detailed proposal for using a rigorous approach to instructional design in the organization. Be sure to describe the relative costs and benefits of the approach, preferably compared to methods of instructional design already in use.
3. Prompt adoption of a rigorous, systematic approach to instructional design by the organization and/or the human resource development department.	Press the issue, since persistence often leads to success. Make a simple, straightforward presentation to key decision makers, ending with a plea for adopting the approach in the future and identifying specifically what each member of the audience would need to *do*.
4. Prompt reconsideration of a rigorous systematic approach to instructional design if such an approach has previously been considered but rejected.	Monitor reasons for initial rejection of the approach. If conditions change, raise the issue again. Identify which decision makers resisted the approach. If the organization experiences a change in leadership, raise the issue again with the new decision makers.

Then select appropriate promotional strategies. Generally speaking, it is better to select at least two such strategies at the same time so that the chances of success are doubled.

Ensuring That Promotional Strategies Are Appropriate for the Stage of Adoption of the Client

In the past few years, numerous authors have noted that organizations and human resource development departments progress through predictable stages called *life cycles* (Kimberly, Miles, and Associates, 1980; Rothwell, 1983b; Sredl and Rothwell, 1987). In many respects, theories of life cycle development are comparable to theories of innovation (Rogers and Shoemaker, 1971). Each deserves brief review.

Each life cycle stage of an organization or human resource development department corresponds to an individual's stage of development. Whereas empirical proof of organizational life cycles is elusive and those who accept the idea completely tread perilously close to personifying an abstraction, the notion of organizational life cycles has a strong intuitive appeal. Moreover, useful clues can be offered about appropriate leadership strategies for each stage of development (Cribbin, 1981). In many ways, organizational life cycle theories bear close resemblances to similar notions of product life cycles in marketing, individual life cycles in psychology, group formation life cycles in organizational dynamics, and diffusion theory in anthropology, sociology, and communications (Buzzell, 1966; Cox, 1967; Erikson, 1959; Levinson, 1978; Weber, 1982).

In each stage of a life cycle, an organization confronts critical issues in much the same way that individuals confront critical issues in each phase of their development. To address those issues, different leadership strategies should be employed (Cribbin, 1981), just as different counseling strategies should be used in guiding individuals through various stages in their development (Erikson, 1959).

During the conception and birth stage, entrepreneurs have an idea for a profitable venture. The challenge they face, however, is making the idea a reality. The appropriate leader must be an innovator; management is usually a "one-person" operation; the organization's central focus is a struggle for existence; and the leader devotes energy to the new and unusual. Entrepreneurs have to arrange for necessary growth capital, locate adequate physical facilities, and secure the other resources necessary to establish their organization. They must also enter their market, create a vision of the organization's future, and maximize profits.

The same general principles hold true for the conception and birth of a human resource development department, even though the human resource development function's genesis does not always coincide with that of the host organization (Rothwell, 1983b). Appropriate leaders must be innovators and entrepreneurs (Pinchot, 1985), willing to seize opportunities to create highly visible successes through the application of instructional design. A key issue that leaders must confront: Can they persuade decision makers to provide adequate support for the function? They must also be masterful in competing for scarce resources with other—and usually established—parts of the organization.

During the infancy stage, an organization must maximize the opportunities with which it is confronted. Leaders must be opportunists, willing to make the most of environmental conditions. The focus must be on achievement. Planning is typically "catch-as-catch-can" (Cribbin, 1981). Management consists of a small group of people. The central concern is continued survival.

The same general principles hold true for the infancy stage of a human resource development department. The operation is limited in scope. Attention is focused on activities in which maximum success can be demonstrated quickly and visibly—and with minimal expenditure of money, energy, and staff time. The central concern is continued survival, since few decision makers are necessarily convinced that the function is worthwhile. The staff size of the department is limited and must be highly leveraged to achieve maximum results.

During the adolescent stage of an organization, decision makers focus on accelerated growth. Appropriate leaders function as consultants, those who provide advice to others but do not necessarily impose their own opinions. Managers at this stage want to establish a reasonable market share, and their planning methods reflect that preoccupation. However, managers increasingly seek planned profits in ways they did not seek them in earlier stages of the organization's development.

Human resource development departments also progress through adolescence. Appropriate leaders are knowledgeable about the relevant professional practices. They function as consultants. Staff members of the department should devote their attention to meeting specific and identifiable instructional needs. Departmental planning reflects a preoccupation with establishing an identifiable market niche within the organization — that is, with serving justifiable learning needs in a cost-effective manner.

During an organization's middle age, the focus of management attention is on sustained, balanced, and systematic growth. Appropriate leadership styles vary, though most organizations have nurtured those who are professionally trained and knowledgeable about the business, industry, and market. Planning methods may be sophisticated.

During a human resource development department's middle age, the leaders are usually professionally trained. The work is divided up by function or organizational component. The methods used are adequate, if not sophisticated.

During an organization's old age, leaders devote their attention to the continued existence of the enterprise. They are administrators, preoccupied with preserving existing conditions rather than introducing innovations. The organization's self-image is complacent, and a central problem is preservation of stability, often through bureaucratic rules. By this time the organization's culture has become quite strong and tradition-bound (Cribbin, 1981). Managers defend their turf.

During a human resource development department's old age, leaders also devote their attention to the continued existence of the function. They, too, are preoccupied with preserving the status quo, tend toward complacency, and worry about preserving stability and tradition.

Of course, the life cycle of organizations and departments may be renewed through efforts to change the culture by changing the leadership, policies, procedures, work methods, rewards, and structure.

Appropriate goals and strategies for promoting rigorous, professional approaches to instructional design may vary by life cycle stage of the organization and/or department. For example:

Life Cycle Stage	Goal	Promotion Strategy
Conception and birth	Inform others about professional approaches to instructional design.	˙Apply performance analysis to identify improvement opportunities. Describe a current, rigorous approach to instructional design.
Infancy	Persuade others to adopt a professional approach to instructional design.	Train opinion leaders. Train assigned human resource development staff.
Adolescence	Apply the approach.	Advertise successes. Enlist supporters who can offer testimonials.
Middle Age	Refine the approach.	Continue to advertise successes. Keep in close contact with supporters so that continuing refinements can be made. Hire individuals skilled in up-to-date professional approaches to instructional design.
Old Age	Identify complaints, problems, or concerns about applications of professional approaches to instructional design in the organization and reenergize support.	Call in outsiders to interview learners and operating managers, providing advice about improving the approach adopted.

Efforts to promote the use of rigorous, professional approaches to instructional design in organizations are comparable to other efforts to introduce innovation. In *Communication of Innovations,* Rogers and Shoemaker (1971) provide a general framework by which to guide the introduction of innovation and change in any social system. They distinguish between *invention,* defined as "the process by which new ideas are created or developed," and *diffusion,* defined as "the process by which these new ideas are communicated to the members of a social system" (p. 7).

In most organizations, innovation usually begins as a result of some crisis, large or small (Beer, 1969). An active search for new approaches stems from dissatisfaction with existing conditions by advocates of change called *idea champions* (McCall and Kaplan, 1985). Hence, innovation is rarely serendipitous; rather, it stems from vague but uncomfortable feelings about existing conditions (Hassinger, 1959).

Rogers and Shoemaker (1971) describe four key stages in the adoption of organizational innovations following exploration:

1. Knowledge
2. Persuasion
3. Decision
4. Confirmation

Their paradigm of the innovation-decision process is complex and encompasses many variables.

During the *knowledge stage,* the first stage in innovation, an individual or group is exposed to a new idea and becomes aware of what it means. This stage is influenced by receiver and social system variables. *Receiver variables* include the decision makers' attitudes about change, their receptiveness to new ideas, and the perceived need for the change. *Social system variables* are functions of the organizational culture, including group norms and tolerance for nonconformity, among other issues.

To introduce an innovation to an organization — such as a rigorous and systematic approach to the instructional design — years of organizational research suggest the best way is to identify key decision makers who are early adopters of innovation. Like their consumer counterparts who adopt new products or services before others do, they are the first to consider new ideas and are willing to introduce change if they can readily see benefits from it. Their interest can be piqued by providing them with information, such as articles, "white paper" descriptions, or one-on-one "briefings." Their support will increase when they can see a use for the approach in helping them address their immediate problems.

During the *persuasion stage,* the second stage in innovation, individuals or groups form a favorable or unfavorable impression of an idea. Of crucial importance for innovation to be successfully introduced, the persuasion stage is influenced by a host of factors. To consider these factors, instructional designers should ask themselves the following questions: (1) How much will decision makers view a possible innovation as offering distinct advantages and relatively few disadvantages when compared to existing conditions? (2) How compatible is the proposed innovation with the organization's present ways of doing things? (3) How easily can the proposed innovation be explained to others? (4) How easily does the proposed innovation lend itself to trial tests? (5) How easily observable are the consequences of the innovation? Use the answers to these questions to identify ways to persuade decision makers to accept a rigorous, systematic approach to the instructional design process.

During the *decision stage,* the third stage in innovation, key decision makers either adopt or reject a new idea. This stage is heavily influenced by how the innovation was introduced. Participation of affected parties is of crucial importance to success in this stage (Kirkpatrick, 1985). If an idea is adopted, it may either be retained in its original form or gradually supplanted, over time, by refinements. If an idea is rejected, it may either be adopted at a later time or dropped forever from consideration. Both adoption and rejection over time are influenced by decision makers, problems confronting the organization, or prospects for future challenges confronting the organization.

During the *confirmation stage,* the fourth and final stage in innovation, key decision makers either remain committed to the innovation or grow disenchanted with it. If experience leads to complete acceptance, then additional resources may be devoted to it, or else the idea may be further refined; if experience with the idea leads to rejection, then resources may be removed from it. Of course, a rejected innovation can be revived when key decision makers change through retirement, removal, or reorganization or when changing conditions make the innovation appealing.

Ensuring That Promotional Strategies Are Congruent with the Value Systems of Decision Makers

Each organization is governed by a dominant coalition, consisting of its key decision makers (Cyert and March, 1963; March, 1962; Rogers, 1971). Each organization's culture is influenced, to a great extent, by that coalition (Deal and Kennedy, 1982). Members of the dominant coalition are responsible for allocating work assignments and distributing rewards. They are also advocates and apologists for the culture, since their own rise to authority can be traced to their adherence to values implicit in the culture. Although that is not always true — Lee Iacocca was brought into Chrysler and Michael Eisner was brought into Disney Corporation precisely so they could change the culture and redirect corporate strategy — it often is.

To promote rigorous, planned approaches to instructional design, then, instructional designers should make sure that the methods they use are congruent with the value systems of the dominant coalition. But how is that done? First, identify members of the dominant coalition. Just who are the "movers and shakers"? When that question has been answered, the members of the dominant coalition have been identified. These are the people who "make things happen." Every organization has them. They are not always members of top management. Sometimes they are high-potential managers located in middle or lower management.

Second, clarify the values, goals, and aspirations of the dominant coalition. According to Rokeach (1973, p. 5), a value is "an enduring belief that a specific mode of conduct or end-state of existence is personally or socially preferable to an opposite or converse mode of conduct or end-state of existence." A goal is simply a "desired end-state." It is usually not capable of measurement, as an objective is (Rothwell and Kazanas, 1989). An aspiration is comparable to a vision, a view of what the future should look like.

To clarify the values, goals, and aspirations of the dominant coalition, audit the culture (Wilkins, 1983). Observe the setting carefully to see what is rewarded. Watch for any existing rituals, backed by tradition, that receive attention from important individuals. (Rituals include Christmas parties, going-away parties, or retirement dinners.) In addition, listen to what members of the dominant coalition talk about and say they want. Compare what they talk about to what they do, what they spend their time on, and what they reward. Listen also to stories told about members of the dominant coalition and their predecessors (Deal and Kennedy, 1982). If possible, administer a value survey to members of the organization (Francis and Woodcock, 1990; Rokeach, 1973).

Rokeach distinguishes between two kinds of values: instrumental and terminal. *Instrumental values* are those leading to a desired end state; *terminal values* are equated directly with the end state itself. Values include expressions or actions pertaining to any of the following (Schmidt and Posner, 1982):

Values	*Descriptions of the Values (Relative Importance)*
Organizational effectiveness	How well the organization achieves desired results
High productivity	The ratio of inputs to outputs
Organizational leadership	Top management's ability to meet challenges facing the organization
High morale	High job satisfaction among members of each work group and in the organization as a whole
Organizational reputation	The organization's standing in the industry and in all industries
Organizational efficiency	How well the organization is able to use its resources to achieve desired results
Profit maximization	The ratio of profits to expenses
Organizational growth	The organization's ability to grow in assets, staff, or market share
Organizational stability	The organization's ability to cope with change created by conditions in the environment
Organizational value to community	The organization's relative contributions to the quality of life in each community of which it is a part

Generally speaking, supervisors and executives place different values on different activities and results (Schmidt and Posner, 1982).

Selecting Strategies for Promoting Instructional Design
Consistent with the Values of the Dominant Coalition

Efforts to promote a professional approach to instructional design must be geared to the values, goals, and aspirations of the dominant coalition. For instance, if members of the dominant coalition seem to value organizational effectiveness most highly, then instructional designers should decribe how a rigorous approach to instructional design can improve that effectiveness. On the other hand, if members of the dominant coalition wish to increase organizational efficiency, then instructional designers should describe how a rigorous approach to instructional design can help achieve that end. In short, promotional efforts should be based on the values and goals of the dominant coalition.

Justifying Promotional Strategy and Tactics

According to *The Standards* (1986), instructional designers should be able to justify the methods they use to promote a rigorous, systematic approach to instructional design. As in most activities, instructional designers should be prepared to explain what they have done and why they have done it to such interested stakeholders as other instructional designers, operating managers, supervisors, and targeted learners. The same holds true for their efforts to promote instructional design. However, they will usually find that, in most cases, they will be asked to justify their methods of promoting instructional design only to other instructional designers. They tend to be most interested in this subject.

When justifying the strategy used to promote instructional design, be prepared to answer the following questions:

1. What key decision makers were targeted, and why were they selected rather than others?
2. What goals were established for the promotional effort? Why were they selected?
3. What consideration was given to the organization's life cycle stage? its stage in adopting a rigorous, systematic approach to instructional design?
4. What consideration was given go the personal value systems of key decision makers?

By answering these questions, instructional designers should be able to explain why and how they chose to promote a rigorous, systematic approach to instructional design.

Conclusion

This chapter began with a brief case study to dramatize important issues in promoting instructional design. We then described ways to make others aware of instructional design. Our final notes were about justifying these promotional efforts.

A rigorous and systematic approach to instructional design will only be accepted if it is promoted by advocates and if the benefits are widely communicated to training and development practitioners, instructional designers, managers of human resource development, line managers, and others. *Mastering the Instructional Design Process: A Systematic Approach* was intended to take up where *The Standards* (1986), a competency study of the instructional design field, left off. While *The Standards* focused on *what instructional designers do,* this book focuses on *how to demonstrate competencies of instructional design work.* Its purpose is thus to point the way toward developing and improving competencies associated with instructional design work. In this respect, this book is itself intended as a means of promoting instructional design work.

The last chapter, Chapter Nineteen, closes this book with some personal reflections on our experiences.

CHAPTER NINETEEN

Being an Effective Instructional Designer: Lessons Learned

We feel it is fitting to close the book with some personal reflections, gained through our experience, about what it takes to be effective as an instructional designer. In the enumerated items below we will share lessons we have learned, our personal opinions, and thoughts about professional development. We will close the chapter with an activity that is intended to help you, the reader, think about the changing instructional design process and the competencies you should work toward acquiring as the future unfolds.

Being an Effective Instructional Designer

The following eight points sum up what we feel are the keys to success in instructional design.

Point 1: Emphasize Performance Analysis

We have found over the years that conducting a first-rate performance analysis is central to the professional practice of instructional design. Indeed, we feel it is the single most important competency for success in this field.

In many cases, however, operating managers will pressure you to take a shortcut. More often than not, we have found, they would like you to skip the analysis, jump into action, and do what they want you to do. (There is a bias, in the United States at least, toward highly visible action but not necessarily toward thoughtful analysis.)

The lesson we have learned, and that we would like to share with you, is to beware of giving customers what they want but not what you are genuinely convinced they need! Too often, that path leads down blind alleys fraught with perils on every side. Even worse, it can eventually damage the credibility of the training department if the causes of performance problems operating managers identify are incorrect, the solutions they offer are ill-advised, or they are simply seeking trendy solutions to otherwise complex problems. Remember that the ultimate responsibility for failures will quickly return to you but that many people will help you take credit for successes.

Point 2: Exercise Performance Analysis Creatively

Although we emphasized performance analysis in point 1, we have to admit that we often feel that present-day models of performance analysis are too simplistic. Our opinion is that, since it is sometimes difficult to be clear in print, writers on the subject have sometimes erred on the side of clarity rather than bringing out the true complexity that may be involved in analyzing problems. In practice, we do not always limit ourselves, as popular models of performance analysis suggest you should, to the simple pigeonholing of all problems into (1) those stemming from skill deficiencies (what Gilbert [1978] calls deficiencies of execution), and (2) those stemming from nonskill deficiencies (what Gilbert calls deficiencies of environment). We find that, too often, such pigeonholing does not reflect the actual complexity of problems. Indeed, many problems stem from both deficiencies of environment and deficiencies of execution.

Nor is it the dizzying complexity of the problems alone that poses a challenge. The broad range of potential solutions, instructional and noninstructional, easily exceeds the fifteen performance improvement interventions formally identified to date (Hutchison, 1990). To make matters more confusing, each solution can be combined with others.

The lesson we have learned is that it is our own inability to be creative enough that often stymies our search for effective solutions. So our advice to you is this: *hold nothing sacred.* Be willing to experiment. Think about otherwise crazy ideas. Challenge assumptions others blithely take for granted in your quest for the causes of performance problems and innovative solutions. As examples of what we mean, consider: Is it really necessary to structure an organization into jobs rather than groups or teams? Must all organizations have pay structures? Is an organization chart essential? Should every group in an organization have a "boss"? Are performance appraisals or job descriptions always necessary if other means can be found to provide feedback, document performance, or outline responsibilities? Always be willing to ask "why?". Listen carefully to the answers you receive.

Our thinking is that eventually the instructional design field will move beyond performance analysis, with its problem-oriented focus, and will begin to concentrate on designing work systems themselves. Productivity can be directly affected by such strategies as spreading more work across fewer workers, broadening the responsibilities of work groups, or linking up groups more closely to those supplying them or distributing for them. As we confront such challenges, we should direct our attention more often to anticipating, and avoiding, problems before they arise rather than troubleshooting them after they become apparent.

Point 3: Take Steps to Educate Managers About Performance Analysis

Although the instructional design field may be gradually moving away from performance analysis toward actual work systems design, we still remain staunch defenders and believers in performance analysis at present. We also believe that instructional designers should not be content to practice performance analysis as a solitary pursuit, something treated sacrosanctly as a well-kept professional secret. They should, instead, work energetically to educate operating managers about it. They can do that by offering training on performance analysis, writing and circulating organizational "white papers," holding executive briefings, writing articles for company publications, and talking to management groups.

It has been our experience that many benefits can flow from these efforts. First, frivolous or ill-advised requests for instruction will diminish as managers become more sophisticated. (Initially, though, you will receive many requests for help in applying performance analysis to special situations or in unusual conditions.) Second, publicizing performance analysis is a subtle way to educate others about the importance of instructional design itself. Third, training others to do troubleshooting may eventually lead to a day when you can devote more time to solving problems than to analyzing them.

Point 4: Pay Attention to the Future and to the Consequences of Solutions

Looking back over time, we have to say that we feel that most of the operating managers we have encountered are a bright, impressive group of people. Yet we have found, in too many cases, that they tend to think in a linear chain like this:

1. We have a problem;
2. We search for a solution; and
3. Having identified a solution, we implement it.

Think of this approach as akin to problem solving on a staircase, because the conditions giving rise to problems and conditions affecting solutions do not move. As the "ground," or steps, on a staircase, conditions are stationary. If an implemented solution introduces new problems not initially considered, managers repeat anew the steps listed above.

But you should do better than that if you are to save your clients time and spare yourself grief. We find that the following approach works better:

1. We have a problem or can anticipate one before it manifests itself;
2. We search for a solution while trying to find out if any conditions presently affecting the problem will change in the future;

3. We tentatively identify a solution and consider how future changes in the organization's environment or in the organization itself may affect it;
4. We play a game called "If . . . what" ("if we implement the solution . . . what is likely to happen?");
5. We step back into the present and modify the solution to avert or minimize the problems that we expect will arise during implementation;
6. We implement the solution; and
7. We follow up continuously to ensure that the solution works as expected as the future unfolds.

Think of this approach as akin to problem solving on an escalator. The "ground" — meaning conditions affecting the problem and solution — *is* capable of moving. What is more, the consequences of solutions are considered before implementation.

We cannot stress too much the importance of (1) scanning the future to see if anything will change the conditions causing a problem, (2) considering future consequences of steps taken in the present to address problems, (3) scanning the future to see if anything will change the assumptions we make about a problem's solution, and (4) following up continuously to ensure that the solution works as expected.

Point 5: Be Flexible When Applying a Model of Instructional Systems Design

Although we have devoted much time to the steps in a model of instructional systems design (ISD), we do not want you to come away from reading this book with the impression that instructional design is inflexible and never lends itself to modification. To apply it properly, you must be creative, not mechanical, in your approach. You must be willing to add, modify, or subtract steps in the process to match up with the culture of the organizations in which you use it. That may require spur-of-the-moment decisions or quick-witted action.

Point 6: Take Steps to Develop Yourself Professionally but Realize That Professional Development Means More Than Just Keeping Knowledge and Skills Current

We define professional development as an individual's gradual and continuing mastery of a field's body of knowledge, methods, and procedures. In addition, it also implies that practitioners adhere to ethical standards appropriate to the field. (See Exhibit 19.1 for more about the professional ethics of performance technologists and instructional designers.)

In a very real sense, then, professional development is never "finished." It requires constant effort. Even the most experienced instructional designers, like the most experienced professionals in other fields, should continuously strive to build their knowledge, maintain their awareness of new developments and approaches, and preserve their adherence to ethical standards.

Exhibit 19.1. A Credo for Performance Technologists and Instructional Designers.

These statements reflect a consensus from the International Board of Standards for Training, Performance, and Instruction (IBSTPI) Delphi Respondents. This, the study concludes, is what Performance Technologists are, what they stand for, and what they believe about their profession.

I.   Performance Technology is a profession. It may have other names, but in general, Performance Technologists:

   − Provide efficient, effective, workable, and cost-effective solutions related to a specific task or organizational performance.

   − Systematically improve human performance through technologies of instruction, motivation, and ergonomics to accomplish valid and appropriate individual and organizational goals.

   − Systematically assure a link between human performance improvement efforts, results, and consequences.

   − Systematically improve human performance through the use of systems engineering concepts.

II. The tasks of the profession are definable and have a valuable, unique place in modern society. Performance Technologists:

   − Improve the effectiveness and efficiency of organizations and the resources within them.

   − Aid the client in solving performance problems by demonstrating systematic approaches to problem identification and problem solving.

   − Facilitate individual accomplishment and remove obstacles to achievement of organizational mission outcomes.

   − Establish, support, and demonstrate results of performance that affect organizational outcomes.

III. The profession has a specific social mandate. Performance Technologists:

   − Use Performance Technology only in support of humane, socially responsible, and life-fulfilling ends for both the individual and organization.

   − Serve individuals and organizations in the context of work.

   − Maintain the widest view of the usefulness for, and impact of, their interventions.

   − Support organizational goals and be aware of the impacts on society as a whole.

   − Take moral/ethical positions on societal issues and make professional decisions according to those positions.

IV. The profession is responsible for the success and well-being of its clients. Performance Technologists:

   − Help clients make informed decisions by providing supportable intervention options with objective data, consequences, and recommendations.

   − Use the highest professional standards of ethics, honesty, and integrity in all facets of their work. They withdraw from clients who cannot act ethically.

   − Protect the privacy, candidness, and confidentiality of client information and communication.

V.   The profession is accountable to its members and they each to the other. Performance Technologists:

**Exhibit 19.1. A Credo for Performance Technologists
and Instructional Designers, Cont'd.**

   —Have a peer relationship with anyone engaged in the improvement of worthy performance.

   —Deal with fellow practitioners ethically, honestly, and with integrity.

   —Share skills and knowledge with other professionals.

   —Do not represent the ideas of others as their own.

VI.   Each professional is responsible for the development and growth of the profession,
      its body of knowledge and its disciplines.

   —By definition, the intelligent practice of Performance Technology includes the education and transfer of the technology to clients.

   —Performance Technologists commit time and effort to the development of the
   profession.

   —The skills and knowledge of Performance Technology are available for examination by colleagues and clients.

   —Performance Technologists give and get support and professional aid from colleagues.

VII. Every professional is responsible for the ethical conduct of him/herself and other
      practitioners. Specifically, it's unethical for a Performance Technologist to:

   —Violate professional, academic (exchange of knowledge), or business (contracting)
   ethics.

   —Take credit for the work of another.

   —Use client information for personal gain.

   —Make false claims about any professional's behaviors or potential accomplishments.

Source: Odin Westgaard, chair of the Ethics Committee, International Board of Standards for Training, Performance, and Instruction. Used with permission.

Point 7: Recognize and Overcome Barriers to Professional Development

It has been our experience that many instructional designers — even the most
ambitious and dedicated — are sometimes unwilling or unable to make time
for such professional development activities as reading, participating in local chapters of organizations like NSPI or ASTD, attending professional
conferences, or taking college courses.

   It is not uncommon to hear a plethora of excuses when staff members
are asked about their professional development. Lack of time is frequently
cited. Here is a sample of typical excuses we have heard:

* If the company thinks professional development is important, then the
  company can send me on work time. Otherwise, I have to get my kids
  to school every day. I also need to be home at night.
* It is worthwhile attending chapter meetings. But I do not like to travel at
  night [or during the day] to these meetings. I just do not have time for it.

- I would enroll in school to continue my education, but I just don't have the time for commuting, attending classes, and doing the homework.

It is ironic that these and similar excuses are also offered frequently by the trainees that instructional designers work so hard to satisfy in the workplace.

To address these excuses, we find it helpful to counsel employees one-on-one. The purpose of the counseling is to reemphasize the importance of professional development and convey the message that it is not entirely the company's — or the boss's — responsibility to address professional development needs. The lion's share of that responsibility always belongs to the individual.

Lack of motivation is also a barrier to professional development. We see it often enough among seasoned instructional designers who feel so smug about their experience or educational credentials that they see no reason to pursue further development unless there is an obvious or immediate personal gain to be had. If asked about their professional development, those lacking motivation are likely to make statements like these:

- I don't really feel a need. The articles and books I look at seem too superficial. The conferences I have attended waste time and are geared to novices. Chapter meetings always seem to be dominated by a clique of insiders. I feel I am doing pretty well without these time wasters.
- Experience is the best teacher. I feel that I am developing professionally by working in the field every day.

Managers of instructional designers should address these objections by pointing out that everyone, no matter how experienced, can and should develop professionally. If need be, managers should ask these instructional designers how they would address similar objectives raised by trainees who attend courses they designed. Then managers should be quite obvious about turning the approach around, applying it directly to the instructional designer who offered excuses!

Finally, very real barriers to professional development can stem from organizations rather than from instructional designers themselves. Chief among these barriers is what instructional designers perceive to be lack of support for professional development activities. It is a barrier most keenly felt by the most ambitious staff members.

Lack of funding is one way that organizations show lack of support. Some cost-conscious organizations pinch pennies on journal subscriptions, association membership fees, and book purchases. Likewise, many organizations limit attendance at professional conferences and chapter meetings. Employees interpret such miserly practices as direct assaults on their efforts to develop themselves professionally. Worse yet, managers of instructional designers are not always capable of single-handedly reversing these trends because final budgetary decisions are made by others.

What managers can do, however, is make sure they encourage professional development in spite of the circumstances. One approach that may work is to poll staff about the journals they would like the organization to subscribe to, the associations they wish to belong to, the books that should be purchased, and the conferences they would like to be sent to. The managers should then make the budget requests based on this information. Each item should be justified for a work-related reason.

As an alternative when that strategy fails, managers in large organizations may find that there is a possibility of forming networks of instructional designers internal to the organization. That can be an inexpensive vehicle for professional development. It can also have a payback in other ways because it forges ties to other instructional designers in the organization.

On the other hand, instructional designers in small or medium-sized organizations may find that they simply have to absorb more of the funding for their own professional development without expecting their employers to do so. While that is a bitter pill to swallow — it does amount to a pay cut — it preserves participation in professional development activities even when employers cut expenses and undergo downsizing or rightsizing efforts. For innovative and committed people, no barrier is so insurmountable that they are unable to find the means to fuel their learning.

Lack of supervisory encouragement is the single worst barrier to professional development. Instructional designers will not participate in professional development activities when they feel that their bosses do not support them. The best way for managers of instructional design to foster professional development is to set the example, not by just talking about it but also by participating.

While there is no simple solution to lack of supervisory encouragement, some instructional designers are honest enough to confront their bosses when they encounter this problem. In those cases, instructional designers may have to undertake the delicate task of pointing out to their bosses that the example they set is the one many people will be influenced to follow.

Point 8: Changing Environmental Conditions Will Prompt Modifications in the Instructional Design Process and in the Competencies Required for Instructional Designers

As our final point in this book, we want to stress that instructional design is not a static field; rather, like so many other things, it is influenced by trends in the economy, government, technology, and demographics.

To maintain professional competence and adapt to changing conditions, you should willingly revisit the steps in the instructional design process and periodically reassess your own competencies relative to it. As our parting gift to you, we offer you an activity to help you do that. (See Exhibit 19.2.) Use the activity to make notes about the changes you expect to see in the instructional design process as it is applied in your organization. Also use it to note the actions you should take on a continuing basis to prepare yourself professionally for the skills necessary to carry out that process. Use the results as a means of updating your professional competencies.

Exhibit 19.2. An Activity for Preparing
for the Future of Instructional Design.

Directions: Use this activity periodically to help you think about the future. In the left column, you will find the model of the steps in the instructional design process that we have used in this book. In the center column, make notes about any changes in the steps of the process that you expect to see in your organization's future. In other words, how will the step be carried out? (Feel free to add, subtract, or modify the steps shown in the left column.) Then, in the right column, jot down ideas about the knowledge or skill you will need to carry out the changing steps of the instructional design process as the future unfolds. When you finish the activity, meet with your immediate supervisor and/or professional colleagues to help you prepare an action plan to acquire new knowledge or skills and identify resources to aid you in carrying out the action plan.

Steps in the instructional design process	How will this step be carried out in the future?	What knowledge, skills, or other abilities will you need to carry out the steps in the future?

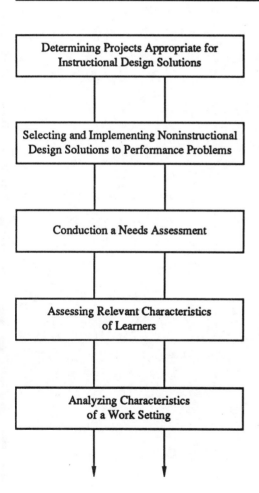

Determining Projects Appropriate for Instructional Design Solutions

Selecting and Implementing Noninstructional Design Solutions to Performance Problems

Conduction a Needs Assessment

Assessing Relevant Characteristics of Learners

Analyzing Characteristics of a Work Setting

Exhibit 19.2. An Activity for Preparing
for the Future of Instructional Design, Cont'd.

Steps in the instructional design process	How will this step be carried out in the future?	What knowledge, skills, or other abilities will you need to carry out the steps in the future?

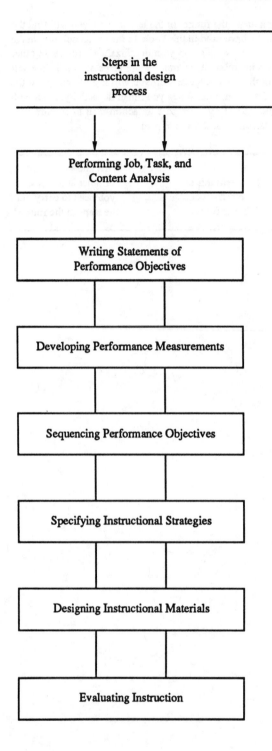

RESOURCE AID

Resource Aid: Instructional Design Competencies and Performances.

Competencies   Performances

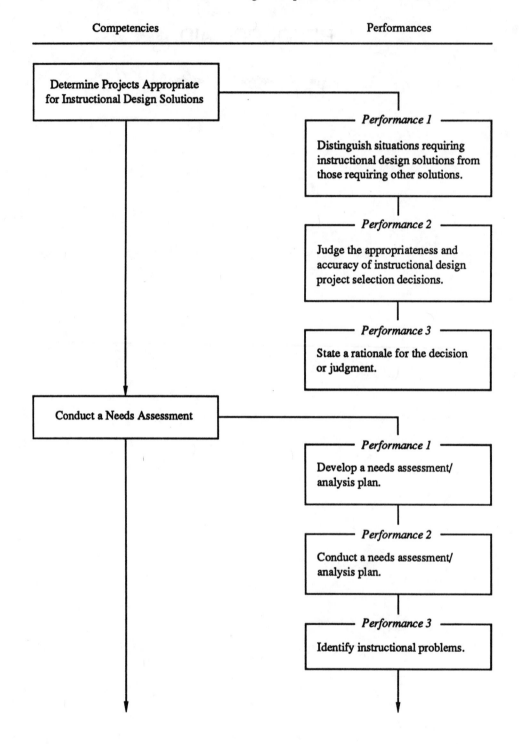

Determine Projects Appropriate for Instructional Design Solutions

Performance 1

Distinguish situations requiring instructional design solutions from those requiring other solutions.

Performance 2

Judge the appropriateness and accuracy of instructional design project selection decisions.

Performance 3

State a rationale for the decision or judgment.

Conduct a Needs Assessment

Performance 1

Develop a needs assessment/ analysis plan.

Performance 2

Conduct a needs assessment/ analysis plan.

Performance 3

Identify instructional problems.

Resource Aid: Instructional Design Competencies and Performances, Cont'd.

Competencies   Performances

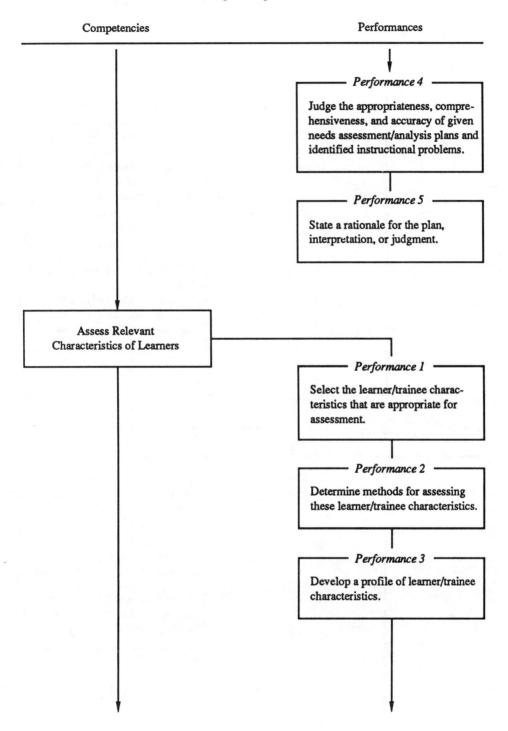

Performance 4

Judge the appropriateness, comprehensiveness, and accuracy of given
needs assessment/analysis plans and
identified instructional problems.

Performance 5

State a rationale for the plan,
interpretation, or judgment.

Assess Relevant
Characteristics of Learners

Performance 1

Select the learner/trainee characteristics that are appropriate for
assessment.

Performance 2

Determine methods for assessing
these learner/trainee characteristics.

Performance 3

Develop a profile of learner/trainee
characteristics.

Resource Aid: Instructional Design Competencies and Performances, Cont'd.

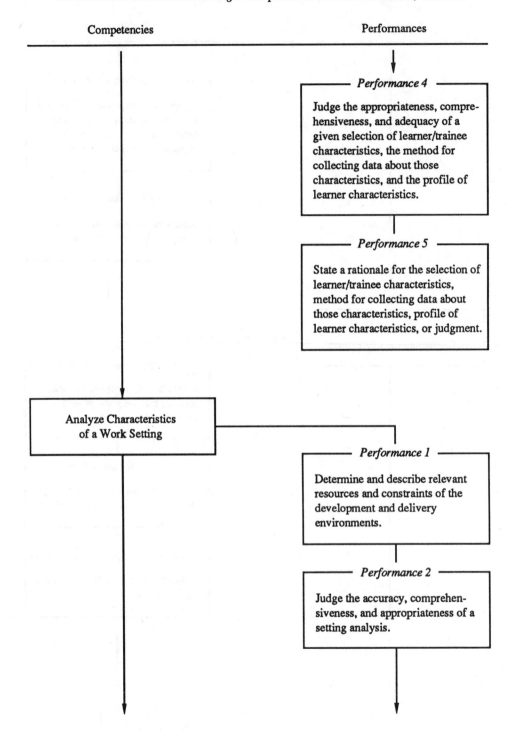

Competencies   Performances

Performance 4

Judge the appropriateness, comprehensiveness, and adequacy of a
given selection of learner/trainee
characteristics, the method for
collecting data about those
characteristics, and the profile of
learner characteristics.

Performance 5

State a rationale for the selection of
learner/trainee characteristics,
method for collecting data about
those characteristics, profile of
learner characteristics, or judgment.

Analyze Characteristics
of a Work Setting

Performance 1

Determine and describe relevant
resources and constraints of the
development and delivery
environments.

Performance 2

Judge the accuracy, comprehensiveness, and appropriateness of a
setting analysis.

Resource Aid: Instructional Design Competencies and Performances, Cont'd.

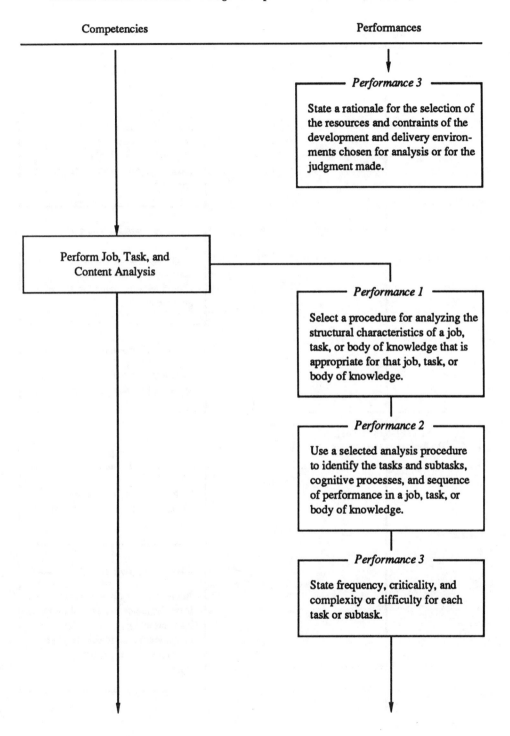

Competencies

Performances

Performance 3

State a rationale for the selection of the resources and contraints of the development and delivery environments chosen for analysis or for the judgment made.

Perform Job, Task, and Content Analysis

Performance 1

Select a procedure for analyzing the structural characteristics of a job, task, or body of knowledge that is appropriate for that job, task, or body of knowledge.

Performance 2

Use a selected analysis procedure to identify the tasks and subtasks, cognitive processes, and sequence of performance in a job, task, or body of knowledge.

Performance 3

State frequency, criticality, and complexity or difficulty for each task or subtask.

Resource Aid: Instructional Design Competencies and Performances, Cont'd.

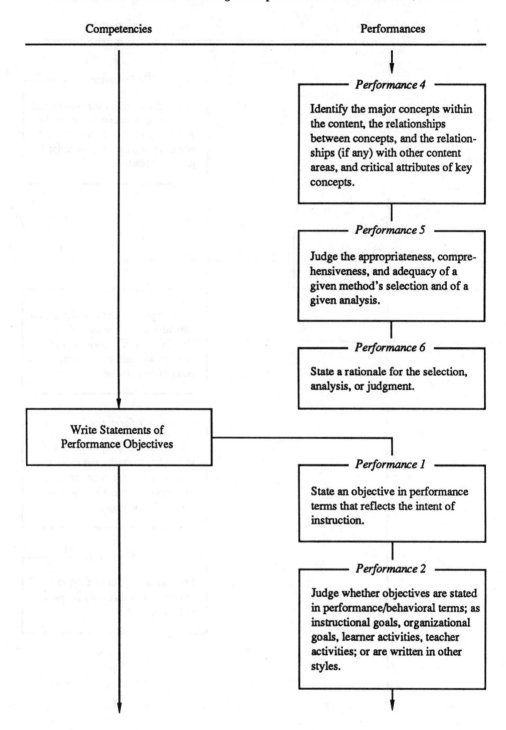

Competencies   Performances

Performance 4

Identify the major concepts within the content, the relationships between concepts, and the relationships (if any) with other content areas, and critical attributes of key concepts.

Performance 5

Judge the appropriateness, comprehensiveness, and adequacy of a given method's selection and of a given analysis.

Performance 6

State a rationale for the selection, analysis, or judgment.

Write Statements of Performance Objectives

Performance 1

State an objective in performance terms that reflects the intent of instruction.

Performance 2

Judge whether objectives are stated in performance/behavioral terms; as instructional goals, organizational goals, learner activities, teacher activities; or are written in other styles.

Resource Aid: Instructional Design Competencies and Performances, Cont'd.

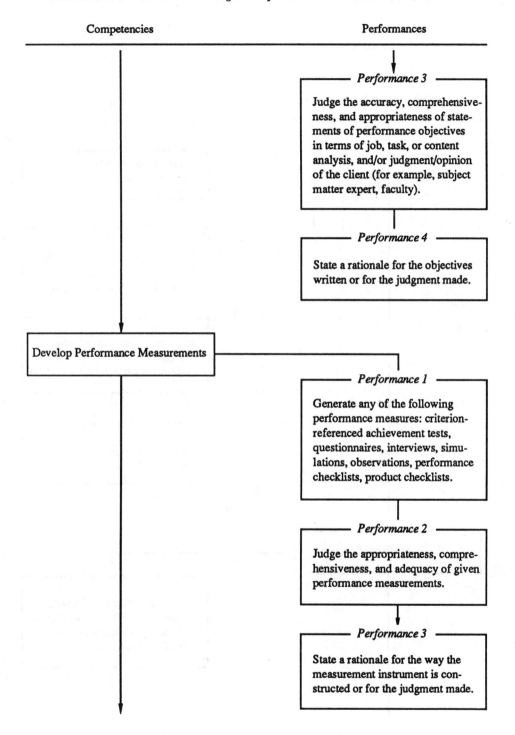

Competencies   Performances

Performance 3

Judge the accuracy, comprehensiveness, and appropriateness of statements of performance objectives in terms of job, task, or content analysis, and/or judgment/opinion of the client (for example, subject matter expert, faculty).

Performance 4

State a rationale for the objectives written or for the judgment made.

Develop Performance Measurements

Performance 1

Generate any of the following performance measures: criterion-referenced achievement tests, questionnaires, interviews, simulations, observations, performance checklists, product checklists.

Performance 2

Judge the appropriateness, comprehensiveness, and adequacy of given performance measurements.

Performance 3

State a rationale for the way the measurement instrument is constructed or for the judgment made.

Resource Aid: Instructional Design Competencies and Performances, Cont'd.

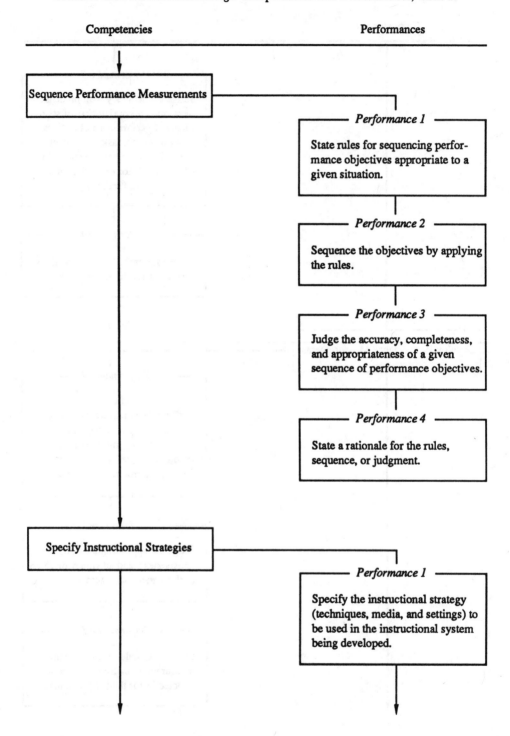

Competencies   Performances

Sequence Performance Measurements

Performance 1

State rules for sequencing performance objectives appropriate to a
given situation.

Performance 2

Sequence the objectives by applying
the rules.

Performance 3

Judge the accuracy, completeness,
and appropriateness of a given
sequence of performance objectives.

Performance 4

State a rationale for the rules,
sequence, or judgment.

Specify Instructional Strategies

Performance 1

Specify the instructional strategy
(techniques, media, and settings) to
be used in the instructional system
being developed.

Resource Aid: Instructional Design Competencies and Performances, Cont'd.

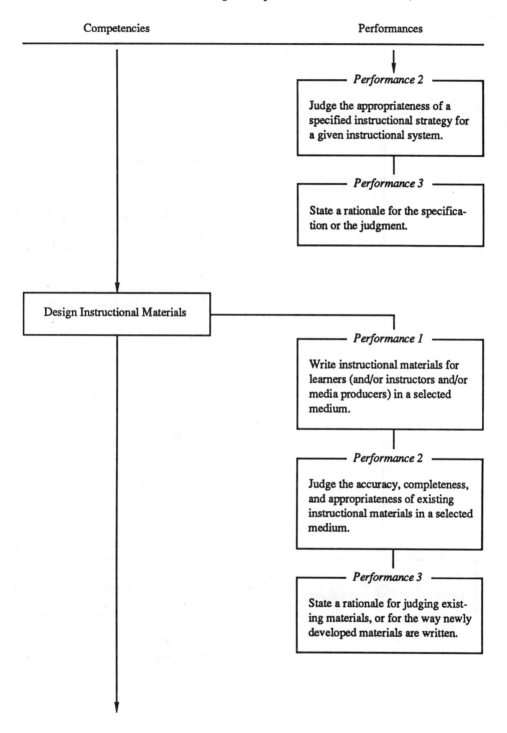

Competencies

Performances

Performance 2

Judge the appropriateness of a specified instructional strategy for a given instructional system.

Performance 3

State a rationale for the specification or the judgment.

Design Instructional Materials

Performance 1

Write instructional materials for learners (and/or instructors and/or media producers) in a selected medium.

Performance 2

Judge the accuracy, completeness, and appropriateness of existing instructional materials in a selected medium.

Performance 3

State a rationale for judging existing materials, or for the way newly developed materials are written.

Resource Aid: Instructional Design Competencies and Performances, Cont'd.

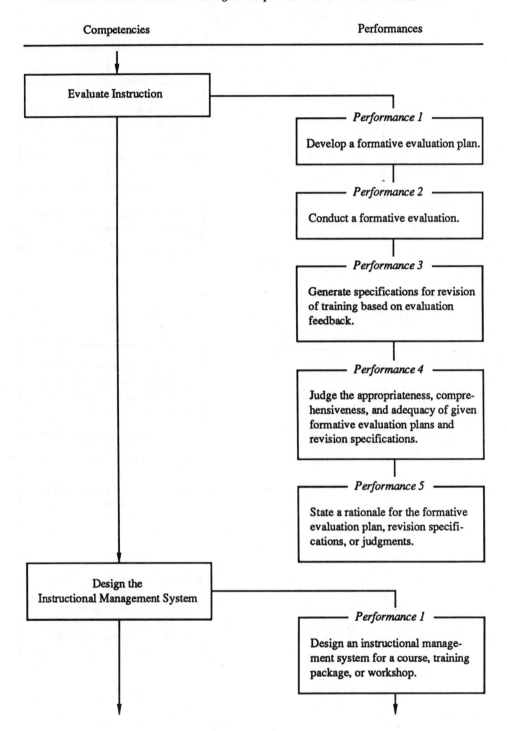

Competencies   Performances

Evaluate Instruction

Performance 1
Develop a formative evaluation plan.

Performance 2
Conduct a formative evaluation.

Performance 3
Generate specifications for revision of training based on evaluation feedback.

Performance 4
Judge the appropriateness, comprehensiveness, and adequacy of given formative evaluation plans and revision specifications.

Performance 5
State a rationale for the formative evaluation plan, revision specifications, or judgments.

Design the Instructional Management System

Performance 1
Design an instructional management system for a course, training package, or workshop.

Resource Aid: Instructional Design Competencies and Performances, Cont'd.

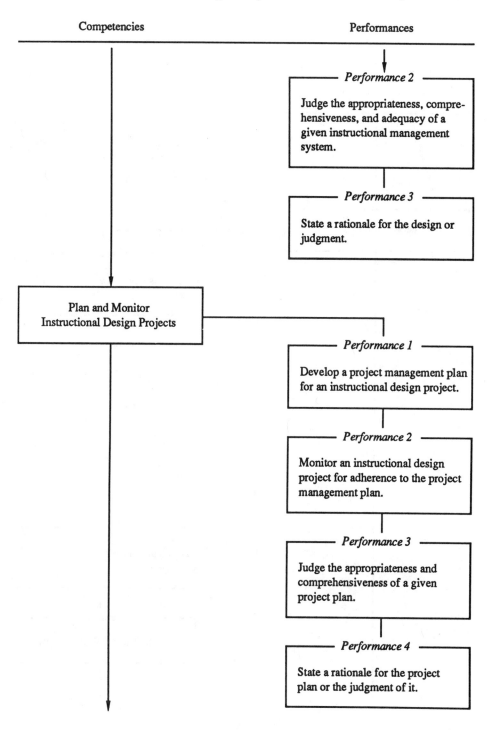

Competencies   Performances

Performance 2

Judge the appropriateness, comprehensiveness, and adequacy of a
given instructional management
system.

Performance 3

State a rationale for the design or
judgment.

**Plan and Monitor
Instructional Design Projects**

Performance 1

Develop a project management plan
for an instructional design project.

Performance 2

Monitor an instructional design
project for adherence to the project
management plan.

Performance 3

Judge the appropriateness and
comprehensiveness of a given
project plan.

Performance 4

State a rationale for the project
plan or the judgment of it.

Resource Aid: Instructional Design Competencies and Performances, Cont'd.

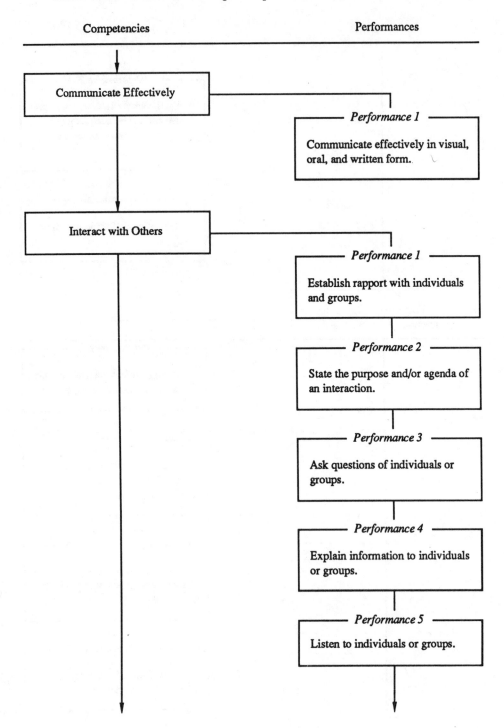

Competencies   Performances

Communicate Effectively

Performance 1

Communicate effectively in visual, oral, and written form.

Interact with Others

Performance 1

Establish rapport with individuals and groups.

Performance 2

State the purpose and/or agenda of an interaction.

Performance 3

Ask questions of individuals or groups.

Performance 4

Explain information to individuals or groups.

Performance 5

Listen to individuals or groups.

Resource Aid: Instructional Design Competencies and Performances, Cont'd.

Competencies	Performances

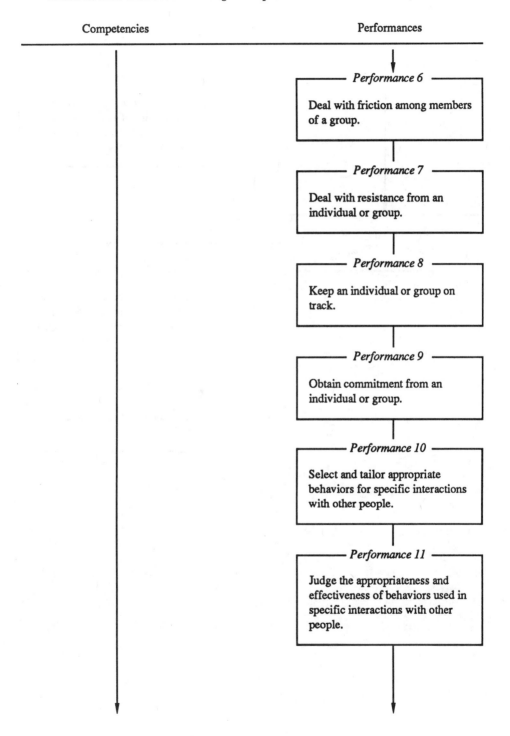

Performance 6

Deal with friction among members of a group.

Performance 7

Deal with resistance from an individual or group.

Performance 8

Keep an individual or group on track.

Performance 9

Obtain commitment from an individual or group.

Performance 10

Select and tailor appropriate behaviors for specific interactions with other people.

Performance 11

Judge the appropriateness and effectiveness of behaviors used in specific interactions with other people.

Resource Aid: Instructional Design Competencies and Performances, Cont'd.

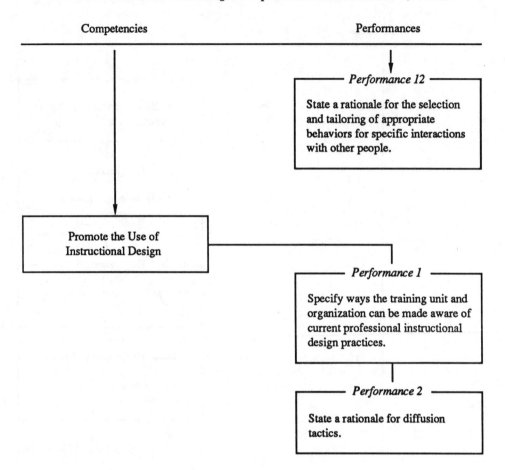

Competencies   Performances

Performance 12

State a rationale for the selection
and tailoring of appropriate
behaviors for specific interactions
with other people.

Promote the Use of
Instructional Design

Performance 1

Specify ways the training unit and
organization can be made aware of
current professional instructional
design practices.

Performance 2

State a rationale for diffusion
tactics.

References

Allred, H., and Clark, J. "Written Communication Problems and Priorities." *Journal of Business Communication,* 1980, *59*(2), 31–35.

The American Heritage Dictionary. (2nd college ed.) Boston: Houghton-Mifflin, 1982.

American Society for Training and Development. *Get Results from Simulation and Role Play. Info-Line,* no. 412. Alexandria, Va.: American Society for Training and Development, 1984a.

American Society for Training and Development. *How to Prepare and Use Effective Visual Aids. Info-Line,* no. 410. Alexandria, Va: American Society for Training and Development, 1984b.

American Society for Training and Development. *Audio, Film, Video. Info-Line,* no. 509. Alexandria, Va.: American Society for Training and Development, 1985a.

American Society for Training and Development. *Be a Better Needs Analyst. Info-Line,* no. 502. Alexandria, Va.: American Society for Training and Development, 1985b.

American Society for Training and Development. *Be a Better Task Analyst. Info-Line,* no. 503. Alexandria, Va.: American Society for Training and Development, 1985c.

American Society for Training and Development. *Build a Strong Assessment Center. Info-Line,* no. 512. Alexandria, Va.: American Society for Training and Development, 1985d.

American Society for Training and Development. *Career Guidance Discussions. Info-Line,* no. 508. Alexandria, Va.: American Society for Training and Development, 1985e.

American Society for Training and Development. *Computer-Based Learning: What, Why, and How. Info-Line,* no. 501. Alexandria, Va.: American Society for Training and Development, 1985f.

American Society for Training and Development. *Getting Inside Interactive Video. Info-Line,* no. 510. Alexandria, Va.: American Society for Training and Development, 1985g.

American Society for Training and Development. *How to Create a Good Learning Environment. Info-Line,* no. 506. Alexandria, Va.: American Society for Training and Development, 1985h.

American Society for Training and Development. *Succeed in Facilities Planning. Info-Line,* no. 504. Alexandria, Va.: American Society for Training and Development, 1985i.

American Society for Training and Development. *Write Better Behavioral Objectives. Info-Line,* no. 505. Alexandria, Va.: American Society for Training and Development, 1985j.

American Society for Training and Development. *Write, Design, and Produce Effective Training Materials. Info-Line,* no. 507. Alexandria, Va.: American Society for Training and Development, 1985k.

American Society for Training and Development. *Alternatives to Lecture. Info-Line,* no. 602. Alexandria, Va.: American Society for Training and Development, 1986a.

American Society for Training and Development. *Be a Better Writer. Info-Line,* no. 611. Alexandria, Va.: American Society for Training and Development, 1986b.

American Society for Training and Development. *Create Quality Videos. Info-Line,* no. 607. Alexandria, Va.: American Society for Training and Development, 1986c.

American Society for Training and Development. *Essentials for Evaluation. Info-Line,* no. 601. Alexandria, Va.: American Society for Training and Development, 1986d.

American Society for Training and Development. *Find the Right Consultant. Info-Line,* no. 610. Alexandria, Va.: American Society for Training and Development, 1986e.

American Society for Training and Development. *How to Market Your Training Programs. Info-Line,* no. 605. Alexandria, Va.: American Society for Training and Development, 1986f.

American Society for Training and Development. *Make Every Presentation a Winner. Info-Line,* no. 806. Alexandria, Va.: American Society for Training and Development, 1986g.

American Society for Training and Development. *Surveys from Start to Finish. Info-Line,* no. 612. Alexandria, Va.: American Society for Training and Development, 1986h.

American Society for Training and Development. *Ensure Learning from Training Films and Videos. Info-Line,* no. 702. Alexandria, Va.: American Society for Training and Development, 1987a.

American Society for Training and Development. *Get Results with the Case Method. Info-Line,* no. 703. Alexandria, Va.: American Society for Training and Development, 1987b.

American Society for Training and Development. *Off to a Good Start: Successful Orientation Programs. Info-Line,* no. 708. Alexandria, Va.: American Society for Training and Development, 1987c.

American Society for Training and Development. *Participants with Disabilities: How to Address Their Needs. Info-Line,* no. 704. Alexandria, Va.: American Society for Training and Development, 1987d.

American Society for Training and Development. *Team Building at Its Best. Info-Line,* no. 701. Alexandria, Va.: American Society for Training and Development, 1987e.

American Society for Training and Development. *Write Successful Video Scripts. Info-Line,* no. 707. Alexandria, Va.: American Society for Training and Development, 1987f.

American Society for Training and Development. *Be a Better Speaker. Info-Line,* no. 802. Alexandria, Va.: American Society for Training and Development, 1988a.

American Society for Training and Development. *Effective Training Manuals. Info-Line,* no. 801. Alexandria, Va.: American Society for Training and Development, 1988b.

American Society for Training and Development. *Listening to Learn: Learning to Listen. Info-Line,* no. 806. Alexandria, Va.: American Society for Training and Development, 1988c.

American Society for Training and Development. *Make or Buy: How to Decide. Info-Line,* no. 810. Alexandria, Va.: American Society for Training and Development, 1988d.

American Society for Training and Development. *Training and Learning Styles. Info-Line,* no. 804. Alexandria, Va.: American Society for Training and Development, 1988e.

American Society for Training and Development. *Be a Better Job Analyst. Info-Line,* no. 903. Alexandria, Va.: American Society for Training and Development, 1989a.

American Society for Training and Development. *Course Design and Development. Info-Line,* no. 905. Alexandria, Va.: American Society for Training and Development, 1989b.

American Society for Training and Development. *How to Design Training Rooms. Info-Line,* no. 912. Alexandria, Va.: American Society for Training and Development, 1989c.

American Society for Training and Development. *How to Produce Great Job Aids. Info-Line,* no. 904. Alexandria, Va.: American Society for Training and Development, 1989d.

American Society for Training and Development. *Lesson Design and Development. Info-Line,* no. 906. Alexandria, Va.: American Society for Training and Development, 1989e.

American Society for Training and Development. *Testing for Learning Outcomes. Info-Line,* no. 907. Alexandria, Va.: American Society for Training and Development, 1989f.

American Telephone and Telegraph Company. "Developing Training Media." In *The Trainer's Library*. Vol. 4. Reading, Mass.: Addison-Wesley, 1987a.

American Telephone and Telegraph Company. "Developing Training Tests." In *The Trainer's Library*. Vol. 5. Reading, Mass.: Addison-Wesley, 1987b.

American Telephone and Telegraph Company. "Instructor and Student Guides." In *The Trainer's Library*. Vol. 6. Reading, Mass.: Addison-Wesley, 1987c.

American Telephone and Telegraph Company. "Measurement and Evaluation." In *The Trainer's Library*. Vol. 7. Reading, Mass.: Addison-Wesley, 1987d.

American Telephone and Telegraph Company. "Planning and Analysis." In *The Trainer's Library*. Vol. 2. Reading, Mass.: Addison-Wesley, 1987e.

American Telephone and Telegraph Company. "Techniques of Instructional Development." In *The Trainer's Library*. Vol. 3. Reading, Mass.: Addison-Wesley, 1987f.

Amidon, E., and Hough, J. *Interaction Analysis: Theory, Research, and Application*. Reading, Mass.: Addison-Wesley, 1967.

Anderson, R. *Selecting and Developing Media for Instruction*. (2nd ed.) New York: Van Nostrand Reinhold, 1983.

Andrews, D., and Goodson, L. "A Comparative Analysis of Models of Instructional Design." *Journal of Development*, 1980, *3*(4), 2–16. (ED EJ 228 351)

Antaki, C. *Analyzing Everyday Explanation: A Casebook of Methods*. Newbury Park, Calif.: Sage, 1988.

Arvey, R., and Faley, R. *Fairness in Selecting Employees*. (2nd ed.) Reading, Mass.: Addison-Wesley, 1988.

Ausubel, D. "A Subsumption Theory of Meaningful Verbal Learning and Retention." *Journal of General Psychology*, 1962, *66*, 213–214.

Bailey, R. *Human Performance Engineering: A Guide for System Designers*. Englewood Cliffs, N.J.: Prentice-Hall, 1982.

Baird, L., Beatty, R., and Schneier, C. *The Performance Appraisal Sourcebook*. Amherst, Mass.: Human Resource Development Press, 1982.

Baker, H., and Morgan, P. "Building a Professional Image: Handling Conflict." In F. Stone (ed.), *The American Management Association Handbook of Supervisory Management*. (Originally printed in *Supervisory Management*, Sept. 1980.) New York: Amacom, 1989.

Baldwin, T., and Ford, J. "Transfer of Training: A Review and Directions for Future Research." *Personnel Psychology*, 1988, *41*(1), 63–105.

Bard, R., Bell, C., Stephen, L., and Webster, L. *The Trainer's Professional Development Handbook*. San Francisco: Jossey-Bass, 1987.

Bard, R., and Loftin, B. "Building a Learning Network." In R. Bard, C. Bell, L. Stephen, and L. Webster. *The Trainer's Professional Development Handbook*. San Francisco: Jossey-Bass, 1987.

Barra, R. *Putting Quality Circles to Work*. New York: McGraw-Hill, 1984.

Becker, W., and Wellins, R. "Customer Service Perceptions and Reality." *Training and Development Journal,* 1990, *44*(3), 49–51.

Beer, M. *Organization Change and Development: Strategies and Models.* Reading, Mass.: Addison-Wesley, 1969.

Bishop, H. "Accurate Job Descriptions: First Things First." *Performance and Instruction,* 1988a, *27*(2), 15–18.

Bishop, H. *Employment Testing and Incentives to Learn.* Ithaca, N.Y.: State University of New York and School of Industrial and Labor Relations, Cornell University, 1988b.

Blanchard, K., and Johnson, S. *The One Minute Manager: The Quickest Way to Increase Your Own Prosperity.* New York: Berkley Books, 1981.

Blank, W. *Handbook for Developing Competency-Based Training Programs.* Englewood Cliffs, N.J.: Prentice-Hall, 1982.

Bloom, B. *Taxonomy of Educational Objectives, the Classification of Educational Goals — Handbook I: Cognitive Domain.* New York: McKay, 1956.

Bloom, B., Hastings, J., and Madaus, G. (ed.). *Handbook of Formative and Summative Evaluation.* New York: McGraw-Hill, 1971.

Bond, T. *Games for Social and Life Skills.* New York: Nichols, 1986.

Brandenburg, D., and Smith, M. *Evaluation of Corporate Training Programs.* TME report 91. Princeton, N.J.: Educational Testing Service, 1986.

Braskamp, L., Brandenburg, D., and Ory, J. *Evaluating Teaching Effectiveness: A Practical Guide.* Newbury Park, Calif.: Sage, 1984.

Brennan, E. *Performance Management Workbook.* Englewood Cliffs, N.J.: Prentice-Hall, 1990.

Brennan, J. *Applications of Critical Path Techniques.* New York: Elsevier, 1968.

Briggs, L. "Designing the Strategy of Instruction." In L. Briggs (ed.), *Instructional Design: Principles and Applications.* Englewood Cliffs, N.J.: Educational Technology Publications, 1977a.

Briggs, L. *Instructional Design: Principles and Applications.* Englewood Cliffs, N.J.: Educational Technology Publications, 1977b.

Brinkerhoff, R. "The Success Case: A Low-Cost High-Yield Evaluation." *Training and Development Journal,* 1983, *37*(8), 58–61.

Brinkerhoff, R., and Dressler, D. *Productivity Measurement: A Guide for Managers and Evaluators.* Newbury Park, Calif.: Sage, 1989.

Brown, J. (ed.). *An Investigation of Motivation's Role in Postsecondary Vocational Training Programs for At-Risk Learners and Their Entry into the Work Force.* St. Paul: Minnesota Research and Development Center for Vocational Education, 1989.

Bruce, S. *Encyclopedia of Prewritten Job Descriptions.* Madison, Conn.: Business and Legal Reports, 1986.

Bruner, J. *Towards a Theory of Instruction.* New York: W. W. Norton, 1966.

Buchanan, D. *The Development of Job Design Theories and Techniques.* New York: Praeger, 1979.

Bullough, R., Sr. "Display Boards." In *The Instructional Media Library.* Vol. 3. Englewood Cliffs, N.J.: Educational Technology Publications, 1981.

Burack, E. "The Sphinx's Riddle: Life and Career Cycles." *Training and Development Journal,* 1984, *38*(4), 52–61.

Bureau of Labor Statistics, U.S. Department of Labor. *The Dictionary of Occupational Titles.* Washington, D.C.: Government Printing Office, 1977.

Bureau of Law and Business. *How to Write Job Descriptions — The Easy Way.* Madison, Conn.: Bureau of Law and Business, 1982.

Buros, O. (ed.). *Mental Measurements Yearbooks.* 9 vols. Highland Park, N.J.: Gryphon Press, 1938–1985.

Business Research Publications. *The Encyclopedia of Managerial Job Descriptions.* Plainville, N.Y.: Business Research Publications, 1976.

Buzzell, R. "Competitive Behavior and the Product Life Cycle." In J. Wright and J. Goldsucker (eds.), *New Ideas for Successful Marketing.* Chicago: American Marketing Association, 1966.

Campbell, D., and Stanley, J. *Experimental and Quasi-Experimental Designs for Research.* Chicago: Rand McNally, 1966.

Carlisle, K. *Analyzing Jobs and Tasks.* Englewood Cliffs, N.J.: Educational Technology Publications, 1986.

Carnevale, A., Gainer, L., and Meltzer, A. *Workplace Basics: The Skills Employers Want.* Alexandria, Va.: American Society for Training and Development and Employment and Training Administration, U.S. Department of Labor, 1988.

Carnevale, A., Gainer, L., and Villet, J. *Training in America: The Organization and Strategic Role of Training.* San Francisco: Jossey-Bass, 1990.

Carr, C. "Designing Systems for the 90s." *Performance Improvement Quarterly,* 1990, *3*(1), 14–26.

Carroll, S., Jr., Paine, F., and Ivancevich, J. "The Relative Effectiveness of Training Methods — Expert Opinion and Research." *Personnel Psychology,* 1972, *25*(3), 495–509.

Carter, J. "Lessons in Text Design from an Instructional Perspective." In T. Duffy and R. Waller (eds.), *Designing Usable Texts.* San Diego, Calif.: Academic Press, 1985.

Center for Public Resources. *Basic Skills in the U.S. Work Force.* New York: Center for Public Resources, 1983.

Chase, R., and Tansik, D. "The Customer Contact Model for Organization Design." *Management Science,* 1983, *29,* 1037–1050.

Chase, W., and Chi, M. "Cognitive Skill: Implications for Spatial Skill in Large-Scale Environments." In J. Harvey (ed.), *Cognition, Social Behavior, and the Environment.* Hillsdale, N.J.: Erlbaum, 1980.

Christopher, E., and Smith, L. *Leadership Training Through Gaming.* New York: Nichols, 1987.

Clark, R. "Defining the 'D' in ISD: Part 2: Task-Specific Instructional Methods." *Performance and Instruction,* 1986, *25*(3), 12–17.

Cleland, D. "Why Project Management?" *Business Horizons,* 1964, *7*(Winter), 81–88.

Coch, L., and French, J., Jr. "Overcoming Resistance to Change." *Human Relations,* Aug. 1948, pp. 512–532.

Collins, A. "A Sample Dialogue Based on a Theory of Inquiry Teaching." In C. Reigeluth (ed.), *Instructional Theories in Action: Lessons Illustrating Selected Theories and Models.* Hillsdale, N.J.: Erlbaum, 1987.

The Conference Board. *Total Quality Performance.* New York: The Conference Board, 1988.

The Conference Board. *Flexible Staffing and Scheduling in U.S. Corporations.* New York: The Conference Board, 1989a.

The Conference Board. *A Manager's Guide to Corporate Culture.* New York: The Conference Board, 1989b.

The Conference Board. *Organization Designs for the '90s.* New York: The Conference Board, 1989c.

Connor, P., and Lake, L. *Managing Organizational Change.* New York: Praeger, 1988.

Converse, J. *Survey Question: Handcrafting the Standardized Questionnaire.* Newbury Park, Calif.: Sage, 1986.

Cooper, H. *Integrating Research: A Guide for Literature Reviews.* Newbury Park, Calif.: Sage, 1989.

Cox, W., Jr. "Product Life Cycles as Marketing Models." *Journal of Business,* 1967, *40,* 375–384.

Cribbin, J. *Leadership: Strategies for Organizational Effectiveness.* New York: Amacom, 1981.

Crowe, M., Hettinger, L., Weber, J., and Johnson, J. *Analysis of Students' Basic Skills Performance in Selected Instructional Delivery Systems: Final Report.* Columbus, Ohio: National Center for Research in Vocational Education, Ohio State University, 1986.

Cummings, L., and Schwab, D. *Performance in Organizations: Determinants and Appraisal.* Glenview, Ill.: Scott-Foresman, 1973.

Cyert, R., and March, J. *A Behavioral Theory of the Firm.* Englewood Cliffs, N.J.: Prentice-Hall, 1963.

Dale, E. *Audiovisual Methods in Teaching.* (3rd ed.) Troy, Mo.: Holt, Rinehart & Winston, 1969.

Dalton, G., Thompson, P., and Price, R. "The Four Stages of Professional Careers: A New Look at Performance by Professionals." *Organizational Dynamics,* Summer 1977, pp. 19–42.

Dalton, M. "Conflict Between Staff and Line Managerial Officers." In A. Etzioni (ed.), *A Sociological Reader on Complex Organizations.* (2nd ed.) Troy, Mo.: Holt, Rinehart & Winston, 1969.

Davis, H. *Super Think: A Guide for Asking Thought-Provoking Questions.* San Luis Obispo, Calif.: Dandy Lion, 1982.

Davis, R., Alexander, L., and Yelon, S. *Learning Systems Design.* New York: McGraw-Hill, 1974.

Deal, T., and Kennedy, A. *Corporate Culture.* Reading, Mass.: Addison-Wesley, 1982.

DeBloois, M. (ed.). *Videodisc/Microcomputer Courseware Design.* Englewood Cliffs, N.J.: Educational Technology Publications, 1982.

Denova, C. *Test Construction for Training Evaluation.* New York: Van Nostrand Reinhold, 1979.

DeWar, D. *Quality Circle Guide to Participative Management.* Englewood Cliffs, N.J.: Prentice-Hall, 1982.

Dick, W., and Carey, L. *The Systematic Design of Instruction.* (2nd ed.) Glenview, Ill.: Scott-Foresman, 1985.

Digman, L. "Determining Management Development Needs." *Human Resource Management,* Winter 1980, pp. 12–17.

Dormant, D. "The ABCDs of Managing Change." In M. Smith (ed.), *Introduction to Performance Technology.* Washington, D.C.: The National Society for Performance and Instruction, 1986.

Dosher, R. "Records and Information Systems." In R. Craig (ed.), *Training and Development Handbook: A Guide to Human Resource Development.* (3rd ed.) New York: McGraw-Hill, 1987.

Drew, R., Mikulecky, L., and Pershing, J. *How to Gather and Develop Job-Specific Literacy Materials for Basic Skills Instruction.* Bloomington: Office of Education and Training Resources, School of Education, Indiana University, 1988.

Drucker, P. *Management: Tasks, Responsibilities, Practices.* New York: HarperCollins, 1973.

Duffy, T. "Readability Formulas: What's the Use?" In T. Duffy and R. Waller (eds.), *Designing Usable Texts.* San Diego, Calif.: Academic Press, 1985.

Dyer, W. *Team Building: Issues and Alternatives.* Reading, Mass.: Addison-Wesley, 1977.

Eder, R., and Ferris, G. *The Employment Interview: Theory, Research, and Practice.* Newbury Park, Calif.: Sage, 1990.

Edosomwan, J. *Integrating Productivity and Quality Management.* New York: Dekker, 1987.

Egan, K. "What Is Curriculum?" *Curriculum and Inquiry,* 1978, *8*(1), 65–72.

Eilbirt, H. "The Development of Personnel Management in the United States." *Business History Review,* 1959, *33*(3), 345–364.

Ellington, H. *Producing Teaching Materials: A Handbook for Teachers and Trainers.* New York: Nichols, 1985.

"Employee Training in America." *Training and Development Journal,* 1986, *40*(7), 35.

Erikson, E. *Identity and the Life Cycle.* New York: International Universities Press, 1959.

Felker, D., Redish, J., and Peterson, J. "Training Authors of Informative Documents." In T. Duffy and R. Waller (eds.), *Designing Usable Texts.* New York: Academic Press, 1985.

Feuer, D. "Training in the *Fortune* 500." *Training,* 1986, *23*(7), 61.

Fidel, R. "The Case Study Method: A Case Study." *Library and Information Science Research,* 1984, *6*(3), 273–288.

Fiedler, F. *A Theory of Leadership Effectiveness.* New York: McGraw-Hill, 1967.

Fiedler, F. "How Do You Make Leaders More Effective? New Answers to an Old Puzzle." *Organizational Dynamics,* Autumn 1972, pp. 3–8.

Fiedler, F., and Chemers, M. *Leadership and Effective Management.* Glenview, Ill.: Scott-Foresman, 1974.

Fink, A., and Kosecoff, J. *How to Conduct Surveys: A Step-by-Step Guide.* Newbury Park, Calif.: Sage, 1985.

Finnegan, G. "Job Aids: Improving Employee Performance in Healthcare." *Performance and Instruction Journal,* 1985, *24*(6), 10–11.

Fitz-Enz, J. *How to Measure Human Resources Management.* New York: McGraw-Hill, 1984.

Fitz-Gibbon, C., and Morris, L. *How to Analyze Data.* Newbury Park, Calif.: Sage, 1987.

Flanagan, J. "Critical Requirements: A New Approach to Employee Evaluation." *Personnel Psychology,* 1949, *2,* 419–425.

Flanagan, J. "The Critical Incident Technique." *Psychological Bulletin,* 1954, *51,* 327–358.

Fleishman, E. "On the Relationship Between Abilities, Learning, and Human Performance." *American Psychologist,* 1972, *27,* 1017–1032.

Fleming, M., and Levie, W. *Instructional Message Design: Principles from the Behavioral Sciences.* Englewood Cliffs, N.J.: Educational Technology Publications, 1978.

Foshay, W. "Choosing the Best Alternative Technique for Task Analysis." In M. Smith (ed.), *Introduction to Performance Technology.* Washington, D.C.: National Society for Performance and Instruction, 1986.

Foshay, W., Silber, K., and Westgaard, O. *Instructional Design Competencies: The Standards.* Iowa City, Iowa: International Board of Standards for Training, Performance, and Instruction, 1986.

Foshay, W., Silber, K., and Westgaard, O. *Instructors' Competencies.* Vol. 1: *The Standards.* Iowa City, Iowa: International Board of Standards for Training, Performance, and Instruction, 1988.

Fournies, F. *Why Employees Don't Do What They're Supposed to Do.* Blue Ridge Summit, Pa.: Tab Books, 1988.

Fowler, F., Jr. *Survey Research Methods.* Newbury Park, Calif.: Sage, 1988.

Fowler, H. *Modern English Usage.* (2nd ed.) Oxford, England: Oxford University Press, 1965.

Frame, J. *Managing Projects in Organizations: How to Make the Best Use of Time, Techniques, and People.* San Francisco: Jossey-Bass, 1987.

Francis, D., and Woodcock, M. *Unblocking Organizational Values.* Glenview, Ill.: Scott-Foresman, 1990.

French, J., Jr., and Raven, B. "The Bases of Social Power." In D. Cartwright (ed.), *Studies in Social Power.* Ann Arbor: University of Michigan Press, 1959.

Frey, J. *Survey Research by Telephone.* (2nd ed.) Newbury Park, Calif.: Sage, 1989.

Gagne, R. "Analysis of Objectives." In L. Briggs (ed.), *Instructional Design: Principles and Applications.* Englewood Cliffs, N.J.: Educational Technology Publications, 1977a.

Gagne, R. *The Conditions of Learning.* (3rd ed.) Troy, Mo.: Holt, Rinehart & Winston, 1977b.

Gagne, R. "Instructional Programs." In M. Marx and M. Bunch (eds.), *Fundamentals and Applications of Learning.* New York: Macmillan, 1977c.

Gagne, R., and Briggs, L. *Principles of Instructional Design.* (2nd ed.) Troy, Mo.: Holt, Rinehart & Winston, 1979.

Gagne, R., Briggs, L., and Wager, W. *Principles of Instructional Design.* (3rd ed.) Troy, Mo.: Holt, Rinehart & Winston, 1988.

Gaither, N. *Production and Operations Management: A Problem-Solving and Decision-Making Approach.* Hinsdale, Ill.: Dryden Press, 1980.

Galbraith, J., and Nathanson, D. *Strategy Implementation: The Role of Structure and Process.* St. Paul, Minn.: West, 1978.

Galosy, J. "Curriculum Design for Management Training." *Training and Development Journal,* 1983, *37*(1), 48–51.

Gardner, J. *Choosing Effective Development Programs: An Appraisal Guide for Human Resources and Training Managers.* New York: Quorum Books, 1987.

Gayeski, D. "From SME to CBT (in a day)." *Educational Technology,* 1990, *30*(4), 84–90.

Georgenson, D. "The Problem of Transfer Calls for Partnership." *Training and Development Journal,* 1982, *36*(10), 75–78.

Gerlach, V., and Ely, D. *Teaching and Media: A Systematic Approach.* (2nd ed.) Englewood Cliffs, N.J.: Prentice-Hall, 1980.

Ghorpade, J. *Job Analysis.* Englewood Cliffs, N.J.: Prentice-Hall, 1988.

Gibbons, A. *A Review of Content and Task Analysis Methodology.* San Diego, Calif.: Courseware, 1977. (ED 143 696)

Gibson, J., Ivancevich, J., and Donnelly, J., Jr. *Organizations: Behavior, Structure, Processes.* (5th ed.) Plano, Tex.: Business Publications, 1985.

Gilbert, T. *Human Competence: Engineering Worthy Performance.* New York: McGraw-Hill, 1978.

Gilmore, T. *Making a Leadership Change: How Organizations and Leaders Can Handle Leadership Transitions Successfully.* San Francisco: Jossey-Bass, 1988.

Giorgini, M. "Training and the Law: What You Don't Know Might Hurt." In L. Baird, C. Schneier, and D. Laird (eds.), *The Training and Development Sourcebook.* Amherst, Mass.: Human Resource Development Press, 1983.

Glueck, W., and Jauch, L. *Business Policy and Strategic Management.* (4th ed.) New York: McGraw-Hill, 1984.

Goldhaber, G., Dennis, H., Richetto, G., and Wiio, O. *Information Strategies: New Pathways to Corporate Power.* Englewood Cliffs, N.J.: Prentice-Hall, 1979.

Goldhaber, G., and Rogers, D. *Auditing Organizational Communication Systems: The ICA Communication Audit.* Dubuque, Iowa: Kendall/Hunt, 1979.

Gordon, J. "Where the Training Goes." *Training,* 1990, *27*(10), 51–54, 58–62, 64, 66–69.

Gould, D. *Personnel Skills Inventory Study.* BLR Management Report. Madison, Conn.: Bureau of Law and Business, Business and Legal Reports, 1986.

Graen, G., Orrin, J., and Alvares, K. "Contingency Model of Leadership Effectiveness: Some Experimental Results." *Journal of Applied Psychology,* 1971, *55,* 196–201.

Greenblatt, C., and Duke, R. *Principles and Practices of Gaming-Simulation.* Newbury Park, Calif.: Sage, 1981.

Gropper, G. "A Lesson Based on a Behavioral Approach to Instructional Design." In C. Reigeluth (ed.), *Instructional Theories in Action: Lessons Illustrating Selected Theories and Models.* Hillsdale, N.J.: Erlbaum, 1987.

Gross, R. *The Lifelong Learner.* New York: Simon & Schuster, 1977.

Gross, R. (ed.). *The Independent Scholar's Handbook.* Reading, Mass.: Addison-Wesley, 1982.

Guba, E., and Lincoln, Y. *Effective Evaluation: Improving the Usefulness of Evaluation Results Through Responsive and Naturalistic Approaches.* San Francisco: Jossey-Bass, 1981.

Guest, R. *Work Teams and Team Building.* In *Highlights of the Literature,* no. 44. New York: Pergamon Press, 1986.

Gunning, R. *The Technique of Clear Writing.* New York: McGraw-Hill, 1952.

Hackman, J., and Oldham, G. *Work Redesign.* Reading, Mass.: Addison-Wesley, 1980.

Hagberg, J., and Leider, R. *The Inventurers.* Reading, Mass.: Addison-Wesley, 1982.

Hall, D. *Careers in Organizations.* Pacific Palisades, Calif.: Goodyear, 1976.

Halson, B. "Teaching Supervisors to Coach." *Personnel Management,* 1990, *22*(3), 36–39, 53.

Harless, J. "Performance Technology and Other Popular Myths." *Performance and Instruction Journal,* 1985, *24*(6), 4–6.

Harless, J. "Guiding Performance with Job Aids." In M. Smith (ed.), *Introduction to Performance Technology.* Washington, D.C.: National Society for Performance and Instruction, 1986.

Harrow, A. *A Taxonomy of the Psychomotor Domain—A Guide for Developing Behavioral Objectives.* New York: McKay, 1972.

Hartley, J. "Eighty Ways of Improving Instructional Text." *IEEE Transactions on Professional Communication,* 1981, *24,* 17–27.

Hartley, J. *Designing Instructional Text.* (2nd ed.) New York: Nichols, 1985.

Hassinger, E. "Stages in the Adoption Process." *Rural Sociology,* 1959, *24,* 52–53.

Havighurst, R. *Developmental Tasks and Education.* (2nd ed.) New York: McKay, 1970.

Head, G. *Training Cost Analysis: A Practical Guide/A How-To Publication for Managers and Specialists.* Washington, D.C.: Marlin Press, 1985.

Heinich, R., Molenda, M., and Russell, J. *Instructional Media and the New Technologies of Instruction.* (2nd ed.) New York: Macmillan, 1985.

Henerson, M., Morris, L., and Fitz-Gibbon, C. *How to Measure Attitudes.* Newbury Park, Calif.: Sage, 1987.

Hennessy, D., and Hennessy, M. *Instructional Systems Development: Tools and*

Procedures for Organizing, Budgeting, and Managing a Training Project from Start to Finish. Frederiksted, St. Croix, U.S. Virgin Islands: TRC Press, 1989.

Hensey, M. "Conflict: What It Is and What It Can Be." In D. Cole (ed.), *Conflict Resolution Technology.* Cleveland, Ohio: Organization Development Institute, 1983.

Herbart, J. *The Application of Psychology to the Science of Education.* (Beatrice C. Mulliner, trans.) New York: Charles Scribner's Sons, 1898.

Herman, J., Morris, L., and Fitz-Gibbon, C. *Evaluator's Handbook.* Newbury Park, Calif.: Sage, 1987.

Herrmann, N. "Brain Dominance Technology." In R. Craig (ed.), *Training and Development Handbook: A Guide to Human Resource Development.* (3rd ed.) New York: McGraw-Hill, 1987.

Hinrichs, J. "Communications Activity of Industrial Research Personnel." *Personnel Psychology,* 1964, *17,* 193–204.

Hodgetts, R. "Leadership Techniques in the Project Organization." *Academy of Management Journal,* 1968, *11,* 211–219.

Horabin, I., and Lewis, B. "Algorithms." In *The Instructional Design Library.* Vol. 2. Englewood Cliffs, N.J.: Educational Technology Publications, 1978.

Houle, C. *The Inquiring Mind.* Madison: University of Wisconsin Press, 1961.

House, E. *School Evaluation: Politics and Process.* Berkeley, Calif.: McCutchan, 1973.

Huczynski, A. *Encyclopedia of Management Development Methods.* London: Gower, 1983.

Hutchison, C. "A Performance Technology Process Model," *Performance and Instruction,* 1990, *29,*(2), 18–21.

Hutchison, C. "What's a Nice P.T. Like You Doing . . . ?" *Performance and Instruction,* 1990, *29*(9), 1–6.

Hutchison, C., Stein, F., and Shepherd, J. *Instructor Competencies Volume I: The Standards.* Batavia, N.Y.: The International Board of Standards for Training, Performance, and Instruction, 1988.

Ingle, S. *Quality Circles Master Guide.* Englewood Cliffs, N.J.: Prentice-Hall, 1982.

"Instructional Designer." *News and Notes,* 1988, *1*(2), 6.

Isaac, S., and Michael, W. *Handbook of Research and Evaluation for Education and the Behavioral Sciences.* (2nd ed.) San Diego, Calif.: EDITS, 1984.

Ivey, A., and Gluckstern, N. *Basic Attending Skills.* (2nd ed.) North Amherst, Mass.: Microtraining Associates, 1982.

Jackson, S. "Task Analysis." In M. Smith (ed.), *Introduction to Performance Technology.* Washington, D.C.: National Society for Performance and Instruction, 1986.

Jacobs, R. *Human Performance Technology: A Systems-Based Field for the Training and Development Profession.* Columbus: ERIC Clearinghouse on Adult, Career, and Vocational Education, National Center for Research in Vocational Education, Ohio State University, 1987.

Jacobs, R. *Effects of Feedback for Training and Development: Selected Research Abstracts.* Columbus: College of Education, Ohio State University, 1988. (ED 305 464)

Janis, I. *Victims of Groupthink: A Psychological Study of Foreign Policy Decisions and Fiascos.* Boston: Houghton Mifflin, 1973.

Johnson, S. "Critical Incident." In F. Ulschak (ed.), *Human Resource Development: The Theory and Practice of Need Assessment.* Reston, Va.: Reston Publishing, 1983.

Johnson, S. "Cognitive Analysis of Expert and Novice Troubleshooting Performance." *Performance Improvement Quarterly,* 1988, *1*(3), 38–54.

Jonassen, D., Grabinger, S., and Harris, N. "Analyzing and Selecting Instructional Strategies and Tactics." *Performance Improvement Quarterly,* 1990, *3*(2), 29–47.

Jones, M. "Job Descriptions Made Easy." *Personnel Journal,* 1984, *63*(5), 31–34.

Jorgensen, D. *Participant Observation: A Methodology for Human Studies.* Newbury Park, Calif.: Sage, 1989.

Kalton, G. *Introduction to Survey Sampling.* Newbury Park, Calif.: Sage, 1983.

Katz, D., and Kahn, R. *The Social Psychology of Organizations.* (2nd ed.) New York: Wiley, 1978.

Kaufman, R. *Educational System Planning.* Englewood Cliffs, N.J.: Prentice-Hall, 1972.

Kaufman, R. "Assessing Needs." In M. Smith (ed.), *Introduction to Performance Technology.* Washington, D.C.: National Society for Performance and Instruction, 1986.

Kaufman, R., and English, F. *Needs Assessment: Concept and Application.* Englewood Cliffs, N.J.: Educational Technology Publications, 1979.

Kearsley, G. "Analyzing the Cost and Benefits of Training." *Performance and Instruction,* 1986, *25*(1), 30.

Keefer, C., Mortlock, H., and Smith, H. "Instructional Developers' Skills and Knowledges." *Performance and Instruction,* 1987, *26*(9 & 10), 58–60.

Keller, J., and Kopp, T. "An Application of the ARCS Model of Motivational Design." In C. Reigeluth (ed.), *Instructional Theories in Action: Lessons Illustrating Selected Theories and Models.* Hillsdale, N.J.: Erlbaum, 1987.

Kelly, G. *The Psychology of Personal Constructs.* New York: W.W. Norton, 1955.

Kelly, G. *Organizational Behavior: Its Data, First Principles, and Applications.* Homewood, Ill.: Irwin, 1980.

Kemmerer, F., and Thiagarajan, S. "What Is an Incentive System?" *Performance and Instruction,* 1989, *28*(3), 11–16.

Kemp, J. *Instructional Design: A Plan for Unit and Course Development.* Belmont, Calif.: Lear Siegler, 1971.

Kemp, J. *The Instructional Design Process.* New York: HarperCollins, 1985.

Kemp, J., and Dayton, D. *Planning and Producing Instructional Media.* (5th ed.) New York: HarperCollins, 1985.

Kemp, J., and Smellie, D. *Planning, Producing, and Using Instructional Media.* New York: HarperCollins, 1989.

Kerr, J., and Slocum, J. "Managing Corporate Culture Through Reward Systems." *Academy of Management Executive,* 1988, *1*(2), 99–109.

Kerr, S. "On the Folly of Rewarding A, While Hoping for B." *Academy of Management Journal,* 1975, *18,* 769–783.

Kimberly, J., Miles, R., and Associates. *The Organizational Life Cycle: Issues in the Creation, Transformation, and Decline of Organizations.* San Francisco: Jossey-Bass, 1980.

Kirkpatrick, D. *No-Nonsense Communication.* (2nd ed.) Elm Grove, Wis.: K & M Publishers, 1978.

Kirkpatrick, D. *How to Manage Change Effectively: Approaches, Methods, and Case Examples.* San Francisco: Jossey-Bass, 1985.

Kirkpatrick, D. "Evaluation." In R. Craig (ed.), *Training and Development Handbook: A Guide to Human Resource Development.* (3rd ed.) New York: McGraw-Hill, 1987.

Kirkpatrick, D. (ed.). *Evaluating Training Programs.* Madison, Wis.: American Society for Training and Development, 1975.

Kirkpatrick, D. (ed.). *More Evaluating Training Programs.* Alexandria, Va.: American Society for Training and Development, 1988.

Kirrane, D. "The Case Method." *Training and Development Journal,* 1989, *44*(3), 17–25.

Klare, G. *Readability Standards for Army-Wide Publications.* Evaluation report 79-1. Fort Benjamin Harrison, Ind.: U.S. Army Administrative Center, 1979.

Knowles, M. *Self-Directed Learning: A Guide for Teachers and Learners.* New York: Cambridge Book Company, 1975.

Knowles, M. *The Modern Practice of Adult Education: Andragogy Versus Pedagogy.* New York: Association Press, 1980.

Knowles, M. *The Adult Learner: A Neglected Species.* (3rd ed.) Houston, Tex.: Gulf, 1984.

Knowles, M. *Using Learning Contracts: Practical Approaches to Individualizing and Structuring Learning.* San Francisco: Jossey-Bass, 1986.

Knox, A. *Adult Development and Learning.* San Francisco: Jossey-Bass, 1977.

Kolb, D. *Experiential Learning: Experience as the Source of Learning and Development.* Englewood Cliffs, N.J.: Prentice-Hall, 1984.

Kotler, P. *Marketing Essentials.* Englewood Cliffs, N.J.: Prentice-Hall, 1984.

Krathwohl, D., Bloom, B., and Masia, B. *Taxonomy of Educational Objectives, the Classification of Educational Goals — Handbook II: Affective Domain.* New York: McKay, 1964.

Krueger, R. *Focus Groups: A Practical Guide for Applied Research.* Newbury Park, Calif.: Sage, 1988.

Kruger, M. "How to Make a Management Advisory Committee Work for You." *Training and Development Journal,* 1983, *37*(6), 86–90.

Laird, D. *Approaches to Training and Development.* (2nd ed.) Reading, Mass.: Addison-Wesley; 1985.

Lawler, E., III. "Reward Systems." In J. Hackman and J. Suttle (eds.), *Improving Life at Work.* Santa Monica, Calif.: Goodyear, 1977.

Lawrence, P., and Lorsch, J. *Organization and Environment.* Homewood, Ill.: Irwin, 1969.

Lawson, T. *Formative Instructional Product Evaluation: Instruments and Strategies.* Englewood Cliffs, N.J.: Educational Technology Publications, 1974.

Lazer, R. "Performance Appraisal: What Does the Future Hold?" *Personnel Administrator,* 1980, *25*(7), 69–73.

Lee, C. "Using Customers' Ratings to Reward Employees." *Training,* 1989, *26*(5), 40–46.

Leeds, D. *Smart Questions.* New York: McGraw-Hill, 1988.

Leibler, S., and Parkman, A. "Selection of Personnel." In M. Smith (ed.), *Introduction to Performance Technology.* Washington, D.C.: National Society for Performance and Instruction, 1986.

Leibman, M., and Weinstein, H. "Money Isn't Everything." *HRMagazine,* 1990, *35*(11), 48–51.

Lerch, R. *Effective Adult Literacy Programs: A Practitioner's Guide.* New York: Cambridge Books, 1985.

Levine, E. *Everything You Always Wanted to Know About Job Analysis.* Tampa, Fla.: Mariner Publishing, 1983.

Levinson, D. *The Seasons of a Man's Life.* New York: Knopf, 1978.

Likert, R. *The Human Organization.* New York: McGraw-Hill, 1967.

Lineberry, C., and Bullock, D. "Job Aids." In *The Instructional Design Library.* Vol. 25. Englewood Cliffs, N.J.: Educational Technology Publications, 1980.

Lippitt, G., and Lippitt, R. *The Consulting Process in Action.* San Diego, Calif.: University Associates, 1978.

Lockyear, K. *Introduction to Critical Path Analysis.* Woodstock, N.Y.: Beekman, 1969.

Lombardo, M., and Eichinger, R. *Eighty-Eight Assignments for Development in Place: Enhancing the Developmental Challenge of Existing Jobs.* Greensboro, N.C.: Center for Creative Leadership, 1989.

London, M. *Change Agents: New Roles and Innovation Strategies for Human Resource Professionals.* San Francisco: Jossey-Bass, 1988.

Lynn, R. *Learning Disabilities: An Overview of Theories, Approaches, and Politics.* New York: Free Press, 1979.

McArdle, G. "What Is Training?" *Performance and Instruction,* 1989, *28*(6), 34–35.

McCall, M., Jr. *Developing Executives Through Work Experiences.* Technical report no. 33. Greensboro, N.C.: Center for Creative Leadership, 1988.

McCall, M., Jr., and Kaplan, R. (1985). *Whatever It Takes: Decision Makers at Work.* Englewood Cliffs, N.J.: Prentice-Hall, 1985.

McCarthy, E. *Basic Marketing: A Managerial Approach.* (6th ed.) Homewood, Ill.: Irwin, 1978.

McCauley, C. *Developmental Experiences in Managerial Work: A Literature Review.* Technical report no. 26. Greensboro, N.C.: Center for Creative Leadership, 1986.

McCormick, E. *Job Analysis.* New York: Amacom, 1979.

McEwan, B. "Mediating Between Disputing Employees." In F. Stone (ed.), *The American Management Association Handbook of Supervisory Management.* New York: Amacom, 1989. (Originally published in *Supervisory Management,* May 1984, *29,* 2–5.

McLagan, P. *Models for Human Resource Development Practice.* 4 vols. Alexandria, Va.: American Society for Training and Development, 1989.

McLinden, D., Cummings, O., and Bond, S. "A Comparison of Two Formats for an Instructor's Guide." *Performance Improvement Quarterly,* 1990, *3*(1), 2–13.

McMurray, R. *Tested Techniques of Personnel Selection.* (Rev. ed.) Chicago: Dartnell, 1979.

Mager, R. *Goal Analysis.* Belmont, Calif.: Fearon-Pitman, 1972.

Mager, R. *Measuring Instructional Intent (or Got a Match?).* Belmont, Calif.: Fearon-Pitman, 1973.

Mager, R. *Preparing Instructional Objectives.* (2nd ed.) Belmont, Calif.: Fearon-Pitman, 1975.

Mager, R., and Pipe, P. *Analyzing Performance Problems or "You Really Oughta Wanna."* Belmont, Calif.: Lake Publishing Company, 1984.

Mahler, W. *Diagnostic Studies.* Reading, Mass.: Addison-Wesley, 1974.

Malasky, E. "Instructional Strategies: Nonmedia." In L. Nadler (ed.), *The Handbook of Human Resource Development.* New York: Wiley-Interscience, 1984.

March, J. "The Business Firm as a Political Coalition." *Journal of Politics,* 1962, *24*(2), 662–678.

Marrow, A. *The Failure of Success.* New York: Amacom, 1972.

Marshall, C., and Rossman, G. *Designing Qualitative Research.* Newbury Park, Calif.: Sage, 1989.

Marshall, H., and Weinstein, R. *Classroom Dimensions Observation System Manual.* Berkeley: Department of Psychology, University of California, 1982.

Martinetz, C. "The Missing Link: A Bridge Between Task Analysis and Training Strategy." Paper presented at the 26th annual conference of the National Society for Performance and Instruction, Washington, D.C., April 1988. (ED 304 108)

Martinez, M. "Creative Ways to Employ People with Disabilities." *HRMagazine,* 1990, *35*(11), 40–44, 101.

Martinko, M., and Gepson, J. "Nominal Grouping and Needs Analysis." In F. Ulschak (ed.), *Human Resource Development: The Theory and Practice of Need Assessment.* Reston, Va.: Reston Publishing, 1983.

Merrill, M. "Component Display Theory." In C. Reigeluth (ed.), *Instructional-Design Theories and Models: An Overview of Their Current Status.* Hillsdale, N.J.: Erlbaum, 1983.

Milkovich, G., and Glueck, W. *Personnel/Human Resource Management: A Diagnostic Approach.* (4th ed.) Plano, Tex.: Business Publications, 1985.

Mill, C. *Activities for Trainers: 50 Useful Designs.* San Diego, Calif.: University Associates, 1980.

Miller, D., and Barnett, S. *The How-To Handbook on Doing Research in Human Resource Development.* Alexandria, Va.: American Society for Training and Development, 1986.

Mitchell, J. (ed.). *Tests in Print III.* Lincoln: University of Nebraska Press, 1983.

Moos, R. *Work Environment Scale Manual.* Palo Alto, Calif.: Consulting Psychologists Press, 1981.

Moos, R., and Trickett, E. *Classroom Environment Scale Manual.* Palo Alto, Calif.: Consulting Psychologists Press, 1974.

Morgan, D. *Focus Groups as Qualitative Research.* Newbury Park, Calif.: Sage, 1988.

Morris, L. *Critical Path: Construction and Analysis.* New York: Pergamon Press, 1967.

Morris, L., Fitz-Gibbon, C., and Freeman, M. *How to Communicate Evaluation Findings.* Newbury Park, Calif.: Sage, 1987.

Morris, L., Fitz-Gibbon, C., and Lindheim, E. *How to Measure Performance and Use Tests.* Newbury Park, Calif.: Sage, 1987.

Morrisey, G., and Sechrest, T. *Effective Business and Technical Presentations.* (3rd ed.) Reading, Mass.: Addison-Wesley, 1987.

Moses, J. "Assessment Centers." In R. Craig (ed.), *Training and Development Handbook: A Guide to Human Resource Development.* (3rd ed.) New York: McGraw-Hill, 1987.

Myers, D. *Human Resources Management: Principles and Practice.* Chicago: Commerce Clearinghouse, 1986.

Myers, M. *Every Employee a Manager.* New York: McGraw-Hill, 1970.

Nadler, D. *Feedback and Organization Development: Using Data-Based Methods.* Reading, Mass.: Addison-Wesley, 1977.

Nash, M. *Managing Organizational Performance.* San Francisco: Jossey-Bass, 1983.

National Center on Education and the Economy. *America's Choice: High Skills or Low Wages.* Rochester, N.Y.: National Center on Education and the Economy, 1990.

Newstrom, J. "Evaluating the Effectiveness of Training Methods." *Personnel Administrator,* January 1980, pp. 55–60.

Newstrom, J., and Lilyquist, J. "Selecting Needs Analysis Methods." *Training and Development Journal,* 1979, *33*(10), 52–56.

Newstrom, J., and Scannell, E. *Games Trainers Play: Experiential Learning Exercises.* New York: McGraw-Hill, 1980.

Nichols, R. *Successful Management.* New York: Doubleday, 1957.

Nickens, J., Purga, A., and Noriega, P. *Research Methods for Needs Assessment.* Washington, D.C.: University Press of America, 1980.

Nystrom, P., and Starbuck, W. *Handbook of Organizational Design.* 2 vols. New York: Oxford University Press, 1983.

Odiorne, G. *MBO II: A System of Managerial Leadership for the 80s.* Belmont, Calif.: Fearon-Pitman, 1979.

Odiorne, G. *The Change Resisters.* Englewood Cliffs, N.J.: Prentice-Hall, 1981.

Pace, R. *Organizational Communication: Foundations for Human Resource Development*. Englewood Cliffs, N.J.: Prentice-Hall, 1983.

Paris, S., Lipson, M., and Wixson, K. "Becoming a Strategic Reader." *Contemporary Educational Psychology*, 1983, *8*, 293–316.

Patton, M. *How to Use Qualitative Methods in Evaluation*. Newbury Park, Calif.: Sage, 1987.

Pearce, J., II, and David, F. "A Social Network Approach to Organization Design—Performance." *Academy of Management Review*, 1983, *8*, 436–444.

Pedler, M. "Management Self-Development." In B. Taylor and G. Lippitt (eds.), *Management Development and Training Handbook*. (2nd ed.) London: McGraw-Hill, 1983.

Pensyl, O. "The Library's Role in Human Resources Development." In W. Tracey (ed.), *Human Resources Management and Development Handbook*. New York: Amacom, 1985.

Peoples, D. *Presentations Plus: David Peoples' Proven Techniques*. New York: Wiley, 1988.

Peters, D. *Directory of Human Resource Development Instrumentation*. San Diego, Calif.: University Associates, 1985.

Peters, T., and Waterman, R. *In Search of Excellence: Lessons from America's Best-Run Companies*. New York: HarperCollins, 1982.

Pfeiffer, J., and Ballew, A. "Using Case Studies, Simulations, and Games in Human Resource Development." In *The Training Technologies Series*. Vol. 5. San Diego, Calif.: University Associates, 1988a.

Pfeiffer, J., and Ballew, A. "Using Instruments in Human Resource Development." In *The Training Technologies Series*. Vol. 2. San Diego, Calif.: University Associates, 1988b.

Pfeiffer, J., and Ballew, A. "Using Role Plays in Human Resource Development." In *The Training Technologies Series*. Vol. 4. San Diego, Calif.: University Associates, 1988c.

Pfeiffer, J., and Jones, J. *The Annual Handbook for Group Facilitators*. 19 vols. San Diego, Calif.: University Associates, 1972–1990 (annual).

Pfeiffer, W. *Instrumentation Kit*. 3 vols. San Diego, Calif.: University Associates, 1988.

Pigors, P., and Pigors, F. "The Pigors Incident Process of Case Study." In *The Instructional Design Library*. Vol. 29. Englewood Cliffs, N.J.: Educational Technology Publications, 1980.

Pigors, P., and Pigors, F. "Case Method." In R. Craig (ed.), *Training and Development Handbook: A Guide to Human Resource Development*. (3rd ed.) New York: McGraw-Hill, 1987.

Pinchot, G., III. *Intrapreneuring: Why You Don't Have to Leave the Corporation to Become an Entrepreneur*. New York: HarperCollins, 1985.

"A Poor Report Card." *Business Month*, May 1990, p. 9.

Priestley, M. *Performance Assessment in Education and Training*. Englewood Cliffs, N.J.: Educational Technology Publications, 1982.

Pucel, D. *Performance-Based Instructional Design*. New York: McGraw-Hill, 1989.

Rae, L. *How to Measure Training Effectiveness.* New York: Nichols, 1986.

Randhawa, B., and Fu, L. "Assessment and Effect of Some Classroom Environment Variables." *Review of Educational Research,* 1973, *43,* 303–322.

Rath, G., and Stoyanoff, K. "The Delphi Technique." In F. Ulschak (ed.), *Human Resource Development: The Theory and Practice of Need Assessment.* Reston, Va.: Reston Publishing, 1983.

Reddout, D. "What Is a Task?" *Performance and Instruction,* 1987, *26*(1), 5–6.

Reigeluth, C. "Introduction." In C. Reigeluth (ed.), *Instructional Theories in Action: Lessons Illustrating Selected Theories and Models.* Hillsdale, N.J.: Erlbaum, 1987.

Revans, R. "Action Learning Projects." In B. Taylor and G. Lippitt (eds.), *Management Development and Training Handbook.* (2nd ed.) London: McGraw-Hill, 1983.

Reynolds, A. "Computer-Based Learning Center." In W. Tracey (ed.), *Human Resource Management and Development Handbook.* New York: Amacom, 1985.

Ribler, R. *Training Development Guide.* Reston, Va.: Reston Publishing, 1983.

Richey, R. *The Theoretical and Conceptual Bases of Instructional Design.* New York: Nichols, 1986.

Robinson, J., Athanasiou, R., and Head, K. *Measures of Occupational Attitudes and Occupational Characteristics* (Rev. ed.) Ann Arbor: Institute for Social Research, University of Michigan, 1969.

Robinson, J., and Shaver, P. *Measures of Social Psychological Attitudes.* (Rev. ed.) Ann Arbor: Institute for Social Research, University of Michigan, 1969.

Rogers, E., and Shoemaker, F. *Communication of Innovations: A Cross-Cultural Approach.* (2nd ed.) New York: Free Press, 1971.

Rogers, R. *The Political Process in Modern Organizations.* New York: Exposition Press, 1971.

Rokeach, M. *The Nature of Human Values.* New York: Free Press, 1973.

Romiszowski, A. *Designing Instructional Systems: Decision Making in Course Planning and Curriculum Design.* New York: Nichols, 1981.

Rosenbaum, B. *How to Motivate Today's Workers: Motivational Models for Managers and Supervisors.* New York: McGraw-Hill, 1982.

Rossett, A. *Training Needs Assessment.* Englewood Cliffs, N.J.: Educational Technology Publications, 1988.

Rothwell, W. "Conducting an Employee Attitude Survey." *Personnel Journal,* 1983a, *62*(4), 308–311.

Rothwell, W. "The Life Cycle of HRD Departments." *Training and Development Journal,* 1983b, *37*(11), 74–76.

Rothwell, W. "Strategic Needs Assessment." *Performance and Instruction,* 1984, *23*–(5), 19–20.

Rothwell, W. "Administering the Climate Survey: A Toolkit." *Journal of Technical Writing and Communication,* 1985, *15*(4), 323–338.

Rothwell, W. "Performance Improvement Methods and Company Policy: Should the Tail Wag the Dog?", *Performance and Instruction,* 1989, *28*(10), 6–9.

Rothwell, W. *The Employee Selection Workshop.* 2 vols. Amherst, Mass.: Human Resource Development Press, 1990.

Rothwell, W., and Brandenburg, D. "Solutions to Literacy Deficiencies in the Workplace: A Survey of Current Practices." *Performance and Instruction,* 1990a, *3*(2), 16–28.

Rothwell, W., and Brandenburg, D. *The Workplace Literacy Primer: An Action Manual for Training and Development Professionals.* Amherst, Mass.: Human Resource Development Press, 1990b.

Rothwell, W., and Kazanas, H. "Participation: Key to Integrating Planning and Training?" *Performance and Instruction,* 1987, *26*(9 & 10), 27–31.

Rothwell, W., and Kazanas, H. "Curriculum Planning for Training: The State of the Art. *Performance Improvement Quarterly,* 1988a, *1*(3), 2–16.

Rothwell, W., and Kazanas, H. *Strategic Human Resources Planning and Management.* Englewood Cliffs, N.J.: Prentice-Hall, 1988b.

Rothwell, W., and Kazanas, H. *Strategic Human Resource Development.* Englewood Cliffs, N.J.: Prentice-Hall, 1989.

Rothwell, W., and Kazanas, H. "Informal Learning in the Workplace." *Performance and Instruction,* 1990a, *29*(3), 33–35.

Rothwell, W., and Kazanas, H. "Structured On-the-Job Training as Perceived by HRD Professionals." *Performance Improvement Quarterly,* 1990b, *3*(3), 12–25.

Rowntree, D. *Assessing Students: How Shall We Know Them?* London: HarperCollins, 1977.

Rummler, G. "The Performance Audit." In R. Craig (ed.), *Training and Development Handbook: A Guide to Human Resource Development.* (2nd ed.) New York: McGraw-Hill, 1976.

Rummler, G. "Human Performance Problems and Their Solutions." In L. Baird, C. Schneier, and D. Laird (eds.), *The Training and Development Sourcebook.* Amherst, Mass.: Human Resource Development Press, 1983.

Rummler, G. "Organizational Redesign." In M. Smith (ed.), *Introduction to Performance Technology.* Washington, D.C.: The National Society for Performance and Instruction, 1986.

Rummler, G. "Determining Needs." In R. Craig (ed.), *Training and Development Handbook: A Guide to Human Resource Development.* (3rd ed.) New York: McGraw-Hill, 1987.

Sanders, N. *Classroom Questions: What Kinds?* New York: HarperCollins, 1966.

Schein, E. *Process Consultation: Its Role in Organization Development.* Reading, Mass.: Addison-Wesley, 1969.

Schein, E. *Organizational Culture and Leadership: A Dynamic View.* San Francisco: Jossey-Bass, 1985.

Schmidt, W., and Posner, B. *Managerial Values and Expectations: The Silent Power in Personal and Organizational Life.* New York: American Management Association Membership Publications Division, 1982.

Schmitt, N., and Robertson, I. "Personnel Selection." *Annual Review of Psychology,* 1990, *41,* 289–319.

Schneider, M. "Exit Interview." In F. Ulschak (ed.), *Human Resource Development: The Theory and Practice of Need Assessment.* Reston, Va.: Reston Publishing, 1983.

Schoonover, S. *Managing to Relate: Interpersonal Skills at Work.* Reading, Mass.: Addison-Wesley, 1988.

Sener, C. "Facilities." In P. Craig (ed.), *Training and Development Handbook: A Guide to Human Resource Development.* (3rd ed.) New York: McGraw-Hill, 1987.

Shaw, M., and Wright, J. *Scales for the Measurement of Attitudes.* New York: McGraw-Hill, 1967.

Sheehy, G. *Passages: Predictable Crises of Adult Life.* New York: Dutton, 1974.

Sherman, A., Jr., Bohlander, G., and Chruden, H. *Managing Human Resources.* (8th ed.) Cincinnati, Ohio: South-western Publishing, 1988.

Smillie, R. "Design Strategies for Job Performance Aids." In T. Duffy and R. Waller (eds.), *Designing Usable Texts.* San Diego, Calif.: Academic Press, 1985.

Smith, B., Stanley, W., and Shores, H. *Fundamentals of Curriculum Development.* New York: World Book, 1957.

Smith, G. "The Use and Effectiveness of the Case Study Method in Management Education — A Critical Review." *Management Education and Development,* 1987, *12,* 51–61.

Smith, R. *Learning How to Learn: Applied Learning Theory for Adults.* New York: Cambridge Books, 1982.

Snowman, J. "Learning Tactics and Strategies." In G. Phye and T. Andre (eds.), *Cognitive Classroom Learning: Understanding, Thinking, Problem Solving.* San Diego, Calif.: Academic Press, 1986.

Society for Human Resource Management. *Performance and Rewards: Linking Pay to Performance.* Alexandria, Va.: Society for Human Resource Management, 1989a.

Society for Human Resource Management. *Training/Retraining Survey Report.* Alexandria, Va.: Society for Human Resource Management, 1989b.

Springer, J. *Job Performance Standards and Measures.* Washington, D.C.: American Society for Training and Development, 1980.

Sredl, H., and Rothwell, W. *The American Society for Training and Development Reference Guide to Professional Training Roles and Competencies.* 2 vols. Amherst, Mass.: Human Resource Development Press, 1987.

Steelcase. *Office Environment Index: 1989 Summary Report.* Grand Rapids, Mich.: Steelcase, 1989.

Steele, F. *Physical Settings and Organization Development.* Reading, Mass.: Addison-Wesley, 1973.

Stephen, L. "Assessing Your Learning Style." In R. Bard, C. Bell, L. Stephen, and L. Webster, *The Trainer's Professional Development Handbook.* San Francisco: Jossey-Bass, 1987.

Stowell, S., and Starcevich, M. *The Coach: Creating Partnerships for a Competitive Edge.* Salt Lake City, Utah: Center for Management and Organization Effectiveness, 1987.

Strunk, W., Jr., and White, E. *The Elements of Style.* (3rd ed.) New York: Macmillan, 1979.

Swanson, R., and Gradous, D. *Performance at Work: A Systematic Program for Analyzing Work Behavior.* New York: Wiley-Interscience, 1986.

Swanson, R., and Gradous, D. *Forecasting Financial Benefits of Human Resource Development.* San Francisco: Jossey-Bass, 1988.

Sweeney, A., and Wisner, J., Jr. *Budgeting Fundamentals for Nonfinancial Executives.* New York: Amacom, 1975.

Tessmer, M., and Jonassen, D. "Learning Strategies: A New Educational Technology." In G. Phye and T. Andre (eds.), *Instructional Development: The State of the Art.* Vol. 2. Dubuque, Iowa: Hunt, 1988.

Thiagarajan, S., and Stolovich, H. "Instructional Simulation Games." In *The Instructional Design Library.* Vol. 12. Englewood Cliffs, N.J.: Educational Technology Publications, 1978.

Thomas, K., and Kilmann, R. "The Thomas-Kilmann Conflict Mode Instrument." In D. Cole (ed.), *Conflict Resolution Technology.* Cleveland, Ohio: Organization Development Institute, 1983.

Thorndike, E., and Woodworth, R. "The Estimation of Magnitudes." *Psychological Review,* 1901a, *8,* 384–395.

Thorndike, E., and Woodworth, R. "Functions Involving Attention, Observation, and Discrimination. *Psychological Review,* 1901b, *8,* 553–564.

Thorndike, E., and Woodworth, R. "The Influence of Improvement in One Mental Function upon the Efficiency of Other Functions." *Psychological Review,* 1901c, *8,* 247–261.

Tiemann, P., and Markle, S. *Analyzing Instructional Content: A Guide to Instruction and Evaluation.* Champaign, Ill.: Stipes Publishing, 1985.

Torrence, D. "Building a Lesson Plan." *Training and Development Journal,* 1987, *41*(5), 91–95.

Torrence, D., and Torrence, J. "Training in the Face of Illiteracy." *Training and Development Journal,* 1987, *41*(8), 46.

Tosti, D. "Feedback Systems." In M. Smith (ed.), *Introduction to Performance Technology.* Washington, D.C.: National Society for Performance and Instruction, 1986.

Tough, A. *The Adult's Learning Projects.* (2nd ed.) Toronto: Ontario Institute for Studies in Education, 1979.

Ulery, J. *Job Descriptions in Manufacturing.* New York: Amacom, 1981.

Ulschak, F., Nathanson, L., and Gillan, P. *Small Group Problem Solving: An Aid to Organizational Effectiveness.* Reading, Mass.: Addison-Wesley, 1983.

U.S. Air Force. *Handbook for Designers of Instructional Systems.* Washington, D.C.: U.S. Air Force, 1973.

U.S. Department of Labor and U.S. Department of Education. *The Bottom Line: Basic Skills in the Workplace.* Washington, D.C.: Government Printing Office, 1988.

Uretsky, M. "Simulated Reality—The Key to More Effective Training." *Employment Relations Today,* 1989/1990, *16*(4), 305–314.

Van Gundy, A. *Techniques of Structured Problem Solving.* New York: Van Nostrand Reinhold, 1981.

Van Ments, M. *The Effective Use of Role-Play: A Handbook for Teachers.* New York: Nichols, 1983.

Van Patten, J., Chao, C., and Reigeluth, C. "A Review of Strategies for Sequencing and Synthesizing Instruction." *Review of Educational Research,* 1986, *56,* 437–471.

Vroom, V. *Work and Motivation.* New York: Wiley, 1964.

Walker, J. *Human Resource Planning.* New York: McGraw-Hill, 1980.

Walton, R. *Interpersonal Peacemaking: Confrontations and Third Party Consultation.* Reading, Mass.: Addison-Wesley, 1969.

Warren, M. *Training for Results: A Systems Approach to the Development of Human Resources in Industry.* (2nd ed.) Reading, Mass.: Addison-Wesley, 1979.

Wasserman, P. (eds.). *Learning Independently.* (2nd ed.) Detroit, Mich.: Gale Research, 1987.

Waters, L., Roach, D., and Batlis, N. "Organizational Climate Dimensions and Job-Related Attitudes." *Personnel Psychology,* 1974, *27,* 465–476.

Webb, E., Campbell, D., Schwartz, R., and Sechrest, L. *Unobtrusive Measures.* Chicago: Rand McNally, 1966.

Weber, R. "The Group: A Cycle from Birth to Death." In L. Porter and B. Mohr (eds.), *Readingbook for Human Relations Training.* Arlington, Va.: National Training Laboratories Institute, 1982.

Webster, E. *The Employment Interview — A Social Judgment Process.* Ontario, Canada: S.I.P. Publications, 1982.

Weller, S., and Romney, A. *Systematic Data Collection.* Newbury Park, Calif.: Sage, 1988.

Werther, W., and Davis, K. *Personnel Management and Human Resources.* (2nd ed.) New York: McGraw-Hill, 1985.

West, J., and Levy, F. *A Management Guide to PERT/CPM.* (2nd ed.) Englewood Cliffs, N.J.: Prentice-Hall, 1977.

Westgaard, O., and Hale, J. *The Competent Manager's Handbook for Measuring Unit Productivity.* Chicago: Hale Associates, 1985.

Wileman, R. *Exercises in Visual Thinking.* New York: Hastings House, 1980.

Wilemon, D., and Cicero, J. "The Project Manager — Anomalies and Ambiguities." *Academy of Management Journal,* 1970, *13,* 269–282.

Wilkins, A. "The Culture Audit: A Tool for Understanding Organizations." *Organizational Dynamics,* 1983, *12*(2), 24–38.

"Win New Allies with a Training and Education Committee." *Training,* 1982, *19*(2), 67.

Wlodkowski, R. *Enhancing Adult Motivation to Learn: A Guide to Improving Instruction and Increasing Learner Achievement.* San Francisco: Jossey-Bass, 1985.

Wohlking, W., and Gill, P. "Role Playing." In *The Instructional Design Library.* Vol. 32. Englewood Cliffs, N.J.: Educational Technology Publications, 1980.

Wong, M., and Raulerson, J. *A Guide to Systematic Instructional Design.* Englewood Cliffs, N.J.: Educational Technology Publications, 1974.

Woodward, J. *Industrial Organization: Theory and Practice.* London: Oxford University Press, 1965.

Workman, M., Jr., and Sperling, J. *Defining the Manager's Job: A Manual of Position Descriptions.* (2nd ed.) New York: Amacom, 1975.

Wren, D. *The Evolution of Management Thought.* (2nd ed.) New York: Wiley, 1979.

Zemke, R. "In Search of a Training Philosophy." *Training,* 1985, *22,* 93–94, 96, 98.

Zemke, R., and Kramlinger, T. *Figuring Things Out: A Trainer's Guide to Needs and Task Analysis.* Reading, Mass.: Addison-Wesley, 1982.

Zemke, R., and Zemke, S. "Thirty Things We Know for Sure About Adult Learning." *Training,* 1981, *18*(6), 45–52.

Name Index

Subject Index